D0965516

THE
WORLD FOOD
PROBLEM

THE WORLD FOOD PROBLEM

Tackling the Causes of Undernutrition in the Third World

Phillips Foster

Lynne Rienner Publishers • Boulder
Adamantine Press Limited • London

HD
9018
-D44
F68
1992

Published in the United States of America in 1992 by
Lynne Rienner Publishers, Inc.
1800 30th Street, Boulder, Colorado 80301

and in the United Kingdom by
Adamantine Press Limited
3 Henrietta Street, Covent Garden, London WC2E 8LU

Library of Congress Cataloging-in-Publication Data
Foster, Phillips Wayne, 1931-
  The world food problem : tackling the causes of
undernutrition in the Third World / Phillips Foster.
  Includes bibliographical references and index.
  ISBN: 1-55587-296-4 (hc)
  ISBN: 1-55587-274-3
  1. Food supply—Developing countries. 2. Poor—
Developing countries—Nutrition. 3. Malnutrition—Developing
countries. 4. Food supply—Government policy—Developing
countries. 5. Food supply—Developing countries—
International cooperation. I. Title.
HD9018.D44F68 1992
363.8'09172'4—dc20   91-31493
                                                           CIP

British Cataloguing in Publication Data
A Cataloguing in Publication record for this book
is available from the British Library.
ISBN: 0-7449-0072-7(hc)
ISBN: 0-7449-0073-5

Printed and bound in the United States of America

The paper used in this publication meets the requirements
of the American National Standard for Permanence of
Paper for Printed Library Materials Z39.48-1984.
5 4 3 2 1

Contents

☐

Tables

Figures

Foreword   *by John W. Mellor*

Food is emotional, political, life-determining. Naturally, it fills the cultural outlook and colors life for the half-billion rich people of the world. But the quest for food and the worry as to how that quest will fare bear with terrible immediacy on well over 1 billion people in the world, the hungry and undernourished. It is central to the worries of another billion or two who are at risk of falling into the ranks of the hungry or who, having only recently reasonably ensured their departure from those ranks, remember hunger all too well.

Many rich countries of the world, as this book makes clear, are only a generation or two away from where much of the world is still mired. And in many countries, Finland and Japan, for example, the remembrance of hunger in war is still in the minds of senior political leaders and affects their approach to many issues of our international world.

The centrality of food is perhaps best marked by noting that for about 2 billion people, it is the direct employment in food and agricultural production, or the indirect employment created by expenditures of those who directly labor in agriculture, that determines their income—how much money they have to devote to food consumption. And it is the price of food that is the dominating determinant of what that money is worth. Or, to offer a numerical example, in rural India the proportion of the rural population in poverty so severe that they are undernourished and hungry fluctuates between 40 and 60 percent, depending on the weather and its effects on food production and food prices. No wonder so many of the poor are fatalistic and do not believe they have significant control of their lives.

Truly important, emotional, political subjects carry with them the controversy and irrationality that impedes progress. This is particularly true of food, the world food problem, and the remedies proffered. It applies to people of good will, dedicated to helping the hungry and the malnourished, as well as to the opportunists who also flock to misery.

Phillips Foster gives us facts about the world food problem—an extraordinary array of facts, all important to understanding the issues. And because food touches so much, these facts cover a wide range of knowledge, about food directly and about the broad processes of development, growth, and distribution that largely determine access to food. But the myriad of facts we are given are built around a conceptual framework that selects the facts to be presented and weaves them into a coherent story, leading us to usable, applicable conclusions.

The conclusions that come out of this vast, complex story are just that: vast and complex. Many of the fortunate in the world who are driven to help those less fortunate owe it to the hungry and malnourished to read this book, to understand the processes which in a generation can abolish hunger and undernutrition, but which cannot so operate if quick fixes are pursued. The title of this book tells us it deals with a problem, and the subtitle that it tackles the causes. This is not a book of quick fixes and treatment of symptoms.

I have emphasized the immensity of the food problem. Phillips Foster documents that. It is important to do so and to grasp the immensity. If the problem is modest in extent, then it is reasonable to think that modest redistribution of food and income will solve the problem: perhaps only redistribution within poor countries. And perhaps we can diffuse our focus to related problems. But if the problem is immense, redistribution has to move to the point at which it hurts in the rich countries as well, and even that is not enough. Incomes must be raised, growth and development must occur. Trade-offs must be faced.

Our guide takes us through these issues step by step. And he leads us to a terribly important and central conclusion. Yes, in one sense there is enough food in the world for everyone. But to get adequate purchasing power into the hands of the billions of poor, they must be made more productive, and since they are so much either directly or indirectly in the food and agriculture sector, we must wrestle with the food production problem. Thus, food production is central to the solution of the world food problem, but as much or more from an income generation and employment point of view as from a consumption point of view. Or to use the jargon of the day, most of the hungry get their "entitlement" to food by producing food. This issue requires facts, analysis, and synthesis. We get these in full measure.

I would like to close this foreword on a personal note. In laboriously building the International Food Policy Research Institute to its premier status, I was driven by the importance of facts as the basis for finding causes and then solutions to the world's problems and by the recognition that facts in our complex world are hard to come by. Thus the institute was built on the pursuit of facts in the context of a strategic vision. But weaving those facts into the policy determination fabric is in itself an immense task. Nothing could more delight and excite me than to see that work, and of course that of many others as well, woven so skillfully and thoughtfully and to such good effect as in this book by Phillips Foster.

But if the subject is so important and complex, why have we not had this book before? Perhaps because the emotion of the subject is so great that it required time for unearthing the facts, and the maturing process of the decade-plus of continual effort, dedication, and interaction that have gone into it. It is now for the rest of us to avoid disappointment by reading, absorbing, and acting, each in our own small way.

Preface

Millions of people in the Third World are hungry, but not because there is not enough food in the world to feed them. There is more than enough food.

Why are people hungry? There are a number of causes. Sometimes one cause is enough to create hunger; sometimes two or more causes work together. What are the causes that deliver hunger? Among the most important are

- *Poverty:* some people simply do not have the purchasing power to obtain enough food for themselves
- *Income and wealth inequalities:* great disparities in income and wealth distribution enable the rich (who tend to be overnourished) to bid food away from the poor (who tend to be undernourished)
- *Large family size:* some families have more children than they can support
- *Illness:* some people would have reasonably good nutrition except for a disease that is taxing their nutritional well-being

What can we do about hunger? We will examine not only food-linked income transfer programs (designed to cope with poverty through supplementing the purchasing power of the poor), but list and analyze policies aimed at alleviating the causes of hunger. These policies fall into the following four broad categories: (1) improving purchasing power (through increasing employment and income among the poor and through lowering the price of the food they eat); (2) reducing disparities in income and wealth distribution; (3) controlling human fertility; and (4) promoting better health.

■ THE PLAN OF THIS BOOK

We begin with an emphasis on definitions and facts. As the material develops, our emphasis changes to behavioral models of society (e.g., economic, demographic) and how these models relate to undernutrition. In the last section I show how these models can be applied in evaluating nutrition policy alternatives.

In Part I malnutrition is found to be a leading killer throughout the world, but in the Third World, undernutrition is the main nutrition problem. Before considering the causes of undernutrition and policy alternatives to alleviate it, I examine the facts and provide the best answers I can to questions such as: What is malnutrition? What are its effects? How do we measure it? Who is malnourished? What are the trends?

In Part II we look at the main causes of undernutrition—the vehicles by which undernutrition is delivered to families—and attribute these causes mainly to economic, demographic, and health variables. A number of models are introduced to help in understanding how economic, demographic, and health variables deliver undernutrition. The concept of food security is used to demonstrate the interrelatedness of these variables.

In Part III we explore applications of the above-mentioned models as tools for the formulation and evaluation of public policy alternatives of interest to nutrition planners. This part is introduced by a section in which I tell how failure to account for conflicting worldviews of the hunger problem can erode the efforts of activists who would seek to improve Third World nutrition. It ends with a set of recommendations on how to achieve policy reform.

■ THE DISCIPLINES INVOLVED IN THIS BOOK

I have attempted to integrate knowledge from a number of disciplines, taking as a central premise the thought, well articulated by Beatrice Rogers (1988b) of Tufts University, that "the solution to the world hunger problem will be achieved only through the integration of knowledge from the whole range of relevant scientific disciplines." Thus, I have drawn on nutrition, economics, demography, biology, health science, geography, agronomy, history, anthropology, philosophy, and public policy analysis.

Nevertheless the book is problem-oriented rather than discipline-oriented. The problem is taken to be Third World undernutrition, and the disciplines are brought to bear on the problem only to the extent that they contribute to an understanding of it or to its solution.

■ TECHNIQUES OF PRESENTATION

To a large extent, this book is data-driven. From the opening chapter, in which I quote the Carl Mabbs-Zeno famine figures, through the data on malnutrition in Part I, and the numbers behind elasticity calculations and population issues in Part II, to the results of alternative public policies measured in terms of food production and prices in Part III, the text is larded with illustrative tables and figures. It is my hope that the data themselves will, in large measure, back up my argument. The text set in numerous boxes serves not only to provide visual variety, but to bring to the reader's attention interesting related material, in many cases consisting of authoritative, expert statements (and often with the added advantage of presenting the material in rather more colorful language than I would dare to use).

Phillips Foster

Acknowledgments

Some of the ideas and materials in this book were developed for seminars presented for the State Department in Washington, Manila, and Jakarta, as well as some presented at Allahabad University in India, the Shanshi Agricultural College in China, and the University of New England in Armidale, Australia. Some appear in a chapter titled "Malnutrition, Starvation, and Death" (Foster 1991) in the book *Horrendous Death, Health and Well-Being*. And some were developed for a Distinguished Lecturer Series at South Dakota State University.

But my thinking on this topic was particularly sharpened during the period 1982–1991 by my experiences teaching a class in world hunger, population, and food supplies at the University of Maryland. Interaction with challenging students was invaluable in stimulating my mind and in improving my capacity to present information to others.

I wish to thank so many who have given me advice, encouragement, and assistance in bringing this book to completion. Particular appreciation goes to Lynne Rienner for her encouragement almost from the inception of this work. Per Pinstrup-Andersen, the present director general of the International Food Policy Research Institute (IFPRI), whose seminal work on food policy is cited so liberally in this book, has been another early supporter of this project and offered many helpful comments during his review of the manuscript. Jim Dever, now of the United States Department of Agriculture (USDA), helped greatly in the preparation of Chapters 2, 3, and 4.

Richard Ahrens, Phylis Moser-Veillon, and Steve Read (University of Maryland) stood by ready to answer my never-ending stream of questions on nutrition, as did Richard Erdman from our Animal Science Department, and Julie Kelment of AID. Claire Cassidy instructed me on nutritional anthropology. Kathleen Cravero of the United Nations Children's Fund reviewed materials on nutrition and health. My son, Dean Foster (University of Chicago), helped both in matters of nutrition and statistics. Carl Haub of the Population Reference Bureau checked my thinking on demography and supplied much useful information. Throughout the whole process Arthur Dommen of the USDA Economic Research Service, Developing Economies Branch, was ready and willing to supply me with information from the encyclopedic fund of knowledge that he stores in his office or simply carries around in his head.

The sections on economics and public policy benefited from comments and criticisms from Earl Brown, Bruce Gardner, John Horowitz, John Moore, and

Jim Russell (all in my department at Maryland). My thinking was frequently influenced by other authors whose material I have discussed with them and quoted in this book. Others who helped in steering me in the right direction include Jock Anderson (World Bank), Dana Dalrymple (USDA/AID), Goeff Edwards (Latrobe University), Brian Hardaker (University of New England), Hope Sukin (State Department), Schlomo Reutlinger (World Bank), Jim Roumasset (East-West Center), Al Thieme (Inter-American Development Bank), and Amanda Wolf (School of Public Affairs, University of Maryland).

The entire book was read and criticized by Arthur Dommen (USDA), Bea Rogers (Tufts), and two anonymous reviewers, all of whom provided much helpful criticism. My wife, Denny, was particularly helpful by insisting that she actually be able to understand everything I said, and her suggestions have been most useful in adding to the readability of the text. Lynn Rodgers, a former student, kindly helped in sharpening concepts and language.

We all owe a debt of gratitude to John Mellor, who encouraged and guided his staff at IFPRI over the 13-year period from 1977 to 1990 during which they produced a wealth of empirical studies that have sharpened the thinking of the entire community of scholars working in the food policy field. I cite, for example, 28 studies published by IFPRI during John's tenure as director.

Thanks go to Carol Warrington and her staff at the Computer Science Center at the University of Maryland for the preparation of all the figures, to Dianne Walbasser and Lien Trieu for preparing the tables for publication, to Pam Ferdinand for her very careful copyediting, and to Steve Barr for managing the project.

P.F.

□ 1

Introduction

Hunger. It was prevalent everywhere. Hunger was pushed out of the tall houses, in the wretched clothing that hung upon poles and lines; Hunger was patched into them with straw and rag and wood and paper; Hunger was repeated in every fragment of the small modicum of firewood that the man sawed off; Hunger stared down from the smokeless chimneys, and started up from the filthy street that had no offal, among its refuse, of anything to eat. Hunger was the inscription on the baker's shelves, written in every small loaf of his scanty stock of bad bread; at the sausage-shop, in every dead-dog preparation that was offered for sale. Hunger rattled its dry bones among the roasting chestnuts in the turned cylinder; Hunger was shred into atomies in every farthing of porringer of husky chips of potato, fried with some reluctant drops of oil.

—Charles Dickens, *A Tale of Two Cities*

■ HUNGER KILLS

A newspaper headline on starvation may conjure up in your mind the image of an emaciated infant, the victim of an Ethiopian famine. And if you are a history buff, words like *Bengal* or *Ukraine* may spring up. Despite massive relief efforts from Europe and North America, some 300,000 people died of hunger-related causes during the Ethiopian famine of 1983–1985 (Hancock 1985). News photographs and television footage of rural Ethiopian families migrating in search of food, of babies with bloated bellies and spindly arms and legs, and of bodies too weak to sit up, have flooded our consciousness with the horror of hunger. Yet that horror pales beside the figures from a long list of 148 earlier famines recently compiled by Carl Mabbs-Zeno of the USDA. In the past it was not unusual for major famines to wipe out people by the millions (see Tables 1.1–1.3). The Ukrainian famine of 1921–1922 may have taken 9 million lives, and the more famous Bengal famine of 1770 claimed perhaps 10 million.

The drama of famine involves not only hunger and death but massive disruptions in the social fabric of the community. Normal social relationships are strained, families disintegrate, and the better-off may take advantage of the situation to exploit the worse-off (see Box 1.1).

Although the drama of famine tends to capture our attention, amazingly most hunger-related deaths do not occur in famines. They happen daily, quietly, largely unchronicled, all around the world. Figures vary, but one conservative

1

Table 1.1 Largest Famines in Europe

Area Affected	Date	Excess Deaths (in Thousands)	Area Affected	Date
Ukraine	1946-47	2,000	England	1321
Greece	1941-43	400	England, Ireland	1314
Lower Volga	1932-34	5,000	England, Scotland,	
Ukraine[1]	1921-22	3,000	Ireland	1302
		9,000	England	1294
Eastern Urals	1911-12	8,000	England	1257-59
Ukraine	1905-06		England	1235
Western Plains,			Russia	1230-31
Russia	1897-98		Ireland	1227
Volga Valley	1891-93		Novogorod, Russia	1215
Ireland	1845-50	1,500	England, France	1193-96
Russia	1833-34		England, Wales	1183
Ireland	1822		England	1124
Poland	1770		Ireland	1116
Bohemia	1770		England	1093
Scotland	1766		Rostor-Volyn', Russia	1070-71
England	1740-41		England	1069
France	1661		England	1042-48
Ireland	1650-51		Suzdal, Russia	1024
Moscow	1601-03	500	England	1004-05
England	1594-95		England	976
Ireland	1588-89		Bolobereg	971
England, Ireland	1586		England, Wales,	
Hungary	1586		Scotland	954-58
England	1549		Scotland	936-39
England	1527		England	310
England	1521		Scotland	306
Hungary	1505		Scotland	228
Ireland	1497		Ireland	192
Ireland	1447		Rome	185
England	1437-39		Italian Peninsula	79-88
Ireland	1410		England	54
England	1392-93		Rome	23
England	1353		Rome	AD 6
Europe[2]	1346-50	40,000	Rome	385 BC
England, Scotland[3]	1341-42		Rome	436 BC

Source: Mabbs-Zeno 1987.

[1]Estimates from two different sources.
[2]Most deaths not due to malnutrition.
[3]No record of excess deaths exists prior to this date.

Table 1.2 Largest Famines in India and Bangladesh Since 1700

Area Affected	Date	Excess Deaths (in Thousands)
Bangladesh	1974	1,000
Bengal	1943	1,500-3,000
Punjab, Central Provinces	1899-1900	2,500
Bangal, Bombay, Central Provinces	1985-97	5,000
Orissa, Ganjam	1888-89	1,500
Madras, Bombay, Hyderabad	1876-78	5,000-8,000
Punjab, Deccan	1868-70	2,500
Orissa, Hyderabad[1]	1865-67	1,900 10,000
Madras, Deccam	1853-55	
North	1837-38	800
Southeast	1933-34	
Madras	1832-33	
Sind, Rajasthan, Madras	1812-13	1,500
West	1802-03	
Bombay, Hyderabad	1790-93	
Mahratta	1787	
Bihar, Madras, Mysore	1781-83	
Argot, Chingleput, Madras	1780-82	
Bengal, Bihar	1770	10,000
Chingleput	1733	
Madurai	1709-21	
Decca	1702-04	2,000

Source: Mabbs-Zeno 1987.

[1]Estimates from two different sources.

estimate, using data provided by the Food and Agricultural Organization (FAO) of the United Nations, is that some 10 million people die annually from hunger (Latham 1984: 55).

The number may be growing. A study done at Brown University Hunger Program estimated that the number of hungry people in the world (not deaths) grew by 50 million from 1949 to 1984, to a total of some 600 million (Kates et al. 1988: 9). It would appear then, that at least 12 percent of the world's 5 billion people are hungry. Other estimates place the number of people with inadequate food intake at higher levels; John Mellor (1986b) gives 800 million, for instance. Of course, not all the hungry die from it; just several million per year. What happens when you die from hunger? An anonymous author (Anon. 1974: 68) writing for *Time* magazine put it eloquently and succinctly, describing famine-related death:

Table 1.3 Largest Famines in China Since 1700

Area Affected	Date	Excess Deaths (in Thousands)
China	1958-60	30,000
Honan	1941	3,000
Northwest	1929-32	5,000
Central	1925	
North	1920-21	500
North	1892-94	
Honan	1887-89	2,000
North	1876-79	10,000
China	1846-49	5,000
China	1810-11	20,000

Source: Mabbs-Zeno 1987.

The victim of starvation burns up his own body fats, muscles and tissues for fuel. His body quite literally consumes itself and deteriorates rapidly. The kidneys, liver and endocrine system often cease to function properly. A shortage of carbohydrates, which play a vital role in brain chemistry, affects the mind. Lassitude and confusion set in, so that starvation victims often seem unaware of their plight. The body's defenses drop; disease kills most famine victims before they have time to starve to death. An individual begins to starve when he has lost about a third of his normal body weight. Once this loss exceeds 40 percent, death is almost inevitable.

While adult males do die of hunger during a famine, the majority of deaths, whether from famine or from chronic undernutrition, occur among preschoolers. Pregnant and lactating women are at substantial risk, although less so than children. Children suffer malnutrition in a multitude of ways. They may be crippled by vitamin D deficiency (rickets), blinded from vitamin A deficiency (xeropthalmia), or stunted by lack of protein (kwashiorkor), for instance. But the most common form of child undernutrition results simply from lack of sufficient calories, from which disease and death can result.

For the most common scenario, played out again and again in the Third World, picture a loving but poorly educated, poverty-stricken mother with several children. Food is scarce. Her youngest child has not been growing for months because of undernourishment. Because of the undernutrition, the baby's resistance to disease has fallen to a very low level. He drinks from the family's supply of unclean water. The older members of his family can handle the microorganisms in the water, but he develops diarrhea. He loses interest in eating. He seems more willing to take liquids, so the mother removes solids from his diet and feeds him on liquids. Since he is unable to obtain sufficient nourishment from the liquids to conquer his illness, his diarrhea continues. Finally in a

Box 1.1 Peasant Perceptions of Famine
Izzedin I. Imam

The structure of relationships in the village community prevents the hardships of famine from being borne equitably by all its members. These relationships allow those who occupy positions of influence and wealth further to widen the gap between themselves and those in a dependent situation. For example, once a natural calamity triggers expectation of a food shortage, the large landowners begin to divert food supplies into storage and wait for the prices to rise—thus turning adversity into their opportunity.

But the landless have no such option. Furthermore, the drop in production also reduces the demand for their labor—the only resource they possess. Wage rates fall and the wage laborers find themselves at the mercy of those who can offer work or who have cash to offer in return for their few possessions.

In such a situation, often the only recourse is to start selling off the only possessions the household may have. Generally, the landless pawn their goods to money lenders, a term generally applied to anyone with surplus assets, such as the landowners. The hope is always that one day the loan will be repaid and the object recovered. But this virtually never happens. The interest charged on the loan is usually so crippling that the debtor has next to no chance of being able to repay the principal in the time allotted and the object passes into the possession of the money lender.

Pawning usually begins with those items which are expendable, such as ornaments or jewelry. Eventually as the desperate need for cash to buy food increases, every household item, including utensils, may be pawned or sold at any available price.

As a last resort the household head may leave his family and set off to an uncertain destination in hope of finding employment. Some of those who migrate return periodically to give any earnings to their families. But anxieties over whether those who migrate will return grow with time, as commonly they do not. The wives left behind may take up employment doing chores in the richer households, living off the leftovers of the rich family's meals. One woman in Rowmari who could no longer stand the cries of her hungry children hung herself—leaving them behind with no one to care for them. A case was reported from Melanda, Jamalpur, of a woman who was said to have sold her four children and turned to begging.

Source: Extracted from Imam 1979.

perate but seemingly logical attempt to stop the diarrhea, his mother removes the liquids from his diet. Although the child by now is feverish, limiting liquids accelerates the baby's loss of fluids. Severe dehydration follows, with death not far behind.

Death traceable to undernutrition can be dramatically reduced, even virtually eliminated, if we are willing to make appropriate, albeit difficult, policy changes. Appropriate policy changes are the subject of the latter part of this book. The discussion of policy alternatives in this chapter will give only the briefest introduction to this important topic.

■ THE MAIN NUTRITION POLICY ALTERNATIVES

When you stop and think about it, food has some of the most important emotional associations in our culture. What a positive association most people have of a mother feeding her baby. Or consider the food associations with some of our important festivals and rituals—Thanksgiving, Christmas, Passover, Communion. And what would a birthday party or a wedding reception be without a cake? The immediacy and presence of the nutrition problem, the fact that it involves human suffering, and the fact that that particular suffering is tied up with one of the most emotion-laden facets of our lives, make the hunger problem cry out for a solution—not only a solution, but a solution *soon*.

☐ Treating Symptoms

Our immediate reaction to hunger tends to be one of charity. If people are hungry, why not feed them? And so we develop a multitude of charitable programs. In high-income countries churches set up soup kitchens, rock music groups perform special concerts, and governments install food-stamp plans. The international aid community makes surplus food available to food-deficit areas through Food for Peace (US government–sponsored) and the World Food Program of the United Nations.

With severely limited budgets for out-and-out charity, Third World governments set up food-rationing schemes and place ceiling prices on basic foods. They forcibly procure food from farmers at below-market prices and resell it to consumers at below-market prices in government "fair-price" shops. In an attempt to make food more readily available to their consumers, Third World governments control the movement of food from one region of the country to another and limit the export of food grains.

Both industrial and Third World governments attempt to improve the quality of the food their people eat through food fortification programs, adding, for example, vitamins and minerals to white bread.

One characteristic that all these urgent and timely programs have in common is that they intervene somehow in the food-marketing system and attempt to redistribute food among households so as to reduce hunger. As such they can be called nutrition intervention programs. When nutrition intervention programs provide needy people with food purchased in the marketplace, charitable donors, or taxpayers in general, pick up the tab for the costs. But many intervention programs lower the cost of food to the needy in other ways. Governments, for instance, may pass laws setting food-price ceilings, or they may subsidize food consumption by procuring food from farmers, using police power, and then redistributing this food to the nonfarm population. In these sorts of cases resource holders in agriculture (landowners, farm managers, farm workers) provide the food subsidy.

But whether paid for by charitable organizations, taxpayers, or the farmers themselves, nutrition intervention programs do not treat the causes of hunger. If we make an analogy to medical science, we might say that nutrition intervention is more concerned with treating the symptoms than the causes of hunger.

☐ Treating Causes

Treating the causes of hunger is a slower, more complex task than the activities just described. As the international aid community and the Third World countries work together in treating the causes of hunger, they have a number of avenues open to them, discussed in some detail in Part III of this book. In this section I provide only a preview of these avenues.

Programs and policies to subsidize food production (rather than food consumption) attempt to lower the cost of food in the marketplace through increasing the quantity offered for sale. Food production subsidies, including public investment in agriculture, take a multitude of forms such as sponsoring agricultural research and development programs, financing rural education programs, or providing farmers with low-cost irrigation water (see Box 18.3 for a discussion of the way the word *subsidy* is used in this book).

Most Third World countries have embarked on programs to reduce their birth rates in hopes that this will alleviate the pressures of population on food supplies. Public health programs (e.g., supplying cities with cleaner drinking water) improve nutrition as healthier people make more-efficient use of the food they consume. Improving employment opportunities for families at risk to undernutrition is another way of treating the causes of hunger. And taxing the rich in order to provide social programs (e.g., education) for the poor is a way of improving the lot of those who might otherwise end up hungry.

■ A NUTRITION POLICY DILEMMA

Treating the causes of hunger is a complex undertaking because the causes themselves are many and complex. Later in this book I devote several chapters to understanding the causes of hunger, but in summary here I simply state that the main causes can be grouped under three headings: (1) economic; (2) demographic; and (3) health. Particular economic, demographic, and health situations result in malnutrition in individual families or family members. We call these variables the *nutrition impact vehicles*, because it is through these variables that malnutrition is delivered.

The particular economic, demographic, and health situation found in any one country or region can be traced to the particular policies, programs or projects (or lack of them) that that country's or region's leaders have promulgated through its history. For instance, the lack of a supply of clean drinking water in a particular city can be attributed to past policies, programs, or projects; or, if you prefer, to the lack of appropriate policies, programs, or projects. The presence of a largely illiterate (and therefore underproductive) farm population can be attributed to the education policies and programs of the country or region.

In any case, if we are to treat the causes of malnutrition, we will have to adjust the public policies, programs, or projects of a given country or region so that the nutrition impact vehicles no longer combine to deliver malnutrition. International aid donors and recipient countries have been working together over the years to improve levels of living, including nutritional status, of people in the Third World. Many of their efforts have focused on changing the economic, demographic, and health situations for the better.

Table 1.4 Ranking of 25 Major Recipients of Aid, 1973-1983

By Total Cumulative Receipts (in Millions of US Dollars)		By Average Annual Receipts per Capita (in US Dollars)	
1. Egypt	17,750.9	1. Jordan	209.87
2. India	16,789.6	2. Israel	185.53
3. Syrian Arab Republic	10,193.9	3. Oman	118.06
4. Bangladesh	10,185.1	4. Syrian Arab Republic	97.55
5. Pakistan	8,364.1	5. Mauritania	95.71
6. Israel	8,163.4	6. Papua New Guinea	92.28
7. Indonesia	8,086.8	7. Lebanon	56.17
8. Jordan	7,156.7	8. Somalia	54.27
9. Sudan	4,972.5	9. Southern Yemen	45.38
10. Tanzania	4,817.4	10. Jamaica	41.86
11. Morocco	4,026.4	11. Congo, People's Republic	41.63
12. Turkey	3,978.7	12. Lesotho	40.98
13. Viet Nam	3,386.8	13. Egypt	36.43
14. Zaire	3,199.6	14. Senegal	36.24
15. Papua New Guinea	3,246.7	15. Yemen Arab Republic	35.37
16. Kenya	2,993.8	16. Nicaragua	33.22
17. Sri Lanka	2,965.0	17. Tunisia	31.45
18. Yemen Arab Republic	2,918.4	18. Liberia	30.49
19. Philippines	2,884.6	19. Central African Republic	27.64
20. Thailand	2,822.8	20. Zambia	27.36
21. Somalia	2,686.4	21. Costa Rica	27.19
22. Senegal	2,392.1	22. Niger	26.13
23. Tunisia	2,318.0	23. Togo	24.94
24. Burma	2,218.9	24. Mali	22.86
25. Republic of Korea	2,051.1	25. Burkina Faso	22.76

Source: Burki and Ayres 1986.

Note: These figures do not include military aid.

Table 1.5 Ranking of the 17 Largest Donors of Aid, 1987

	Amount (in Millions of US Dollars)	Percentage of Total		Percentage of GNP
1. United States	8,945	21.5	1. Norway	1.09
2. Japan	7,454	17.9	2. Netherlands	0.98
3. France	6,525	15.7	3. Denmark	0.88
4. Germany	4,391	10.6	4. Sweden	0.88
5. Italy	2,615	6.3	5. France	0.74
6. Netherlands	2,094	5.0	6. Finland	0.50
7. Canada	1,885	4.5	7. Belgium	0.49
8. United Kingdom	1,865	4.5	8. Canada	0.47
9. Sweden	1,337	3.2	9. Germany	0.39
10. Norway	2,094	2.1	10. Italy	0.35
11. Denmark	859	2.1	11. Australia	0.33
12. Belgium	689	1.7	12. Japan	0.31
13. Australia	627	1.5	13. Switzerland	0.31
14. Switzerland	547	1.3	14. United Kingdom	0.28
15. Finland	433	1.0	15. New Zealand	0.26
16. Austria	19	6.5	16. United States	0.20
17. New Zealand	8	7.2	17. Austria	0.17

Source: World Bank 1989:200.

Note: These figures exclude military aid.

The magnitude of nonmilitary international aid is shown in Tables 1.4 and 1.5. Major aid recipients are among those countries with lower per capita incomes, although it is clear from the data here that aid flows are influenced by geopolitical as well as humanitarian considerations. On the right-hand side of Table 1.4, for instance, notice that Jordan and Israel are credited with approximately $200 per capita per year of international aid, while Costa Rica received only about $27 dollars per capita, and Bangladesh and Ethiopia did not even show up in the top 25 in per capita recipients. The World Bank (1988: 222–223) estimates 1986 per capita incomes in these countries to be: Jordan, $1,540; Israel, $6,210; Costa Rica, $1,480; Bangladesh, $160; and Ethiopia, $120.

Notice also that donor countries provide substantially different proportions of their gross national product (GNP) for aid (Table 1.5). For instance, although the United States provided the largest amount of aid during 1987, it stood sixteenth in terms of percentage of GNP allocated to aid. The $41 billion that the aid donors (Table 1.5) provided to Third World countries finances a range of programs from food donations to assistance in agricultural research.

Resources are scarce, and competition for charitable funds, international donor assistance, and Third World government expenditures is keen. But for those who want to spend more resources on reducing hunger, one of the toughest decisions is how to allocate expenditures between direct food assistance, or

---

Figure 1.1 A Nutrition Policy Dilemma

Policies, Programs, Projects
(or lack of them)

Causes of Malnutrition
(Nutrition impact vehicles -- Economic, Health, Demographic)

Malnutrition

Alternatives:	• Treat symptoms (nutrition intervention)	• Treat causes (adjust nutrition impact vehicles)
Trade-off:	• More resources to treating symptoms • Fewer resources left for treating causes	•More resources to treating causes •Fewer resources left for treating symptoms
What mix to use?	• Present Time Orientation: Emphasize treating symptoms	Future Time Orientation: Emphasize treating causes

nutrition intervention, which helps alleviate suffering sooner (treating symptoms) and programs to adjust the nutrition impact vehicles (treating causes) so that, later, they will not deliver so much malnutrition. A difficult trade-off is involved. Spending more resources on nutrition intervention leaves fewer resources for adjusting the nutrition impact vehicles.

Those with a short, or present, time orientation tend to emphasize treating symptoms. Since the first task of any government is to stay in power, politicians tend to be present time–oriented. On the other hand, academics and government technocrats tend to have longer time horizons; they tend to be more future time–oriented, and therefore they tend to favor treating causes. Most everyone would prefer to both feed the hungry today and end hunger in the future. But resources are limited and choices must be made. Figure 1.1 organizes the main points of the dilemma we have been discussing.

■ Part I

MALNUTRITION— WHAT ARE THE FACTS?

Malnutrition is a leading killer. In high-income countries one variant of malnutrition—overnutrition—is the main nutrition problem. In the Third World another variant—undernutrition—is the main problem. The problem of Third World undernutrition is exacerbated by secondary malnutrition—malnutrition stemming from causes such as disease.

Before considering the causes of undernutrition, and policy alternatives to alleviate it, we need to examine the facts and provide the best answers we can to questions such as: What is malnutrition? What are its effects? How do we measure it? Who is malnourished? What are the trends?

☐ 2

Malnutrition and Undernutrition

Different studies done in several countries of the less developed world show that only a third of the children of low-income families suffer from malnutrition, qualifying it as an important defect in growth, with a weight deficit of 25% or more. This information is not exact. . . . experience . . . shows that the real figures are much higher. The majority of the prevalent studies do not take into consideration: 1) that the study is always done by weighing and measuring the children who are found in the village and that this group constitutes, in reality, the survivors, while many malnourished children are already in their graves as a consequence of their malnutrition and infections; 2) that in the samplings there are many small children who have not yet become malnourished because the mother's breast protects them during the first months, although there is no doubt that many of them will become malnourished; and finally, 3) that the older children have already recovered from malnutrition though at some prior moment they were malnourished. Very probably the truth may be that at least two-thirds of the children in the world suffer, or have suffered at some time in their lives, this syndrome of moderate, chronic malnutrition, if not so glaring in its symptoms, certainly glaring in its consequences.

This moderate, chronic malnutrition rarely kills directly, but it always leaves its mark on child development.

—Chávez and Martínez 1982

■ MALNUTRITION DEFINED

Malnutrition is difficult to define. It is commonly defined as a nutritional disorder or condition resulting from faulty or inadequate nutrition, but that does not tell us much. We can understand more about malnutrition if we look at the various types that exist. The internationally famous nutritionist Jean Mayer (1976) president of Tufts University, identifies four types of malnutrition: (1) overnutrition; (2) dietary deficiency; (3) secondary malnutrition; and (4) undernutrition.

☐ Overnutrition

When an individual takes in too many calories the resulting condition is called overnutrition. Overnutrition is the most common nutritional difficulty in high-income countries such as the United States, although high-income people in low-income countries also suffer from this type of malnutrition. The diet of the world's high-income people is usually overladen with calories, saturated fats, salt, and sugar. Their diet-related illnesses include obesity, diabetes, hypertension, and atherosclerosis.

Figure 2.1 shows the rather pronounced relationship between body weight and income among males in the United States. Table 2.1 shows a similar relationship among males in an Indian village. Interestingly, US females deviate from the usual trends, weighing less as their income goes up (Table 2.2). Perhaps wealthy US women, being conscious of their weight, can afford to spend more effort keeping their weight under control than can their lower-income compatriots.

Figure 2.1 Body Weight and Income, US Males, 1971-1974

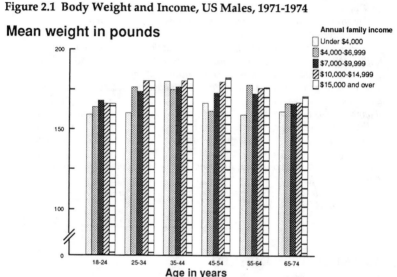

Source: Adapted from US Department of Health and Human Resources 1981:15.

☐ Dietary Deficiency

A diet may lack sufficient amounts of one or more essential nutrients such as a vitamin or a mineral, resulting in dietary deficiency. A special set of diseases accompany dietary deficiencies. Some were mentioned in Chapter 1: Xeropthalmia, caused by vitamin A deficiency, leads to blindness; rickets, a childhood disease resulting from a lack of sufficient vitamin D, leads to deformed skeletal development. However, the list goes on, including anemia (iron deficiency), goiter (iodine deficiency), and scurvy (vitamin C deficiency).

When compared with the other types of undernutriton listed by Jean Mayer, dietary deficiencies appear relatively easy to cope with. The missing elements are inexpensive, and programs to deal with them are relatively easy to mount.

Table 2.1 Adult Male Mean Weight, Bagbana Village, India, 1981

| | Weight (in Kilograms) by Age | | |
Income (in Rupees)	20-39	40-59	60 +
Under 525	46.9	43.5	*
525 to 1,161	49.3	47.3	44.0
1,162 to 2,050	50.6	51.4	50.0
Over 2,050	52.0	53.0	*

Note: Number of observations = 384. Average per capita family income is 1,162. The income range is from 223 to 9,000 rupees.

*Fewer than three observations.

For instance, dietary anemia was greatly reduced in a rural community in Guatemala after the peasants were persuaded to substitute iron cooking pots for aluminum. Goiter can be prevented through the use of iodized salt, at virtually the same cost as the uniodized product. Enough vitamin A to prevent blindness can be purchased for less than 25 cents per year. Similarly, preventing scurvy, which results in loss of one's teeth, is relatively inexpensive. In the 1700s, scurvy was dramatically reduced among British sailors when it was discovered that consuming citrus would prevent the disease. The British practice of loading on citrus fruits for long voyages is the reason that, to this day, British sailors are called limeys.

Dietary deficiencies are what most people think of first when they think of malnutrition, but they are far from the leading cause of today's nutrition-related problems.

Table 2.2 Adult Female Mean Weight, Ages 18-74, United States, 1971-1974

Annual Family Income in Dollars	Mean Weight (Age-Adjusted) in Pounds
Under 4,000	150
4,000 - 6,999	146
7,000 - 9,999	145
10,000 - 14,000	142
15,000 and over	139

Source: US Department of Health and Human Resources 1981:34.

☐ Secondary Malnutrition

When an individual has a condition or illness that prevents him from properly digesting or absorbing some of his food, he suffers what is called secondary malnutrition. (It is called secondary because it does not result directly from the nature of the diet, as do the other types, which are therefore classed as primary.)

Common causes of secondary malnutrition are diarrhea, respiratory illnesses, measles, and intestinal parasites. The mechanisms through which secondary malnutrition is delivered usually include one or more of the following:

- *Loss of appetite (anorexia)*
- *Alteration of normal metabolism:* the body shifts some of its attention to fighting the infection. Among other things, production of disease-fighting white blood corpuscles may be increased and body temperature may be raised.
- *Prevention of nutrient absorption:* for instance, diarrheal infections irritate the lining of the gastrointestinal tract, creating difficulty in absorbing nutrients and at the same time causing it to shed its contents prematurely and before full digestion has had time to occur.
- *Diversion of nutrients to the parasitic agents themselves:* parasites such as hookworm, tapeworm, and schistosome worms (that cause schistosomiasis) rob the body of nutrients it would otherwise have all to itself (Briscoe 1979, Martorell 1980).

Public health measures such as providing appropriate means for human waste disposal and a sanitary water supply are especially important in reducing the incidence of secondary malnutrition.

Secondary malnutrition often accompanies and exacerbates the fourth type of malnutrition: undernutrition.

☐ Undernutrition

Undernutrition occurs when an individual simply does not get enough food. He or she is short on the calories or protein necessary for normal growth, body maintenance, and the energy necessary for ordinary human activities (Gopalan & Rao 1979). Technically, the condition is usually called protein-calorie malnutrition (PCM), although you will sometimes see it referred to as protein-energy malnutrition (PEM).

PCM hardly ever occurs among families that have enough income to satisfy their basic needs for food, shelter, clothing, and heat. It is found largely in the low-income countries in the Third World. Nutritionists commonly feel that it is this condition that accounts for the fact that Third World populations are, on the average, shorter and lighter in weight than European and North American populations.

In extreme forms, PCM manifests itself as the potentially fatal nutritional disorders known as marasmus and kwashiorkor (see Boxes 2.1 and 2.2). Kwash-

Box 2.1 Kwashiorkor
Eleanor Whitney and Eva Hamilton

The word kwashiorkor originally meant "the evil spirit which infects the first child when the second child is born." It is easy to see how this superstitious belief arose among those Ghanaians who named the disease. When a mother who has been nursing her first child bears a second child, she weans the first and puts the second on the breast. The first child soon begins to sicken and die, just as if an evil spirit had accompanied the new baby into the world and set out to destroy the older child. What actually happens, of course, is that protein deficiency follows soon after weaning, for while breast milk provides these children with sufficient protein, they are generally weaned to a protein-poor gruel.

Millions of children in the world are affected by kwashiorkor. It typically sets in around the age of two. By the time children with kwashiorkor are four, their growth is stunted; they are no taller than they were at two. Their hair has lost its color; their skin is patchy and scaly, sometimes with ulcers or open sores which fail to heal. Their bellies are swollen with edema; they sicken easily, and are weak, fretful, and apathetic.

The swollen belly of the kwashiorkor child is due to edema; blood protein is so low that fluid leaks out into the body. Since the child is too weak to stand much of the time, the fluid seeks the lowest available space—in this case the belly. The picture of such a child is one of skinny arms and legs and a greatly swollen belly. On first glance you might think the child is fat, but if the fluid could be drawn off, his true condition would be revealed: he is actually a wasted skeleton, just skin and bones.

The body follows a priority system when there is not enough protein supplied to meet all its needs. It abandons its less vital systems first. When it cannot obtain amino acids enough from dietary sources, the body switches to a metabolism of wasting, and begins to digest its own protein tissues in order to supply the amino acids needed to build the most vital internal proteins and keep itself alive. Hair and skin pigments (which are made from amino acids) are dispensable and are not manufactured. The skin needs less integrity in a life-and-death situation than the heart, so its maintenance ceases and skin sores fail to heal. Many of the antibodies are also degraded in order that their amino acids may be used as building blocks for heart and lung and brain tissue. Children with a lowered supply of antibodies cannot resist infection and readily contract dysentery, a disease of the digestive tract. Dysentery causes diarrhea, leading to rapid loss of those nutrients—including amino acids—which these children may be receiving in food. Thus dysentery worsens the protein deficiency, and the protein deficiency in turn increases the likelihood of a second or third or tenth attack of dysentery.

The water loss in diarrhea increases losses of the water soluble B vitamins and vitamin C. The children's inability to manufacture protein carriers for the fat-soluble vitamins makes them deficient in vitamins A and D as well. Their inability to manufacture protein carriers for fat often leaves them with fat accumulated in the liver tissue, from which it would normally be carried away. As the liver clogs with fat, its cells become unable to carry out their other normal functions, and gradually they atrophy and die.

Source: Reprinted by permission from *Understanding Nutrition* by Whitney, Hamilton, and Rolfes, copyright 1990 by West Publishing Company.

iorkor is most likely to be encountered among populations that are dependent on diets heavy in cassava, popular in West Africa, or cooking bananas (called *plátanos*), popular in Latin America and also southern Uganda. These particular plant foods are almost totally devoid of available protein, and children that are weaned on them are at high risk for severe protein deficiency. Marasmus is most likely to occur under conditions of extreme poverty in which children are weaned onto a gruel that contains modest amounts of protein, but where total amounts of available food are severely inadequate. Marasmus is thus more common among the poorest populations in the world, such as those of Ethiopia, Nepal, and Bangladesh. Without warmth, loving care, and expert medical attention, children with marasmus or kwashiorkor may die within a short time.

Box 2.2 Marasmus
Eleanor Whitney and Eva Hamilton

When children are almost totally deprived of food, they cannot obtain the energy necessary to maintain their body systems, much less that necessary for growth. Marasmus, a wasting disease, results. Invariably, protein deficiency occurs with this condition, as available protein is used not to build body protein but to supply energy (which takes priority). As a result, the marasmic child has many, though not all, of the same symptoms as the child with kwashiorkor.

Marasmic children are wizened little old people in appearance, just skin and bones. They are often sick because their resistance to disease is low. Their hearts are weak, and all their muscles are wasted. Their metabolism is slow. They have little or no fat under their skin to insulate against cold. Their body temperatures may be subnormal. The experience of hospital workers with victims of this disease is that their primary need is to be wrapped up and kept warm. They need love, since they have often been deprived of maternal attention as well as food.

Unlike the kwashiorkor child, who is fed milk until weaning, the marasmic child may have been neglected from early infancy. The disease occurs most commonly in children from six to eighteen months of age in all the overpopulated city slums of the world. Since the brain normally grows to almost its full adult size within the first two years of life, marasmus impairs brain development and so may have a permanent effect on learning ability.

Marasmus also occurs in adults in countries where calorie deficiency is prevalent.

Source: Reprinted by permission from *Understanding Nutrition* by Whitney, Hamilton, and Rolfes, copyright 1990 by West Publishing Company.

■ **UNDERNUTRITION: THE LEADING PROBLEM**

While all four types of malnutrition are serious problems in today's world, it is the fourth type, undernutrition, that is by far the most common and that causes by far the most grief. Therefore our focus will be on ways to reduce the prevalence of undernutrition.

As you saw from the above discussion, there is a close relationship between nutrition and health. Inadequate nutrition diminishes the body's immune response. This may, in turn, lead to infection. Infection often diminishes the body's capacity to utilize nutrients (secondary malnutrition). In other words, faulty nutrition can lead to poor health, and poor health can lead to faulty nutrition. It is a vicious circle or, if you prefer engineering terminology, a feedback loop. Similarly, good nutrition can lead to better health, and good health reduces the tendency toward bad nutrition. These relationships are important and will be referred to more than once in this book.

☐ Symptoms of Undernutrition

I said that undernutrition occurs when an individual has insufficient calories or protein for normal growth, body maintenance, and the energy necessary for ordinary human activities. But how can you tell when someone is undernourished? What are the symptoms? Or if you wish, what are the indicators of poor nutritional status? Identifying undernutrition commonly consists of comparing characteristics of individuals (or populations) with a reference population. Therefore, the symptoms of undernutrition are generally expressed as a comparison to a reference population, such as a sample of the US populace.

Low birth weight, high infant mortality rate. Average birth weight is sometimes used as an indicator of a population's nutritional status. A group with a subnormal average birth weight is assumed to be one with a high number of undernourished mothers. Such a population normally experiences high rates of spontaneous abortions. It also usually experiences high rates of infant mortality. All these indicators are used as clues to nutritional status.

Low height-for-age. An individual whose height is low for his or her age, relative to the reference population, may have suffered from chronic undernutrition at some time during the growth years. Low height-for-age is a symptom of past undernutrition. The person may or may not be undernourished today.

The curves in the top part of Figure 2.2 show the usual reference population against which the height of girls under three years of age is measured. A 21-month-old girl who is 85 centimeters in length is on the fiftieth percentile. That is, half of the girls in the reference population are taller than she and half of them are shorter. Her height for her age is normal. But if her height is only 79 centimeters at 21 months, more than 95 percent of the reference population is taller than she. She would be at only 89 percent of the reference population on this measure, that is, she would have a low height-for-age—a symptom of past undernutrition.

Low weight-for-height. An individual whose weight is low for their height as compared to the reference population may be suffering from undernutrition

Figure 2.2 NCHS Percentiles of Girls' Height-for-Age and Weight-for-Age, Birth to 36 Months

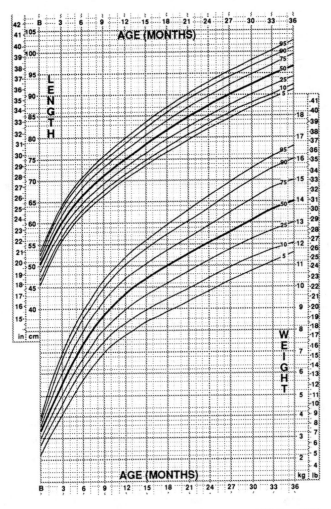

Source: Reprinted from US Department of Health, Education and Welfare 1976.

today. The person appears excessively thin. Low weight-for-height is thus a symptom of present undernutrition.

The curves in Figure 2.3 show the usual reference population against which the weight of young girls is compared to their height. (Note that age is omitted in this comparison.) A girl who is 65 centimeters long and weighs seven kilograms is on the fiftieth percentile. That is, half of the girls of her height weigh

Figure 2.3 NCHS Percentiles of Girls' Weight-for-Height, Birth to 36 Months

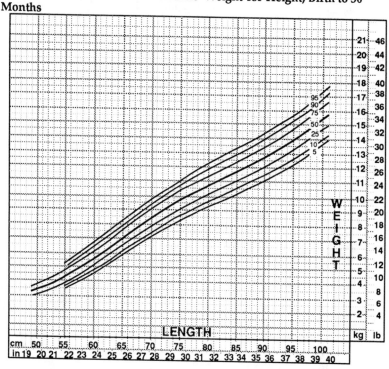

Source: Reprinted from US Department of Health, Education and Welfare 1976.

more than she does and half of them weigh less than she does. She has normal weight-for-height. If she is 65 centimeters long but weighs only 6 kilos, then more than 95 percent of the girls in the reference population of her height weighed more than she does. She is at only 79 percent of the reference population on this measure. She has a low weight-for-height—a symptom of undernutrition today.

A person who is short for his age, but of normal weight-for-height is probably not undernourished right now, but could have been undernourished in the past.

Low weight-for-age. Low weight-for-age is a symptom of either past or present (chronic or acute) undernutrition and may be an indication of both. Look at the curves in the bottom half of Figure 2.2. A 24-month-old girl who weighs 12 kilos is on the fiftieth percentile. If she weighs 9.8 kilos, more than 95 percent of the reference population weigh more than she does. At 9.8 kilos she is at only 82 percent of the reference mean on this measure. She may have been undernourished in the past and is possibly undernourished now.

Delayed age of menarche. Delayed age of menarche (age of first menstruation) is an indicator of low levels of calorie intake. The female sex hormone, estrogen, is produced from cholesterol, a fat (Pike & Brown 1984: 42). The fatter a woman is, the more estrogen she is likely to produce. Girls in the United States reach menarche earlier today than they did a century ago because they now have a higher percentage of fat (and estrogen) in their bodies. Because vigorous exercise reduces body fat, well-fed young girls who are also athletes tend to reach menarche later in life than their more sedentary counterparts.

Table 2.3 shows something of the geography of menarche. Notice how much higher is the age of menarche in the Third World populations listed in the bottom half of the table than in the presumably better-nourished industrialized populations in the top half.

Not all the advantages lie with the well-nourished populations. Recent research suggests that women who have fewer ovarian cycles (late menarche) are at reduced risk for breast cancer. There is also evidence that lean women are less prone to cancer because the lower levels of estrogen in lean women may reduce the growth of cells that can start tumors.

☐ **Effects of Undernutrition**

Undernutrition is responsible for a number of adverse effects on the individual, on his family, and on society.

Table 2.3 Median Age of Menarche, by Location of Population Studied

Place	Median Age	Year of Observation
Santiago, Chile (middle class)	12.3	1971
Hong Kong (affluent)	12.5	1961-65
Madrid (affluent)	12.8	1968
United States, all	12.8	1960-70
Hong Kong (middle class)	12.8	1961-65
Sydney, Australia	13.0	1970
Hong Kong (lower class)	13.3	1961-65
India, all urban	13.7	1956-65
Baghdad (poor)	14.0	1969
India, all rural	14.4	1956-65
South Africa (Bantu, rural)	15.0	---
Rwanda (Tutsi)	16.5	1957-58
Rwanda (Hutu)	17.0	1957-58
New Guinea (Lumi)	18.4	1967

Source: Evelth and Tanner 1967:Table 15.

Disease and death. Death is the most dramatic of the adverse effects. A limited number of deaths are caused primarily by undernutrition, but childhood diseases in which undernutrition plays a part, through weakening the immune system, are major killers of Third World children (Dever 1983). Intestinal disorders that lead to diarrhea are the leading Third World child killers, but other diseases associated with malnutrition, such as pneumonia, influenza, bronchitis, whooping cough, and measles, are also important. This set of largely preventable childhood diseases accounts for over 40 percent of childhood deaths in Third World countries (see Table 2.4).

Table 2.4 Percentage of Deaths of Children Under One Year Old Attributable to Causes Commonly Related to Malnutrition, 1967

Cause	Average of 12 Third World Countries[1]	Sweden
Gastritis and enteritis[2]	20.2	0.6
Pneumonia and influenza	13.8	2.2
Bronchitis	5.3	*
Whooping cough	2.1	*
Measles	1.3	0.8
All five causes	42.7	3.6

Source: Adapted from Latham 1984:56.

[1]Chile, Colombia, Ecuador, Guatemala, Mexico, Nicaragua, Peru, Egypt, Angola, Nigeria, Mauritius, Philippines. Data for Nigeria, 1963; Egypt, 1964; Angola, 1965; Guatemala and Nicaragua, 1966.

[2]Includes all gastrointestinal diseases.

*Less than 0.05%.

The death rate is especially high for Third World infants (children under one year of age). World Bank (1982) data indicate that infant mortality is 10 to 20 times higher in Third World than in developed countries, and J. M. Bengoa (1972), a leading authority on the relationship between undernutrition and death, has estimated that 52 percent of infant deaths in developing countries are nutritionally related. Using data gathered in the Punjab, Keilmann and McCord (1978) showed infant mortality to double with each 10 percent decline below 80 percent of the Harvard median weight-for-age (a commonly used nutritional status reference discussed briefly in the next chapter). Figure 2.4 is a graphic representation of their results.

The risk of death from nutrition-related disease in the Third World decreases dramatically after two years of age (Figure 2.5).

Differences in death rates among children under five between the Third World and the developed world are startling and are dramatized by comparing the data for representative Third World countries (top two-thirds of Table 2.5) with representative developed countries (bottom third of the same table). Again, these differences are heavily related to differences in nutrition.

Figure 2.4 Mortality in Children Age 1 to 36 Months by Nutritional Status, Punjab, India

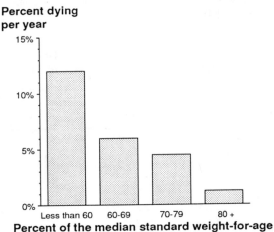

Source: Adapted from Galway, et al. 1987:31. Data from Keilmann and McCord 1978.

The emphasis in this section has been on deaths caused by disease related to undernutrition. Disease related to undernutrition is not always fatal, of course. Interactions between nutrition and health are discussed in Chapter 11.

Undernutrition, intellect, and education. Ancel Keys, working with conscientious objectors during World War II, found that male adults subjected to diets that led to measurable undernutrition first experienced intellectual problems—loss of memory and difficulty concentrating. Later, as their period of undernutrition continued, the men experienced problems with physical dexterity (Keys et al. 1950).

More-recent research has tended to focus on the potential effect of childhood undernutrition on later intellectual development and achievement. Researchers note that undernutrition, with its associated childhood diseases, may result in growth delays that are never made up. Figure 2.6 illustrates the pattern. When full-grown, the adult is shorter than he would otherwise be; he is stunted. Since 80 percent of a child's brain weight is achieved by the time he is two years old, it is tempting to wonder if early childhood undernutrition results in a similar stunting of intellect. Moreover, it seems reasonable to assume that a

Figure 2.5 Third World, Age-Specific Diarrheal Mortality Rates

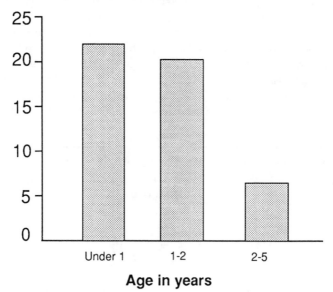

Deaths per 1,000 per year

Age in years

Source: Adapted from de Zoysa, et al. 1985:9.

Table 2.5 Child Mortality Rates in Selected Countries, 1970

	Percentage in Age Group Who Die Each Year		Percentage That Die Before Fifth Birthday	Age at Which Same Percentage as in Column 3 Have Died in United States
	Under 1 (1)	1-4 (2)	(3)	
India	13.9	4.40	28.1	63
Pakistan	14.2	5.30	31.0	66
Egypt	11.7	3.93	24.8	61
Guinea	21.6	5.20	36.7	68
Cameroon	13.7	3.93	26.5	62
Guatemala	8.9	2.75	18.5	57
Taiwan	2.0	0.43	3.6	20
Japan	1.5	0.14	1.9	1
United States	2.1	0.10	2.5	5
Sweden	1.3	0.07	1.7	1

Source: Adapted from Latham 1984:56.

child who is better nourished will be more likely to be alert, active, and demanding of its environment (Myers 1988) and will therefore be more likely to advance intellectually to its fullest capacity.

As to whether or not early childhood undernutrition degrades future intellect, the jury is still out. Empirical investigations of the relationship between present undernutrition and future mental capacity have produced mixed results. In a study conducted in Hyderabad, India, children who had previously suffered from kwashiorkor scored an average of 35 points below their matched controls on IQ tests administered up to six years after their recovery. However, the authors note that it was difficult "to determine to what extent this is a result of the episode of kwashiorkor and to what extent it is due to other factors" (Cham-

---

Figure 2.6 Effect of Protein-Calorie Malnutrition on Growth

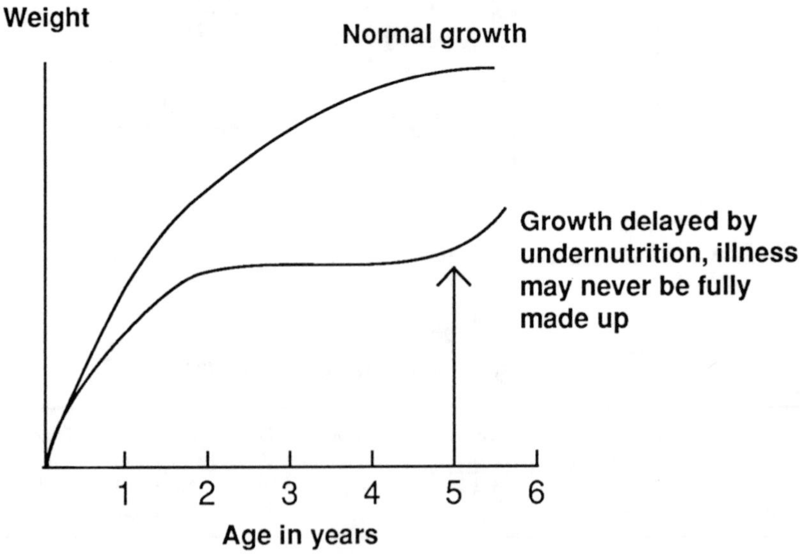

Source: Adapted from UNICEF 1982.

---

pakam, Srikantia & Gopalan 1968). Winick and coworkers (1973) tracked severely undernourished Korean orphans and found no signs of mental impairment years after their adoption by US families.

Chávez and Martínez (1982) studied child development among poor Mexican peasant families. They set up a controlled experiment in which one set of families was given supplemental food for the child through three years of age, and for the mother while she was pregnant and lactating. The control group was a set of families matched to the treated group so as to have similar genetic and socioeconomic characteristics, but given no food supplements. A large number of tests of neurological maturation and mental performance were given to each set of children. In virtually every instance (walking, control of bladder, and language development, for instance), the control children lagged behind the treated children. The better-nourished children were found to be more precocious in constructing three-word sentences, for example (see Figure 2.7).

Chávez and Martínez stress that it is not possible, at this time, to determine the ultimate significance of the gap between the undernourished and better-nourished children. The undernourished children may well catch up later on in life.

Using the Bayley scales for cognitive skills, Gretl Pelto (1987), professor of nutritional science at the University of Connecticut, in a seven-year longitudinal study of nutrition and cognitive development among 78 Mexican preschool children, tested short-term memory, responsiveness to stimulus, attention and distractability, abstract categorization skills, and sedentary passivity. She found that

Figure 2.7 Age at Which Child Constructs First Three-Word Sentence, Cumulative Percentages, Mexico

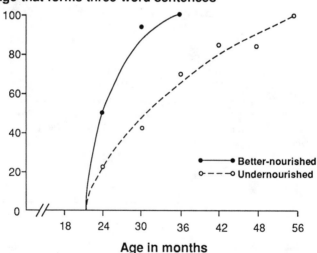

Source: Adapted from Chávez and Martínez 1982:90.

children with less animal food in their diet were shorter in stature and were delayed in their cognitive development, and that delays in intellectual development result from nutritionally induced growth stunting. But, she points out that there is nothing in her study to lead to the conclusion that these delays are permanent.

Janina Galler (1986), in a longitudinal study in Barbados, matched 183 children who had a history of PEM or kwashiorkor with 129 classmates without any history of malnutrition but of similar age and sex, and from the same socioeconomic group. Both sets of children were followed from age five to 18 years. By the time of sexual maturation, the previously undernourished children had essentially caught up with the matched group in terms of physical growth, but demonstrated small deficits in IQ throughout the growth period. The most striking difference between the groups was a fourfold increase in the frequency of attention deficit disorder among the previously undernourished. This syndrome is characterized by decreased attention span, impaired memory, high distractability, restlessness, and disobedience, and was found to reduce educational progress among the previously undernourished children to a far greater degree than the slight deficit in IQ they experienced.

Box 2.3 Nutrition and Schooling
Alan Berg

Nepalese children whose height was less then 70 percent of the norm were found, after accounting for income differences, to be 14 times less likely to be enrolled in school than children whose height was 85 percent of the norm. A similar relationship was found for weight: children at 70 percent of the norm were four times less likely to be enrolled in school than those at 85 percent of the norm and 13 times less likely than those at the norm. The relationship between height and weight and school enrollment was much stronger for boys than girls. These findings are consistent with those for three provinces in China where data collected by Bank staff showed that low height-for-age was consistently related inversely to performance, as measured by the number of grades a child was behind his age group. Studies in Brazil showed a 15 percent advantage in school performance among those who were part of a preschool nutrition program.

Source: Berg 1987: 87–88

Undernutrition seems to affect an individual's educational development not only by lessening attention span and making him or her apathetic to learning while in school, but also by increasing the school days missed through sickness. World Bank nutrition specialist Alan Berg (1973) cites the case of four Latin American countries where "illness caused children to miss more than 50 days of school a year." It appears that, if there is a relationship between childhood undernutrition and long-term intellectual development or achievement, it may be working itself out through such variables as frequency of attendance in school and attentiveness while there (see Box 2.3).

Undernutrition and the capacity to work. Undernutrition can reduce productivity through work time lost to sickness, lower productivity when working, and decreasing the total number of working years during a lifetime.

In a study of agricultural workers in Colombia and the United States, Spurr, Barac-Nieto, and Maksud (US Dept. of State 1976) looked at the relationship between nutritional status as measured both by indices of weight and height and by physical work capacity in terms of maximum capacity to consume oxygen. Their results suggest that some nutritional status variables have a high enough correlation to maximal oxygen capacity to be utilized as predictors for work capacity. They also found that the productive capacity of Colombian sugarcane cutters was directly related to their current nutritional status. Reduction in maximal aerobic power on the order of 50 percent was not uncommon among undernourished workers.

Undernutrition and demographic variables. The tendency for improved nutrition to increase population growth rates through a reduction in infant and child mortality is widely accepted. The evidence also suggests, however, that improved nutrition may cause at least temporary increases in population growth rates through increased fertility rates. Improved nutrition may increase fertility through reduced incidence of spontaneous abortion; increased fecundity or reproductive capacity (probability of conception at any given point in a woman's reproductive period) resulting from higher levels of body fat (and therefore estrogen); increased length of the reproductive period by lowering the age of menarche and raising the age of menopause; increased coital frequency; and reduced adult mortality, which reduces the number of widows of childbearing age (women not so likely to be exposed to conception).

On the other hand, the very reduction in infant mortality rates caused by improved nutrition may eventually be a major factor in reducing fertility over the long run. Parents seem to adjust their fertility in order to achieve a desired number of surviving children. If this is true, and if improved levels of nutrition result in reductions in infant and child mortality, then couples may be increasingly motivated to reduce the number of births.

Measuring
Undernutrition

To explain with some precision the differences in body-size existing over a smaller or larger area in terms of genetic and environmental factors is not at all easy. Partly this is because these factors interact, partly because of the complexity of the genetic determination of stature and other dimensions, and partly because climate or disease factors may in some cases be more important than nutritional.

—Weiner 1977: 420

Because resources for coping with undernutrition are scarce and therefore need to be spent wisely, we need to be able to accurately identify and measure it.

■ INDIRECT MEASURES

A common approach to identifying undernutrition is to examine aggregate data and make inferences from it. For instance, low birth weights or high infant mortality rates in a country or region of a country are assumed to flag high rates of undernutrition (e.g., Table 2.5). Aggregate data like this can provide a pretty good first approximation on where in the world you are likely to find substantial numbers of undernourished people. Since undernutrition and poor health tend to go together, aggregate data on morbidity can also provide indirect measures of the incidence of undernutrition in that country or region.

The Philippines does one of the most careful jobs of nutrition surveillance of any Third World country. Because of the accuracy and detail of Philippine data, from time to time in this chapter I refer to them for illustrations suggestive of the incidence of Third World nutritional problems. For example, according to the 1982 Nationwide Nutrition Survey (Philippines, National Science and Technology Authority 1984), 52 percent of the country's population was afflicted with roundworms (ascariasis). Hookworm infection was noted among 19 percent of the male population between 13 and 59 years of age. Of the 14,785 subjects examined, 69 percent were found to be positive for some type of parasite. With morbidity data such as this, one could expect to find substantial rates of undernutrition in the Philippines.

So far in this chapter I have mentioned low birth weights, high infant mortality rates, and high morbidity rates as suggestive of undernutrition in a population. But these variables do not measure nutritional status directly. Using these indicators, undernutrition is merely inferred from the nonnutritional aggregate data. Therefore these measures are called indirect indicators of nutritional status. They are normally used to identify countries or regions where undernutrition rates can be expected to be high.

Another indirect approach to identifying regions with nutritional problems is to look at food balance sheets. Table 3.1 is a simple food balance sheet for corn (maize) in Swaziland for the year 1987/88. Annual human consumption for one commodity such as corn is estimated by adding up beginning-of-the-year stocks, production, and imports, and subtracting from this total, exports, amount used as livestock feed, amount used for seed, and end-of-the-year stocks.

Table 3.1 Annual Food Balance Sheet for Corn, Swaziland, 1987/88

Category	1,000 Tons
Beginning stocks (carryover from last year)	3
Production	88
Imports	54
Exports	5
Fed to livestock	37
Seed	3
Ending stocks (carryover into next year)	4
Human consumption	96

Source: US Department of Agriculture 1988:40.

Once human consumption is estimated for every food commodity in a country, the food consumed can be converted to calories and nutrients, and per capita consumption figures can then be derived. Table 3.2 is such a completed food balance sheet for India. If a country's per capita consumption turns out to be below amounts recommended by nutritionists, there is good cause to assume that a substantial block of its population is undernourished.

Infant mortality rates, birth rates, nutrition-related disease rates, and food balance sheets serve as indirect measures of nutritional status. Useful as such measures are in identifying nutritional trouble spots, they do not give us good information on the nature and extent of malnutrition. For this we must turn to direct measures of nutritional status.

Table 3.2 Food Balance Sheet, India, Average 1984-1986

Population 684,534,000

Units = 1,000 Metric Tons

	Production	Imports	Stock Changes	Exports	Processed Trade (E-1)	Domestic Supply	Feed	Seed	Manuf. Use	Nonfood Use	Food Waste	Food	Kilograms/Year	Grams	Per Day Calories	Per Day Protein	Per Day Fat Grams
Grand total															2056	49.7	32.6
Vegetable products															1952	44.2	25.6
Animal products															104	5.5	7.0
Grand total exc. alcohol															2056	49.7	32.6
Cereals													183.3	502.2	1369	32.5	6.4
Wheat	34550	676	-1333	159	17	36383	415	2739			2771	30459	44.5	121.9	380	11.1	1.8
Paddy rice	74716	61	-6130		895	80012	299	4562	2		4450	70700	103.3	283.0	683	12.8	1.5
Barley	2020	2		16		2006	242	145	4		133	1482	2.2	5.9	14	.4	.1
Maize	6440	9	60			6389	122	444	52		798	4973	7.3	19.9	64	1.6	.6
Millet	9124		-329			9453	122	313			433	8585	12.5	34.4	107	3.1	1.2
Sorghum	11216	1	792			10425	135	381			728	9182	13.4	36.8	120	3.5	1.3
Cereals NES	52	10				62						61	.1	.2	1		
Prepared cereals NES					-1												
Roots and tubers													19.6	53.6	42	.6	.1
Cassava	5904					5904					403	5501	8.0	22.0	19	.1	
Potatoes	9353			17		9336		1412			1455	6468	9.5	25.9	18	.4	
Sweet potatoes	1491					1491					75	1416	2.1	5.7	5	.1	
Sugars and honey													20.2	55.3	186		
Sugar cane	143670	6				143676	1580	9483	131886		727		1.1	2.9	1		
Raw sugar	5385		-931	2	286	6028			6			6022	8.8	24.1	86		
Noncentrifugal sugar	7910					7910	432	413				7065	10.3	28.3	99	.3	
Pulses													12.5	34.3	120	7.0	1.1
Dry beans	2561	48		1		2608	130	273			130	2073	3.0	8.3	28	1.8	.1
Dry peas	295					295	15	23			15	242	.4	1.0	3	.2	
Chick-peas	4474	3		1		4476	570	256			90	3561	5.2	14.3	52	2.8	.8
Pigeon peas	1867					1867	93	57			93	1624	2.4	6.5	22	1.3	.1
Lentils	408	15				423	21	28			21	353	.5	1.4	5	.6	.1
Pulses NES	901	2		1		902	45	99			45	713	1.0	2.9	10	.7	
Nuts and oilseeds													5.2	14.4	28		2.4
Cashew nuts	183	34			134	83				37	46		.1	.2			
Almonds		4				4						4					
Walnuts	16					16						15					
Soybeans	433					433		31	260		13	130	.2	.5	2	.2	.1
Groundnuts in shell	6009		303		47	5659		635	4501		322	200	.3	.8	3	.1	.2
Coconuts	4444				-62	4506			1606			2900	4.2	11.6	17	.2	1.5
Castor beans	220	1				221		5		210							
Sunflower seed	55					55			55								
Rapeseed	1845	24				1869		23	1759			87	.1	.3	2	.1	.2
Safflower seed	274					274		7	262		5						

Table 3.2 *(continued)*

	Production	Imports	Stock Changes	Exports	Processed Trade (E-1)	Domestic Supply	Feed	Seed	Manufacturer Use	Nonfood Use	Food Waste	Food	Kilograms/Year	Grams	Per Day Grams	Calories	Protein Grams	Fat Grams
Sesame seed	436		-20	9		447		10	317		10	111	.2	.4	3		.1	.2
Cottonseed	2621					2621	460	144	1492	393	131							
Linseed	411	1				412		28	310		8	66	.1	.3	1			.1
Oilseeds NES	131			6		125		8	89		3	26						
Vegetables													58.6	160.4	37		2.3	.3
Cabbages	463					463					23	440	.6	1.8	1			
Tomatoes	743					743					74	669	1.0	2.7	1			
Cauliflower	650					650					32	617	.9	2.5				
Dry onions	2579			159		2420					129	2291	3.3	9.2	3		.1	
Garlic	202			4		198					10	187	.3	.8	1			
Green beans	41					41					4	37	.1	.1				
Green peas	253					253					25	228	.3	.9				
Fresh vegetables NES	35667			3		35664			143			35521	51.9	142.2	31		2.0	.3
Fruit																		
Bananas	4535					4535					907	3628	23.1	63.4	29		.3	.2
Oranges	1153					1153					115	1038	5.3	14.5	9		.1	
Lemons and limes	485			1		484					49	436	1.5	4.2	1			
Grapefruit and pomelo	20					20					2	18	.6	1.7				
Citrus fruit NES	30					30					3	27	.1	.1				
Apples	734			1		733					73	660	1.0	2.6	1			
Pears	64					64					6	57	.1	.2				
Apricots	15					15					1	13		.1				
Cherries	4					4						4						
Peaches and nectarines	15					15					1	13						
Plums	28					28					3	25	.1	.1				
Grapes	196	8			-26	230					21	209	.3	.8				
Figs	2				-1	3						3						
Mangoes	8365					8365			33		837	7495	10.9	30.0	13			.1
Pineapples	548					548			55			493	.7	2.0	1			
Dates	34				34					1								
Papayas	262					262					39	222	.3	.9				
Fresh tropical fruit NES	1215			7		1208			24		182	1001	1.5	4.0	2			
Fresh fruit NES	493	3				496					50	446	.7	1.8				
Meat and Offals													1.3	3.7	6		.5	.4
Mutton and lamb	120			4		116						116	.2	.5	1		.1	.1
Goat meat	268					268						268	.4	1.1	2		.2	.1
Pig meat	70					70						70	.1	.3	1		.1	.1
Chicken meat	111					111						111	.2	.4	1		.1	.1
Eggs																		
Hen eggs	733					733		18			73	642	.9	2.6	4		.3	.3

Item	Production	Imports	Stock var.	Exports	Domestic supply	Feed	Processing	Waste	Food	Per caput kg/yr	g/day	Calories	Protein	Fat
Fish and seafood	928				928				928	3.1	8.4	5	.9	.2
Freshwater diadrom	449				448				401	1.4	3.7	3	.4	.1
Demersal fish	653		1		617				492	.6	1.6	1	.2	
Pelagic fish			36	125		47				.7	2.0	1	.2	
Milk										38.2	104.7	66	3.8	3.6
Whole cow milk	13033		-44		13077			156	12921	18.9	51.7	31	1.5	1.7
Skim cow milk			-448		448				448	.6	1.8	1	.1	
Buffalo milk	17000			4303	17000			819	11878	17.4	47.5	32	2.1	1.7
Goat milk	923				923			11	912	1.3	3.7	2	.1	.1
Oils and fats										6.4	17.5	153		17.3
Vegetable oils and fats		4								5.3	14.7	130		14.7
Soya bean oil	47	517			564		32		564	.8	2.2	20		2.2
Groundnut oil	1260	1			1257		35		1226	1.8	4.9	43		4.9
Coconut oil	189	23			212		42		177	.3	.7	6		.7
Palm oil		439			439				397	.6	1.6	14		1.6
Sunflower seed oil	16	1			17		3		18	.1	.1	1		.1
Rapeseed oil	580	136			716				713	1.0	2.9	25		2.9
Safflower oil	73				73				73	.1	.3	3		.3
Sesame seed oil	127				127		11		116	.2	.5	4		.5
Cottonseed oil	209	9			218				218	.3	.9	8		.9
Linseed oil	102	1			103		48		55	.1	.2	2		.2
Rice bran oil	109				109		11		98		.4	3		.4
Animal oils and fats										1.0	2.8	24		2.7
Tallow	10	31			41				41	.1	.2	1		.2
Ghee of buffalo milk	515				515				515	.8	2.1	18		2.0
Butter of buffalo milk	124				124				124	.2	.5	4		.4
Spices										1.2	3.4	10	.4	.4
Pepper, white/long/black	29	22	-1		8			1	6		.1			
Anise, badian, fennel	20	1			21				20					
Pimento, allspice	529	6			523			26	496		2.0	6	.2	.2
Cloves, whole & stems		1			1									
Nutmeg, mace, cardamom	5	2			5				6					.2
Spices NES	415	87			330			8	321		1.3	4		
Stimulants										.7	1.5			
Green coffee	126	76	3		47			6	41	.1	.2	1	.1	
Cocoa beans								6						
Tea	559	223			336			6	330	.5	1.3	1	.1	.1
Areca nuts (betel)	185				185		179							

Source: FAO 1991: 158-159.

■ DIRECT MEASURES

Direct assessment of nutritional status involves the actual examination of individuals. The common methods of direct assessment are clinical, biochemical, dietary, and anthropometric. Each method has shortcomings and each results in a somewhat different assessment of the nature and extent of nutritional disorders.

☐ Clinical Assessment

Clinical assessment of nutritional status relies on the examination of physical signs on the body that are symptomatic of nutritional disorders (Jelliffe 1966). Kwashiorkor, for instance, is accompanied by loss of pigment in the hair (it often turns reddish) and by edema (swelling) of the ankles. Using clinical observation (looking for a generalized swelling at the base of the neck above the collarbone), the Philippine nutrition survey found that the goiter rate in subjects nine years old and over was high—3.1 percent.

Correct identification of nutritional disorders using physical signs depends not only on the training and skill of the clinician but on how well the signs are manifested in the particular individual. Clinical signs are difficult to quantify and are usually obvious only in the advanced stage of the disease, so clinical assessment can be used in only the most severe and specific types of nutritional disorders.

☐ Biochemical Assessment

Biochemical assessment requires examination of body fluids such as blood or urine for the complex metabolic changes that accompany nutritional disorders. In the Philippine nutrition survey over 14,000 blood samples were drawn and analyzed. From these samples and using standards of the World Health Organization (WHO) of the United Nations, 27 percent of the population were found to be anemic. The highest rates of anemia were for those below one year (51 percent) and for pregnant women (49 percent).

Biochemical tests provide an accurate indication of the nature of short-term nutritional problems, but their complexity and expense are an impediment to their widespread use in field surveys. Imagine the problems associated with persuading a sample of over 14,000 individuals all over the Philippines to submit to having blood drawn (in addition to providing a stool sample—remember the parasitism data cited earlier) and then getting these materials to appropriate laboratory apparatus for analysis before the samples deteriorate in the heat!

☐ Dietary Assessment

Dietary surveys are often employed to assess nutritional status. Two approaches are used: (1) dietary recall, in which the subject is asked to remember what he or she ate, say during the past 24 hours or the past seven days; and (2) dietary record, in which someone actually records the amount of food consumed at mealtimes, often by weighing it. Both methods have their unique advantages and drawbacks.

Dietary recall has the advantage of being able to catch the subjects when they are not expecting to be surveyed. They are less likely to adjust their consumption because of the survey. On the other hand, it is often difficult to remember exactly what you or members of your family ate during the past 24 hours, much less during the past week. And estimates of quantity consumed are particularly prone to error in recall surveys.

When making food records, especially if every portion of food must be weighed, there is a strong tendency for the cook to simplify the diet to make the record–keeping easier (Quandt 1987). People participating as subjects in a food record keeping survey are especially prone to adjust their diet so that things will "look better" to the surveyor, especially if the surveyor is in the household for the purpose of making and recording the measurements.

In both types of surveys measurement of quantity of food consumed by breast-fed babies presents difficulties. And in both cases seasonal variation in consumption may confound the data unless appropriate adjustments are made. For instance, the Philippine survey was done during February through May, a time when access to the countryside is made easier by the relative absence of monsoon rains and typhoons. The retail price of tomatoes, for example, is typically 250 percent higher in November than it is in April. Similarly the price of rice tends to be low during the survey period, while the price of corn tends to be high (Philippines, Ministry of Agriculture 1981a, b). The unadjusted survey data thus tend to overestimate annual consumption of tomatoes and rice, which are in abundant supply during the survey period, and to underestimate the consumption of corn.

In either case (dietary recall or record) results of the survey can be used to determine amounts of various nutrients consumed, and these amounts can then be compared to a dietary standard appropriate to the particular country being observed, in order to determine nutritional status.

In the Philippine survey food energy intake was 1,808 kilocalories per capita per day, which was 89 percent of the national target of 2,031. Protein intake was at 50.6 grams, or 99.6 percent of the target level. Consumption steadily increased with increasing per capita income, especially for food items such as refined sugar, soft drinks, cooking oil, pork, chicken, eggs, evaporated milk, and mangos. The proportion of the households found as having met 100 percent adequacy level for various nutrients is given in Table 3.3.

Dietary assessment is useful in studies relating consumption and income, or determining food allocation patterns within the family. But care must be taken in interpreting the results of such surveys. Food intake is not always a good index of nutritional status. For instance, secondary malnutrition can substantially degrade the nutritional status of an otherwise appropriately fed individual.

Table 3.3 Households Meeting 100-Percent Adequacy Levels for Various Nutrients, Philippines, 1982

Nutrient	Percentage of Households
Energy (calories)	32.9
Protein	46.0
Iron	35.5
Calcium	26.3
Thiamine	19.3
Riboflavin	8.1
Niacin	66.5
Ascorbic Acid	35.2

Source: Philippines National Science and Technology Authority 1984.

☐ **Anthropometric Assessment**

Anthropometry is the science of measuring the human body and its parts. Human physical growth (increase in size) and development (differentiation) are both responsive to variations in calorie and protein intakes. Because of this, measurements of the human body, when compared to some reference standard, provide clues as to protein and calorie nutrition. This is especially true during youth, when growth is so rapid, but to some extent also true during adulthood, when various dimensions change gradually with aging. Thus anthropometry can be used to suggest the protein and/or calorie nutritional status of adults as well as children. For instance, measurements showing adequate muscle but low fat suggest calorie deficiency; measurements showing inadequate muscle but adequate fat suggest protein deficiency. (The method of estimating fat content and, therefore by deduction, muscle content of the body is described later in this chapter. The necessary measurements are usually taken on the arm.)

We should note immediately that nutrition is not the only influencer of bodily growth and development. Growth and development can also be affected by variables such as genetic disposition, health, hormonal abnormalities, or deficiencies of micronutrients (for instance, zinc deficiency is associated with poor growth). Since anthropometry does not provide particularly useful clues as to dietary deficiencies (micronutrient shortages), it is not normally used to measure them. Nevertheless, since nutritional status is by far the most common variable normally influencing bodily growth and development, and since deficiencies in calories and/or protein are by far the most important causes of subnormal growth and development in the Third World, anthropometry is generally assumed to provide strong clues as to protein and calorie nutrition in the Third World. In the Philippine National Nutrition Survey, for example, using a cut-off point of less than 85 percent of the standard weight-for-height, 10 percent of preschool children were found to be moderately to severely undernourished. Using an alternative anthropometric measure, less than 75 percent of standard weight-for-age, 27 percent of preschoolers were found to be moderately to severely undernourished.

In developed countries anthropometry is used largely as a measure of overnutrition, which is the most common nutritional problem among high-income people. Adults who are trying to keep their weight down are using the anthropometric measure weight-for-age as a reference standard, although they seldom think of their activity in such technical terms. Using a body-mass index, which is determined by dividing weight in kilograms by height in centimeters squared, the US National Center for Health Statistics (NCHS) found 8 percent of the adult men and 11 percent of the adult women in the United States to be severely overweight (US, Dept. of Health and Human Services 1987).

Low-income people in Third World countries are at risk for undernutrition (insufficient calories), which is very commonly exacerbated by secondary malnutrition (e.g., a diarrheal infection that robs the body of nutrients). Anthropometric measures are useful in flagging this type of nutritional disorder, that is, some combination of undernutrition and secondary malnutrition. Because of the strong link between the two, undernutrition and secondary malnutrition are commonly grouped together and called, simply, undernutrition. And that is what we will do throughout the rest of this book.

Since 1966, when the WHO published a monograph by D. B. Jelliffe titled *The Assessment of the Nutritional Status of the Community*, which provided a set of standardized anthropometric measurements useful in nutritional assessment, anthropometry has become the most widely used tool in nutritional assessment. The most common measures used for anthropometric assessment of nutritional status are height, weight, and a combination of arm circumference and skinfold thickness. They are usually used in conjunction with sex and age (as in weight-for-age or height-for-age) and sometimes in combination with each other (as in weight-for-height).

Low cost and a relatively high degree of accuracy combine to make this method so popular. Training time of field surveyors is cut to a minimum. All the measures are relatively easy to do, and the tools required are easy to use: scales, tape measures, measuring boards, skinfold calipers. Intelligent amateurs can be trained in a matter of days to take accurate measurements using these tools. In contrast, training technicians to recognize and diagnose undernutrition from clinical symptoms may take weeks or months. (From the point of view of accuracy, age data may be the biggest problem in using anthropometry. Third World adults often have only a vague idea of how old they are, and illiterate mothers sometimes have difficulty telling the age of their children.) Capital requirements for anthropometry are minimal. Compared to the laboratory apparatus involved in biochemical analysis, anthropometric tools are inexpensive. And anthropometry measures the results of nutrition (the size and shape of the body) rather than nutritional inputs (as in dietary intake). Because of its quantitative nature, anthropometry can be used to judge varying degrees of undernutrition—not just its presence or absence. And by using a mix of anthropometric indices, one can make judgments about the nature of a nutritional disorder (protein or calorie) as well as the time dimension of the disorder (past or present).

■ USING ANTHROPOMETRY TO CLASSIFY NUTRITIONAL STATUS

If you decide to use anthropometry to measure degrees of undernutrition, three issues are immediately raised: (1) What set of variables (e.g., weight-for-age or weight-for-height) do you use to measure undernutrition; (2) which group of people do you use as your reference population; and (3) what kind of deviation, and how much of this deviation from the reference standard, constitutes undernutrition?

It is an unsettling and vexatious fact that no clear consensus exists on any of these questions. It may be comforting to know that the WHO has recently recommended using NCHS data (sometimes called the Atlanta standards because NCHS headquarters is in Atlanta, Georgia) as the reference population for the world, that the most commonly quoted index of undernutrition is stated in terms of weight-for-age, and that a deviation of 25 percentage points or more below the reference standard (equal to or less than 75 percent of standard weight-for-age) is the most commonly used definition of undernutrition. But that by no means indicates that the controversy surrounding our three questions is settled. For instance, WHO currently recommends the use of weight-for-height and height-for-age, instead of the more popular weight-for-age measure.

We will now examine some of the problems associated with the three issues raised above. We will look at some popular and widely used systems for classifying nutritional status, and see how the people who developed them dealt with these problems.

☐ Within-Population Variables

The purpose of a reference population is to provide an optimal standard against which to judge the growth and maturation of particular individuals—a reference against which deviations of individuals can be measured and from which nutritional status can be inferred. But before considering the selection of a reference population we will first look at some normal changes we can expect of an individual as he goes through life.

After seeing how certain characteristics that provide clues to nutritional status change through the life cycle, we will look at examples of how these changes differ from one population to another. Then we will consider the issue of how much these differences among populations may be the result of heredity and how much of environment. If the variations in the nutritional status variables among populations are found to be largely due to heredity, this will argue for the use of more than one reference population. On the other hand, if variations in these variables among populations are found to be largely caused by the environment, this will argue for the use of a single reference population to be used worldwide.

Whenever you try to guess someone's age you use, as at least some of your clues, body size and configuration. To the extent that you do that, you are using informal anthropometric measurements to deduce age. That is, you learn what to expect in the way of variations in height, weight, even fatness, as people grow and develop, and you can deduce age fairly well from what you see of these characteristics, although you use other clues to age as well. Anthropometry, usually in conjunction with known age, uses deviations from these expected changes as clues to nutritional difficulties. We will review the most commonly used anthropometric standards used in nutritional surveillance.

Age, sex, and weight. Table 3.4 shows the median weight of men and women 18 to 74 years of age in the United States. The table is easy to read, but if you are not on the median, it does not say much about how you compare with others who are off the median. This sort of comparison is most easily made on charts such as the one shown in the lower half of Figure 2.2 (p. 20). The charts are harder to read but they contain much more information.

Charts such as Figure 2.2 are extremely useful for monitoring growth in children. By plotting her own child's progress on such a chart, a mother (or her health care worker) can easily spot deviations from the normal growth pattern that may signal a health or nutritional problem. (It is easy to mistake some growth for adequate growth unless the child's progress is charted against an appropriate reference population.) Around the world, charts such as these are in widespread use for monitoring growth.

Age, sex, and height. The top half of Figure 2.2 shows a typical height-for-age chart. Since babies cannot stand up it is customary to measure children under the age of two lying down. And since the reclining measurement is a bit different from the standing measurement, the two are distinguished by calling the first "length" and the second "height." Thus the top half of Figure 2.2 technically shows length, not height.

Sex, height, and weight. As the body grows, we expect the proportions between height (or length) and weight to change according to standard patterns, with the male pattern being different from that of the female. Such standard ratios between height and weight are commonly graphed, and one such graph, for US preschool girls, is shown in Figure 2.3 (p. 21).

Age, sex, and fat. There is a marked tendency for the human body to add fat as it ages. On Table 3.5 you see how the percentage of the total body that is fat

Table 3.4 Median Weight of Adults, United States, 1971-1974

Sex and Height	18-74	Age Group in Years					
		18-24	25-34	35-44	45-54	55-64	65 and over
	Weight in Pounds						
Men							
62 inches	140	*	*	*	*	*	148
63 inches	148	*	155	*	154	*	144
64 inches	151	145	148	160	159	154	148
65 inches	155	134	150	159	161	162	156
66 inches	161	155	157	164	165	165	159
67 inches	167	153	167	172	168	167	167
68 inches	168	153	164	177	173	171	167
69 inches	169	161	167	169	176	172	168
70 inches	176	162	180	185	184	177	177
71 inches	181	170	175	186	190	187	190
72 inches	185	168	185	197	193	182	185
73 inches	192	180	192	204	192	194	*
74 inches	196	197	182	*	*	*	*
75 inches	192	*	*	*	*	*	*
76 inches	197	*	*	*	*	*	*
Women							
57 inches	121	*	*	*	*	*	133
58 inches	119	112	115	118	*	119	130
59 inches	131	112	126	132	148	141	131
60 inches	131	115	120	124	135	145	136
61 inches	133	118	121	128	140	148	140
62 inches	132	119	127	134	134	139	142
63 inches	137	129	131	136	143	147	144
64 inches	138	130	131	138	147	147	150
65 inches	140	130	134	147	150	151	150
66 inches	144	131	137	145	151	151	147
67 inches	144	138	144	146	152	*	168
68 inches	154	140	152	160	186	*	171
69 inches	144	134	143	167	*	*	*
70 inches	159	*	*	*	*	*	*

Source: US Department of Health, Education and Welfare 1976.

Note: Examined persons were measured without shoes: Clothing weight ranged from 0.20 to 0.62 pound, which was not deducted from weights shown.

*Data missing or sample size too small to be reliable.

Table 3.5 NCHS Median Percentage of Total Body That Is Fat, Adult Males and Females by Age

Age	Males	Females
18-24	16	27
25-29	18	29
30-34	23	31
35-39	23	32
40-44	26	35
45-49	26	36
50-54	27	39
55-59	27	39
60-64	27	40
65-69	26	38
70-74	26	38

Source: Adapted from Frisancho 1990:Table IV.19, p. 57.

increases from early adulthood to old age. Over the eons of human evolution it may have been the case that older people in the family, no longer being involved in the hunt (men) or childbearing (women) would tend to be shortchanged on food during periods of hunger. But these older people could be of some use to the clan. There may have been survival value to the clan if the older people had some fat reserves to tide them over seasons of short food supplies.

Notice that throughout adulthood women, on the average, have a greater percentage of fat in their bodies than men. In childbearing, women have to provide nutrients for the growing fetus before birth, and during lactation, food for the child after birth. Throughout most of the eons of human evolution it was probably difficult for the mother to consume as many calories as both she and her offspring needed during the last few months of pregnancy and the first few months of lactation. There was therefore survival value in the woman's being provided with a reserve supply of fat to tide her and the baby over this critical period. At the same time, for the family as a whole there was probably survival value in the man's having a greater proportion of his body composition be muscle.

No part of the body represents the fat content of the whole body. Even if you get total body density by weighing people and then comparing their weight with the weight of the water they displace while submerged in a tank, it is almost impossible to estimate accurately the percentage of the entire body that is fat. Nevertheless, the midupper arm has been selected as being fairly representative of the body as a whole and is used as an indicator of nutritional status.

Figure 3.1 shows how the fat content of the midupper arm changes with age for US males and females. If you will compare the data in Figure 3.1 with that of Table 3.5, you will notice that the midupper arm tends to be a bit fattier than the body as a whole.

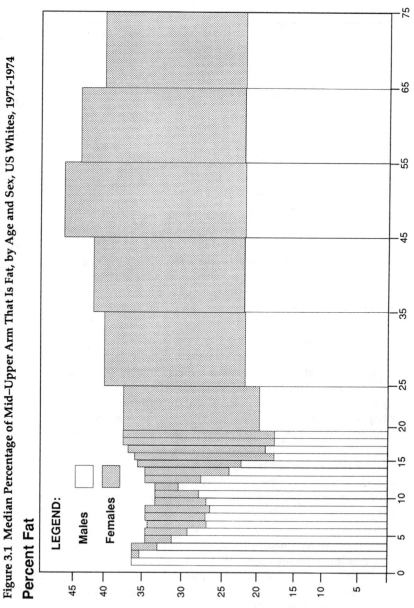

Figure 3.1 Median Percentage of Mid–Upper Arm That Is Fat, by Age and Sex, US Whites, 1971-1974

Source: Frisancho 1981 (Table III)

Figure 3.2 Changes in Spontaneous Physical Activity and Caloric Intake in Male Rats During Growth

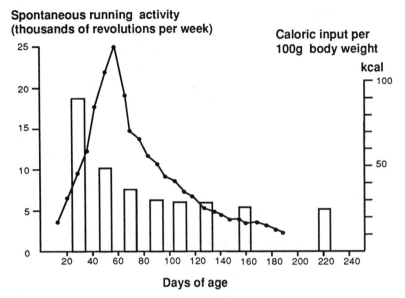

The dots show running activity (measured on the left-hand scale), and the vertical bars show caloric intake per day per 100 grams of body weight (measured on the right-hand scale).

Source: Adapted Parizokova 1977:16.

In Figure 3.1 you see the tendency for fat percentage to fall after birth and then rise again in adulthood. Although born with a reserve fat supply, often called baby fat, humans, like other mammals, tend toward intense activity during their growing period. (See Figure 3.2 for a good illustration of spontaneous physical activity and calorie intake by rats during their growth phase.) What with the energy requirements of growth plus all that youthful physical activity, humans tend to reduce their fat reserve during their growth years, only to build it back up in adulthood.

☐ **Choosing a Reference Population**

Variations from one population to another. We have looked at expected variations in weight, height, and fat by age and sex within a given population. Often these data sets change from one population to another.

In Figure 3.3 you see variations in body weights in seven Latin American countries and the United States. Boys in all eight countries start life with fairly similar weights, but by adulthood there is considerable variation among countries.

Figure 3.3 Median Male Weight-for-Age in Seven Latin American Countries and the United States

Weight in kilograms

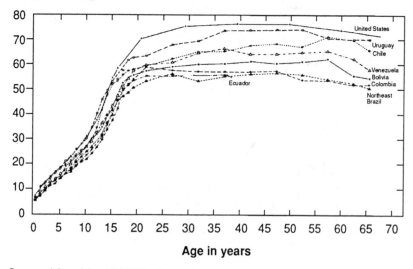

Age in years

Source: Adapted from US White House, President's Science Advisory Committee 1967:37.

In Table 3.6 weight-for-age in the Philippines and in the United States is contrasted. Note that, for the first 20 years of life, Filipinos' weights tend to be from 70 to 80 percent of those in the United States. Although, because of different age breaks, the data are not strictly comparable in later years, as the populations age the differences in weight appear to increase.

In Figure 3.4 the height of the US population is contrasted with that of an Indian village (Bagbana) that I surveyed in 1981. Both males and females track the fifth percentile of the NCHS data. That is, 95 percent of the US population is taller than an average Bagbana villager of comparable age.

In Figure 3.5 the weight of the US population is compared with that of Bagbana. The villagers track the US data fairly closely during the first couple of years of life, but the difference increases with age, especially for females. By 70 years of age, the village females' weight is only slightly over 50 percent of the weight for 70-year-old US females. Are 70-year-old Bagbana village women underweight? Are 70-year-old US women overweight? To what extent are the differences in these two populations the result of nutrition? To what extent do they stem from heredity, climate, or other factors?

Nature vs. nurture, or heredity vs. environment. It is a widely held view among geneticists that the body has a built-in genetic code that determines maximum height (see Box 3.1). Provide an optimal environment, including appro-

Table 3.6 Philippine and US Mean Weight-for-Age, by Sex

	Weight in Kilograms				Percentage That Column	
	US American		Philippine			
	Male	Female	Male	Female	3 is	4 is
Age	1	2	3	4	of 1	of 2
1	11.8	10.8	9.1	8.8	77	81
2	13.6	13.0	11.1	10.7	81	82
3	15.7	14.9	12.9	12.3	82	83
4	17.8	17.0	14.2	13.8	78	81
5	19.8	19.6	15.7	15.6	79	79
6	23.0	22.1	17.3	16.8	75	76
7	25.1	24.7	18.8	18.7	75	75
8	28.2	27.9	20.5	21.1	73	76
9	31.1	31.9	22.7	22.8	73	71
10	36.4	36.1	24.7	25.2	68	70
11	40.3	41.8	26.6	27.7	66	66
12	44.2	46.4	29.2	32.7	66	70
13	49.9	50.9	34.0	36.5	68	72
14	57.1	54.8	37.6	41.2	66	75
15	61.0	55.1	43.0	43.9	70	80
16	67.1	58.1	47.8	44.6	71	77
17	66.7	59.6	49.9	45.8	75	77
18	71.1	50.0	53.1	46.1	72	78
19	71.7	60.2	52.5	45.9	73	76
	United States					
18-24	73.8	60.6				
25-34	78.7	64.2				
35-44	80.9	67.1			Data	
45-54	80.9	68.0				
55-64	78.8	67.9				
65-74	74.8	66.6				
					not	
			Philippine			
20-29			55.3	47.5		
30-39			56.9	49.1	comparable	
40-49			55.9	48.6		
50-59			52.8	47.2		
60-69			52.2	54.5		
70+			51.3	41.7		

Source: US Department of Health and Human Services 1987; Philippines National Science and Technology Authority 1983:203.

priate nutrition backed up by good health, and the individual will attain that height. Subject the growing child to prolonged undernutrition, significant periods of disease, or both, and he will never attain his full height potential.

Given variations among individuals within a population, to what extent are

Figure 3.4 NCHS (US) Median Height-for-Age vs. Median Height-for-Age, Bagbana Village, India

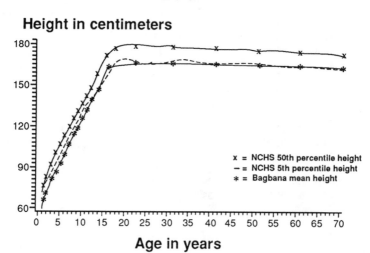

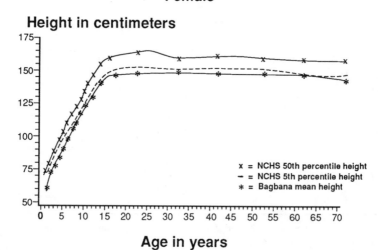

Source: Adapted from Dever 1983:71.

Figure 3.5 NCHS (US) Median Weight-for-Age vs. Median Weight-for-Age, Bagbana Village, India

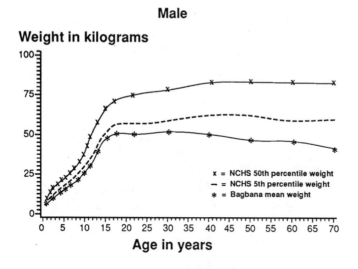

Source: Adapted from Dever 1983:73.

the variations in stature among populations the result of differences in genetic potential, and to what extent do they stem from living conditions, including nutrition?

D. F. Roberts (1953) examined the question: Does climate affect stature? He reviewed the evidence from 149 sample surveys representing all major human varieties from many parts of the world and found an inverse relationship

---

Box 3.1 Human Growth: Heredity Versus Environment
J. M. Tanner

The height, weight, or body-build of a child or an adult always represents the resultant of both the genetical and environmental forces, together with their interaction. It is a long way from the possession of certain genes to the acquisition of a height of 2 [meters].

In modern genetics it is a truism that any particular gene depends for its expression firstly on the internal environment created by all the other genes, and secondly on the external environment. Furthermore, the interaction of genes and environment may not be additive. That is to say, bettering the nutrition by a fixed amount may not produce a 10 per cent increase in height in all persons irrespective of their genetical constitutions; instead a 12 per cent rise may occur in the genetically tall and an 8 per cent rise in the genetically short.

Thus it is very difficult to specify quantitatively the relative importance of heredity and environment in controlling growth and physique under any given circumstances; the particular circumstances must always be made clear. In general the nearer optimal the environment the more the genes have a chance to show their potential actions.

Source: Extracted from Tanner 1977:339.

---

between body weight and environmental temperature. In hot climates people tend to get linear—they grow lanky. They tend to maximize surface relative to mass so as to lose heat easily. In cold climates they tend to maximize their mass relative to body surface, that is, they become round, chunky. This seems reasonable because a chunky body holds body heat efficiently and helps keep you warm in cold weather, whereas a lanky body radiates heat easily and helps keep you cool in the tropics. To what extent is it heredity, to what extent is it environment? It is reasonable to suppose that over the generations in a hot climate, natural selection has resulted in a gene pool producing lanky bodies, with the opposite happening in cold climates. Has that, in fact, happened?

Good data exist on height-for-age among Caucasian, black, and Chinese peoples in comparably high-income circumstances, with presumably near-optimal nutrition. There seems to be little difference in height between the Caucasians and blacks in this group, yet the Chinese are growing up shorter (Tanner 1977: 342). There is certainly evidence that there are differences in human growth potential by groups or race (Pygmies, for example, appear to have a clear genetic proclivity for shortness), but the evidence is less clear-cut than is the evidence on nutrition affecting growth and development.

It is easy to show impacts of environment on body dimensions. In temperate areas children grow in height fastest during the spring and in weight fastest in the fall. All over the world, undernutrition and disease delay growth. During a short period of undernutrition or disease the body slows its growth and seems to wait for better times in order to to catch up, which it commonly does. If growth is delayed long enough, however, the body may never reach its full genetic height potential.

Girls appear to withstand periods of undernutrition or illness better than boys. Perhaps this explains why, in their late teens, Philippine girls are significantly closer in weight to US girls than Philippine boys are to US boys (see Table 3.6). Tanner (1977: 343) speculates that girls may be better buffered against malnutrition and disease than boys because "the two X-chromosomes provide better regulatory forces than one X- and the small Y-chromosome."

Within a given population, children from upper socioeconomic levels are taller than children from lower levels. In Figure 3.6 you see the heights at age seven of a national sample of British children born during one week in 1958. Children were broken into five classes depending on their father's occupation. Children of the upper classes were taller than those in the lower classes, and presumably differences in nutrition accounted for at least some of the height differences. That children in larger families tend to be shorter than children in small families, as shown in Figure 3.6, has been found to be true among non-Caucasian as well as Caucasian families (Walker & Stein 1985: 335).

During the period from 1880 to 1950 the populations of Northern Europe and North America were growing taller at the rate of approximately one centimeter per decade. The trend has stopped in most well-off sections of these communities but is going strong presently in Japan (Tanner 1977: 349). In 1981, 61 percent of the adult sons in Bagbana were taller than their fathers; on the av-

---

Figure 3.6 Height Differences Among British Children by Social Class of Father and Number of Children in the Family

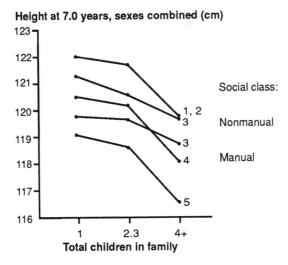

Source: Adapted from Tanner 1977:347; data from Goldstein 1971.

erage the sons were 3.1 centimeters (1.25 inches) taller. (Data on daughters were not available because daughters normally leave the village on marriage.) Presumably this secular trend in height of populations during the past hundred years or so is largely the result of better health and nutrition.

Bone length is closely tied to protein nutrition. In the developing individual a bone begins life as collagen, the same pure protein that you see growing out from the edges of a wound when the tissue is growing back together. The collagen protobone gradually turns to gristle and eventually hardens into bony structure. During growth, bones lengthen at the ends, laying down new collagen that then goes through the cycle of hardening into gristle and bone. During prolonged illness or undernutrition, bone lengthening may be retarded or stopped altogether. If succeeding catch-up growth is insufficient to make up for lost growth, the resulting body ends up short of its genetic potential. There is considerable empirical evidence of the positive relationship between protein consumption and height of humans (see Box 3.2).

Stephenson, Latham and Jansen (1983: 53) compared growth data from US children, privileged African children, and underprivileged African children, and concluded that ethnic differences were less important than other factors as determinants of growth in children: "Poverty, poor food intakes, infectious and parasitic diseases and other environmental factors combine together to prevent children from realizing their growth potential. There are, of course, genetic influences which lead to differences of body size, and especially of stature, but it seems that in pre-pubertal children, heredity is a much less significant cause of below average growth than are other factors."

We are left with the impression that environmental influences are major determinants of the anthropometric characteristics of a population, but we must bear in mind that, especially for a particular individual, anthropometric measurements are the product of the *interactions* of heredity and environment.

Note also that, despite substantial genetic variation in height and weight-for-height within any population, the growth trajectories of infants and very young children are much more uniform than those of older children. Therefore the application of the same growth standards to various racial groups makes more sense than might, at first, appear.

Reference populations. If you look at the literature on nutrition surveillance during the past quarter century you will find frequent references to two reference populations: (1) the Boston or Harvard, and (2) Tanner. First appearing in a textbook (Stuart & Stevenson 1950), the Boston data were collected by a Harvard researcher and concerned a sample of relatively well-nourished children in the Boston area. This data set became the basis of weight-for-age growth charts used extensively in Latin American and Asia. The Tanner data (Tanner, Whitehouse & Takaishi 1966) were developed by the same Tanner who is being quoted so liberally in this chapter, and concerned a sample of relatively well-

Box 3.2 Nutrition and Body Size
J. S. Weiner

In India the greater stature, stronger constitution, and superior physical resistance of the Sikhs of northern India, as compared to the Madrassi of the south, seem directly related to the high protein of the Sikh diet derived from meat, milk, and milk derivatives as compared to the vegetarian diet of the Madrassi. McCarrison fed rats on these two types of diet; those on the Sikh diet weighed an average of 225 [grams] compared to 155 g on the other. Of the two genetically similar populations of Hutu in Ruanda, studied by Hiernaux, those living in the more fertile and healthier regions were on average 7 [kilograms] heavier and had greater thigh- and chest-measurements.

In the studies of Boyd Orr and Gilks in East Africa, on the Kikuyu and the Masai tribes of Kenya, we are faced with the operation probably of both genetic and nutritional factors. The Kikuyu are farmers, living on a diet of cereals, tubers, and legumes; the Masai, on the other hand, are cattle-raisers, whose diet includes meat, milk, and ox-blood which they take from the animals. These two human groups, living side by side in the same natural environment and the same climate, differed markedly in their physical measurements. The Masai men were 7.5 [centimeters] taller and 10.25 kg heavier than their Kikuyu counterparts. This difference in Boyd Orr and Gilks's opinion is a direct result of their fundamentally different diets. The Masai, through an abundant use of food of animal origin, enjoy a diet balanced in proteins, while the Kikuyu live under conditions of permanent protein hunger.

De Castro observed something similar in the north-east of Brazil. In the littoral regions and in the dry backland area far from the coast the diet is high in proteins because the inhabitants live by fishing. In the backland also the protein intake is high, since it is a cattle-raising region with abundant production and consumption of meat, milk, and cheese. But in the jungle zone, where sugar-cane monoculture established itself and drove out all other food-producing activities, the diet is very poor, being based on cassava or manioc flour, the protein content of which is extremely low. These dietary differences, particularly of protein, would explain the differences in body-size among three human groups living within a fairly restricted geographical area.

Source: Weiner 1977:419–420. Reprinted by permission of Oxford University Press.

nourished British children. These data have been used extensively on growth charts in Europe and Africa.

In the United States, from 1976 to 1980, the NCHS conducted its second National Health and Nutrition Examination Survey (NHANES II). Anthropometric data were collected from 20,322 people in the United States, making NHANES II by far the largest anthropometric survey ever conducted. Data on age, height, weight, midupper-arm circumference, skinfolds, head and chest circumferences, and so forth were collected on a cross section of the American population six months to 74 years of age, not just on children as in the Boston and Tanner data.

The population for the NCHS data was more representative of the US population than the Boston/Harvard data in that it included all US ethnic groups, not just whites, and all income groups. The resulting weights-for-age for children, therefore, are somewhat below the Boston/Harvard data as well as the Tanner data (see Figure 3.7 on page 56) and at the same time are more representative of a modern industrial nation's population. This, plus the fact that household survey data accompany the anthropometric data, makes the NCHS data attractive as a reference population. WHO, the US Centers for Disease Control in Atlanta, and others are urging the adoption of the NCHS reference population as an international standard (Griffiths 1985: 14–16).

**Box 3.3 Should the Reference Population
Be Country-Specific?**
Marcia Griffiths

Which population to use for comparison purposes is a controversial question. The debate continues about whether children from different areas of the world have the same genetic potential for growth. Some experts argue that genetic background does make a difference, particularly for age-specific rates of growth, while others argue that for children 0–5 growth rates are the same and only begin to be influenced by genetic potential at puberty. Investigators exploring the effect of environmental factors, such as extremely high altitudes, on growth conclude that perhaps in countries and even in regions where environmental factors are extreme, special reference values should be established based on more realistic expectations of growth in these populations.

Several studies indicate that presumably well-nourished, upper-class children in developing countries grow at the same rate as upper-class children in developed countries. This implies that growth patterns may be influenced more strongly by such environmental factors as dietary adequacy and frequency of illness than by genes. If this is true, reference values based on the growth of healthy children in industrialized countries are suitable for use in less developed countries or in ethnically distinct communities.

Source: Griffiths 1985:14.

Despite the fact that a number of countries have adopted reference standards specific to their own situation the NCHS data seem destined to become the international standard (see Box 3.3). In 1981 FAO, WHO, and the United Nations University (UNU) jointly convened a most prestigious panel of experts in Rome to consider the question of energy and protein requirements. Their report (WHO 1985a: 23) contains the following statement: "The Consultation feels it desirable that the growth potential of children should be fully expressed, and estimates of energy and protein requirements should allow for this." They then explain that their new estimates of protein and calorie requirements for children up to 10 years are based on the reference growth standards sponsored for international use by WHO (Waterlow et al. 1977), which are derived from the NCHS data.

☐ Measuring Deviation From the Reference Population

The whole point of having a reference population is to see if a particular individual deviates sufficiently from it to be of concern. If an individual's deviation exceeds a certain amount, which WHO calls the cut-off point, then he or she may be presumed to have a nutritional problem. The three most commonly proposed candidates for measuring cut-off points, all based on deviation from the median score are: (1) percentile; (2) percentage of the median; and (3) standard deviation unit. We will use Figure 3.7, weight-for-age in girls from birth to 36 months (NCHS data), to illustrate these concepts.

Percentile. The median weight is the fiftieth percentile. This weight is plotted as the top solid line. At any point on this line half of the girls in the sample at that age weighed more than this. Half weighed less. The other solid line in Figure 3.7 plots the fifth percentile. At any point on this line 95 percent of the children of that age weighed more and 5 percent weighed less.

Percentage of the median. To get percentage of the median you find what percentage the observed weight of the individual is of the fiftieth percentile (median weight). Among the NCHS girls shown in Figure 3.7, the median girl of 14 months weighed approximately 10 kilos. Ninety percent of this median weight is 9 kilos. Seventy-five percent of this median weight is 7.5 kilos, and 60 percent is 6 kilos. For children up to five years, the 75 percent of the median line tracks the third percentile (not shown) rather closely (Griffiths 1985: 17).

Standard deviation unit, or Z-score. Standard deviation is a statistical measure of dispersion away from the mean. An observation that is two standard deviation units below the mean will be approximately on the second percentile. It would track fairly close to the "75 percent of the median" line plotted in Figure 3.7.

In anthropometric data the mean is usually close to the median, and since nutritionists commonly use the median instead of the mean it has become customary for them to substitute the median for the mean, and then measure two standard deviation units from this as a measure of undernutrition. They commonly call this measurement a Z-score (Krick 1988: 326–328).

☐ Three Popular Classification Systems

Choosing a classification system for undernutrition involves selecting an appropriate anthropometric measure or measures in conjunction with an appropriate set of criteria (deviations from the reference standard) in order to identify under-

Figure 3.7 NCHS Weight-for-Age, Girls, Birth to 36 Months

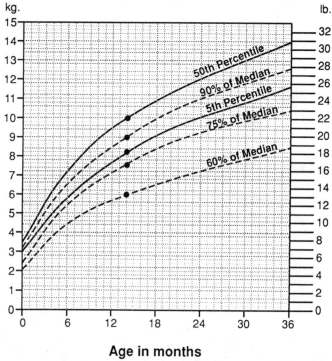

Weight

This chart compares the 50th and 5th percentile weight-for-age curves with weight-for-age curves at 90, 75, and 60 percent of the median, using the NCHS reference population.

Source: Adapted from US Department of Health, Education and Welfare growth charts (undated).

nutrition or various levels of it. No matter which system is chosen, the aim is to flag those individuals in most need of help, either because they are undernourished or because they are in danger of becoming so.

I will describe and briefly discuss three very different but widely used classification systems: (1) Gómez weight-for-age; (2) Waterlow weight-for-height combined with height-for-age; and (3) Shakir arm circumference.

Gómez weight-for-age. Gómez and his colleagues (1956) developed the first widely used method of classifying nutritional disorders on the basis of growth. They used percentage of the median weight-for-age of their reference population to classify nutritional status in children. Those greater than 90 percent of the median were called normal; those from 76 to 90 percent were called mildly mal-

Table 3.7 Philippine and US Weight-for-Age Reference Standards for
Preschool Children (in Kilograms)

Age in Years	US (median weight)			Philippines (4)	Percentage That Column 4 Is of Column 3
	Boys (1)	Girls (2)	Average (3)		
1	11.7	10.7	11.2	11.2	100
2	13.5	12.7	13.1	13.1	100
3	15.4	14.7	15.0	14.7	98
4	17.6	16.7	17.2	16.1	94
5	19.4	19.0	19.2	17.8	92
6	22.0	21.3	21.6	19.4	90

Sources: US Department of Health and Human Services 1987; Philippines National Science and Technology Authority 1984:218.

nourished; those 61 to 75 percent, moderately malnourished; and those 60 percent or less, severely malnourished. These latter three categories are sometimes designated simply as first-, second-, and third-degree malnutrition with no reference made to Gómez. In this case, third-degree means severely malnourished.

Since preschool children, particularly weaning children, are the most-at-risk group for undernutrition, the nutrition classification systems have concentrated on this group. The Gómez system, or variations of it, has become the most widely used method of monitoring preschool children's growth in the Third World. It is sensitive to small changes in weight. The only tool required is portable and widely available. It is usually a good indicator of present and/or past undernutrition and is regarded as a valid measure during the preschool years.

Because Third World populations tend to track well below the European and US data (review Figures 3.4 and 3.5), there is a strong motivation for Third World governments to build their own reference tables. Colombia, India, Brazil, and the Philippines have established their own reference populations. In Table 3.7 the Philippine and US reference standards are compared. The Philippine data track the US data for the first two years, but by the sixth birthday the Philippine data have dropped to 90 percent of the US. The Gómez-like cut-off point applied to the Philippine data and quoted earlier in this chapter—that is, that weight under 75 percent of (Philippine) standard weight-for-age put 27 percent of preschoolers in the moderately to severely undernourished category—is somewhat more forgiving than using Gómez cut-off points with the NCHS standards.

It is questionable how useful applying Gómez cut-off points to adult data is. In Figure 3.8 Bagbana villagers are tracked against the NCHS reference population. Examining Figure 3.8 yields some interesting speculations: middle-aged to older Indian villagers are mostly moderately to severely undernourished; middle-aged to older people in the United States are overweight; or optimal nutrition lies between that of the Indian village and that of the United States.

Figure 3.8 Gómez Classification by Age, Bagbana Village, 1981

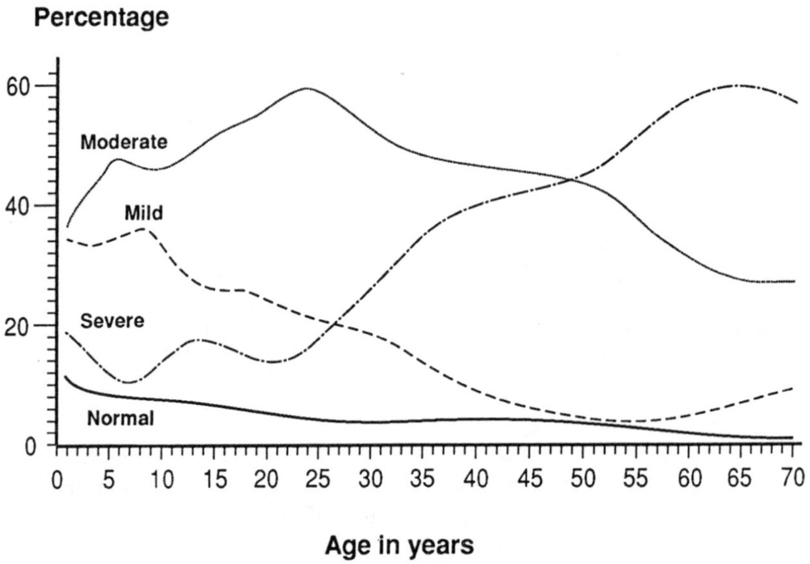

Percentage

Age in years

Source: Adapted from Dever 1983:88.

We also see in Figure 3.8 a phenomenon commonly found in low-income Third World populations; namely, the indicated severe undernutrition rate (look at the line for severe undernutrition) tends to decline during the first six years of life. This is partially because as the child grows up he more easily commands his share of the family's food resources (weaning children are notoriously difficult to feed) and partially because the weakest individuals have already succumbed to malnutrition and disease. With their early death the remaining population of older children "looks better."

Waterlow weight-for-height combined with height-for-age. Although the Gómez system is usually a good indicator of undernutrition, it may fail to flag as a problem an unusually tall child who is presently undernourished, and it may erroneously flag as a problem the unusually short child who is adequately nourished. To avoid these types of problems Waterlow and colleagues (1977) developed a classification system that ingeniously, yet logically, combines height-for-age (which identifies past undernutrition) with weight-for-height (which identifies present undernutrition). The classification system is summarized in Figure 3.9.

The beauty of this system is that it is likely to correctly identify individuals who are presently at risk for undernutrition and eliminate from present consideration those who merely have been undernourished in the past. A disadvantage

Figure 3.9 Waterlow Weight-for-Height Combined with Height-for-Age

Height-for-age	Weight-for-height	Status
90% or better	80% or better	Normal
90% or better	Less than 80%	Wasted (current undernutrition)
Less than 90%	80% or better	Stunted (past undernutrition)
Less than 90%	Less than 80%	Wasted and stunted (both present and past undernutrition)

Note: The reference standard is the NCHS median.

Figure 3.10 Waterlow Nutritional Status Classifications, Bagbana Village, 1981

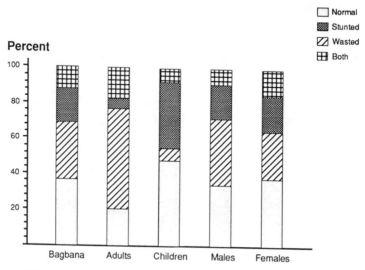

Source: Adapted from Dever 1983:90.

of the system is that it requires height (length) measurements in addition to age and weight data. Length is considerably more difficult to obtain than weight, especially for children under two. The operation requires a special board and two trained individuals. While one holds the baby's legs straight and moves the baby's feet close up against the footboard, the other moves the headboard up against the top of the baby's head, taking care to hold the head in the prescribed position. Needless to say, when two strangers, no matter how gentle they try to be, hold a baby tightly in the prescribed position on this new contraption for the first time in his life, a certain amount of kicking and screaming, and occasionally urinating and defecating, can be expected. The exercise can end up traumatic for all concerned.

The results of using the Waterlow classification with the NCHS data in Bagbana is shown in Figure 3.10.

Shakir arm circumference. One of the more intriguing facts of child growth and development is that, while the body of a well-nourished child is gaining in length and weight from one to five or six years of age, his or her midupper-arm circumference remains essentially the same! Using this fact, Shakir (1975) developed a screening device to identify severely undernourished preschoolers that is simplicity itself. It consists of a tape that is wrapped around the child's midupper arm, lightly enough so as to not compress the skin but firmly enough to fit exactly. The reference standard used is 16.5 centimeters. A circumference of greater than 14 centimeters (85 percent of standard) is considered normal. Between 12.5 and 14 centimeters (76–85 percent of standard) is classed as undernutrition. Under 12.5 centimeters (less than 76 percent of standard) is classed severe undernutrition.

The tape is cheap and can be made by hand, if necessary. If the tape is coded with culturally appropriate colors (e.g., green, yellow, and red), even illiterate health workers can do the classification.

The accuracy of the system is good for severe cases and only moderate for mild cases. Nevertheless, because of its simplicity and the fact that it works on preschoolers without any age data, it has become an important screening tool.

☐ 4

The Protein/Calorie Debate

Sugar baby disease—Jamaica
Enfant rouge—Cameroons
Kwashiorkor—Ghana
Mehlnahrschaden—Germany
Culebrilla—Mexico
Polycarencil infantile—Central America

(Local names for severe protein deficiency among preschoolers, various cultures.)
—US, White House, President's Science
Advisory Committee 1967: 310

As I pointed out in Chapter 2, undernutrition, technically called protein-calorie malnutrition, or PCM, is the leading form of malnutrition in the world today. But as the technical name implies, there are two elements involved in PCM, protein and calories. And a controversy exists over the relative importance of the deficiency of calories versus proteins in the diet of the Third World.

We must have energy (calories) for physical activity and for driving the multitude of activities that go on within our bodies, as well as for maintenance of body heat. And we must have protein for body building and repair as well as for a host of other essential functions: Proteins carry oxygen around our body; confer disease resistance; carry nutrients into and out of cells. Some proteins act as enzymes. Proteins are involved in the clotting of blood. The list goes on.

The body gets energy from carbohydrates (e.g., starch, sugar) and fats (e.g., corn oil, butter). It makes the millions of different proteins that it needs from some 20 amino acids, which are the building blocks of our body's proteins. Such simple organisms as yeasts and algae can synthesize all or most of the amino acids they need. But humans cannot synthesize some amino acids, and we make insufficient quantities of others for our requirements. (Over the eons of evolution, our ancestral line seems to have lost some of its capacity to synthesize amino acids.)

To live, therefore, we must consume sufficient quantities of these essential amino acids (the ones we either cannot make at all or make in insufficient quan-

61

tity) through our diet. The list of essential amino acids includes half of the total number we need for life. We get these essential amino acids by eating protein that contains them. Egg white is an example of a protein that contains all of the essential amino acids. The protein in milk is similarly well supplied.

If a human overconsumes protein but is short on carbohydrates and fats, the body can burn the surplus protein as energy (see Box 4.1). But it does not work so well the other way around. If the body is short of protein and long on carbohydrates and fats, it can make limited quantities of some of the essential amino acids, but cannot do the whole job. So we end up short on enough protein for an active, healthy life.

Box 4.1 The Energy Value of Carbohydrates, Fats, and Proteins

Gram for gram, you get about the same energy value from proteins as you get from carbohydrates. Dried egg whites, which are almost pure protein, contain 372 kilocalories per 100 grams. White sugar, which is almost pure carbohydrate, contains 385 kilocalories per 100 grams. Since the common foods we eat typically contain considerably more carbohydrate than protein (100 grams of wheat flour contains 10.5 grams of protein and 76.1 grams of carbohydrates), let us take the value for sugar as representative of the mix of proteins and carbohydrates in our diet and compare it to the energy value of fat, taking butter oil (which is butter with the water removed) as representative of the fat we eat. Butter oil contains 867 kilocalories per 100 grams. Divide the Calories in 100 grams of butter oil by the Calories in 100 grams of white sugar:

$$\frac{867 \text{ Calories in 100 g. butter oil}}{385 \text{ Calories in 100 g. white sugar}} = 2.25$$

In other words, fat contains about two and a quarter times the calories per gram as do carbohydrates and proteins.

If protein in foods were more abundant than carbohydrates and fat, then there would be no controversy about whether poor people in the Third World are getting enough protein. If they were short of food, they would be tending to substitute protein for carbohydrates and fat in their diet. But in this real world of ours protein is scarce relative to carbohydrates and fat. Thus there is a tendency for poor people to substitute carbohydrates and fat for protein in their diet and therefore end up underconsuming protein.

Before we examine the relative costs of major nutrients in the diet, we should first look at the various methods of comparing nutrient contents of foods.

■ METHODS OF COMPARING
NUTRIENT CONTENTS OF FOODS

There are three commonly used methods of comparing the relative amounts of carbohydrates, fats, and proteins of various foods. Each has its advantages and disadvantages. All three methods refer to the edible portion of food and disregard parts not commonly eaten, such as banana peels and date pits.

1. *Grams of protein, carbohydrates, and fat per 100 grams, as purchased:* The most common method of comparing the big three nutrients in food is to list the weight of each nutrient in some specified amount of the food, as purchased. Food product companies in the United States typically confuse the issue by listing number of grams per serving, but giving the serving size in ounces! But many published food composition tables, such as the authoritative *Composition of Foods, Raw, Processed, Prepared*, prepared by the US Department of Agriculture (1963) as Agricultural Handbook no. 8, simplify matters by listing grams of each nutrient per hundred grams of the food. Thus you can read percentages of the nutrient, by weight, directly from the tables. This method has the advantage of presenting the data on foods as they are purchased, but because foods contain varying amounts of water, comparisons among foods using this system can be difficult.

2. *Grams of protein, carbohydrates, and fat per 100 grams, dry weight:* Lean hamburger as purchased is 68 percent water. Dry rice as purchased is actually 12 percent water (all "dried" grains contain some water). So, to make nutrient comparisons, some people like to compare the weight of the big three nutrients per hundred grams of food with all the water extracted. The calculations can be easily made from the tables such as those in Agricultural Handbook no. 8 mentioned above. Nice as this comparison may be for showing relative ratios of the main nutrients, it does not show the relative amounts of energy derived from the various nutrients.

3. *Percentage of calories from protein, carbohydrates, and fats:* As you saw in Box 4.1, fat has 2.25 times as many calories per gram as does carbohydrate. The ratio is about the same for calories from protein versus calories from fat. So, comparing these three nutrients by weight ignores the difference in calories that may be delivered through similar weights of a fatty versus a nonfatty food. Again, using data such as that found in Agricultural Handbook no. 8, and the conversion factor of 2.25 for fat, you can readily determine the number of calories from each of the big three nutrients in a hundred grams of food, either as purchased or with the water extracted.

Keep the advantages and disadvantages of these three methods of comparing nutrient content in mind as you read about food comparisons in this book. Nutrient values produced using the three different methods are given for three different foods in Table 4.1.

Table 4.1 Nutrient Values for Rice, Hamburger, and Carrots, Using Three Common Measures of Nutritional Content of Foods

Food (percentage water)	Grams per 100 Grams and Kilocalories per 100 Grams of Food as Purchased	Grams per 100 Grams of Carbohydrate, Protein, and Fat, All Water Extracted	Percentage of Total Calories from Carbohydrate, Protein, and Fat
Rice, dry, white raw (12.0%)			
Carbohydrate	80.4	91.9	91.4
Protein	6.7	7.7	7.6
Fat	0.4	0.5	1.0
Kilocalories	363		
Hamburger, lean, raw (68.3%)			
Carbohydrate	0.0	0.0	0.0
Protein	20.7	67.4	47.9
Fat	10.0	32.6	52.1
Kilocalories	179		
Carrots, Raw (88.2%)			
Carbohydrate	9.7	88.2	86.2
Protein	1.1	10.0	9.8
Fat	0.2	1.8	4.0
Kilocalories	42		

Source: Calculated from US Department of Agriculture 1963.

■ PROTEIN: MORE EXPENSIVE THAN CARBOHYDRATE OR FAT

Most of the foods we eat contain a combination of carbohydrates, fat, and protein. We are generally aware that we pay a premium for protein-rich foods. For instance, you probably know that hamburger is a richer source of protein than rice and that hamburger costs more per pound than rice.

In 1990 a pound of lean hamburger in a Washington, DC, supermarket cost $1.70, while a pound of common dry rice cost $0.24. Hamburger was seven times as expensive per pound as rice. Lean hamburger is 20.7 percent protein, while common rice is only 6.7 percent protein. Yet, pound for pound, dry rice contains over twice the food energy of hamburger. (Hamburger is less energy dense than dry rice because hamburger is 68 percent water, while dry rice is only 12 percent water. When cooked up with water a pound of dry rice becomes about three pounds of cooked rice.) One hundred grams of common dry rice contains 363 Calories of energy (see Box 4.2) while 100 grams of lean hamburger contains only 179 Calories (US, Dept. of Agriculture 1963). A little arithmetic will show that to get 1,000 Calories of food energy from hamburger you have to pay some 14 times as much as you do to get 1,000 Calories from dry rice.

Box 4.2 Calories and Kilocalories

In physics, chemistry, and engineering, a calorie is the amount of heat energy required at sea level to raise the temperature of one gram of water one degree centigrade. A kilocalorie (abbreviated Kcal) is the energy it takes at sea level to raise the temperature of 1,000 grams of water (a kilogram—also a liter) one degree centigrade.

Nutritionists always quote their data in kilocalories, but unfortunately commonly shorten the word to Calories. Usually people capitalize the word *Calorie* when intending to indicate a kilocalorie as distinguished from calorie. But the convention is not always observed. At any rate, when you are reading nutrition literature and see the word *calorie*, (note the lower case c) it is safe to assume that it means kilocalorie.

There is another thing to bear in mind when comparing nutritional calories to those in the physical sciences. The energy value of foods found in the standard handbooks, such as Agricultural Handbook no. 8, represents the energy available after deductions have been made for losses in digestion and metabolism. The system for determining these energy values was developed through the classic investigations of W. O. Atwater and his associates at the Connecticut Agricultural Experiment Station.

For more information on this subject, consult US Dept. of Agriculture 1963.

We pay a premium for protein-rich foods because protein is scarcer and harder to make than carbohydrate or fat. Green plants fix energy from the sun through photosynthesis: Carbon dioxide plus water plus radiant energy from the sun yield (in the presence of chlorophyll) a carbohydrate plus oxygen plus water; or, written as a chemical equation:

$$6CO_2 + 12H_2O + Light\ energy \xrightarrow{Chlorophyll} C_6H_{12}O_6 + 6O_2 + 6H_2O$$

Using enzymes, a plant can rearrange the carbon, hydrogen, and oxygen atoms of the carbohydrate, or sugar ($C_6H_{12}O_6$), produced in the above equation, to form starch or fat. The conversion of sugar to starch is very energy-efficient: Practically all of the energy in the original sugar can be released in burning the starch made from it. The conversion of sugar to fat, however, is about 77 percent energy-efficient, so we can only say that most of the energy in the original sugar can be released in burning the fat that is made from it.

The process of making amino acids is not so easy. Like carbohydrates and fat, amino acids contain carbon, hydrogen, and oxygen. But they also contain nitrogen, and nitrogen in the form that can be used to build amino acids is scarce. Plants can use carbon dioxide (CO_2) straight out of the atmosphere, but they cannot use the nitrogen (N_2) in the atmosphere. It has to be converted to more-complex forms, such as ammonia (NH_3), before the plant can use it.

The process of converting atmospheric nitrogen to usable nitrogen compounds is called nitrogen fixation. It can be done in a commercial fertilizer plant where energy is combined with some raw organic stock such as naptha. Or it can be done by nature, which provides three other ways of fixing nitrogen: (1) lightning storms; (2) nitrogen-fixing bacteria; and (3) blue-green algae. By and large, the nitrogen fixed by blue-green algae is not available to plants useful to man. Leguminous plants, such as beans, peas, and alfalfa, provide a suitable environment on their roots for some nitrogen-fixing bacteria and thus have an extra boost of nitrogen available to them (for more on legumes, see Box 4.3).

Box 4.3 Types of Edible Seeds

Most of the calories consumed in the world come from edible seeds. Even in high-income countries where livestock products are so important in the diet, the livestock themselves eat substantial quantities of these edible seeds.

There are two kinds of edible seeds: cereals and pulses. Cereals are characterized by one seed leaf (the seed does not split easily), pulses by two seed leaves (the seed splits easily). Cereals, also called grains, come from grasses, while pulses come from legumes. In general the cheapest calories are available through the cereals. The cheapest fats are from the pulses or palms like the coconut. The cheapest proteins are often from the pulses, with soybeans being the prizewinner for lowest cost. In the Third World, corn (i.e., maize) sometimes competes with the pulses for the lowest-cost protein.

The major edible seeds, together with their percentage of protein content, are:

Cereals		Pulses	
Rice	6.7	Beans, white	22.3
Corn (Maize)	7.8	Peas, dry	24.2
Millet	9.9	Lentils	24.7
Sorghum	11.0	Peanuts	26.0
Wheat, hard		Soybeans	34.1
red winter	12.3		

You notice that the protein content of the cereals is in all cases under 14 percent, while the pulses provide protein content of over 20 percent.

The coconut palm is more similar to a grass than to a legume and its protein content reflects this fact. The protein content of dried coconut meat is 7.2 percent. Dried coconut meat is about 4 percent water. The dried cereals in our list generally run from 10 to 14 percent water, by weight.

So, plants can get fixed nitrogen derived from natural sources (this supply is scarce) or from commercial fertilizer (which is costly). The fixed nitrogen taken up by plants is available in the food chain to make amino acids and, ultimately, proteins. Plants and animals have to spend energy (use up sugar) to synthesize amino acids. They have to spend still more energy to recombine these amino acids into the enormous molecules of protein they need for their life activities. As a result of using up so much sugar to assemble protein, the energy released in the burning of a protein is substantially less than the energy it took to make it in the first place. In contrast, the energy released in the burning of a carbohydrate or fat is closer to the energy it took to make it in the first place.

Plant proteins are used primarily in the form of enzymes to "run the cell." Carbohydrates and fats are basically either structural components or energy storage units.

Because complex nitrogen compounds from natural sources are scarce and because proteins are relatively difficult to make, plants have not evolved in such a way that they try to store energy as protein. They make only the amount of protein they need to live on. Proteins, therefore, are always going to be scarce relative to carbohydrates and fats. And therefore they are going to be more expensive. There is nothing we can do about it; it is a matter of physics and chemistry.

Finding the cheapest sources of protein, carbohydrates, and fats is not of particular interest to high-income people. They are more interested in such issues as food palatability, fine-tuning their nutritional intake for optimal nutrition, or keeping their weight down. But the cost of nutrients is a major issue for low-income Third World people. Imagine how much more important the cost of food is to Filipinos, whose per capita income in 1986 was $560 than to people in the United States, whose per capita income that year was $17,480 (World Bank 1988: 222–223).

Table 4.2 is a compendium of interesting information on diet in the Philippines. The prices are given in Philippine pesos. At this writing a peso is worth about 5 US cents, but this is not important. What is important in Table 4.2 are the relative prices at retail level of nutrients from various sources in a representative Third World country. Notice that in the Philippines you can buy 100 grams of the carbohydrate white sugar for P 0.75. You can buy corn grits for P 0.40 pesos per 100 grams but corn grits are only 78 percent carbohydrate. To get 100 grams of carbohydrate as corn grits you would have to buy 128 grams of grits, which would cost P 0.51. In the Philippines, corn grits are the cheapest source of carbohydrate.

In the seventh column of Table 4.2 you see the price per 100 grams of protein (column 3, price, divided by column 6, protein per 100 grams of product, multiplied by 100). The cheapest sources of protein are the cereals and pulses (soybeans, peanuts, and mongo beans). The cheapest protein, at P 3.37 per 100 grams (from soybeans) is over six times as expensive as the cheapest carbohydrate (from corn). A similar calculation using 1978 village prices in West Java (Indonesia, Diro Pusat Statik 1981; Indonesia Oleh Direktorat Gizi Departemen

Table 4.2 Relative Importance of Foods in the Diet, and Retail Peso Price of Nutrients, Philippines, 1984

	1 Kcal Available for Consumption per Capita per Day 1981	2 Percentage of Calories in Diet	3 Price per 100 g as Purchased	4 Kilocalories per 100 g Edible Portion	5 Price per 1,000 Kcal	6 Protein per 100 g Edible Portion	7 Price per 100 g Protein	8 Fat per 100 g Edible Portion	9 Price per 100 g Fat
Cereals	1465.3	56.6							
Rice, milled, ordinary	981.1	37.9	.463	363	1.27	6.7	6.91	0.4	115
Corn, grits, white	368.8	14.2	.405	362	1.1	8.7	4.66	0.8	50
Wheat flour	98.6	3.8	.752	364	2.06	10.5	7.16	1.0	75
Others	16.8	.6							
Starchy Roots and Tubers	199.4	7.6							
Sweet potato	61.9	2.4	.304	119	2.52	.97	31.34	.35	87
Cassava, white sweet	128.1	4.9	.241	108	2.23	.44	54.77	.15	161
White potato (Irish)	1.2	-	.875	64	13.67	2.0	43.75	.08	1094
Gabi (taro)	3.4	.1	.554	86	6.44	1.8	30.77	.15	369
Other roots	3.0	.1							
Cassava flour and starch	1.8	.1							
Sugars and Syrups	258.0	9.9							
Centrifugal sugar, white	222.5	8.5	.751	387	1.94	0	-	0	-
Banochs and muscovado	4.0	.2		376		0.2		0.4	
Others	31.5	1.2							
Pulses and Nuts	34.2	1.3							
Peanuts, shelled	4.7	.2	1.807	564*	3.20	26.0*	6.95	47.5*	4
Mongo, green	9.7	.3	1.392	354	3.93	24.4	5.70	1.0	139
Other dried beans except soy	1.8	.1							
Soybeans and products	1.9	.1	1.148	403*	2.84	34.1*	3.37	17.7*	6
Coconut for food	11.8	.5							
Mature coconut in shell	8.6	.3	.215	169	1.27	2.1	10.24	14.5	1
Young coconut in shell	3.2	.1							
Other nuts, unshelled	0.3	-							
Other pulses and nuts	4.0	.2							
Vegetables	33.8	1.3							
Cabbage	10.6	.4	.958	18	53.32	1.1	87.09	.24	399
Yardlong beans, green (sitao)	9.4	3.6	.640	33	19.39	2.9	22.07	.18	355
Tomatoes	2.5	.1	.747	27	27.69	.89	83.93	.29	258
Others	11.0	.4							

Fruits									
Banana (latundan)	168.0	6.5	.825	69	11.95	.87	94.83	.21	393
Calamansi	110.3	4.2	.933	12	82.28	.15	622	.38	245
Other vitamin C-rich fruits	2.2	.1							
Other fresh fruits	19.3	.7							
Meat	35.8	1.4							
Beef (rump)	8.8	.3	3.939	110	35.80	20.7	19.03	2.4	164
Carabao (rump)	6.9	.3		90		19.3	0.9		
Pork (ham)	110.6	4.3	3.288	281	11.70	14.8	22.22	24.2	14
Poultry (broiler)	13.1	.5	2.349	81	29.00	14.4	16.31	2.2	107
Milk and Milk Products	27.1	1.0							
Fresh milk	0.4	.0		64		3.3		3.6	
Powdered and other dry	7.2	.3		476		24.1		22.5*	
Dry skimmed milk	18.0	.7	3.523	363*	9.70	35.9*	9.81	0.8*	440
Eggs	20.4	.8							
Chicken	16.4	.6	2.460	143	17.20	10.8	22.78	9.5	26
Duck	4.0	.2	2.860	156	18.33	10.1	28.31	10.9	26
Fish	74.3	2.9							
Milkfish	54.8	2.1	1.269	90	14.10	12.5	10.15	4.0	32
Small shrimps (susha)	10.5	.4	2.842	60	41.36	11.8	24.08	.49	580
Mollusk	7.1	.3							
Fats and Oils	103.3	4.0							
Vegetable (coconut)	91.8	3.5	1.541	883	1.74	.0		99.1	
Butter (commercial)	3.6	.1		720		0.5		81.6	
Butter (homemade)	7.1	.3							
Miscellaneous	55.7								
Beer and other alcohol	22.9	.9							2
TOTAL	2590.7								

Sources: Nutrients per 100 grams: Food Composition Tables, Food and Nutrition Research Institute, February 1980, except cereals and items marked *, for which see Food Composition Table for Use in East Asia, FAO, USDHEW, 1972. Relative Importance in the diet: NEDA Food Balance Series Number 8, Food Balance Sheet for the Philippines CY 1977 to CY 1981, pp. 58-62. Prices: white sugar, National Sugar Trading Corporation; wheat flour, NFA, July 1, 1984, retail price; coconut oil and coconut for food, United Coconut Association of the Philippines; powdered milk, Pampanga Market, May 1985, deflated by estimate to July 1984; soybeans, US wholesale price 1984/85 times 2.5; all others, Bureau of Agricultural Economics, average retail price, Philippines, 1984.

Kesehatan R. I. 1979) produced a twelve-fold difference in the cheapest carbohydrate (from dried cassava) and the cheapest protein (from soybeans). (Soybeans cost 40.18 rupiahs (Rp.) per 100 grams and provided 34.1 grams of protein per 100 grams, while dried sweet cassava cost Rp. 8.43 per 100 grams and provided 81.3 grams of carbohydrates per 100 grams. The cost of soy protein was thus Rp. 1.18 per gram, which was almost twelve times the cost of cassava carbohydrate at Rp. 0.10 per gram.)

Since your body can get calories from carbohydrates, proteins, and fats, it makes sense to compare the cost of calories from various foods rather than to concentrate on the differences in the cost of protein and carbohydrate. Column 5 in Table 4.2 allows us to compare the price of 1,000 kilocalories from various foods. The cereals plus coconut oil win hands down in this contest.

Notice (column 2) that Filipinos eat 56.6 percent of their calories as cereals. They have made the cheapest sources of proteins and calories major constituents of their diet. Despite their low-cost protein, pulses do not figure much in the Philippine diet, probably because their calories are too costly. The Filipinos have evidently found, over the generations, that if you buy enough (inexpensive) calories as rice or maize, you get enough protein. But they have also found that it does not work the other way around: If you buy enough (inexpensive) protein as soybeans, you do not get enough calories. So all things considered, rice and corn are a more economical diet than soybeans.

Coconut oil, the cheapest source of fat in the Philippines, outside of breaking open the coconut yourself, provides 3.5 percent of the calories in the Philippine diet.

Countries with even lower incomes than the Philippines tend to consume an even greater proportion of their calories as cereals. India, with a 1989 per capita income of $340 (about half that of the Philippines) consumes 67 percent of its calories as cereals (calculated from Table 3.2).

Contrast these figures with those of the United States (Table 4.3), where people consume only 24 percent of their total calories as cereals. This is typical for cereal consumption in high-income countries where greater proportions of the calories in the diet come from animal products. (For a list of countries that gain more than 40 percent of their food energy from cereals, see Box 4.4.) It should be noted that the food balance sheets overstate calories derived from livestock products because they estimate consumption of meat from carcass weight and not from dietary intake surveys. Considerable fat is trimmed from the meat by the meat packer, the butcher, and by the consumer himself at the dinner plate.

■ HOW MUCH PROTEIN DO WE NEED?

Until recently, the history of recommended protein intake has been one of declining amounts. In 1865 Playfair, a professor of chemistry in Edinburgh, pro-

Table 4.3 Daily per Capita Supply of Nutrients by Food Source, US Average, 1984-1986

Food Sources	Kcal Available for Consumption	Percentage of Calories in Diet	Protein Grams	Fat Grams
Grand total	3595	100.0	106.6	165.0
Vegetable products	2388	66.4	35.4	72.1
Animal products	1227	34.1	71.2	92.8
Cereals (excluding beer)	876	24.4	20.7	2.9
Wheat	538	15.0	17.5	2.3
Rice (paddy)	44	1.2	0.8	
Barley	5	.17	0.2	
Maize	59	1.64	1.1	0.2
Rye	3	.08	0.1	
Oats	13	.36	0.5	0.2
Millet				
Sorghum				
Cereals, other	15	.44	0.5	0.2
Starchy Roots	95	2.6	2.5	0.2
Potatoes	89	2.5	2.4	0.2
Sweet potatoes	4	.11	0.1	0.2
Cassava	2	.0		
Roots, other				
Sugar Crops				
Sugar cane				
Sugar beet				
Sweeteners	571	15.9	0.2	
Sugar (raw equivalent)	310	8.6		
Sweeteners, NES	257	7.1	0.2	
Honey	5	0.14		
Pulses	29	.81	1.9	0.1
Beans	26	.72	1.7	0.1
Peas	2	.06	0.1	
Pulses, other	1	.03		
Tree nuts	15	.42	0.4	1.4
Oilcrops	58	1.61	2.4	5.0
Soybeans				
Groundnuts	44	1.2	2.0	3.8
Sunflowerseed	3	.08	0.1	0.2
Rape and mustardseed	3	.08	0.2	0.2
Cottonseed				
Coconuts (incl. copra)	3	.08		0.3
Sesameseed	2	.05	0.1	0.2
Olives	2	.05		0.2
Oilcrops, other				
Vegetables	72	2.0	3.5	0.8
Tomatoes	16	.46	0.8	0.2
Onions	7	.19	0.2	
Vegetables, other	49	1.4	2.5	0.5
Fruit (excluding wine)	117	3.2	1.3	0.8
Oranges and mandarins	29	.81	0.5	
Lemons and limes	1	.03		
Grapefruit	3	.08		
Citrus, other				
Bananas	18	.5	0.2	0.1
Apples (excl. cider)	18	.5		0.1
Pineapples	5	.14		
Dates	1	.03		
Grapes (excl. wine)	13	.4	0.1	0.1
Fruit, other	29	.81	0.4	0.4

Table 4.3 *(continued)*

Food Sources	Kcal Available for Consumption	Percentage of Calories in Diet	Protein Grams	Fat Grams
Stimulants	16	.4	1.3	0.7
Coffee	6	.17	0.8	
Cocoa Beans	10	.28	0.4	0.7
Tea			0.1	
Spices	3	.08	0.1	0.1
Pepper	1	.03		
Pimento	1	.03		
Cloves				
Spices, other	1	.03		
Alcoholic beverages	185	5.1	0.8	
Wine	17	.47		
Barley beer	115	3.2	0.8	
Beverages, fermented				
Beverages, alcoholic	53	1.5		
Meat	660	18.3	38.6	54.9
Bovine meat	268	7.4	17.6	21.4
Mutton/goat meat	5	.14	0.3	0.4
Pig meat	259	7.2	8.9	24.6
Poultry meat	125	3.5	11.4	8.4
Other meat	3	.08	0.4	0.1
Offal	19	.53	3.1	0.6
Milk (excl. butter)	356	9.9	21.3	20.6
Eggs	56	1.6	4.3	3.9
Fish and Seafood	25	.7	3.8	0.9
Freshwater fish	2	.05	0.3	0.1
Demersal fish	6	.17	1.0	0.1
Pelagic fish	11	.31	1.2	0.6
Marine fish, other	1	.03	0.1	
Crustaceans	4	.11	0.5	
Molluscs, other	2	.05	0.3	
Cephalopods				
Aquatic Products, Other				
Aquatic animals, other				
Aquatic plants				
Vegetable oils	533	14.8	0.2	60.1
Soybean oil	427	11.9	0.2	48.2
Groundnut oil	6	.17		0.7
Sunflowerseed oil	4	.11		0.4
Rape and mustard oil				
Cottonseed oil	26	.7		3.0
Palm kernel oil	5	.14		0.6
Palm oil	13	.36		1.5
Copra oil	13	.36		1.5
Sesameseed oil				
Olive Oil	5	.14		0.5
Maize germ oil	33	.92		3.8
Oilcrops oil, other				
Animal fats	106	2.9	0.1	12.0
Butter, ghee	43	1.2	0.1	4.8
Cream				
Fats, animals, raw	64	1.8		7.1
Fish, body oil				
Fish, liver oil				

Source: FAO 1991: 361-362.

Box 4.4 Fifty-Three Developing Countries in Which More Than 40 Percent of All Food Energy Is Derived from Cereals

Afghanistan	Iraq	Panama
Algeria	Jordan	Peru
Bangladesh	Kenya	Philippines
Botswana	Korea, Republic of	Senegal
Burkina Faso	Lesotho	Sierra Leone
Burma	Liberia	Somalia
Chad	Libya	Sri Lanka
Chile	Malawi	Sudan
Egypt	Malaysia	Suriname
El Salvador	Mali	Swaziland
Ethiopia	Mauritania	Syria
Gambia	Mexico	Thailand
Guatemala	Morocco	Trinidad and Tobago
Guyana	Nepal	Tunisia
Honduras	Nicaragua	Turkey
India	Niger	Zambia
Indonesia	Nigeria	Zimbabwe
Iran	Pakistan	

Note: This list does not include centrally planned economies. Centrally planned economies where more than 40 percent of all food energy is derived from cereals would probably include China, Viet Nam, and Laos.

Source: Reutlinger et al. 1986:65.

posed 71 to 184 grams of protein per day according to the degree of physical activity. In 1881 Voit, who had studied German workers, thought 118 grams per day adequate for male workers unless they were doing hard work, in which case they needed 145 grams. In 1901 Chittenden at Yale decided to challenge these high figures and began a series of experiments, in which he himself was one of the subjects. He concluded that men could be maintained in good health on as little as 50 to 55 grams of protein per day (Guggenheim 1981: 151–152), the amount contained in slightly over half a pound of lean, raw hamburger.

The Chittenden standard was still in place when, in 1967, the US government issued a report by a blue-ribbon committee assigned to study the world food problem (US, White House, President's Science Advisory Committee 1967). Partially because large segments of the Third World adult population received less than the Chittenden quantity of protein, the committee concluded that the main nutrition problem in the Third World was a shortage of protein. They were further concerned that most of the Third World protein was not animal in origin and therefore must be of poor quality. The following is illustrative of their position: "Proper protein nutrition involves the provision of adequate calories and a proper amount of protein of suitable *quality*. The mass of the population in the developing countries gets most of its protein and most of its calories from grain. Thus, for these people, the central protein problem is the *provision of more protein* (p. 300, my emphasis). Later in the same paragraph they stressed the need to fortify Third World diets with protein concentrates such as oilseeds (like soybeans) and fish.

A later paragraph is illustrative of their concern with protein deficiency in Third World diets even in countries where the data suggested protein availability approached the Chittenden recommendation. "Calculations of average protein consumption in many areas fail to reveal a great deficiency in the quantity of protein available. For example, it has been calculated that the per capita requirement in India is 48.3 grams daily, but food balance data indicate that the average supply in India is 55.6 grams daily. These data do not reflect the true situation since a major cause of morality (*sic*) among young children is protein malnutrition" (p. 310).

By the 1970s a feeling was developing that protein deficiency was not the major Third World nutritional problem. In 1970 Gopalan published the results of a study of 15,000 Indian preschool children. He found that 92 percent of the Indian preschoolers showed evidence of calorie deficiency, and that about a third of those (35 percent of the total population) were also protein-deficient. Only 8 percent of the preschoolers were found calorie-sufficient, and virtually all of these were also found to be protein-sufficient. The implication of this study was that if one could simply increase the quantity of foods that these preschoolers were eating, the protein shortage among them would disappear as the calorie shortage disappeared.

■ EFFICIENCY AND BALANCED PROTEIN

In 1971 Frances Moore Lappe shifted popular thinking in the Western world somewhat away from the problem of Third World protein scarcity through the publication of her best-selling book, *Diet for a Small Planet*, which popularized the idea that by appropriately mixing pulses and cereals you could achieve a balance of amino acids approximately equal to that of high quality animal protein.

The concept Moore was pushing is illustrated in Figure 4.1. The percentage of the daily recommendation of selected essential amino acids is represented on the horizontal axis. The three boxes show the degree to which each of the selected nutrients meets these requirements when one is consuming a certain weight of a particular grain or grain mix. A representative pulse—beans—is shown in the top box. A representative cereal—wheat—is shown in the middle box. And a 50-50 mixture of the two is shown in the bottom box. Consuming the given (unfortunately unspecified) weight of seeds as beans provides you with more than your needs for lysine while leaving you short on methionine and cystine. Consuming the given weight of seeds as wheat leaves you shy on all the

Figure 4.1 Protein Complementarity Between a Cereal and a Pulse

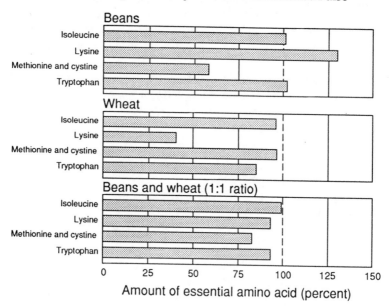

Source: Adapted from Scrimshaw and Young 1976:32.

listed acids but especially short on lysine. Consuming a 50-50 mixture provides a reasonably balanced mix.

Consuming a nutritionally balanced mix of amino acids is important for both nutritional and economic efficiency. Protein molecules are made up of

Table 4.4 Balanced Protein for a Healthy Adult Male, NAS Standard

Essential Amino Acid	RDA in Milligrams
Phenylalanine	1,100
Tyrosine	1,100
Methionine	1,100
Cystine	1,100
Leucine	1,000
Lysine	800
Valine	800
Isoleucine	700
Threonine	500
Tryptophan	250

fixed proportions of amino acids. A balanced protein is one in which the essential amino acids appear in the same ratio to each other as the body needs them for constructing its protein molecules. You can see this ratio (or at least an approximation of it) for the body as a whole in Table 4.4, containing the recommended daily allowance (RDA) for a healthy adult male (National Academy of Science standard).

If you get more of one of these acids than you need, your body cannot use it for making proteins, so it just burns it for energy. If you get less of one of them than you need, some portion of the others goes to waste for lack of the needed part to manufacture protein molecules. Whitney and Hamilton (1977: 92) provide a delightful analogy:

> Suppose that a signmaker plans to make 100 identical signs, each saying LEFT TURN ONLY. He needs 200 L's, 200 N's, 200 T's and 100 each of the other letters. If he has only 20 L's, he can make only 10 signs, even if all the other letters are available in unlimited quantities. The L's limit the number of signs that can be made. The quality of dietary protein depends first on whether or not the protein supplies all the essential amino acids, and second on the extent to which it supplies them in the relative proportions needed.

It is not economical to consume an unbalanced protein. If you consume more of a particular amino acid than your body can use, you burn it as fuel. And you can probably buy that fuel as carbohydrate or fat for one-eighth the cost. If you consume too little of one amino acid, then you burn the other amino acids (which you could have made into useful proteins) as fuel. Again that is an expensive way to buy fuel. Furthermore, the lack of protein may cut down on your productivity if you get sick because protein undernutrition has weakened your immune system.

You can get balanced protein by consuming animal products like meat, milk, eggs, and cheese. But these proteins are relatively expensive. After all, we use a lot of grains to produce these animal products, grains you could have consumed yourself without going to the expense of putting them through livestock.

The cheapest way to eat balanced protein is to consume a mix of pulses and cereals. Through their history various cultures have wisely, but most certainly unconsciously, developed traditional ways of mixing cereals and pulses to obtain a balanced protein. (Those that did not develop a tradition of eating a balanced protein did not have such good survival value as others.) To balance the protein you do not need much pulse relative to the cereal, and therefore the pulse in the mixture is sometimes called the "go with" food (Mintz 1989: 117). For instance, in the Caribbean Islands, beans (pulse) go with the rice (cereal). Asian Indians put a little *dahl* on their rice. Dahl is a mixture of one or more pulses with cooking oil and often includes a blend of fiery hot spices. Mexicans mix corn (cereal) with beans and call it a tortilla. In the United States schoolchildren and office workers put peanut butter (pulse) on bread (cereal) and call it lunch.

■ SHIFTS IN RECENT THINKING ON NUTRITIONAL REQUIREMENTS

In 1974 the FAO published the report of a panel of world-famous experts it had convened to consider the problem of recommended nutrient intake level. The FAO panel recommended 37 grams of protein for the moderately active adult man and 29 grams for the moderately active adult woman (see Table 4.5).

That same year, the most prestigious group of US scientists, the National Academy of Sciences (NAS), published a new set of recommended dietary allowances that were considerably more generous than those of the FAO (Table 4.6). Although the NAS recommendation was for somewhat bigger people, the difference in level was substantially more than justified by the weight difference. The protein recommendation for the adult male, for instance, was 56 grams daily—one and a half times the FAO recommendation!

Despite the NAS position on protein, much professional opinion continued to come down on the side of a calorie shortage, rather than a protein shortage. Leonard Joy (1973) capsulized the thinking that was to prevail throughout the 1970s, stating that the conventional policy approaches to nutrition are based on false notions of the nature of the nutrition problem. The problem is one of calorie rather than protein deficiency, he said, and arises from inadequate effective demand for food rather than insufficient supply. Policies should therefore emphasize generating incomes among the poor. Ryan (1977) was more specific. He claimed that, in India, the overriding nutritional deficiencies among low-income groups are calories, calcium, copper, iron, zinc, vitamin A, and vitamin B complex. For him, protein and amino acids did not appear to be limiting factors, as had for so long been the conventional wisdom.

The 1980s saw a shift in thinking in the direction of higher recommended allowances for protein on the Third World scene. In 1981 the FAO and WHO again called together a panel of internationally famous experts, this time with backing from the UNU, to reexamine the findings of the previous committee with regard to energy and protein requirements. In their 1985 report (WHO 1985a: 132) these experts set 0.75 grams of protein with the quality and digestibility of milk or egg, per kilogram of body weight per day, as the safe level of protein intake for adults. Their recommendations for all ages are summarized in Table 4.7. Up until age 10 the new UN figures run at about two-thirds of the NAS recommendations, and thereafter the UN figures track the NAS figures fairly closely, running only a few grams lower in most cases.

Remember that all of these recommendations are designed for the majority of the population when it is in good health. How these recommendations are designed is shown in Figure 4.2. On the normal (bell-shaped) curve D is the mean requirement for the population. The statistical unit of variation from the mean is known as the standard deviation (SD) and is shown on either side of the mean (C and E). An intake of F, obtained by adding two SDs to the mean value, would cover the requirements for nearly all (97.5 percent) of the individuals in

Table 4.5 Recommended Daily Intakes of Nutrients, FAO, 1974

Age	Body Weight	Energy		Protein[1,2]	Vitamin A[3,4]	Vitamin D[5,6]	Thiamine[3]	Ribo-flavine[3]	Niacin[3]	Folic acid[5]	Vitamin B$_{12}$[5]	Ascorbic acid[7]	Calcium[5,8]	Iron
	kilo-grams	kilo-calories	mega-joules	grams	micro-grams	micro-grams	milli-grams	milli-grams	milli-grams	micro-grams	micro-grams	milli-grams	grams	milli-grams
Children														
<1	7.3	820	3.4	14	300	10.0	0.3	0.5	5.4	60	0.3	20	0.5-0.6	5-10
1-3	13.4	1360	5.7	16	250	10.0	0.5	0.8	9.0	100	0.9	20	0.4-0.5	5-10
4-6	20.2	1830	7.6	20	300	10.0	0.7	1.1	12.1	100	1.5	20	0.4-0.5	5-10
7-9	28.1	2190	9.2	25	400	2.5	0.9	1.3	14.5	100	1.5	20	0.4-0.5	5-10
Male adolescents														
10-12	36.9	2600	10.9	30	575	2.5	1.0	1.6	17.2	100	2.0	20	0.6-0.7	5-10
13-15	51.3	2900	12.1	37	725	2.5	1.2	1.7	19.1	200	2.0	30	0.6-0.7	9-18
16-19	62.9	3070	12.8	38	750	2.5	1.2	1.8	20.3	200	2.0	30	0.5-0.6	5-9
Female adolescents														
10-12	38.0	2350	9.8	29	575	2.5	0.9	1.4	15.5	100	2.0	20	0.6-0.7	5-10
13-15	49.9	2490	10.4	31	725	2.5	1.0	1.5	16.4	200	2.0	30	0.6-0.7	12-24
16-19	54.4	2310	9.7	30	750	2.5	0.9	1.4	15.2	200	2.0	30	0.5-0.6	14-28
Adult man (moderately active)	65.0	3000	12.6	37	750	2.5	1.2	1.8	19.8	200	2.0	30	0.4-0.5	5-9
Adult woman (moderately active)	55.0	2200	9.2	29	750	2.5	0.9	1.3	14.5	200	2.0	30	0.4-0.5	14-28
Pregnancy (later half)		+350	+1.5	38	750	10.0	+0.1	+0.2	+2.3	400	3.0	30	1.0-1.2	(9)
Lactation (first 6 months)		+550	+2.3	46	1200	10.0	+0.2	+0.4	+3.7	300	2.5	30	1.0-1.2	(9)

[1]Energy and protein requirements: report of Joint FAO/WHO Expert Group, FAO, Rome, 1972. [2]As egg or milk protein. [3]Requirements of vitamin A, thiamine, riboflavin and niacin: report of a Joint FAO/WHO Expert Group, FAO, Rome, 1965. [4]As retinol. [5]Requirements of ascorbic acid, vitamin D, vitamin B$_{12}$, folate, and iron: Report of a Joint FAO/WHO Expert Group, FAO, Rome, 1970. [6]As cholecalciferol. [7]Calcium requirements: Report of a Joint FAO/WHO Expert Group, FAO, Rome 1961. [8]On each line the lower value applies when over 25 percent of calories in the diet come from animal foods, and the higher value when animal foods represent less than 10 percent of calories. [9]For women whose iron intake throughout life has been at the level recommended in this table, the daily intake of iron during pregnancy and lactation should be the same as that recommended for nonpregnant, nonlactating women of childbearing age. For women whose iron status is not satisfactory at the beginning of pregnancy, the requirement is increased, and in the extreme situation of women with no iron stores, the requirement can probably not be met without supplementation.

Source: FAO 1974.

Table 4.6 Recommended Daily Dietary Allowances, NAS, 1974[a]

Age (years)	Weight (kg)	Weight (lbs)	Height (cm)	Height (in)	Energy (kcal)	Protein (g)	Vitamin A Activity (RE)[c]	Vitamin A (IU)	Vitamin D (IU)	Vitamin E Activity[e] (IU)	Ascorbic Acid (mg)	Folacin[f] (ug)	Niacin[g] (mg)	Riboflavin (mg)	Thiamin (mg)	Vitamin B6 (mg)	Vitamin B12 (ug)	Calcium (mg)	Phosphorus (mg)	Iodine (ug)	Iron (mg)	Magnesium (mg)	Zinc (mg)
Infants																							
0.0-0.5	6	14	60	24	kgx117	kgx2.2	420[d]	1,400	400	4	35	50	5	0.4	0.3	0.3	0.3	360	240	35	10	60	3
0.5-1.0	9	20	71	28	kgx108	kgx2.0	400	2,000	400	5	35	50	8	0.6	0.5	0.4	0.3	540	400	45	15	70	5
Children																							
1-3	13	28	86	34	1,300	23	400	2,000	400	7	40	100	9	0.8	0.7	0.6	1.0	800	800	60	15	150	10
4-6	20	44	110	44	1,800	30	500	2,500	400	9	40	200	12	1.1	0.9	0.9	1.5	800	800	80	10	200	10
7-10	30	66	135	54	2,400	36	700	3,300	400	10	40	300	16	1.2	1.2	1.2	2.0	800	800	110	10	250	10
Males																							
11-14	44	97	158	63	2,800	44	1,000	5,000	400	12	45	400	18	1.5	1.4	1.6	3.0	1,200	1,200	130	18	350	15
15-18	61	134	172	69	3,000	54	1,000	5,000	400	15	45	400	20	1.8	1.5	2.0	3.0	1,200	1,200	150	18	400	15
19-22	67	147	172	69	3,000	54	1,000	5,000	400	15	45	400	20	1.8	1.5	2.0	3.0	800	800	140	10	350	15
23-50	70	154	172	69	2,700	56	1,000	5,000		15	45	400	18	1.6	1.4	2.0	3.0	800	800	110	10	350	15
51+	70	154	172	69	2,400	56	1,000	5,000		15	45	400	16	1.5	1.2	2.0	3.0	800	800	110	10	350	15
Females																							
11-14	44	97	155	62	2,400	44	800	4,000	400	12	45	400	16	1.3	1.2	1.6	3.0	1,200	1,200	115	18	300	15
15-18	54	119	162	65	2,100	48	800	4,000	400	12	45	400	14	1.4	1.1	2.0	3.0	1,200	1,200	115	18	300	15
19-22	58	128	162	65	2,100	46	800	4,000	400	12	45	400	14	1.4	1.1	2.0	3.0	800	800	100	18	300	15
23-50	58	128	162	65	2,000	46	800	4,000		12	45	400	13	1.2	1.0	2.0	3.0	800	800	100	18	300	15
51+	58	128	162	65	1,800	46	800	4,000		12	45	400	12	1.1	1.0	2.0	3.0	800	800	80	10	300	15
Pregnant					+300	+30	1,000	5,000	400	15	60	800	+2	+0.3	+0.3	2.5	4.0	1,200	1,200	125	18+	450	20
Lactating					+500	+20	1,200	6,000	400	15	80	600	+4	+0.5	+0.3	2.5	4.0	1,200	1,200	150	18	450	25

[a] The allowances are intended to provide for individual variations among most persons as they live in the United States under usual environmental stresses. Diets should be based on a variety of common foods in order to provide other nutrients for which human requirements have been less well defined.

[b] Kilojoules (kJ) = 4.2 X kcal.

[c] Retinol equivalents.

[d] Assumed to be all as retinol in milk during the first six months of life. All subsequent intakes are assumed to be half as retinol and half as B-carotene when calculated from international units. As retinol equivalents, three-fourths are as retinol and one-fourth as B-carotene.

Source: US National Academy of Sciences 1974:129.

Table 4.7 Safe Level of Protein Intake, FAO/WHO/UNO Recommendations, 1985

Age	Weight (Kilos)	Grams of Protein Intake per Day
Both sexes		
Months		
3-6	7	13
6-9	8.5	14
9-12	9.5	14
Years		
1-2	11	13.5
2-3	13.5	15.5
3-5	16.5	17.5
5-7	20.5	21
7-10	27	27
Boys		
10-12	34.5	34
12-14	44	43
14-16	55.5	52
16-18	64	56
Girls		
10-12	36	36
12-14	46.5	44
14-16	52	46
16-18	54	42
Both sexes		
18 or over	50	37.5
	55	41
	60	45
	65	49
	70	52.5
	75	56
	80	60

Source: WHO 1985a:132, 136-137.

Note: At ages three months to 10 years, weights are the average of the median for boys and girls at mid-point of age range, NCHS.

this population and is the value adopted for the recommended allowance. The shaded region to the right on the curve shows the small minority of individuals (2.5 percent) not covered by the recommended allowance. The approach illustrated here is followed by the international committees in estimating daily dietary recommendations.

It is important to recall that there will always be a few individuals who will need more than the recommended amount. But it is equally important to remember that the vast majority of individuals can remain perfectly healthy on some-

Figure 4.2 Distribution of Nutrient Requirements in a Typical Population of Healthy Individuals

Proportion of Individuals

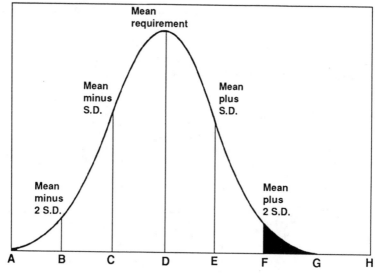

Increasing intake of a given nutrient

Note: The curve is bell-shaped.

Source: Adapted from Scrimshaw and Young 1976:35.

thing less than the recommended allowance. And it should be noted that there is increasing evidence that metabolism responds to caloric scarcity by becoming more efficient. The body can survive (although not necessarily thrive) long-term on intakes well below the recommended number of calories. There are, however, three groups who should have special consideration of dietary needs.

Lactating mothers need about 40 percent more protein in their diet than do nonpregnant/nonlactating women. Pregnant women need some 65 percent more than nonpregnant/nonlactating women. But infants need the most protein-dense diet of anyone. The UN committee recommends that infants below six months consume 2.5 times the protein per kilogram of body weight as do adults, and the NAS recommendation is even higher at almost three times the adult rate.

Fortunately breast milk is high in balanced protein, and breast-fed infants normally get adequate protein, especially if their mothers are reasonably well nourished. Children are not normally at risk for protein deficiency until weaning time. Third World mothers have traditionally breast-fed their children for 18 months or more. For instance, the standard breast-feeding period in Bagbana village, India, is two years.

Unfortunately, many Third World mothers have been tempted to follow the Western practice of early weaning. Selected infant feeding practices in selected countries are shown in Figure 4.3. Pay attention particularly to the triangle in the top right-hand corner of each box. Mothers in Third World rural regions, illustrated by the top row of boxes, tend to breast-feed for more than 16 months.

Figure 4.3 Patterns of Infant Feeding in Selected Countries

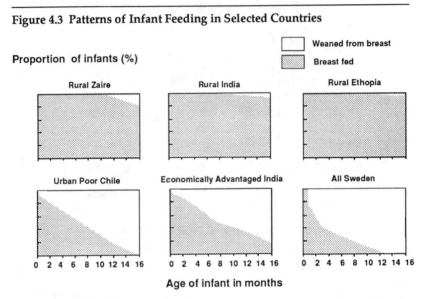

The data, drawn from the preliminary report of the WHO breast-feeding study, show the prevalence of particular practices at intervals of age.

Source: Adapted from Beaton and Ghassemi 1982.

Mothers in the regions represented by the bottom row of boxes, namely Third World urban poor, Third World economically advantaged, and Western mothers, tend to wean their children early. Early weaning and its associated bottle-feeding may be no particular problem when practiced by well-educated mothers in economically advantaged families. But in Third World low-income families, the attempt at bottle-feeding can end in sickness and even death for the infant. Imagine what can happen when an illiterate, low-income, Third World mother, who has no easy means to sterilize her baby bottles in her mud hut with its mud floor, stirs up some baby formula with some water of questionable repute and lets the whole mixture sit overnight on the shelf in the heat of the tropics!

■ SOME POINTS TO KEEP IN MIND

Gram for gram, protein is more expensive than carbohydrates or fat. Infants, pregnant women, and lactating mothers need more protein than they can get from consumption of cereals alone. They benefit substantially from a pulse component in their diet. There needs to be special consideration given to these groups to see that they get adequate protein, as well as calories, in their diets.

But the adult diet in Third World countries does not, typically, seem to be short on protein. As Nevin Scrimshaw, professor emeritus of Massachusetts Institute of Technology and a world-famous advocate of the importance of protein in the diet, put it recently (1988), "it is true that adult protein needs are met by most traditional developing country diets when they are consumed in sufficient quantity to meet normal energy needs." On the other hand, Schrimshaw points out, "this is true only when populations can afford these diets."

For the adult population, protein undernutrition is normally a problem only among families that are so poor that they must abandon their traditional diet and start to depend heavily on cheap, low-protein foods such as cassava or cooking bananas.

But arguments still exist for upgrading the content of protein in the Third World diet. Following weaning, there is a tendency to feed children the same diet as eaten by the adults in the family. If the adult diet is low enough in protein, children suffer. Furthermore there is a tendency for the working male to get first choice of food within the household. If he overconsumes the (tastier) high-quality protein foods, the pulses, for example, there is less protein left over for the weaning children, pregnant women, and lactating mothers in the household. Higher-protein-content diets for all would lessen the protein problem associated with this practice. On the other hand, for those families that have a limited food supply but a reasonable balance of protein in the diet, the mere provision of more food would also reduce the tendency toward protein shortage among the at-risk family members.

□ 5

Undernutrition: Who, Where, When?

Man may live by bread alone, but his wife and children cannot.
—Pellett 1987: 176.

In the previous chapters we saw that there are a number of ways of measuring undernutrition, and that the methods used usually involve somewhat arbitrarily placed cut-off points. On top of that, we learned that there is debate on what constitutes undernutrition. Given this situation, it is no wonder that estimates of the magnitude of the undernutrition problem can only be approximations.

Nevertheless, we know enough about what we mean by undernutrition that useful statements can be made that place the magnitude of the problem in perspective. So in this chapter we consider the questions: How widespread is undernutrition? What kinds of people suffer from it? When do they suffer (or when have they suffered)? And where do they live?

We will examine two authoritative estimates of the number of undernourished people, one by the WHO and the other by the International Bank for Reconstruction and Development (World Bank).

The WHO data (Table 5.1) suggest that some 500 million children under seven years of age, or 11 percent of the 1980 total world population, could be found in any one year to be suffering from protein and energy undernutrition serious enough to stunt their growth. In addition, the WHO estimates that there are a million clinical cases of kwashiorkor and marasmus in any one year, with a combined death rate from all of the above causes of 10 million. In Table 5.1 morbidity (sickness) caused by the other main nutritional difficulties—deficiencies of iron, vitamin A, and iodine—is quantified. Some of the most interesting information in this table is found in the notes.

Schlomo Reutlinger of the World Bank takes a somewhat different approach (Naiken 1988), presenting numbers of people who have different levels of energy-deficient diets in 87 developing countries (Table 5.2). His data include 92 percent of the population in developing countries outside of China. Reutlinger estimates that, in 1980, some 340 million people (10 percent of the world's 1980 population of 3.4 billion excluding China) did not have enough food to provide a diet that would prevent serious health risks and stunted growth

85

Table 5.1 World Population Affected by Malnutrition, WHO Data

Deficiency	Morbidity from malnutrition	Prevalence[1]	Age (Years)	Mortality per Year
Protein and energy	Stunted growth[2, 10] Clinical cases of kwashiorkor and marasmus[4]	500 million 1 million	0-6 1-4	10 million[3, 5]
Iron	Anemia[6]	350 million	Women 18-45	
Vitamin A	Blindness[7]	6 million	All ages	750,000
Iodine	Goiter[8] Cretinism[9]	150 million 6 million	All ages All ages	

Source: Adapted from Latham 1984:55.

[1]The estimates are gross and do not express the significant variations occurring not only from country to country but within countries.

[2]Stunted growth defined by weight below the 2.5 percentile of WHO growth standards. This figure includes mild malnutrition and is therefore higher than the usual estimated 200 million of moderately to severely malnourished.

[3]Often diarrhea is the proximate cause of death. Most cases of death by diarrhea (about 1.5% of 1-4-year-olds or 4.6 million a year) are associated with stunting and wasting.

[4]About 1.5% of those with stunted growth are so malnourished that they will show the life-threatening symptoms of marasmus and kwashiorkor within the year (e.g., 7.5 million cases per year). The mean duration of kwashiorkor is about a month, and of marasmus about three months, for an average of two months. The prevalence at any given time is thus over 1 million.

[5]Of the 7.5 million cases per year of kwashiorkor and marasmus, most die (e.g., 7 million). Of these many die with diarrhea.

[6]Fifty percent of these women have hemoglobin values below the seventeenth percentile of WHO standards, that is, 33% of women aged 18-45 years are anemic.

[7]This is an underestimate of persons affected because it includes only those cases in Southeast Asia. This area does have the highest prevalence in the world, but further cases should be added from Africa and the Americas. Of a million new cases of blindness per year 25% survive that year, so there are 250,000 blind survivors each year. These probably have another 40 years of mean life span, resulting in a prevalence of 6 million.

[8]Two hundred million estimate in 1960. Latham estimates successful campaigns against goiter have reduced the prevalence so that about 150 million suffer from goiter today.

[9]In goitrous populations 1.5% of the children born have severe mental and physical retardation (cretinism); 750 million people live in goitrous areas (overall prevalence of 20% goiter in such areas). Thus about 250,000 cretins are born a year in these areas. Even if their life span is half that of noncretins, 6 million persons living today are mentally deficient because of maternal iodine deficiency.

[10]The first manifestation of stunting appears at birth, defined by low weight for gestational age. A rough estimate has been made of 22 million live-born low-birth-weight infants, equivalent to one-sixth of total number of births. If one-third of these cases are due to other factors, there are at least 14 million nutrition-related stunted babies born each year. Some evidence suggests a higher mortality for these babies than for bigger babies.

Table 5.2 Share and Size of Population with Energy-Deficient Diets, 1980

Region	Not enough calories for an active working life: below 90 percent of FAO/WHO requirement[1]		Not enough calories to prevent stunted growth and serious health risks: below 80 percent of FAO/WHO requirement[2]	
	Share in Population (percentage)	Affected Population (in millions)	Share in Population (percentage)	Affected Population (in millions)
All developing countries[3] (87)[4]	34	730	16	340
Low income[5] (30)	51	590	23	270
Middle income (57)	14	140	7	70
Sub-Saharan Africa (37)	44	150	25	90
East Asia and Pacific (8)	14	40	7	20
South Asia (7)	50	470	21	200
Latin America and Caribbean (24)	13	50	6	20
Middle East and North Africa (11)	10	20	4	10

Source: Reutlinger 1985:8.

[1]Intake at this standard is sufficient for a person to function at full capacity in all daily activities.

[2]Intake at this standard is sufficient to prevent high health risks and growth retardation in children.

[3]The 87 countries had 92 percent of the population in developing countries in 1980, excluding China.

[4]Numbers in parentheses are the number of countries in the sample.

[5]The low-income countries had a per capita income below $400 in 1983.

in children. That is, their diet fell below 80 percent of the 1974 FAO/WHO standard for adequate nutrition (see Table 4.5). But, Reutlinger says, if you take 90 percent of the FAO/WHO standard as your cut-off point for an energy-sufficient diet, you include 730 million people, or about 21 percent of the world's population, again excluding China. Consuming less than 90 percent of the FAO/WHO requirement for adequate nutrition is regarded as not getting enough calories for an active working life.

■ GLOBAL TRENDS IN LONG-TERM PERSPECTIVE

With regard to recent global trends in undernutrition there is good news and bad news. The good news is that the percentage of the world's people suffering from

Figure 5.1 **Changes in the Size and Share of Population with Energy-Deficient Diets in 87 Developing Countries, 1970-1980**

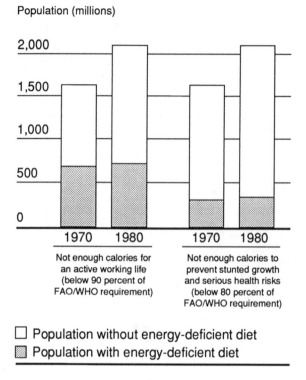

Population (millions)

| | Not enough calories for an active working life (below 90 percent of FAO/WHO requirement) | Not enough calories to prevent stunted growth and serious health risks (below 80 percent of FAO/WHO requirement) |

□ Population without energy-deficient diet
▓ Population with energy-deficient diet

Source: Adapted from Reutlinger, et al, 1986:3.

undernutrition is decreasing. The bad news is that there are more of them in sheer numbers. Within the 87 developing countries studied by Reutlinger, the number of people below 90 percent of FAO/WHO calorie requirement for an active working life increased between 1970 and 1980, while the percentage of the population below the 90 percent cutoff in those countries decreased. A similar phenomenon occurred among those people below the 80 percent cut-off point (Figure 5.1).

Using a different methodology and somewhat different data sources, the Brown University World Hunger Program came to a similar conclusion. They found that during the period from 1949 to 1984 the number of undernourished people increased from about 550 million to just under 600 million, while the percentage declined from the low twenties to the low teens (Figure 5.2).

A more recent study that concentrates on the prevalence of underweight preschool children compares the intensity of undernutrition in three continents.

Figure 5.2 World Population in Households with Dietary Energy Less Than That Required for Minimal Activity, 1949-1984

Food-poor population (millions)   Percentage of world population

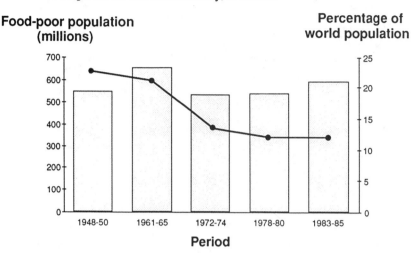

Period

Note: Absolute numbers are shown as bars, and percentages are plotted as a line.

Source: Adapted from Kates, et al, 1988:9.

The prevalence increases as you move from Latin America to Africa and then to Asia (Table 5.3).

During the past 25 years, world production of the three leading food grains—wheat, rice, and corn (maize)—has increased faster than population

Table 5.3 Prevalence of Underweight Preschool Children, by Decades

	Percent Underweight [1]		
	1960s	1970s	1980s
Latin America	21.6 (10)	21.2 (7)	15.3 (7)
Africa	24.6 (5)	26.3 (20)	29.5 (10)
Asia/Near East[2]	36.5 (3)	35.7 (7)	36.6 (5)
Total	29.3 (18)	28.8 (34)	29.2 (22)

Source: McGuire 1988:Table 2.

Note: Parentheses ( ) = number of countries with data.

[1]Generally under two standard deviations below median weight-for-age, but also less than 80 percent or less than 75 percent weight-for-age or prevalence of selected clinical signs.

[2]Excluding Bangladesh, India, Pakistan.

Figure 5.3 World Prices and Production of Wheat, Rice, and Maize, 1960-1984

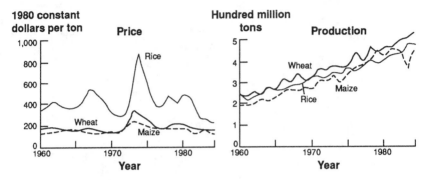

Source: Adapted from Reutlinger, et al, 1986:5.

growth, resulting in a gradual downtrend in the price of these commodities (Figure 5.3). At today's prices, a family can buy calories, protein, and fat for a year on a remarkably modest budget (see Box 5.1).

Why is it then, that since the end of World War II, a period of remarkable growth in per capita income worldwide, the number of undernourished people has increased? Undoubtedly this is due in part to the sheer increase in human population during this period, with an accompanying increase in numbers of poor people. But it may be the result, in part, of a growing distance between the poor and the rich (the greater the economic distance between the rich and the poor the greater is the tendency for the rich to bid food away from the poor.)

A simple data sort of the income growth data contained in the *World Development Report* (World Bank 1988: 222–223) basic indicators table produces

Table 5.4 GNP per Capita in 1986, by Annual Growth Rate of GNP per Capita, 1965-1986

Annual Percentage Growth in GNP Per Capita, 1965-1986	Number of Countries	Population 1986 (Millions)	Percentage of World's Population	GNP per Capita (Average of countries in group) US Dollars, 1986
Negative	19	771	16	1660
0 to 1.9	39	1700	36	3411
2 or more	46	2389	48	3980
Total	104	4930	100	

Source: World Bank 1988:222-223.

the interesting results shown in Table 5.4. Nineteen countries, containing 16 percent of the world's population, experienced negative growth in GNP per capita between 1965 and 1986! The rest of the world's countries were more or less evenly divided between those whose GNP per capita grew between 0 and 1.9 percent and those that grew at 2 percent or more. On the average, the positive-growth countries had about twice the income per capita as the negative-growth countries. In other words, there is a group of relatively poor countries that are experiencing negative income growth while the rest of the world, with higher average income, is experiencing positive income growth.

Box 5.1 Could You Survive for a Year on $100 Worth of Food?

Could one adult survive for a year on what it might cost a couple to eat dinner in a top-rated restaurant in Paris?

Let us assume a very simple diet, yet one not far from what some of the world's poorest live on: corn grits and cooking oil. Actually no one probably lives on a diet that is this simple. People switch from one food to another as prices change during the year, they pick leaves and munch on them as they walk through the countryside, and they vary their diet on special days like holy days. But the basic diet of the world's poorest comes close to this level of simplicity.

Take the 3,000 Calorie recommendation for a moderately active adult male, found in both the FAO and National Academy of Sciences recommendations, and, using the Philippine prices in Table 4.1, do some arithmetic. We will provide 2,400 Calories as corn grits and 600 as cooking oil, yielding a diet that is just over 20 percent fat and provides 57 grams of protein daily. A thousand Calories of corn grits costs P 1.11, so 2,400 (663 g) would cost 2.66. Multiply this by 365 (days per year) and you have P 970 per year for grits.

The fat makes the diet a lot more palatable (and healthier too, since you need linoleic acid, found in vegetable fat, for survival). The tables of recommended amounts do not include fat because fat adequacy is not normally a problem. However, you do need more fat in the diet than would be supplied by corn grits alone. To get 600 calories as fat you need 67 grams of cooking oil (there are 9 calories per gram of fat), which, at P 2 per 100 grams, will cost P 1.24. Multiplying by 365 gives P 452 per year.

The annual cost of this diet is P 1,442 or about $72. Nobody is going to claim that this is a balanced diet. It is short on iron and vitamins, especially the B vitamins, but it provides more calories than some of the poorest people on earth eat, and its deficiencies are representative of common Third World nutritional deficiencies.

With the acceleration of technology during the nineteenth and twentieth centuries, Westerners developed considerable confidence in their rate of progress. We have come almost to expect that "every day in every way we are getting better and better"—that our present state of development is the result of an almost continual improvement since the days of the caveman. There is a strong tendency to look back on life in preagricultural societies as "nasty, brutish, and short."

It is easy to presume that our abundant life today is the culmination of progress on a multitude of fronts, one of which is certainly nutrition. In Chapter 3 I cited data sets that suggested that, during the past 100 years, whole populations have grown taller in such diverse areas as Europe, Japan, and India. So it comes as something of a shock that, during the past few decades, ethnologists, anthropologists, paleopathologists, and agronomists have begun to suggest that life was not totally bad after all, during those millennia before the development of agriculture, which supposedly released us from the brutish life of the hunter-gatherer (Box 5.2).

One of the first chinks in the armor of the progressivist thesis was a famous and widely quoted study by Richard Lee (1968: 30–48) of the !Kung Bushman of the Kalahari desert of Southern Africa. Lee found, when he studied a group of these Bushman of the Dobe area, that, "In all, the adults of the Dobe camp worked about 2 1/2 days a week. Since the average working day was about 6 hours long, the fact emerges that !Kung Bushmen of Dobe, despite their harsh environment, devote from 12 to 19 hours a week to getting food" (p. 37). If 15 hours a week getting food is representative, that is only about two hours a day! Such a life leaves more time than we had previously supposed that the preagricultural societies had for activities such as the creative arts and crafts and other leisure activities.

Figure 5.4 Relative Height of Eastern Mediterranean Adult Males Since 9000 B.C., Based on Correlations Between Leg Bones (From Burial Remains) and Height

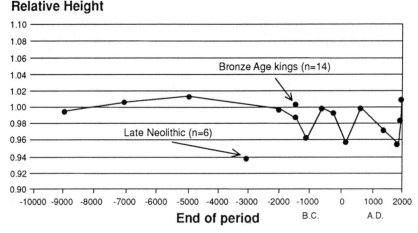

Source: Adapted from Kates, et al, 1988:26; data from Angel 1984.

Box 5.2 Did Settling Down Improve Human Lives?
Mark Cohen

A long-standing debate among prehistorians concerns the impact of early improvements in food-related technology on human health and well being. A traditional view, still popularly held, argues that the development of agriculture, which occurred at various places around the world between 5,000 and 10,000 years ago, generally resulted in the improvement of human health, improvements in the quality and reliability of human food supplies, and the overall lessening of labor demands in the food quest.

Beginning in the 1960s, stimulated by the work of economist Esther Boserup and ethnographer Richard Lee, an alternative view of prehistory was put forward. According to this theory, early farming permitted more mouths to be fed without necessarily increasing leisure—and in fact often increasing the work load. This view also suggested that the adoption of agriculture might have resulted, at least in some areas, in a decline in the nutritional quality of the food supply.

At the same time, according to the new theory, human health began to deteriorate as the intensity of early agriculture increased. Modern epidemiology suggests that many human diseases that pass from person to person in the air or water or by touch will be transmitted more readily by larger, sedentary farming communities than by small, mobile bands of hunter gatherers. Diseases vectored by human feces such as hookworm and various kinds of diarrhea should pass more readily; diseases such as bubonic plague transmitted by rats or other animals attracted to human garbage should become more common; and the increasing size of human groups in combination with increasing trade networks would have permitted some epidemic diseases such as measles, mumps, smallpox, and cholera to appear for the first time.

Whether agriculture increased the reliability of human food supplies is also questionable. Human tending may well protect crop plants from failure; and storage of food certainly helped to alleviate hunger in the short run. But domesticated crops growing under human care are often relatively fragile because human beings have selected them and bred them for qualities other than hardiness and because the crops are often being grown outside the ecological niche to which they were originally adapted. Storage requires that a group be sedentary, which limits options in times of crises. Stored food may spoil, and most important, the storage of food made food supplies vulnerable to expropriation by other human groups for the first time.

Hunter gatherers and early farmers alike probably enjoyed relatively balanced diets; but as intensified farming supported larger populations, agriculture became increasingly focused on individual crops such as maize (corn), wheat, or rice. Diets that rely too heavily on any one crop are likely to create dietary deficiency (anemia, pellagra, beriberi, etc.) as is readily seen in the twentieth century, not among "primitives"—hunter gatherers or farmers—but among the poor of modern states.

The skeletons of prehistoric populations (of which we now have many thousands) appear to support the new view. If we use stature as a measure of well being, as we like to do, it is worth noting that prehistoric hunter gatherers

(continued on next page)

Box 5.2 continued

more often than not are taller than the populations that replace them. In fact, the general trend in human stature since prehistory is downward, the modern trend in Western countries being an exception. The skeletons of hunter gatherers commonly display fewer signs of anemia than the farmers that succeeded them (whether this results from better diets or fewer parasitic infections is unclear). Hunter gatherers also commonly show fewer signs of infection than later farmers. Some specific diseases identifiable in the skeleton, such as tuberculosis, appear relatively recently in prehistory among densely populated, settled groups.

From this perspective, the adoption and intensification of agriculture seems to be a series of compromises with growing numbers—increasing numbers of mouths to feed and increasing competition among groups, rather than "progress."

Source: Adapted from Cohen 1989.

Jack Harlan (1975: 10), in a survey of the literature on preagricultural societies, reports that the pattern of food gathering among the Australian aborigines is similar to that of the !Kung Bushman. Both males and females in Australian aboriginal society tend to work for two days and keep every third day as a holiday. The working adults can supply food for the entire group with only about three to four hours of activity per day (Sahlins 1968).

Not only do we have evidence that preagricultural societies had plenty of leisure time, we also have evidence that they ate rather well. Lee (Harlan 1975: 11) reports that !Kung Bushman consume 93 grams of protein per day, most of which is from meat and nuts. Their food supply is not only abundant most of the time, but reasonably well balanced. Further evidence that preagricultural societies ate rather well is furnished by the record of nutrition they left in their bones. Bone length is one indicator of nutritional status. The height of eastern Mediterranean people at the beginning of agriculture seems to have exceeded the height of these people since the days of Plato and Aristotle (Figure 5.4).

It seems that, around the world since the beginnings of agriculture, as populations have grown and people have therefore exerted increasing pressure on their supply of land, they have at the same time tended to concentrate their food consumption on those crops that make the most efficient use of the land for converting the sun's energy to food. Jack Harlan (1975: 57) again:

The trend for more and more people to be nourished by fewer and fewer plant and animal food sources has reached the point today where most of the world's population is absolutely dependent on a handful of species. . . . This is a relatively recent phenomenon and was not characteristic of the traditional subsistence agricultures abandoned over the past few centuries. . . .

Man once enjoyed a highly varied diet. He has used for food several thousand species of plants and several hundred species of animals. . . . With the beginnings of agriculture there was a tendency to concentrate on the species that were more productive and the most rewarding in terms of labor and capital invested.

If, as the new thinking implies (see Box 5.2), there are still substantial blocks of modern society that are less healthy and less well nourished than pre-agricultural society, then our present-day much-vaunted accomplishments seem a bit tarnished. We should be all the more motivated to improve the level of health and nutrition of modern mankind, at least to the level attained by our preagricultural hunter-gatherer ancestors!

■ THE SEASONALITY OF UNDERNUTRITION

People who are at risk for undernutrition are not usually at risk all of the time. It tends to come in fits and starts. We are all aware of the periodicity of famine— the word connotes a time of extreme food scarcity as contrasted with normal times when food is less scarce. But we are less aware that Third World hunger usually follows a rhythm of the seasons. In the Third World there is usually a strong seasonality in the production, price, and availability of food, as well as in the availability of employment (Sahn 1989). All of these factors can influence the nutritional status of a family at risk for undernutrition.

The seasonality of undernutrition is usually linked to the agricultural year, which in the tropics is usually heavily dependent on rainfall patterns. In monsoon Asia, for instance, rice is usually planted at the beginning of the wet mon-

Figure 5.5 Seasonality of Women's Employment, Rural Tamil Nadu, India

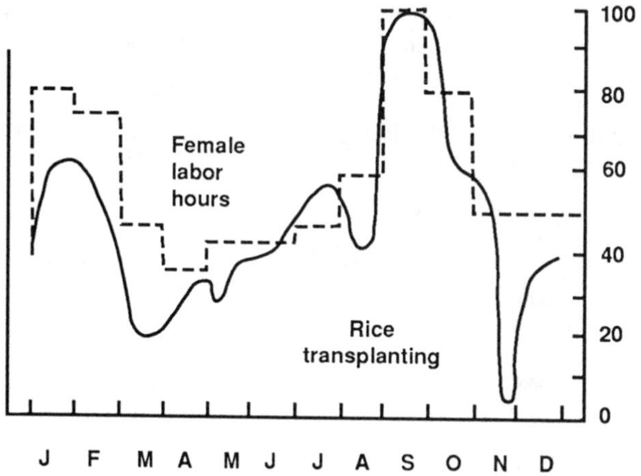

Source: Adapted from Payne 1985:13.

Figure 5.6 Seasonal Price Variation in Rice, Philippines

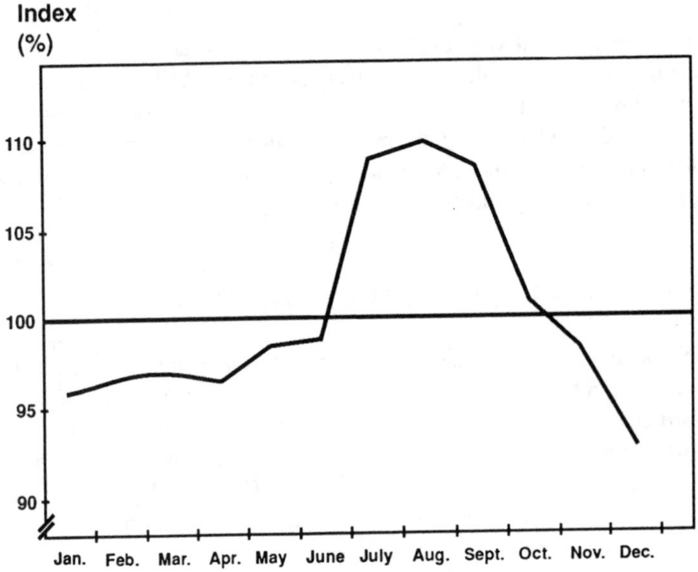

Source: Adapted from Philippines Ministry of Agriculture 1981b.

soon that typically starts in July. For those using the "Japanese method," which involves transplanting seedlings taken from a nursery, there is a particularly heavy labor demand during transplanting (Figure 5.5), which follows planting by a couple of weeks. Harvest begins about four months after planting. With irrigation there can be more than one crop per year, but most of the rice gets its start during the wet monsoon.

Table 5.5 Annual Rate of Consumption of Rice and Rice Products, Philippines, 1980-1981

		Kilos per Capita per Year
1980	March	108.4
	June	110.4
	September	98.2
	December	103.6
1981	March	103.4
	June	115.1

Source: Philippines Ministry of Agriculture 1983.

Consequently the price of rice is lowest just after harvest and rises gradually as supplies dwindle. During the growing season supplies may become short, and prices may rise more sharply. The pattern of seasonal variation in the Philippines is shown in Figure 5.6. Compare this with consumption rates in Table 5.5. Consumption is at its lowest rate in September when the price has been high for three months, and picks up during the following months when the price is below the annual average.

Because of the relationships between food prices, food availability, and the agricultural year, a hunger season is often timed to the onset of the wet season, when food prices are approaching their peak. Some germs die when they dry out or get cold, and so do some diseases, such as diarrhea, spread more easily during the warm, wet season. With the onset of the wet season, increased communicability and lowered resistance caused by reduced food consumption combine to increase infection rates, exacerbating the effects of reduced consumption (the story is told more eloquently in Box 5.3).

■ WHO IS UNDERNOURISHED?

Most of the world's undernourished people live in a belt that extends around the earth from about 30° south latitude to 30° north latitude, or about those latitudes that lie between the southern tip of Brazil and New Orleans, Louisiana. This belt, lying at 30° either side of the equator, contains (according to one authoritative estimate) 65 percent of the world's population and 60 percent of the world's farm animals such as pigs, chickens, and cows, but produces only 20 percent of the world's agricultural product (University of California Food Task Force 1974: 14).

In Figure 5.7 the geographic distribution of the world's hungry is plotted on the basis of daily per capita availability of calories as a percentage of requirements. Such a comparison provides a measure of adequacy of calories on the assumption that the food supply is distributed in proportion to the individual requirements within a population. Its usefulness is limited once we realize that the lack of such distributional equity is, in fact, one of the major causes of undernutrition in developing countries (K. Becker, pers. comm.). This concept is discussed in detail in Chapter 8.

The usefulness of Figure 5.7 is further limited because it does not show the relative numbers of undernourished people by areas. Reutlinger and his colleagues (1986: 1) point out that "about two-thirds of the undernourished live in South Asia and a fifth in Sub-Saharan Africa." The Secretariat of the World Food Council, in their 1988 report, also identified Asia as the region of most-intense undernutrition. Referring to children under five, they state that: "two-thirds of South Asia's children and one-third of those in South East Asia are malnourished as compared to one-fourth in Africa, about one-sixth in China and between 5 and 10 percent in Latin America and the Near East/North African region" (World Food Council 1988: 6).

Box 5.3 The Seasons of Poverty

Robert Chambers, Richard Longhurst, David Bradley, and Richard Feacham

While this is a generalized scenario drawn as a composite from many settings, it illustrates relationships between variables that many settings seem to share. In particular, there is a widespread tendency for adverse factors to operate concurrently during the wet seasons and for these to hit the poor segments of the population harder than the more well-to-do. Typically the scenario develops as follows.

Toward the end of the dry season, water becomes scarce. There is a rise in the labor and energy required to fetch water and to water livestock, and also to gather food and to clear and manure fields. The poorer people begin to suffer more than others. They have less food because they have been able to grow less, because they have fewer livestock, because they may lose a higher proportion of their food reserves in storage, and because they have less money. They may eat less in order to save food for the crucial time of cultivation. Work is scarce and wages are low at this time of year. Some migrate in search of work and food.

The rains bring the start of crisis and of the "hungry season" or "lean period."

For both small farmers and laborers, heavy manual labor for land preparation (often by men), for transplanting (often by women), and for weeding (often by women) comes at this time when food is short. Laborers benefit from being able to get work, but many are in negative energy balance and lose weight. At the same time, food prices are high and transport problems in the rains make it difficult for either central authorities or the open market to relieve local shortages. Anticipating hard work, mothers give their children only a diminished and less regular food supply with their milk. Food preparation becomes more hurried and the diet less varied and nutritious. Less time is spent on cooking, housecleaning, water collection, fuel gathering and childcare, and more of the women's time is spent on agricultural operations.

Diseases vary in their seasonality, but some of the more serious and debilitating peak during or just after the rains. These usually include malaria and sometimes diarrheal diseases, especially where the wet season is also the hot season. Guinea worm also peaks at this time, as do infections of the skin. The development of protein-energy malnutrition contributes to low immune response. Coinciding with a peak labor demand, when failure to cultivate, transplant, weed, or harvest may critically affect future income and food supplies, infections increase the risks and vulnerability of rural people. This is when the poorer people must work in order to earn enough to tide them over until the next agricultural season. This is also a bad time for mothers and children. Births peak, but body weights of mothers and of babies at birth are both low, and neonatal mortality also peaks. The calorific value of the milk supply of lactating mothers is low. Pregnant and lactating women are weakened by disease and work. Those in the poorer, smaller families are especially vulnerable because of the need to work when work is available.

At harvest time wages are high, but the work is also hard—both the harvesting proper and the post-harvest processing. Furthermore, morbidity is still marked and weakness lingers from the food shortages and sicknesses of the lean season. Weight loss is now at its greatest. Mortality, especially among older adults, peaks in response to the high energy demands and the weakened physical condition.

After harvest, things improve for a time. Food is available, and food intake recovers in both quantity and quality. Body weights rise. Morbidity and mortality decline. There are ceremonies, celebrations, marriages. There is a peak in rates of conception. And then gradually the cycle begins all over again.

Source: Extracted from Chambers et al. 1979.

Ironically, many of the world's undernourished live in countries where more than 40 percent of the gross domestic product (GDP) is created in agriculture. Very few of them live in countries that are known as "industrial" (less than 10 percent of the GDP created in agriculture), although some undernutrition can be found in industrial countries (see Box 5.4). Most of the undernourished live in countries with very low average incomes.

Box 5.4 Third-Degree Malnutrition in the United States

One might argue that it's hunger when an American middle-class child leaves for school so late in the morning that he misses breakfast and "feels hungry" before lunch. But that's hardly the problem we have in mind when we talk about undernutrition in today's world.

On the other hand, to say that undernutrition doesn't exist in an affluent society such as America's would be wrong. The *National Nutrition Policy Study— 1974* cited eight cases of kwashiorkor and nine of marasmus, all reported by the Tube City Hospital on the Navajo Reservation in Arizona between 1969 and 1973. Evidently they couldn't find more than these 17 cases of severe undernutrition during this five year period. Undernutrition exists in the United States, although, compared to third world rates, the number of severe cases is small.

Source: US, Congress 1974.

The World Bank (1990: 238) calculated that, among the 42 countries that they classified as low income in 1988, rural people made up 65 percent of the population. Rural incomes are usually considerably below urban incomes and, since undernutrition is so closely associated with low-income populations, a pretty strong argument can be made that the majority of the world's hungry are rural. Because of this and because so many policies affecting the price and availability of food to both rural and urban consumers impinge on the rural sector of the economy, there is a heavy emphasis in this book on policies affecting the rural sector. The tension that exists between the rural and urban sectors of

Figure 5.7 Daily per Capita Calorie Supply as Percentage of Requirement, 1985

Percentage of requirement

Less than 95
95 to 105
106 to 130
Above 130

Source: UNICEF 1988:66-67.

the Third World is discussed in some detail in Chapter 17. As the world moves into the twenty-first century, Third World economies are expected to become increasingly urban, but even then, rural-oriented policies will remain especially significant among those affecting undernutrition.

Children as a group are by far the most vulnerable to undernutrition, especially at weaning time—that transitional period during which an infant's diet is changed from 100 percent breast milk to 100 percent other foods—a transition that can be abrupt but that, in the Third World, often takes place during an 18 months' time span, say, between six months and two years of age. While infants are being moved from breast milk towards other foods, their requirement for a calorie- and protein-dense diet is still very high, and in cultures where the diet is dominated by grains, providing an appropriate diet for weaning children takes a special effort.

Pregnant women and lactating mothers are the next most vulnerable to undernutrition, and evidence is gathering that old women may be next in line. For example, notice again, in Figure 3.5, how the older Indian village women fell further below the NCHS standard than did their older male counterparts.

During times of extreme food shortages or famines the above groups are almost always the most at risk, but at these times a broader segment of the population, including large numbers of able-bodied men, is likely to be affected also.

There are occasional reports of food deprivation based on gender. Roger Winter (1988), director of the US Committee for Refugees, writes about the Dinka people in Sudan, who are plagued by both drought and a scorched-earth strategy the Sudanese army has been using to subdue their rebellious tendencies. Winter reports that many refugee groups consist chiefly of physically weakened young men and boys. "Women and children often are left behind, displaced and without access to international assistance or protection. They are dying in shockingly large numbers. In some areas, virtually all children under 3 are dead. Young girls are rare: In a society beset by war, with an economy based on cattle herding, girls are allowed to starve so that resources can be devoted to their brothers."

The Punjab in northwest India has the highest ratio of males to females in India. A recent study there (Das Gupta 1988) reported that the youngest daughters in families with many children are often selectively deprived of both medicine and the more nutritious foods in order that their brothers may be better cared for. We looked for, but did not find evidence of this practice in our 1981 study of Bagbana village.

When examining the at-risk groups, the emphasis on women and children does not mean that undernutrition never affects adult working men. A significant number of the 730 million estimated in Table 5.2 to consume insufficient calories for an active working life are working adult men. While it is hard to find clinical signs of undernutrition among this group, significant numbers of them appear to be in an energy situation such that their work capacity, and thus their productivity, is limited.

Table 5.6 Correlation of Socioeconomic Variables with Percentage of Standard Body Weight-for-Age, Philippine Preschoolers (Under Six Years Old), 1979

Socioeconomic Variable	Correlation Coefficient	Number of Families Sampled
Number of years of formal education of the mother	.27	721
Number of years of formal education of the father	.26	716
Income, farming families	.12	213
Income, nonfarming families	.35	499
Age of weaning if subject child is weaned	.34	545
Type of infant feeding	-.37	718
1 = breast alone, 2 = mixed, 3 = bottle alone		
Total number of household members	-.25	722
Birth order of subject child	-.21	722

Source: Arnold et al. 1981.

Note: All variables were significant at the .01 level except income, which was significant at the .07 level.

So far we have examined the number of people suffering from undernutrition, as well as the trends, geographic location, and seasonality of hunger, and the people most vulnerable to it. But undernutrition occurs in individuals on a case-by-case basis. If we can identify the characteristics of a family that predispose them to an occurrence of undernutrition, we may, at the same time, uncover clues as to appropriate policies for reducing its prevalence.

Arnold and his coauthors (1981) examined data collected in 1979 by the National Nutrition Council of the Philippines. Their sample contained 722 families from seven provinces. To be included in the sample a family had to have at least one preschool child. The purpose of the study was to see if family data could be used to predict the presence of an undernourished child. So the preshool child with the lowest level of nutrition of all family preschoolers was chosen as the subject. This child, therefore, became the dependent variable, and what Arnold's group tried to predict was the percentage of standard weight-for-age of this child. See Table 5.6 for some of the main findings of the study. Variables with a positive correlation coefficient have a positive influence on percentage of weight-for-age. That is, the higher the value of the variable, the more likely the subject child is to be well nourished. Some of the relationships are fairly obvious. The more education the father and mother have and the more income the family has, the better nourished the subject child is likely to be.

The importance of age of weaning becomes clear when you think about it. The Philippines is a country of rice eaters, and rice is low in both protein and fat. Therefore, the longer a child is breast-fed, the longer is the time when it is getting a an appropriately protein-rich, calorie-dense diet.

Variables with a negative correlation coefficient (those at the bottom of Table 5.6) have a negative influence on percentage of weight-for-age. Thus mothers who bottle-fed their baby almost exclusively were more likely to have an undernourished child than those who breast-fed exclusively. Children of mothers who mixed bottle- and breast-feeding tended to be better off than those who were bottle-fed and worse off than those who were breast-fed. Children in large families were more likely to be undernourished than children in small families. And within the same family, children born later were more likely to be undernourished than their older siblings. There has been speculation that mothers tend to give up, if ever so slightly, on the youngest child after they have already had three or four children (S. Scrimshaw 1978: 389; 1984).

Another study has shown that age of the mother at time of birth may influence nutritional status. Children of mothers who at the time of the child's birth were younger than 20 or older than 30 are more likely to be undernourished than are children whose mothers were between 20 and 30 when they were born (Rustein 1984).

Sometimes special circumstances exacerbate an already unfortunate situation and increase still further the chance that a child will be undernourished. In 1980 I had occasion to visit a number of Filipino families in which there was at least one third-degree undernourished child. In most cases, in addition to the usual problems of low income, low education of the parents, and large number of children in the household, there was some special situation or stressor that might have been a significant contributing factor to child undernutrition; for example, the mother had tuberculosis and was always tired; the mother liked to gamble and left her one-year-old in the care of her four-year-old; the mother had had twins and thought that therefore they were carrying a curse; the father was living with another woman; or the father was working in the city and came home only every other Sunday.

■ Part II

CAUSES OF UNDERNUTRITION

The main causes of undernutrition can be traced to economic, demographic, and health variables. Part II is devoted to each of these causes of undernutrition, or nutrition impact vehicles, as they were called in Chapter 1. The concept of food security demonstrates the interrelatedness of these nutrition impact vehicles, and it is with this concept that we begin Part II.

6

The Concept of
Food Security

*The world has ample food. The growth of global food production has
been faster than the unprecedented population growth of the past forty
years. . . . Yet many poor countries and hundreds of millions of poor
people do not share in this abundance. They suffer from a lack of food
security, caused mainly by a lack of purchasing power.*
                                                —Reutlinger et al. 1986: 1

In the early 1970s rising fertilizer prices, spurred by the OPEC oil cartel, and a
couple of years of lackluster grain harvests that included a really bad crop year
in the Soviet Union combined with gradually increasing demand to draw down
worldwide grain reserves and send the price of grain skyrocketing (see Figure
5.3). Worldwide end-of-crop-year stocks of wheat, coarse grains, and rice carried over to 1975 and 1976 were below 140 million metric tons (Gilmore &
Huddleston 1983), whereas the carryovers of these grains in the 1980s have generally run some 300 million metric tons or more (FAO 1989: 29).

In 1974 the shock of finding that "the global grain bin was nearly empty"
(Gilmore & Huddleston 1983: 31) channeled food policy thinking in the direction of the security of national and international grain reserves. The phrase *food
security* entered the literature, and food security was discussed as a problem of
grain-importing nations (e.g., Chisholm & Tyers 1982).

But, as the worldwide food shortage seemed to evaporate in the 1980s,
while the numbers of hungry continued to increase, the thinking on food security shifted from concern over national food supplies to concern over hungry
people. Reutlinger and his colleagues (1986: 1) captured this shift toward a concern for people when, in 1986, they defined food security as "access by all people at all times to enough food for an active, healthy life."

By focusing on people, food security thinkers have tended to shift the main
concern in the world hunger problem away from an emphasis on food production and toward an emphasis on the purchasing power of those families at risk
for undernutrition. It is not that food production is no longer considered important in the hunger problem. It is. For food shortages result in high prices for
food, which make it difficult for the poor to purchase adequate supplies. What
has happened is a broader recognition of the complexity of the hunger problem:

that food production, income of the poor, and a mix of other variables all influence the incidence of undernutrition.

■ THE FOOD SECURITY EQUATION

Anderson and Roumasset (1985) have developed a series of inequalities for conceptualizing the risk of food insecurity on a national scale. By adapting these inequalities to the household level, we can better understand the concept of food security as well as what delivers the risk of food insecurity to a household.

In simplest form, the food security equation compares the value of the food production deficit in a household with the income and liquid assets that household has available to purchase food. Practically any household, even that of a landless worker, can raise some food at home, if nothing more than a tomato plant near the back door, so we can assume that any household at risk for food insecurity has a food production deficit that will have to be made up by food purchases. In simplest form, therefore, we can develop the food security equation as follows:

$$\text{Value of food production deficit in a household (HH)} \leq \text{Income and liquid assets available to purchase food}$$

The food production deficit in a household is that food needed, over and above any home production, in order to provide all household members at all times, with enough food for an active, healthy life. The value of that deficit is simply the minimum cost of purchasing such a supply of food.

Families make decisions on how to budget or allocate their expenditures among competing needs such as food, housing, clothing, medical care, and entertainment. What the right hand side of the equation says is that, for food security, the income and liquid assets (e.g., savings) available in the household's food budget must be at least enough to purchase enough food to cover the food production deficit.

A household gets more food-secure when the right-hand side of the equation gets bigger relative to the left. It gets less food-secure when the left-hand side of the equation gets bigger relative to the right. *The risk of food insecurity is the probability that the left hand side of the equation will be bigger than the right.*

We said above that, by focusing on people, food security thinkers tended to shift the emphasis in the world hunger problem away from food production and toward purchasing power of those families at risk for undernutrition. But the beauty of an equation is that it forces you to look at the balance between variables. In the food security equation we concern ourselves not only with the right-hand side, the income and liquid assets available in the family food purchase budget, but equally with the left-hand side, the value of the household food production deficit. This left-hand side of the equation can be factored into two components, the food purchase requirement and the price of food, for the value of the food production deficit is the product of these two variables. So the equation can be rewritten as follows:

$$\text{Food purchase requirement} \times \text{Price of food} \leq \text{Income and liquid assets available to purchase food}$$

Now we can demonstrate how the price of food affects food security. If it goes up, the left-hand side gets bigger. There is greater risk of food insecurity. If it goes down, this lessens the risk of food insecurity.

The food purchase requirement in our equation can be broken down into two factors. It is the difference between the household food consumption requirement and household food production. The greater the household food production the less the food purchase requirement; the smaller the household food consumption requirement the smaller the food purchase requirement. We can rewrite the equation again:

$$\left\{ \begin{array}{c} \text{HH food consumption requirement} - \text{HH food production} \end{array} \right\} \times \text{Price of food} \leq \text{Income and liquid assets available to purchase food}$$

For any given family, to the extent that we can adopt policies to assure that the left-hand side of the above equation is smaller than the right-hand side we will reduce the risk of food insecurity. Therefore it makes sense to examine each variable in the equation separately and discuss what sorts of things influence it.

☐ Household Food Consumption Requirement

The household food consumption requirement is affected by the number of people in the household and, as was pointed out in Chapters 3 and 4, by their age, sex, and working status. (It is a simple, but sometimes overlooked, fact that, other things being equal, a family with few children will have an easier time feeding itself than a family with many children.) Since, as we found in Chapter 2, good health reduces the need for food, good health reduces the household food consumption requirement. Childbearing increases the food needs of the mother during pregnancy and lactation and thus increases the consumption requirement.

☐ Household Food Production

The poorest people in the world are generally landless, and the relation between household production and food security is mainly relevant to families with land. Nevertheless, many families with no rights to farmland to grow small amounts of food around their house or keep a few productive scavenging animals such as chickens, ducks, a pig, a goat, or a cow.

The level of food production in a farming household is influenced by a complex set of variables including the amount and quality of land available and the education of the farm manager and farm workers. The quantity and quality of technology and capital available is important. How this technology and capital are used is also important and is usually heavily influenced by a multitude of government incentives and disincentives that can include tariffs, export taxes, price controls, and subsidies of purchased inputs. Agricultural research and education have a powerful influence on quantity produced.

The level of food production of households taken together influences the next variable in the equation—the price of food.

☐ The Price of Food

The price of food is influenced by the quantity produced, discussed above. But all that is on the supply side. The price of food is also influenced by the demand side: the size of the population as well as the per capita income and the tastes and preferences of consumers. Governments often attempt to influence the price of food by activities such as tariffs, export taxes, price controls, and subsidies of purchased inputs mentioned above.

☐ Income and Liquid Assets Available to Purchase Food

The income and liquid assets position of a household is the result of a complex set of factors, among them the education of its members, its capital position, the land position, employment opportunities, attitudes to work, cost of transportation to and from work, and health.

From all of the above, we see that there are a multitude of things that influence each of the variables in the food security equation.

■ IMPORTANCE OF THE FOOD SECURITY EQUATION

In much of the rest of this book we build on the concepts introduced in the food security equation. Once you understand the food security equation and the sorts of things that influence the variables within it, you will be well along the road to rational thinking about policies that can reduce the risk of food insecurity.

The food security equation is summarized in Box 6.1.

Box 6.1 The Concept of Food Security

$$\text{Value of food production deficit in a HH} \leq \text{Income and liquid assets available to purchase food}$$

$$\text{Food purchase requirement} \times \text{Price of food} \leq \text{Income and liquid assets available to purchase food}$$

$$\left\{ \text{HH food consumption requirement} - \text{HH food production} \right\} \times \text{Price of food} \leq \text{Income and liquid assets available to purchase food}$$

You are more food-secure as the left-hand side gets smaller relative to the right, or as the right-hand side gets bigger relative to the left. The risk of food insecurity is the probability that the left-hand sides are bigger than the right.

Factors influencing each element in the final equation are listed below:

- HH food consumption requirement
  Number of people in household
  Age, sex, working status of individuals
  Health status of individuals
  Childbearing status (pregnant, lactating)
- HH food production
  A complex set including amount of land, technology, capital, education of farmer
  Government policies (tariffs, price controls, export taxes, input subsidies, research, etc.).
- Price of food
  Quantity produced
  Size of population
  Income of population
  Government policies (tariffs, price controls, export taxes, input subsidies, research, etc.)
- Income and liquid assets available to purchase food
  A complex set including education of members of household, capital position of household, land position, employment opportunities, attitudes toward work, transportation cost to and from work, and health

7

Purchasing Power: Income and the Price of Food

*Anti-hunger efforts need to focus on the poor, wherever they are: the urban un-
deremployed and unemployed, the rural landless, the rural farmers with inadequate land or other resources. Targeted efforts to alleviate hunger thus need
to use poverty as their main criterion, rather than focusing on a particular sector of the economy or region of the country. Similarly, the alleviation of
poverty should be the criterion of success.*

—Rogers 1988a

■ WHO ARE THE POOR?

There is widespread agreement that a leading cause of undernutrition is low purchasing power—poverty. The World Bank (1988) lists eight countries with a per
capita income of less than $200. These eight countries have a combined popula-
tion of almost 200 million—about 4 percent of the world's population. Because
income distribution in these countries is skewed toward the high end of the
scale, over half of their people live on less than the average income. And they
have needs in life besides food. To merely survive, they need clothing, shelter,
cooking fuel, and cooking utensils.

As you learned in Chapter 5 (e.g., Figure 5.7), not all of the hungry people
in the world live in these eight countries. But the hungry people, by and large,
are existing on incomes that will be very difficult for the typical reader of this
book to imagine.

Who are the poorest of the poor? Mostly they live in the Third World. By
and large they are landless or nearly so. If they do have a bit of land, typically
they earn more than half of their livelihood working for others. Whether they
live packed tightly into city slums or sprinkled across the countryside, they are
poorly educated, often illiterate, and commonly superstitious. When employed,
they accept the most menial of jobs. Some are subsistence fishermen. Some live
in relative isolation in upland farming areas. Often they are squatters, neither
owning nor renting the land on which they put up their hut. Their food larder is
usually almost empty.

Their household is often separated, with one or more members away from home trying to find work so as to send some money home. They are commonly in debt, to a wealthier relative, to a friend, to their employer, or to the local moneylender. The household head is often young, not having had a chance yet to find good employment, but already burdened with the responsibility of raising children. (For a good essay on the poor of a particular region, see Carner 1984.)

■ THE IMPORTANCE OF ELASTICITY

Purchasing power equals income divided by price. Purchasing power can therefore be increased by increases in income or by decreases in prices (for a simple illustration of the concept, see Box 7.1).

Box 7.1 Purchasing Power Equals Income Divided by Price

Purchasing power can be upgraded by increases in income or by decreases in price. A simple illustration shows how important both income and price are in determining purchasing power. Suppose you spend all your income on purchasing rice; now consider the following three situations.

	Income	Price of Rice Per Kilogram	Kilograms Purchased
A	$100	$0.20	500
B	$200	$0.20	1,000
C	$100	$0.10	1,000

Start with situation A. By doubling income from situation A to situation B, you can double the amount purchased. But you can accomplish exactly the same increase in purchasing power by cutting the price of rice in half, as in going from situation A to situation C.

In the real world prices and incomes are constantly changing, yielding corresponding changes in purchasing power. As purchasing power changes, people make changes in their spending patterns. Some of the changes they make involve food purchases that, in turn, influence people's nutritional status. So, policymakers concerned with nutrition must be concerned with the income of the poor as well as with the price of the food they eat. And to know the nutritional impact of policies that affect income and prices, they need to know how people change their spending as prices and incomes change.

By making use of consumption surveys taken at different times, we can learn how people's purchasing patterns change in response to changes in prices and income. How much, and in what directions, they change their purchasing in response to certain changes in prices and income is called their elasticity of demand, or, for short, their demand elasticity. Understanding changes in food consumption that result from changes in prices or income is so important to nutrition policymaking that I devote the rest of this chapter to the concept of elasticity.

■ TYPES OF ELASTICITY

In 1973 the Soviets, after a bad harvest, entered the world grain market and for the first time bought substantial quantities of wheat. Around the world, prices responded (see Figure 5.3). In the United States, the prospects of high livestock feed prices sent up the price of beef, and consumers drastically cut back beef consumption. Some even organized boycotts of beef at supermarkets. The change in consumption of beef resulting from this change in price was an expression of the elasticity of demand for beef with respect to price. This type of response is often called *own-price elasticity* because it is about a change in the consumption of a commodity caused by a change in its own price.

At the same time people were boycotting beef, they were looking around for substitutes, or at least ways to stretch the more limited quantities of beef they were purchasing. Many turned to Italian foods such as spaghetti, ravioli, and pizza, which are usually laced liberally with tomato paste. Tomato paste became scarce and its price shot up. The tomato paste consumption response to the change in the price of beef is called an expression of *cross-price elasticity* because it shows· the consumption response to a change in the price of something across the marketplace.

A change in your consumption of, say, orange juice, as a result of a change in your income, would be an expression of *income elasticity of demand*. In most cases we expect consumption of a product to increase as income increases, whereas increases in price are expected to decrease consumption. Those few products for which people decrease consumption as their income increases are called inferior goods.

Recapitulating the above, we find three kinds of demand elasticity: own-price; cross-price; and income. We will deal mostly with the two most important—own-price elasticity and income elasticity. And on occasion I will refer to own-price elasticity simply as price elasticity.

Since the consumption response to a change in the price of of a commodity, such as rice, is different from the consumption response to a change in income, we need to examine income and price elasticity of demand separately.

☐ Income Elasticity of Demand

How food consumption changes with income. Put in simplest terms, income elasticity of demand is the percentage change in the consumption of something, such as rice, when there is a 1 percent change in income. You can easily see that this elasticity will change depending on your income level. If a poverty-stricken Indian villager suffered a 1 percent decrease in income, he might decrease his consumption of rice by half a percent or so. But a wealthy stockbroker who suffered a 1 percent decrease in income might not change her rice consumption at all! (She might spend less on recreational travel, for instance. But this is getting ahead of our story.)

Let us look at some general ways that food consumption changes as income rises or falls. Table 7.1 provides an illustration, for a Third World country, of how consumption of calories and protein increases as income increases or decreases. (In Table 7.1 expenditure subgroup is used as a proxy for income category.) The table, by the way, provides yet another illustration of the relationship between low income and undernutrition.

In Figure 7.1, more general than Table 7.1, we see differences in food consumption, converted to an equivalent amount of cereal grains, as income changed in a number of countries between 1966 and 1982. The curve is a best-

Table 7.1 Calorie and Protein Intake Estimated from the Fifth National Socioeconomic Survey (Susenas V), All Indonesia, 1976

Expenditure Subgroup (Rupiahs per Capita per Month)	Percentage of Total Population	Calories per Capita per Day	Grams Protein per Capita
Less than 2,000	15.3 } 39.1	1,387	22.2
2,000 - 2,999	23.8	1,870	32.3
3,000 - 3,999	19.5	2,034	40.2
4,000 - 4,999	13.6	2,084	47.0
5,000 - 5,999	8.8	2,288	52.7
6,000 - 7,999	9.4	2,533	60.9
8,000 - 9,999	4.2	2,794	69.7
10,000 - 14,999	3.8	3,066	79.1
Over 15,000	1.6	3,284	93.3
Total	100		
Average		2,064	43.3

Source: Hutabarat 1990, as quoted in Dixon 1982:6.

Note: Dixon (1982:4) reports that minimum nutritional requirements for Indonesia are 1,900 calories and 39.2 grams of protein per day, based on the 1973 FAO/WHO recommendations and the distribution by age and body weight of Indonesians. Groups above the line in the table can therefore be considered undernourished. Note that, because of wastage in marketing and preparation, the amount available for consumption must be greater than the actual calorie or protein intake. For Indonesia, the minimal daily requirements of food available are 2,100 calories and 45.9 grams of protein. In 1976 the exchange rate for rupiahs was US $1 = Rp 145.

Figure 7.1 Food Consumption and Income, Selected Countries, 1966-1982

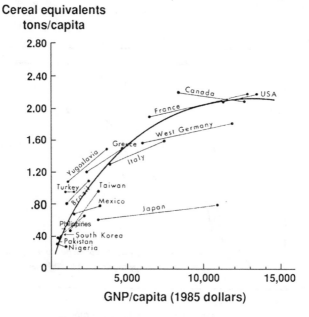

Source: Adapted from Rask 1986.

fit trend line for the data. Notice how the rate of increase in consumption falls off as income increases. What is happening is that the proportion of the household budget spent on food decreases as income increases. The first person to write about this was Ernst Engel, and the phenomenon has become known as Engel's law.

In Figure 7.2 we can see, in some detail, changes in food consumption patterns associated with changes in income for a low-income region of East Java, Indonesia. Only the families in the top half of the income groupings (the right-hand half of Figure 7.2a) were receiving at least the 1,900 Calories cited in Table 7.1 as the minimum appropriate for Indonesians. Figure 7.2b provides a second illustration of Engel's law: As income rises, the percentage of income spent for food declines from 75 for the lowest-income families in the sample population to 60 for the highest-income families. Figure 7.2c shows how the food expenditure mix changes as income increases. As income grows, East Javanese spend a smaller proportion of their food budget on starchy staples—cassava, rice, maize, and wheat flour—and a larger proportion of their food budget on other items, especially on animal products. This phenomenon is called Bennett's law, which states that the "starchy staple ratio" (the ratio of starchy foods such as cereals and root crops to other foods in the diet) falls as income increases. Figure 7.2d shows how the energy derived from various food sources

Figure 7.2   Relationships Between Income Level and Nutritional Status, East Java, 1977-1978

a. Energy (Kcal)

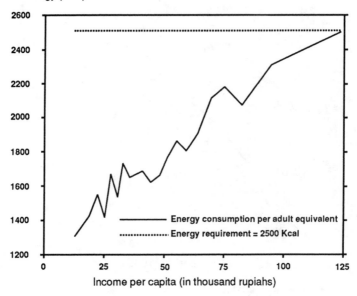

Income per capita (in thousand rupiahs)

b. Food expenditures (percentage of income)

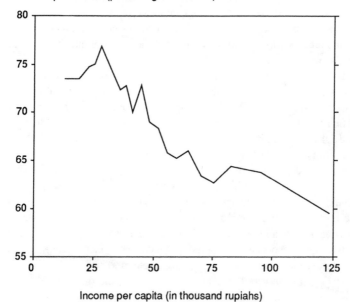

Income per capita (in thousand rupiahs)

c. Percentage of food budget

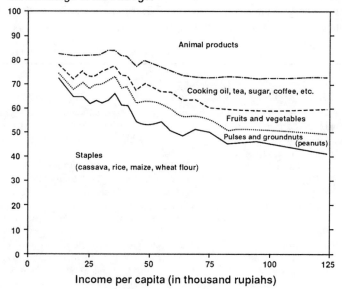

Income per capita (in thousand rupiahs)

d. Percentage of total energy consumption

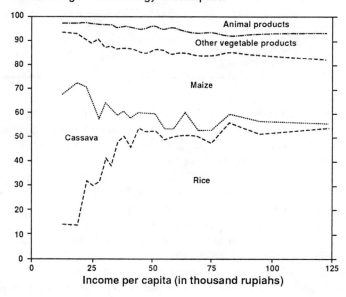

Income per capita (in thousand rupiahs)

Note: Income is shown in thousands of Rupiahs. An income of Rs. 125,000 in 1977-1978 was worth something over $200. The study region included Madura and the nearby regency of Sidorajo.

Source: Ho [1984].

shifts as income rises. The lowest-income people in the sample derive half of their food energy from cassava (see Box 7.2). But as income rises, they quickly substitute other foods, especially rice, for cassava.

Box 7.2 Cassava

Cassava is a common food source in the tropics, especially among low-income people. It is a member of the spurge family (genus *Manihot*) and, in Africa, is usually called manioc. The fleshy rootstock is high in the starch known to English speakers as tapioca.

One source (Indonesia Oleh Direktorat Gizi Departemen Kesehatan R. I. 1979: 19) gives the major nutritional constituents for 100 grams of dried cassava as: Calories, 338; protein, 1.5 g; fat, 0.7 g; and carbohydrate, 81.3 g. There is some feeling among nutritionists that the protein in cassava is largely unavailable. If this is the case, consuming cassava is very close to consuming straight starch.

In the tropics cassava is so easy to grow it has been called "the Lazy Man's Crop." If you want some, just cut a foot or so of stalk from a live plant and stick it in the ground where it can get plenty of sunshine and some rain. Wait six to nine months and dig up the rootstock. The tuberous roots will keep only a week or so out of the ground, but if you are in no hurry do not dig it up, it will usually store for a year or so in the ground. Thus it can be used as insurance against famine during periods of food scarcity.

It is unfortunate that cassava leaves are seldom eaten, for they are high in vitamin A.

To some people, a full-grown cassava plant resembles a miniature papaya tree, while to others it looks more like an overgrown marijuana plant.

Commodities such as cassava, which people consume less of as their income rises, are known by the ignominious name of inferior goods. In Figure 7.3, we see that, for the world as a whole, diet changes follow Bennett's law. Starchy staple carbohydrates make up about 75 percent of the dietary calories of the lowest-income countries and only 30 percent of the dietary calories of the highest-income countries. For the world as a whole, then, the cereals and root crops are inferior goods. Contrast this income consumption response to the change in consumption of fats and sugars as income increases.

The charts shown so far in this chapter certainly do not define the diet for every individual in each of the income categories shown. They do, however, identify clear tendencies toward changes in consumption patterns with changes in income. And it is certainly safe to conclude from the data we have examined so far that, on a worldwide basis, while low-income people are at risk for underconsumption of calories and protein, high-income people are at risk for overconsumption of calories and fat (see Box 7.3). It would be interesting to explore the

Figure 7.3 Percentage of Calories Derived from Fats, Carbohydrates, and Proteins by Annual GNP per Capita, 1962

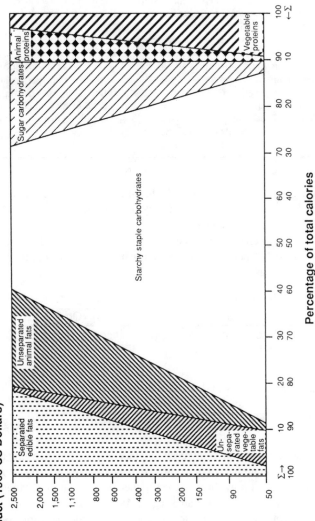

Note: The regression is based on 85 countries. The GNP data are shown with a ratio scale. Separated edible fats are fats that have been separated from their original source such as butter (made from milk) or peanut oil (made from peanuts). Unseparated fats are fats consumed with their natural carrier such as the butterfat in whole milk (unseparated animal fat) or the peanut oil in whole peanuts (unseparated vegetable fat).

Source: Adapted from Perisse, et al, 1969:2.

hypothesis that, by and large, those people in the second quartile from the bottom of the world's income groups have the best diet.

Box 7.3 Fat

For good nutrition adults need some 1 to 2 percent of calorie intake in the form of linoleic acid, a nutritionally essential fatty acid. We need at least 10 percent of our calorie intake as fat in order to have sufficient medium in which to dissolve and transport fat-soluble vitamins. Nutritionists commonly feel that, to be safe, some 20 percent of adult dietary calories should be in the form of fat.

In the high-income industrialized democracies, fat typically runs about 40 percent of total dietary calories. This is considered overconsumption. There is growing evidence that overconsumption of fat is implicated in atherosclerosis, heart attacks, and high blood pressure. Because high-fat diets tend to squeeze out consumption of dietary fiber, they tend to be associated with appendicitis, diverticulosis, and cancer of the colon, all of which fiber in the diet helps protect against. In the summer of 1988 the surgeon general of the United States (US, Dept. of Health and Human Services 1988) recommended that we limit fat consumption to no more than 30 percent of our total calories.

Quantifying income elasticities. As I said earlier, income elasticity of demand is the percentage change in consumption of something, like rice, when there is a 1 percent change in income.

For very small changes in income—for instance, when the percentage change in income is 1 percent or less—we can express income elasticity of demand algebraically as:

$$E = \frac{\%\text{ change in consumption}}{\%\text{ change in income}} = \frac{\dfrac{QD_2 - QD_1}{QD_1}}{\dfrac{Income_2 - Income_1}{Income_1}}$$

where: E = Elasticity of demand with respect to income

QD_1 = Quantity demanded at old income level

QD_2 = Quantity demanded at new income level

In the real world of constantly changing incomes and prices, trying to estimate demand elasticities is a lot more difficult than the above equation suggests. I leave descriptions of how this is done to others (e.g., Deaton & Muellbauer 1980; Huang 1985, Johnson, Hassan & Green 1984). For purposes of this discussion we accept elasticity estimates done by others and concentrate on their meaning and implications for policy planners.

T. J. Ho (1984) made income elasticity calculations for the East Javanese consumers whose food consumption patterns were outlined in Figure 7.2. She found the income elasticity of expenditure on food to be 0.58. That is, for this community, a 1 percent increase in income will produce a 0.58 percent increase in spending for food.

For purposes of illustration, let us hypothesize that this community spends half of its income on food and, to make the computations simple, let us assume that its income is $100. A 1 percent increase in income raises income to $101. If food spending increases by 0.58 percent then these people will spend 29 cents more on food, for a total of $50.29. The remaining 71 cents of increased income will be spent on nonfood items, bringing the total for that category (housing, clothing, paying off debts, etc.) to $50.71. We can deduce, therefore, that the income elasticity of demand for nonfood items in this community is 1.42.

In order for this community to have increased its spending on food exactly by the same percentage (and in this case exactly the same dollar amount) as its spending on nonfood items, its income elasticity of demand for both food and nonfood items would have to have been exactly one (1.0).

Ho estimates the income elasticity of demand for calories to be 0.28 and for protein to be 0.52. These elasticities condense some of the information in Figure 7.5. Review this graph and notice again how these people are substituting rice for cassava as their income increases. To a lesser extent, they are substituting animal products and other vegetable products for cassava at the same time. Calories from cassava are cheaper than calories from rice, other vegetables or meat. So as they increase their spending on food they are buying fewer calories per rupiah and more of other food properties like protein and flavor. That is what the income elasticity figures (low for calories and high for protein) are telling us.

If you are finding this hard to grasp, here is another way of looking at those elasticity figures for calories versus protein. A 1 percent increase in income yields only a 0.28 percent increase in consumption of calories but a more generous 0.52 percent increase in protein consumption. That is, as income changes, these people change their consumption of protein more, in terms of percentages, than they change their consumption of calories. While you could easily have come to this conclusion without the aid of the elasticity figures, what you get from the elasticity calculations is *how much* they change their consumption of these two nutrients when income changes. That is the beauty—and importance—of elasticity! It quantifies things.

Of course, people do not go to the market and buy nutrients like calories and protein. They buy food. So let us look at some income elasticity figures for particular commodities and see how these elasticities change with income.

How income elasticity changes as income changes. Table 7.2 shows some income elasticities for three income groups in rural Brazil. Notice that, except for cassava flour, the income elasticity figures are positive. That is, for most

Table 7.2 Income Elasticities for Calorie Intake, Selected Foods, by Income Group, Rural Brazil, 1974-1975

| | Income Group | | |
	Lowest 30 Percent	Middle 50 Percent	Highest 20 Percent
Cassava flour	-3.50	-1.59	-.356
Rice	1.99	.172	.173
Milk	2.27	.147	.172
Eggs	1.93	.630	.114
Mean per capita calorie intake	1,963	2,432	2,771

Source: Gray 1982:26.

Note: The 1974-1975 National Household Expenditure Survey (ENDEF) of the Brazilian Geographical and Statistical Institute was used as the data base from which to calculate these income elasticities.

foods, consumption increases as income increases. Cassava flour, with a negative income elasticity, is an inferior good.

Notice also that the absolute value (value without regard to sign) of the numbers in this table tends to decrease as you move from low- to high-income consumers. That is, food consumption among low-income consumers is consid-

Table 7.3 Changes in Calorie Consumption Resulting from a 1-Percent Increase in Income, Selected Foods, Lowest 30 Percent of Consumers by Income, Rural Brazil, 1974-1975

	Kilo- Calories	Percentage of Total Kilocalories Consumed	Income Elasticity	Change in Kilocalories Consumed Resulting From a One Percent Increase In Income
Cassava flour	440	22.4	-3.50	-15.4
Rice	296	15.1	1.99	5.9
Milk	41	2.1	2.27	.9
Eggs	7	.5	1.93	.1
Other	1152	59.9		
Total kilocalorie intake	1,963		.46	1,940
Total change in entire diet				9

Source: Calculated from Gray 1982:20, 26.

erably more responsive to changes in income than it is among high-income consumers. This phenomenon is found among all Third World populations.

When the low-income consumer in the Brazilian sample gets a 1 percent increase in income, he tends to increase his rice consumption by about 2 percent. But the high-income consumer tends to change his consumption of rice by less than two-tenths of a percent when his income changes by 1 percent. We call the low-income family's consumption response on rice elastic. That is, a 1 percent change in income yields a greater than 1 percent change in consumption. On the other hand, we call the high-income family's consumption response on rice inelastic. A 1 percent change in its income produces a less than 1 percent change in consumption. If a family changed its consumption of rice by exactly 1 percent when its income changed by 1 percent, we would say it had an income elasticity of demand for rice of one—neither elastic nor inelastic.

Remember that the elasticity figures show percentage change in consumption with a 1 percent change in income. The income elasticity of demand for rice in rural Brazil is about the same as the income elasticity of demand for eggs. But since rice makes up 15 percent of the total calories consumed among this income group and eggs only one-half of 1 percent, a 1 percent change in income results in a far greater change in actual consumption of rice than eggs (see Table 7.3). The nutritional significance of an elasticity, therefore, depends not only on the magnitude of the elasticity but on the magnitude of consumption of the good under consideration.

☐ Price Elasticity of Demand

How food consumption changes with price. As we noted in Box 7.1, purchasing power can be increased either by an increase in income or a decrease in price. The consumption response to a decline in the price of a food item can be complex. Let us think about what might happen to consumption among the poorest 30 percent, in terms of income, in Brazil if the price of rice were to fall substantially.

A fall in the price of rice would likely result in the consumption of more rice. But it might well be that not all of the increased purchasing power that results from a fall in the price of rice will be spent on rice. Some of it might be spent on purchasing more of various other foods, such as eggs, and some of it might be spent on purchasing various nonfood items, such as entertainment.

This percentage change in rice consumption as a result of a 1 percent change in the price of rice is its own-price elasticity. The percentage changes in the consumption of a variety of other things, from eggs to entertainment, resulting from a 1 percent change in the price of rice (a fall in price, in this case) are the cross-price elasticities of rice.

Cross-price elasticities tend to be small. The cross-commodity price impact of a change in the price of rice, for instance, may be spread across a multitude of goods and services. Data on cross-price elasticities are harder to come by and may be less reliable than income and own-price elasticities. Furthermore, much sound analysis of the nutritional impact of policy alternatives can be done with what we know about income and own-price elasticities. So, as mentioned earlier, in this book we will not deal much with cross-price elasticities.

Quantifying own-price elasticities. Remember that price elasticity of demand is the percentage change in consumption of something, like rice, when there is a 1 percent change in its own price.

For very small changes in price (for instance, when the percentage change in income is 1 percent or less) we can algebraically express elasticity of demand with respect to price as:

$$ E = \frac{\% \text{ change in consumption}}{\% \text{ change in price}} = \frac{\dfrac{QD_2 - QD_1}{QD_1}}{\dfrac{Price_2 - Price_1}{Price_1}} $$

where: E = Elasticity of demand with respect to price
QD_1 = Quantity demanded at old price
QD_2 = Quantity demanded at new price

As in the case of income elasticity of demand, trying to estimate these elasticities is a lot more difficult than the above equation suggests. So again I leave descriptions of how this is done to others.

Table 7.4 shows a set of income and price elasticities for major food groups in Indonesia. These figures are for the whole spectrum of incomes, not broken down by income groups. Notice that for Indonesian society as a whole, all of the

Table 7.4 Income and Price Elasticities for Selected Foods, Indonesia

	Income Elasticity	Own-Price Elasticity
Corn and cassava	.3	- .26
Spices	.3	- .25
Rice	.7	- .63
Coconut	1.1	- .88
Tea and coffee	1.1	- .90
Vegetables and fruits	1.2	- .97
Prepared food	1.2	-1.01
Fish	1.3	-1.04
Sugar	1.4	-1.15
Drinks	2.1	-1.71
Livestock and livestock products	2.2	-1.73

Source: Boediono 1978:362.

income elasticities are positive and all the price elasticities are negative. This is normal.

Elasticities quantify consumer behavior in the face of changing purchasing power. If income increases 1 percent, you can expect most consumption responses to be positive. But if price increases by 1 percent, you can expect the usual consumption response to be negative. It is so common for price elasticities to be negative that the minus sign is often omitted. I will use the minus sign when quoting specific price elasticities to remind you of the inverse relationship between change in price and change in consumption.

Elasticity figures show you the relative importance consumers attach to the various foods in their diet. Items considered essential or necessary tend to have elasticities below one. Think of it this way: When income falls by 1 percent, consumption of necessities falls by less than 1 percent. Or if the price of a necessity rises by 1 percent, consumption falls by less than 1 percent. From Table 7.4 it appears that, by and large, Indonesians regard corn and cassava, spices and rice as necessities.

Conversely, items considered luxuries tend to have elasticities above one. If income falls by 1 percent, the consumption of luxuries falls by more than 1 percent, as people cut back on luxuries and concentrate what income is left on necessities. If the price of a luxury rises by 1 percent, people are more likely to cut back substantially on consumption of that luxury than if the price of a necessity rises by one percent. Table 7.4 shows that Indonesians generally regard livestock and livestock products as luxuries. This is commonly the case in Third World countries.

How price elasticities change as income changes. Per Pinstrup-Andersen and coworkers (1976; Pinstrup-Andersen & Caicedo 1978) were the first to show that one could estimate price (and income) elasticities by income groups as well as by the community as a whole. They divided their Cali, Colombia, sample population into five income groups, and estimated elasticities for each income group as well as for their entire sample. Some of the elasticities calculated in their path-breaking study are shown in Table 7.5.

Notice how responsiveness to change in price generally diminishes as you move from low-income to high-income consumers. From this table it appears that high-income consumers in Cali could not care less about small changes in the price of cassava, potatoes, maize, or bread. And even for pork, which the average consumer considers just over the edge into the luxury category, high-income consumers have a demand elasticity with respect to price of less than one (a 1 percent change in the price of pork will generate a less than 1 percent change in pork consumption among these consumers). In contrast, low-income consumers are fairly responsive to changes in food prices. They treat cassava, rice, potatoes, bread, and beans as necessities, but they regard animal products and fresh fruit as luxuries.

Table 7.5 Estimated Direct Price Elasticity of Demand by Income Group, Cali, Colombia, 1969-1970

| | Low Income | | | High Income | | |
	I	II	III	IV	V	Average
Cassava	-.23	-.28	-.25	-.00	-.00	-.19
Potatoes	-.41	-.42	-.31	-.00	-.00	-.26
Rice	-.43	-.40	-.40	-.26	-.18	-.35
Maize	-.63	-.55	-.44	-.00	-.00	-.44
Bread/pastry	-.65	-.56	-.32	-.24	-.00	-.31
Beans	-.82	-.78	-.64	-.45	-.25	-.60
Peas	-1.13	-1.13	-.76	-.59	-.52	-.70
Eggs	-1.34	-1.23	-1.26	-.75	-.35	-.92
Oranges	-1.39	-.96	-.79	-.64	-.29	-.69
Milk	-1.79	-1.62	-1.12	-.64	-.20	-.77
Pork	-1.89	-1.61	-1.12	-.82	-.70	-1.01
Daily calorie intake	89	99	117	132	178	119
as percentage						
of requirement						

Source: Pinstrup-Andersen et al. 1976:137-138.

Since this pioneering study, a number of other studies have been done that relate food price elasticities to income. Alderman provides a useful survey of those studies as of 1986.

■ ELASTICITIES, NUTRITION ECONOMICS, AND PUBLIC POLICY

Armed with their complete set of food elasticity figures by income groups, Pinstrup-Andersen and his team went on to show how price elasticities could be useful in analyzing the differential impact of various agricultural production changes on the nutrition of the poor. Let us look at this subject ourselves now.

Reexamine the elasticity formula on page 126. Notice that this elasticity compares two rates of change: rate of change in consumption and rate of change in price. If we know an elasticity and one of the rates of change, we can easily calculate the other rate of change.

We have been looking at price elasticity from the point of view of a 1 percent change in price. In other words, elasticity is the percentage change in consumption when price changes by 1 percent. Once we know the elasticity for a commodity, say cassava, we can look at things the other way around and ask: How much will price change if consumption changes by one percent? And if we have a closed economy (no imports or exports) and assume all cassava offered to the market is consumed (a reasonable assumption), then consumption equals production. So, given the elasticity equation, we can just as easily ask: How much will price change if production changes by 1 percent?

Table 7.5 shows the *average* price elasticity of demand for cassava to be –0.19. For ease of computation let us call it –0.2. If the elasticity is –0.2 and we set the top half of the elasticity equation to 1—for a 1 percent change in production (which is also consumption)—then the bottom half of the equation must be –0.5. In other words, with an elasticity of –0.2, an increase of 1 percent in the production of cassava will yield a 5 percent decrease in the price.

Using this type of computation, once you have the elasticity figures by income groups, you can estimate changes in consumption among income groups given various production changes. It is useful to be able to do this because governments often successfully promote the production of a particular agricultural commodity or set of commodities, and policymakers may want to know the nutritional consequences of such agricultural policies.

Pinstrup-Andersen and colleagues went through calculations similar to the above for agricultural production in Colombia. For a number of agricultural commodities, they assumed a 10 percent expansion in the quantity supplied to the market and then looked at the resulting amount consumed by the various income groups. The increases in amount consumed are of most interest among the poorest income group, since, as Table 7.5 shows, all of the other income groups are either adequately supplied with calories (group II) or oversupplied (groups III, IV, and V). Calories consumed by the groups with incomes higher than group II's are, by and large, simply wasted.

Notice (Table 7.6) that, although the lowest-income groups have the highest demand elasticity for what they consider the luxuries—peas, eggs, oranges, milk, and pork—they will share in only a small proportion of a 10 percent increase in production of these commodities. This is because their quantity consumed of these goods is so small that, even though they are relatively responsive to price changes, they do not change their consumption, in absolute terms, as much as do the higher-income groups.

The Colombian government might therefore be well advised to promote production of those commodities in the top half of Tables 7.5 and 7.6. The low-income group, which contains 18 percent of the sample population, would consume a larger proportionate share of the increase in production of these commodities. Notice (Table 7.5) that, by and large, the highest-income consumers simply are not going to bother changing their consumption of those commodities in the top half of the table when their prices change. However, a greater than proportionate share of the increases in production of those commodities in the bottom half of the table go to those who already have adequate or more than adequate calories. The Colombian government might equally want to take this into account in allocating resources to agricultural production promotion programs for those commodities.

Table 7.6 Percentage of a 10 Percent Expansion in Quantity Supplied Expected to Be Consumed by Income Group I (the Calorie Deficient Strata) Cali, Colombia, 1969-1970

Commodity and Its Price Elasticity of Demand	Percentage Consumed
Cassava (-.23)	30.4
Potatoes (-.41)	27.5
Rice (-.43)	20.2
Maize (-.63)	27.8
Bread/pastry (-.65)	25.0
Beans (-.82)	19.1
Peas (-1.13)	8.0
Eggs (-1.34)	12.5
Oranges (-1.39)	12.4
Milk (-1.79)	12.0
Pork (-1.89)	11.1

Source: Pinstrup-Andersen et al. 1976:138.

☐ **Relating Demand Elasticities to Different Incomes and Commodities**

We have examined elasticity data from three Third World countries—Brazil, Indonesia, and Colombia. We have used these data to illustrate some interesting and useful generalizations about the relationships between demand elasticities, income, and commodity type in the Third World. I will now re-present these generalizations in geometric diagrams as well as in prose. I introduce the geometric diagrams here because, in the literature, relative demand elasticities are often represented as lines with different slopes.

Income level and income elasticity. As income rises, elasticity of demand for food with respect to income falls (e.g., Table 7.2). That is, low-income people spend a greater proportion of an increase in their income on food than do high-income people. We represent this geometrically with Figure 7.4. In this figure, movement from 1 to 2 represents a 1 percent increase in income. Movement from A to B represents the consumption response of a poor family to the income shift. Movement from E to F represents the (less dramatic) consumption response of a wealthy family to a 1 percent increase in income. The lines labeled C are the locus of points tracing out the consumption responses as income increases. They are like a consumption function. The more steeply sloped line represents the less elastic consumption response (see Box 7.4).

Income level and price elasticity. As income rises, elasticity of demand for food with respect to price falls (e.g., Table 7.5). That is, low-income people are

Figure 7.4 Influence of Income Level on Income Elasticity of Demand for Food

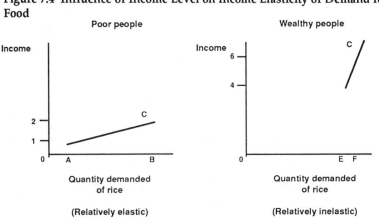

Poor people

(Relatively elastic)

Wealthy people

(Relatively inelastic)

more responsive to a change in the price of food than are high-income people. We represent this geometrically with Figure 7.5. In this figure, movement from 2 to 1 represents a 1 percent decrease in price. Movement from A to B represents the consumption response of a poor family to the price shift. Movement from E to F represents the (less dramatic) consumption response of a wealthy family. The lines labeled D are the locus of points tracing out the consumption responses as price falls. They are demand functions, or demand curves. The more steeply sloped line represents the less elastic demand curve (consumption response).

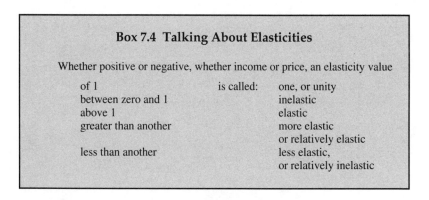

Box 7.4 Talking About Elasticities

Whether positive or negative, whether income or price, an elasticity value

of 1	is called:	one, or unity
between zero and 1		inelastic
above 1		elastic
greater than another		more elastic
		or relatively elastic
less than another		less elastic,
		or relatively inelastic

Commodity type and income elasticity. As income changes, people change their consumption of luxuries by a greater percentage than they change their consumption of necessities. That is, the income elasticity of demand for luxuries is greater than it is for necessities. Third World consumers generally consider rice a

Figure 7.5 Influence of Income Level on Price Elasticity of Demand for Food

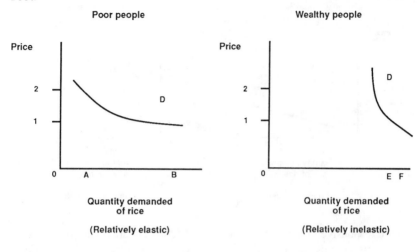

Poor people

Wealthy people

Quantity demanded
of rice

(Relatively elastic)

Quantity demanded
of rice

(Relatively inelastic)

necessity but often regard livestock products as a luxury (e.g., Table 7.4). Alderman (1986: 81) cites several examples of studies that found that income elasticity of demand for livestock products is above one for low-income Third World consumers. This phenomenon is represented graphically in Figure 7.6, where the consumption response to an increase in income of our Third World consumer is shown to be more elastic for livestock products than for rice.

Figure 7.6 Relation Between Commodity Type and Income Elasticity of Demand for Food (Average Consumer)

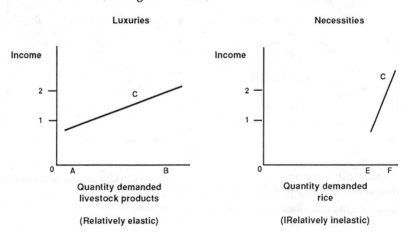

Luxuries

Necessities

Quantity demanded
livestock products

(Relatively elastic)

Quantity demanded
rice

(IRelatively inelastic)

Commodity type and price elasticity. For a necessity, a 1 percent change in price will elicit a relatively small change in consumption. For a luxury, a 1 percent change in price will elicit a relatively large change in consumption. This is true for consumers across the income spectrum as well as for the average consumer (e.g., Table 7.5). Figure 7.7 is a geometric representation of this phenomenon.

Figure 7.7 Relation Between Commodity Type and Price Elasticity of Demand for Food (Average Consumer)

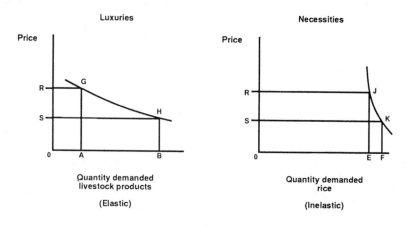

□ **Nutrition Policy Implications**

From our discussion of elasticities we can derive two policy recommendations and a policy dilemma, all of which are of interest to those who would improve Third World nutritional status. The geometric representations of behavior that we just went through will be helpful in developing these recommendations and in understanding the dilemma.

Increase the income of the poor. Increasing the income of the poor is one of the most fundamental things that can be done to reduce Third World undernutrition. Since poor people have a much greater income elasticity of demand for food than do rich people (represented on Figure 7.4), a greater proportion of any increase in income that they experience will go to food consumption. Wealthy people are, by and large, overconsuming calories. Increases in income of the wealthy are far less likely to improve nutrition. In fact, since there is a tendency to induce health risks through gaining excess weight and overconsuming fat as income increases, a case could be made that increasing the income of the wealthy may be detrimental to nutrition.

Promote the production of foods with low elasticities of demand with respect to price. Significant production increases of food commodities will lower their price. People at risk for undernutrition benefit most from price declines among those products that have low overall elasticities of demand with respect to price. There are two important reasons for this.

First, the foods with low demand elasticities are the foods that the poor spend most of their food budget on, the necessities (cassava, potatoes, rice, maize, bread, beans) shown in the top half of Table 7.5, for instance. Even though poor people have greater demand elasticities for the luxury items, they spend such a small proportion of their food budget on them that reductions in their price are not particularly helpful to the poor's nutrition. Notice on Table 7.3 that rural low-income consumers in Brazil get only 2.1 percent of their calories from milk and 0.5 percent from eggs. Rural high-income consumers in the same sample population consume three and a half times as much milk and four and a half times as many eggs as do their low-income counterparts (Gray 1982: 20). Benefits from price decreases resulting from increasing the production of these livestock products, which have relatively high demand elasticities, will go chiefly to the wealthy, who are already well fed—perhaps overfed.

The second reason for increasing the production of foods with low demand elasticities is that increases in the production of these foods will result in greater percentage declines in price than will similar percentage increases in the production of foods with high demand elasticities. This is illustrated in Figure 7.7. Look at the substantial price drop (from R to S) resulting from a small increase in production (from E to F) of the necessity diagrammed in the right-hand side of the figure. Compare that to the very small price drop expected (from R to slightly below R) in the price of the luxury commodity if production increased a small amount from A toward B in the diagram on the left-hand side of the figure.

The substantial price declines associated with increased production of commodities with low demand elasticities are of particular benefit to the poor, who spend most of their food budget on these items. The rich, who spend a smaller proportion of their food budget on these low-elasticity items, will benefit less, proportionally. The increase in purchasing power resulting from a decline in the price of low-elasticity foods enhances purchasing power of the poor by a greater percentage than it does the purchasing power of the rich.

The farm product promotion dilemma. In a closed economy where the market clears, production and consumption will be equal. In this situation, or in situations close to it, an increase in the production of a commodity with a demand elasticity of less than one will result in a decline in total revenue to the producer. You can reason this through using either the elasticity formula or a demand diagram (for a more detailed discussion of this subject see Miller, Rosenblatt & Hushak 1988).

Imagine a commodity with a demand elasticity of –0.5. Substitute –0.5 for elasticity in the equation on page 126. For the elasticity to be –0.5, the top half of the elasticity formula must be half the value of the bottom half. In other words, the market responds to an increase in production (which equals consumption) in such a way that price changes twice as much as production. If production increases by 1 percent then price will fall by 2 percent. And when price falls by a greater percentage than production increases, total revenue to the farmer decreases.

Now let us look at the same situation as diagrammed on the right-hand side of Figure 7.7. Total revenue is price times quantity produced. The total revenue from the sale of rice in this diagram is the price, OR, times the quantity produced (demanded), OE. This total revenue can be represented graphically as the box, ORJE (length times width equals area). If the price of rice falls from R to S, the new total revenue box is represented by OSKF. Notice that, for a product with an inelastic demand such as rice, the size of the total revenue box decreases when price falls.

On the other hand, for products with demand elasticities greater than one, an increase in production will yield an increase in total revenue. Go through the exercise again, only this time assume a price elasticity of demand of –2. The top half of the formula in the price elasticity equation (percentage change in consumption [production]) will have to be twice as big as the bottom half (percentage change in price). Now look at what happens to the size of the total revenue boxes for the luxury product diagrammed in the left-hand side of Figure 7.7. As price falls from R to S, the size of the total revenue box increases!

Now here is the dilemma: When government successfully promotes the production of a farm product with an inelastic price elasticity of demand, such as a grain crop, unless other factors intervene in the market, farmers see their total revenue decrease. Low-income consumers are better nourished, but farmers get hurt.

When government successfully promotes the production of a farm product with an elastic demand with respect to price (in the Third World, livestock products are sometimes in this category and often close to it), farm revenue increases, but the majority of the benefits from the lower price go to the wealthy, who do not really need to consume more food.

Governments want to make everyone happy. But the agricultural policy that does the most to improve nutrition happens to be the policy that is most likely to damage the welfare of farmers (see Box 7.5).

Box 7.5 Farmers Are Also Consumers

Farmers, of course, are also consumers and, to the extent that they buy the farm commodities whose prices fall, they benefit from increased production. But families with significant amounts of farmland are not generally at risk for undernutrition. Remember that the undernourished do not usually own a significant amount of farmland. It is the landless workers who suffer most commonly from poverty and its related undernutrition.

☐ 8

Undernutrition and the Distribution of Income, Wealth, and Education

"Get off this estate!"
"What for?"
"Because it's mine."
"Where did you get it?"
"From my father."
"Where did he get it?"
"From his father."
"And where did he get it?"
"He fought for it."
"Well, I'll fight you for it!"

—Carl Sandburg 1936: 75

■ INCOME DISTRIBUTION AND FOOD CONSUMPTION

☐ Income Elasticity and the Reutlinger Triangles

So far I have presented substantial evidence that, for the world as a whole, low-income people tend to underconsume food while high-income people tend to overconsume it. In an influential monograph published in 1976, Reutlinger and Selowsky attempted to quantify this under- and overconsumption. Figure 8.1 is representative of their work on this subject.

For purposes of developing the data from which Figure 8.1 was drawn, Reutlinger and Selowsky assumed that Third World income elasticity of demand for calories was 0.15. Subsequent estimates based on data from 17 developing countries put the income elasticity of demand for calories at 0.15 or 0.16 (Reutlinger et al. 1986: 64) suggesting that this original assumption was reasonable.

Figure 8.1 plots calorie consumption by income groups in Latin America, given 0.15 as the estimate for overall income elasticity of demand for calories. The dashed horizontal line cutting across the vertical bars represents FAO–

137

recommended per capita daily calorie consumption for adult equivalents. The dotted horizontal line close by represents average daily adult equivalent calorie consumption. With a little imagination you can see two stepped triangles in this figure: one (the shaded triangle) represents the total calorie deficit among low-income people, while the other triangle (the boxes above the dotted line) represents overconsumption among the rich. I refer to these as the Reutlinger triangles.

Figure 8.1 Calorie Consumption by Income Groups, Latin America, 1965 (with Calorie-Income Elasticity Equal to 0.15)

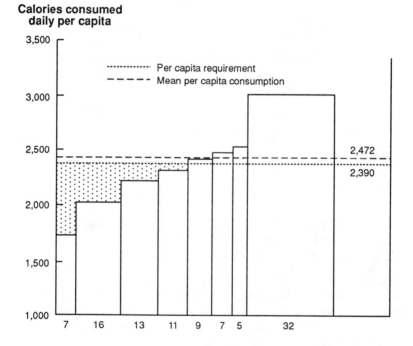

Percentage share of total population by income group, lowest income on left and highest on right

Note: If an income elasticity of 0.15 seems low to you, remember that income elasticities decline as income rises. The income elasticities we have quoted so far are mostly for very low-income. For example, Ho's estimate was 0.58 for the East Javanese sample. The income elasticity estimates shown for calories in Table 7.2 were for rural Brazil, which, by and large, is poorer than urban Brazil, where such elasticity estimates run lower. Remember also that income elasticities for particular foods, (as in the case of Tables 7.2 and 7.3) tend to run higher than income elasticities for calories as a whole. The median calorie elasticity for low- income families (consuming 1,750-2,000 calories per capita per day) among 19 estimates examined by Alderman (1984:37) was 0.405.

Source: Adapted from Reutlinger and Selowsky 1976:20.

Figure 8.1 is a visualization of the nutritional impact of differential purchasing power among Third World income groups. As the rich and the poor both bid for food in the marketplace, the poor simply do not have as much clout as the rich. The rich bid food away from the poor.

As per capita income increases, people, especially the rich, eat more livestock and livestock products. Over the past century the worldwide demand for livestock and livestock products has increased to the point that the world livestock herd, which in the 1800s was largely a scavenging herd (cows ate grass; chickens, pigs, and ducks ate table scraps), is now eating substantial amounts of grain. In 1983 and 1984 about one-third of the world's grain production was fed to livestock (Reutlinger et al. 1986: 24). As the rich consume meat, milk, eggs, and other livestock products, they are, to some extent, bidding grain away from the poor. Almost half of the grain fed to livestock goes into animals in the United States and the Soviet Union, two countries that account for only 10 percent of the world's population yet produce about 40 percent of the world's GDP (Table 8.1).

Let me recapitulate what I have said so far in this chapter. Income distribution is important in nutrition for two reasons: (1) The greater the distance be-

Table 8.1 Income and Population Distribution, Selected Countries

| Country | 1986 GDP | | Population | |
	Trillions of US Dollars	Percentage of Total	Millions	Percentage of Total
USA	4.2	27	244	4.8
USSR	2.1	14	284	5.6
Japan	2.0	13	122	2.4
West Germany	.9	6	61	1.2
France	.7	5	56	1.1
Italy	.6	4	57	1.1
UK	.5	3	57	1.1
Canada	.3	2	26	.5
Subtotal	11.3	74	907	18.0
China	.27	2	1062	21.1
India	.20	1	800	15.9
Subtotal	.5	3	1862	37.0
World total	15.3	100	5026	100.0

Sources: Income for USSR and all population estimates, Population Reference Bureau 1987; all other material, World Bank 1988.

Note: The first eight countries listed have the largest GDP of all countries. The eight countries with the highest per capita income would be a different list and would show a greater intensity of income concentration.

Box 8.1 Can We Solve the World Food Problem by Giving Up Bacon and Eggs?
Arthur Dommen

Some people argue that it is immoral for people in the high-income industrial nations to eat a diet rich in livestock products as long as there are people starving in parts of Africa, Asia, and Latin America who could consume directly the cereals and pulses that are now being fed to cattle, pigs, and chickens. Since approximately a third of the world's grain supply goes to feed livestock, the argument has a certain plausibility to it.

It is certainly true that food energy is lost in putting grain through livestock to convert it to livestock products. For instance, it takes around 2 pounds of grain to produce a pound of chicken, 4 pounds of grain to produce a pound of pork, and 8 pounds of feed (in this case, much of it grass and other materials not usable by man as food) to produce a pound of beef.

The question is, if the rich cut bacon, eggs, steak, butter, and cheese, for example, from their dinner table, to what extent would the grain and pulses currently going to produce these products find their way to the food-short people of the developing countries? To be more specific, how would the food get into the hands of the world's hungry? Who would buy it? Who would store it? Who would ship it? Who would distribute it? How much would it cost? Would the resources spent on this direct feeding activity go further toward solving the hunger problem if spent on alternative activities?

But the story is more complicated than this. Some of the products finding their way into the Western livestock feed market these days are produced by farmers in developing countries—soybeans from Brazil and cassava chips from Thailand, to mention just two. These products enjoy large and expanding markets in Europe and Japan, which do not have enough acreage available to satisfy the feed demand from the livestock sectors of their own countries. These exports of livestock feed add to income in the developing countries.

Even with the enormous grain consumption of the world's livestock herd, there is enough grain-producing capacity left over to feed the world's hungry— if they had the purchasing power to buy the grain they need. Furthermore, the grain-consuming livestock sector acts as an insurance policy against the "seven lean years" or whatever other period of bad harvests we might experience. The commercial livestock sector acts as a huge cushion for human grain consumers. Commercial livestock producers absorb large quantities of grain when supplies are cheap and abundant and reduce livestock feeding when grain supplies are expensive and scarce because of drought or other causes.

The causes of Third World undernutrition are complex. Simple approaches such as giving up bacon and eggs for breakfast may make you feel better about the world food situation, but there are probably more effective actions you can take toward solving the problem.

Arthur Dommen is an agricultural economist specializing in Third World food issues.

tween the rich and the poor, the greater is the capacity and the tendency of the rich to bid food away from the poor; and (2) the greater the concentration of income in the hands of a wealthy few, the greater is their tendency (because of their high-income) to purchase and consume livestock products. The more the wealthy consume livestock products, the more dependent the livestock herd becomes on grain as it switches from scavenging and grass to grain. The more the price of grain is bid up to satisfy the wealthy's demand for animal products, the harder it is for the poor to buy the grain they need for minimal nutrition.

☐ The Redistribution-Incentive Paradox

Programs that transfer purchasing power from the rich to the poor will reduce the size of both of the Reutlinger triangles, thus improving nutrition (the upward-sloping line that is the hypotenuse of the right triangles will become more horizontal). By eliminating all differences in income, the Reutlinger triangles could also be eliminated, and food would, presumably, be fairly evenly distributed across the population.

Two major and vastly different countries—China and the Soviet Union—have experimented with programs that greatly reduced differences in income. As they succeeded in this goal they reduced differences in food consumption, but at the same time they experienced difficulties in food production.

Prior to their respective socialist revolutions, both countries had healthy agricultural economies. In 1917, the year of the Russian Revolution, the world's leading agricultural geographers (Finch & Baker 1917: 13) wrote that "the Russian Empire leads the world in both acreage and production of wheat. . . . Nearly one-fifth of the average harvest is exported." China's socialist revolution was completed after World War II. Before that war, China accounted for 93 percent of the world's soybean exports (*Oxford Economic Atlas* 1959: 33).

Both Russia and China went from being major food exporters before their socialist revolutions to major food importers afterward. And during the 1980s both countries tried to reintroduce market-oriented incentives, in part to bolster their flagging agricultural productivity.

There appear to be nutritional gains from reducing the size of the Reutlinger triangles through redistributing income, yet income redistribution, carried to extremes, appears to introduce incentive problems that could conceivably lead to low levels of food consumption for all. It seems, then, if your goal is to improve nutrition for all, there is not much point in debating the relative merits of laissez-faire, free-enterprise capitalism (which can produce large Reutlinger triangles) versus extreme socialism (which appears to lead to problems in agricultural productivity), for both of these extremes may lead to widespread hunger problems. In terms of reducing undernutrition, then, the appropriate debate with reference to income redistribution should center on how much and by what methods to do it. That is, to what extent should the rich be taxed, and how should the money going into the tax till be spent?

In much of the latter part of this book we will consider the question of policies that affect nutrition, which heavily involve the issue of how to allocate the money going into the tax till. I concentrate here on the issue of income distribution and redistribution. We will look at methods of measuring income distribu-

Figure 8.2 Stylized Representation of Income Distribution Among the Rich in a Typical Community

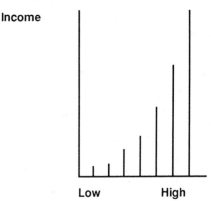

Note: Each vertical bar represents the total income of one individual or family. A line traced across the top of the bars resembles a "J."

tion, some factors influencing income distribution (such as education, fertility control, and the adoption of new technology), and finally at the relationship between these factors and the pace of economic development.

■ MEASURING INCOME DISTRIBUTION

☐ Pareto's Law

In a typical town, if you rank family or individual incomes from low to high and graph them, the resulting graph is suggestive of a J. The J-shape is especially pronounced if you graph just the richest people in the town (Figure 8.2).

In the late 1800s the Italian mathematician-economist-sociologist Vilfredo Pareto examined income distribution among the rich and moderately rich in a number of countries and found the J-shaped distribution pattern among them to be remarkably consistent. Furthermore he was able to fit this pattern to a mathematical formulation that soon became known as Pareto's law. Pareto's law had its problems, and, as it turned out, one of the main benefits of Pareto's work on income distribution was to stimulate others to think about alternative methods of measuring it. (For a concise discussion of Pareto's work on distribution see Steindl 1987.)

☐ The Lorenz Curve

In 1905 the US statistician Max Lorenz proposed a method of comparing distributions of income and wealth through a cumulative income or wealth curve, the

Lorenz curve, an example of which is shown as the dashed line in Figure 8.3. The vertical axis, OC, represents percentage of total income for the group under analysis. The horizontal axis, OE, represents the percentage of individuals (or families) in the group.

To conceptualize how a Lorenz curve is constructed, imagine a group of 100 individuals, each with a different income. Bake a cake that represents the total income of the group. Cut the entire cake into blocks, each of which is of a length proportional to one individual's income, and distribute the cake accordingly. Now arrange all the individuals in a line according to cake size, with the person having the shortest piece of cake first and the person with the longest piece last. Starting with the person with the shortest piece of cake, have the line pass by a point at which each individual stacks his piece of cake on top of the previous piece until all the pieces are placed in a column. Then the column will represent all of the income of the group.

As every tenth person places cake on the column, measure the height of the column at that time and calculate what percentage of total income is represented so far. On the Lorenz diagram, plot the percentage of total income accounted for so far against the percentage of population accounted for at that time until all the

Figure 8.3 A Lorenz Curve

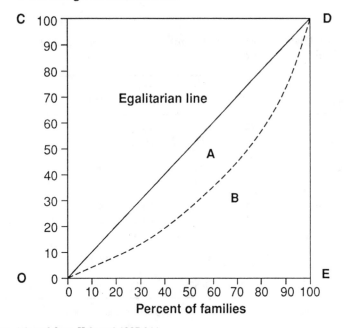

Source: Adapted from Kakwani 1987:244.

people have walked by. Connect the points with a smooth line and you have a Lorenz curve (Cowell 1977: 23).

The straight diagonal line, OD, in Figure 8.3 is called the egalitarian line. If everyone in the group under analysis had exactly the same income, the Lorenz curve would correspond to the egalitarian line. If all the income accrued to one individual, the Lorenz curve would be the right angle represented by OED in Figure 8.3. The more the Lorenz curve bends away from the egalitarian line, the greater the inequality of income.

Figure 8.4a shows a Lorenz curve for the distribution of land owned in Bagbana village, India, during 1968 and 1981. Over 30 percent of the families in this village own no land, which is why both Lorenz curves in Figure 8.4 track the zero line of land owned for more than a third of the way across the horizontal axis. Notice that inequality in land distribution in this village increased during the 13 years from 1968 to 1981.

Figure 8.4b shows the Lorenz curve for farm income in this same village over the same time period. More people have farm income than own land (many are landless farm workers). During the 13 years under consideration the inequality of farm income decreased. A possible explanation for this is discussed later in this chapter in the section on the distributional impact of the green revolution.

In Table 8.2 some raw data from the Philippines is presented, from which several Lorenz curves could be constructed. To fix the concept in your mind you might try constructing a Lorenz curve for Philippine families for 1983.

Table 8.2 Distribution of Total Family Income by Decile and Gini Coefficient, Philippines, 1978-1983

Ranking of	Percentage					
Families	1978	1979	1980	1981	1982	1983
First tenth	0.9	0.8	0.8	0.8	1.0	1.0
Second tenth	2.1	2.0	1.9	1.9	2.0	1.9
Third tenth	3.2	3.1	2.9	2.8	3.2	3.2
Fourth tenth	4.1	4.1	3.9	3.8	3.6	3.7
Fifth tenth	5.3	5.4	5.3	5.1	5.0	5.0
Sixth tenth	6.7	6.7	7.0	6.7	6.4	6.5
Seventh tenth	8.6	8.6	8.9	8.6	8.1	8.3
Eighth tenth	11.4	11.3	11.9	11.6	11.2	11.3
Ninth tenth	16.3	16.0	15.4	16.7	16.1	16.1
Last tenth	41.1	42.0	42.0	42.0	43.4	43.0
Gini coefficient	0.521	0.525	0.527	0.534	0.535	0.533

Source: Philippines, National Economic Development Authority 1983:157.

Figure 8.4 Lorenz Curves for Farm Land and Farm Income, Bagbana Village, India, 1968 and 1981

a. Cumulative land

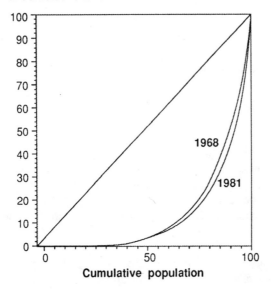

Cumulative population

b. Cumulative farm income

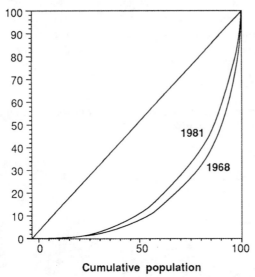

Cumulative population

Source: Field surveys by the author and his assistants. Lorenz curves by Paul Fishstein.

☐ The Gini Coefficient

The search for a better method of measuring income and wealth distribution did not end with Lorenz. In 1912 the Italian economist Corrado Gini proposed yet another measure of inequality, the Gini ratio, often called the Gini coefficient (Dagum 1987). Gini used the Lorenz curve as the basis of his ratio. He simply compared the area of the triangle OED (see Figure 8.3) with the area of the lens-shaped piece taken out of that triangle by the Lorenz curve. Labeling the lens-shaped part A and the remainder of the triangle B, the Gini ratio is:

$$\frac{A}{A + B}$$

If one individual has all the income in the group, the Gini ratio becomes one. If the size of A approaches zero, the Gini ratio approaches zero. The range of the Gini is thus from zero to one. At the bottom of Table 8.2 are Gini ratios for the income distribution data shown in that table.

Although popular, the Gini coefficient is open to criticism (Paglin 1974). It shows nothing about the location of the concentration of income inequality among high- versus low-income groups. The shape of the Lorenz curve could conceivably change (with the poor better off and the middle class worse off, for instance) without any change in the Gini. Furthermore, neither the Lorenz curve nor the Gini take account of expected variation in income as people age.

Imagine a group consisting of working adults with ages distributed evenly from 20 to 50 years and with everyone in their twenties paid the same, everyone in their thirties paid the same but more than those in their twenties, and everyone in their forties paid the same but more than those in their thirties. Calculate the

---

Figure 8.5 Changes in Relative Income Share Between 1979 and 1986, by Income Groups, US Population

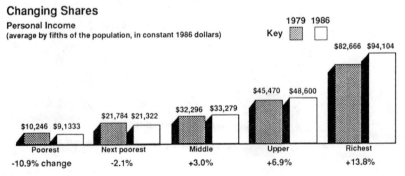

Source: Rose and Fasentast 1988:3.

Gini. (Calculating the Gini is not easy unless you have a computer program to do it for you. For an explanation on how it is done see Cowell 1977.) It would be greater than zero, although you might feel the income distribution was equitable.

Now imagine another group with the same income by age, but in which young and old ages predominate, with few in the middle group. The Gini would be higher than before, indicating greater inequality, but you might not think that the ratio fairly contrasted the two groups.

☐ **Relative Income Share**

Lorenz curves and Gini ratios make for useful comparisons and appear frequently in the literature of income and wealth distribution, but they are hard for the layman to understand and time-consuming to explain to politicians. Increasingly, the easy-to-understand relative income share is being used to describe income inequalities. With relative income share, you array the incomes in the population from lowest to highest and divide the population into equal-sized groups, just as you did on the Lorenz curve. Then you calculate the percentage of the total income in each group. And that is it. You have relative income share.

Given time series data, as in Table 8.2 or Figure 8.5, you can track what is happening to any one income category you may be interested in, such as the poorest, who are the most prone to undernutrition.

Relative income share is equally convenient for making comparisons among countries. A convenient source of such comparisons can be found in the World Bank's annual World Development Report table on income distribution (e.g., 1990: 236–237).

■ **FACTORS INFLUENCING INCOME DISTRIBUTION**

Since unequal distribution of income contributes to Third World undernutrition, we need to examine the causes of unequal income distribution so we can, later, consider policies that might reduce undernutrition through changes in income distribution. The causes are many and complex and not necessarily fully understood.

☐ **Traditional Thinking: Heredity and Environment**

Traditional thinking on the causes of differences in income concentrated on heredity and environment; we can develop a list of the leading schools of thought on this subject. Capsulizing each school of thought in a purposely oversimplified sentence provides an efficient way of leafing through the diversity of causes. Each school of thought (the list here is excerpted from Chu 1982: 18–19) purports to offer at least a partial clue as to that basic income distribution question: Why is A's income greater than B's?

"Because A is smarter," says the *ability school*.

"Because A chose to work harder and/or chose to take more risks, and he was rewarded for this behavior," says the *individual choice school*.

"Because A went to a high-quality, expensive college and got a good education, and he is being rewarded for the educational investment in him," says the *human capital school*.

"Because A came from a well-to-do, supportive family. As a result, he was raised better, learned the habits and attitudes necessary for success, and thus can get and hold a better job," says the *family background school*.

"Because A works in the primary labor market, characterized by large firms and/or labor unions, while B works in the secondary labor market, characterized by small firms and without the protection of labor unions," says the *segmented labor market school*.

"Because A inherited a large fortune from his parents," says the *wealth inheritance school*.

"Because A is a white male and B is a black female," says the *discrimination school*.

"Because A is in his prime years of earnings and B is either substantially younger or older," says the *life cycle school*.

"Because A is lucky," says the *stochastic school*.

Each of these schools of thought could be the subject of considerable discussion as to causes and interrelationships with the other schools. Take the first one, for instance, the ability school. Ability is constrained by both heredity and environment. But we have learned much in this century about how the developmental potential of an individual can be influenced by the mother's behavior during pregnancy. Poor food habits, smoking, drug abuse, alcohol abuse, and other activity during a woman's pregnancy can limit the ultimate potential of her offspring. Is this part of the family background school?

Intelligence tests conducted on over 386,000 Dutch boys as they were inducted into the military were correlated with their family size and birth order (whether they were born first, second, etc.). Belmont and Marolla (1973) found a high level of statistical significance when they correlated intelligence with family size and birth order. With the exception that an only child tended to be less intelligent than children in a family with two or three children total, there was a remarkable tendency for intelligence to decrease as family size and/or birth order increased (Figure 8.6).

In a recent study in the United States, Blake (1989) found that family size is a major influence on verbal and educational attainment, both of which tend to decrease as family size increases. Do parents, to some extent, determine family size? And if so, is family size a variable that issues from the individual choice school?

We have been examining some of the traditional ways of thinking about the causes of inequality of income distribution, schools of thought based largely on heredity and environment or their interaction. Recent research has caused us to

Figure 8.6 Relationship Between Family Size, Birth Order, and Intelligence in 19-Year-Old Dutch Men Tested Between 1963 and 1966, by Occupational Background

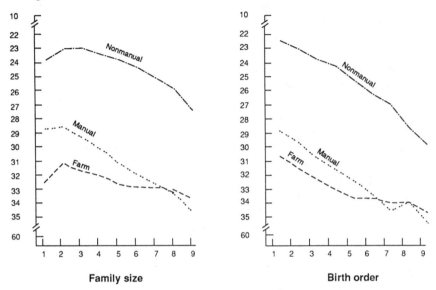

Family size   Birth order

Note: The Raven Progressive Matrices test was used to measure intelligence. Dr. Clayton Stunkard of the Department of Measurement and Statistics, College of Education, University of Maryland, characterizes this test as one that attempts to be culturally unbiased. N=137,823 for nonmanual, 184,334 for manual, and 45,196 for farm. This test has the unusual property that the lower the score, the higher is the intelligence rating.

Source: Adapted from Belmont and Marolla 1973:1100.

look at the impact of other variables such as technology adoption, education, and fertility control on income distribution.

☐ Technology Adoption

The Kuznets curve. In his 1954 presidential address to the American Economic Association, Simon Kuznets (1955) hypothesized that during the early phases of development Third World countries might experience increasing income inequalities before "leveling forces become strong enough to first stabilize and then reduce income inequalities." His idea that the path of income inequality through time in the Third World would trace the shape of an inverted U became known as the Kuznets curve. Subsequent studies have lent support to Kuznets's hypothesis (Adelman & Morris 1973; Ahluwalia 1976b; Chenery, Robinson & Syrquin 1974).

Using cross-sectional data of a sample of 60 countries including 40 Third World countries, 14 developed countries, and six socialist countries, Ahluwalia estimated relative income shares as per capita income changed. The result of one of his multiple regressions, which estimates percentage income share for the lowest 40 percent of the population from income variables, is shown in Figure 8.7. In this diagram the income share of the lowest 40 percent of the population declines from around 17 percent at around $150 per capita to about 12 percent at around $400 per capita, and then is back up to around 17 percent when income increases to $3,000. The U in Figure 8.7 is not inverted because the diagram tracks a measure of income equality instead of inequality, as in the original statement of the Kuznets curve.

It seems reasonable to postulate that the poor may benefit less from development than the rich. As development takes place, those in the more advanced sector of the economy are likely to be the first to take advantage of it. Therefore they reap the first gains. After all, when the new productive techniques come along they often require new knowledge and substantial amounts of capital. The railroads and canals and electric companies, which were originally privately owned, are a case in point. It was difficult for the poor even to imagine "making a killing" in these areas.

Figure 8.7 Estimated Relationship Between Income Share and per Capita GNP, 60 Countries, Various Years Prior to 1975

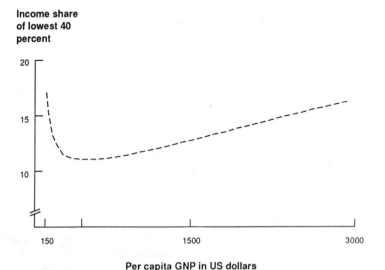

Per capita GNP in US dollars

Source: Adapted from Ahluwalia 1976:133.

Modernization could conceivably make the poor worse off. As Ahluwalia (1976b: 330–331) puts it, "An aggressively expanding technologically advanced, modern sector, competing against the traditional sector for markets and resources (and benefiting in this competition from an entrenched position in the institutional and political context) may well generate both a relative and absolute decline in incomes of the poor." He concludes from his research, however, that though the initial stages of development are likely to make the poor worse off relative to the rich, these same initial stages are not necessarily prone to making the poor worse off in absolute terms.

The distributional impact of the green revolution. Given this background, it was logical for people to be nervous that the green revolution might increase inequality of income; indeed, might make the poor absolutely worse off, in regions where it was adopted (for a briefing on the green revolution see Box 8.2). After all it has been common for new agricultural technologies to be adopted earlier by the leading farmers in a region, who are often those with the biggest or best farms, the best education, and the greatest willingness to take a risk trying something new. Furthermore there is a tendency for public services to be more available to the big farmers than to the small, for technology to carry with it a labor-saving bias that reduces labor's share of the product, and for technological innovations to be more appropriate to some geographical areas than to others. Would not wealthy landlords use the benefits from the green revolution technology as a stepping-stone to increasing the size of their holdings at the expense of small farmers, increasing income inequality?

Some of the above fears turn out to have been justified; most not. Early adopters did tend to be the bigger, better farmers, but this has not prevented the smaller farmers who are slower to change from adopting the green revolution technology.

On the other hand, the benefits of the green revolution have accrued more to farmers in regions where water, especially irrigation water, is plentiful. Growers of lowland rice (rice that spends much of its early growing days with its stalks standing in a few inches of water) benefit more than growers of upland rice. Wheat and rice farmers, who predominate in those tropical regions with 40 inches or more of annual rainfall, benefit more than sorghum and millet farmers who farm the semiarid tropics where rainfall tends to be less than 40 inches per year.

The high-yielding fine grains (wheat and rice) grown with adequate water are far more responsive to fertilizer than are even the best varieties of the coarse grains (sorghum and millet) grown in the dry regions where irrigation water is scarce to nonexistent. The fertilizer subsidies that Third World governments frequently provide to their farmers therefore benefit the fine-grain producers more than the coarse-grain farmers. So the benefits of the green revolution have tended to concentrate in the wetter tropics and especially on the more level lands where irrigation and water management are easier. This phenomenon may well have increased income inequality between regions.

Box 8.2 What Is the Green Revolution?
Dana Dalrymple

In October 1944, about a year before the close of World War II, the Rockefeller Foundation brought to Mexico a young plant scientist to join a team of agriculturalists that had recently started work to assist in the agricultural development of that country. In a few months, the new man, Norman Borlaug (who was later to be awarded a Nobel Prize for his work in Mexico), was put in charge of the wheat program. He and his team set out to develop new varieties of wheat that would do better than the local varieties. Disease resistance (e.g., resistance to the fungus causing the disease rust) was particularly important at first. In the mid-1950s increased emphasis was given to increasing yields and within a few years varieties had been developed which could produce much more than the traditional ones.

Encouraged by this success, in the 1960s Rockefeller Foundation joined with the Ford Foundation to establish two permanent research stations for the development of high-yielding cereals, the International Rice Research Institute (IRRI) in the Philippines and the International Maize and Wheat Improvement Center (CIMMYT) in Mexico. The success of these centers in developing high-yielding varieties led to such enthusiasm for the idea of international agricultural research centers that by the late 1980s thirteen centers, treating various aspects of improving Third World agriculture, had been set up worldwide, and sponsorship had spread to a consortium of donors worldwide including both foundations and government agencies.

The high-yielding varieties of wheat and rice have spread more widely, more quickly, than any other technological innovation in the history of agriculture in the developing countries. First introduced in the mid-1960s, they occupied

Figure a Estimated Proportion of Area Planted to High-Yielding Varieties of Wheat and Rice, South and Southeast Asian Nations, 1965/66-1982/83

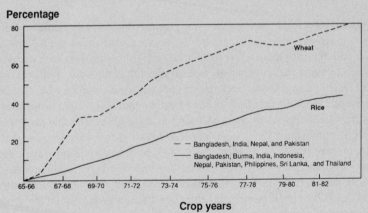

Source: Adapted from Dalrymple 1985.

about half of these countries' total wheat and rice area by 1982–1983 (Dalrymple 1985). Figure a shows the remarkable growth in adoption of high-yielding varieties in South and Southeast Asia.

Struck by the remarkable speed with which high-yielding varieties of wheat and rice were being developed for the Third World and by their potential to alleviate world hunger, William S. Gaud, who was then administrator of the US Agency for International Development, referred, in a 1968 speech, to the phenomenon of their development and spread as "the green revolution" (Dalrymple 1979: 724).

Actually, the green revolution's wheat and rice varieties, also known as high-yielding varieties (HYVs) or modern varieties (MVs), do not do much better than the traditional varieties (they can even do worse) unless they have appropriate amounts of water and fertilizer. In fact, it is largely tolerance of and response to substantial amounts of fertilizer that makes them so successful.

Figure b Lodging and Nonlodging Rice Plants

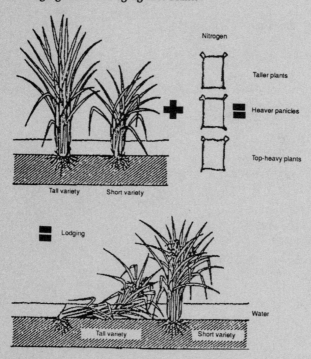

• Plant height increases with nitrogen application and lodging becomes a problem.
• Many leaves on the lodged plants decay since they are soaked in water and do not receive sufficient light.
• Short, stiff stem prevents lodging.

Note: Nonlodging plants are tolerant of fertilizer

Source: Adapted from Vergara 1979:158.

Box 8.2 continued

The traditional varieties of wheat and rice were not tolerant of significant amounts of fertilizer. When Third World farmers attempted to increase rice or wheat yields by adding fertilizer—especially nitrogen fertilizer—to their fields, their plants would grow so tall that they would fall over. The technical term for this is *lodging*. What the plant scientists at the international institutes did was to locate plant varieties with genes for shortness and breed these genes into plants that had other characteristics desirable for the Third World. The new plants, called semidwarfs, borrowed dwarfism genes from Japan (for wheat) and China (for rice). When used with fertilizer, they grew taller than without the fertilizer, but not excessively so. Thus they were much more resistant to lodging (Figure b).

Plant scientists did not stop merely with the development of nonlodging plants. They bred into their new varieties a host of other characteristics such as disease resistance.

One of the more intriguing changes in plant design that they accomplished involved rearranging the location of the seed cluster on the plant. Traditional rice

Figure c Flag Leaf Higher than the Panicle

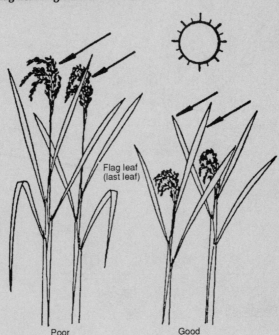

Flag leaf
(last leaf)

Poor   Good

• There is less shading of the upper leaves if the panicle does not extend far above the flag leaf.

Note: Green revolution plant scientists designed a rice plant where the topmost leaves were not shaded by the seed cluster

Source: Adapted from Vergara 1979:161.

plants sent their cluster of seeds (the panicle) high into the air. The seeds themselves store energy, but they do not make it. Photosynthesis is concentrated in the leaves. It did not make sense for the seed cluster to shade the highest leaves on the plant, so the scientists bred rice plants whose topmost leaf, the flag leaf, extended well above the panicle, thus taking maximum advantage of the available sunshine (Figure c).

The green revolution, then, is a whole complex of innovations, such as those described above, that combine to make up new plant varieties. The modern plant varieties, when used with a package of appropriate inputs such as fertilizer and water and good management, are dramatically raising crop yields in the Third World.

For more about the green revolution, see Brown 1970; US, Dept. of State 1986a, b; Stackman, Bradfield & Mangelsdorf 1967.

On the other hand, within regions "the benefits from adopting modern varieties have been remarkably evenly distributed among farmers differing in size of holding and tenure status": This is the conclusion of a major study commissioned to examine the impact of the international agricultural research centers (Anderson et al. 1985: 4).

In a detailed study of the economy of a north Indian village where modern varieties had been widely adopted, Bliss and Stern (1982: 291) found no strong association between size of holding and the intensity of use of inputs associated with the adoption of green revolution technology; in fact, "the adoption of various newer varieties and intensive practices seemed to be particularly associated with the younger educated farmers."

How is it that the benefits could be so evenly distributed among farmers of different size and tenure status? For one thing, the capital requirements of the green revolution are minimal. Unlike hybrid corn, which has done so much to increase corn yields in the United States and Europe, the green revolution fine-grain seeds breed true (i.e., produce offspring almost identical to the parent plant). Hybrid seed corn must be produced annually under technically demanding conditions on specialized farms and sold to farmers each year. A farmer who planted the grain from his hybrid corn crop as seed would be most disappointed in the yield results. Green revolution rice and wheat, although the result of complicated crosses, are not true hybrids. You can plant a little one year, take the resulting grain as seed for next year's crop, and rapidly and cheaply multiply your seed stock. Thus, a handful of green revolution seed is all you need to get started. And it usually does not cost any more than traditional seed.

Green revolution varieties do require capital in the form of commercial fertilizer. On the other hand, fertilizer, like seed, is almost infinitely divisible, and a farmer need purchase only as much as he needs for his particular plot. Unlike capital investment in a tractor, the capital investment in the green revolution is not "lumpy"—that is, it does not come only in large, indivisible clumps.

A second reason for the evenly distributed benefits is that the green revolution technology is not labor saving. In fact, it turns out to be labor using (Hos-

---

Figure 8.8 Impact of Green-Revolution Technology Adoption on the Total Revenue of a Semisubsistence Rice-Farming Household

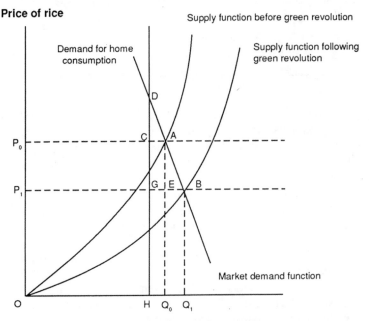

Quantity supplied or demanded of rice

Note: P_0CHO = market value of rice consumed by semisubsistence farm household before the green revolution; CAQ_0H = market value of rice marketed by semisubsistence household before green revolution; P_1GHO = market value of rice consumed by semisubsistence farmer household after green revolution; GBQ_1H = market value of rice sold by semisubsistence farm household after green revolution. Note that, although the market value of the rice consumed at home falls as the green revolution depresses the price of rice, the semi-subsistence farmer experiences no real decrease in welfare from this fall in price because he wasn't selling that rice anyway. His income from rice sales, on the other hand, may increase, even though the demand for rice is inelastic, because the amount of rice he sells after the green revolution (relative to what he sold before) increases so dramatically.

(If you are not familiar with the concept of the supply function read Box 18.2.)

Source: Adapted from Hayami and Herdt 1977.

sain 1988: 12; Ranade & Herdt 1978: 103; Pinstrup-Andersen & Hazell 1985: 11). Much of the Third World grain crop is harvested and threshed by hand, and the increased crop yield requires more labor for harvest. More importantly, though, the fertilizer applied to the crop turns out to stimulate the growth of weeds as well as grain. Farmers are finding it profitable to remove these weeds, and, in the Third World, weeding a field is labor-intensive (weeds are pulled by hand or chopped with a blade, for example).

Because the poor spend a greater proportion of their income on food than do the rich, the benefits from price drops associated with increased production following the adoption of green revolution technology favor the poor over the rich. Because of the very low overall elasticity of demand for cereals, consumers benefit substantially from the price drop caused by increased production, but farmers as a whole experience a decline in total revenue (see the last part of Chapter 7 for a review of why this happens).

In a study of the social returns to rice research, Evenson and Flores (1978: 255) found that in the Philippines, during the period from 1972 to 1975, the annual loss to producers from the adoption of the high-yielding rice varieties was $61 million, while the annual gain to consumers was $142 million, yielding a net annual gain to society of $72 million. Similarly, working with Colombian data, Scobie and Posada (1984) concluded that, during 1970–1974, Colombian rice producers lost $796 million, while consumers benefited by over $1,349 million, for a net gain to society of $553 million. Furthermore, they conclude that "while the lower 50 percent of Colombian households received about 15 percent of household income, they captured nearly 70 percent of the net benefits of the [rice] research program" (p. 383).

The cereal production increases that, because of demand elasticities of well below one, result in the loss of revenue for commercial rice growers may, at the same time, result in an increase in total revenue to the semisubsistence farmer. A semisubsistence farmer is defined as one who purchases less than 50 percent of his food supply in the marketplace. (Almost no one is a subsistence farmer, purchasing no food supplies, not even spices, in the marketplace.)

Consider a semisubsistence farmer who consumes, say, 90 percent of his rice crop. He has a small amount left over for sale in the market. He sees his neighbors on larger farms, who sell most of what they grow, practicing green revolution technology, and copies them, purchasing some seed and fertilizer and irrigating his crop as usual. His yield increases by the same percentage as that of the larger farmers, but, if he consumes the same amount of rice as he used to, the size of the surplus that he has left to sell grows by a much greater percentage than the percentage growth in his total production. Thus, even in the face of sharply declining rice prices, he may experience a gain in total revenue while his more commercially oriented neighbors are experiencing losses. (Figure 8.8 shows what is happening, making use of the concept of total revenue boxes introduced in Chapter 7.)

☐ **Education and Fertility Control**

Ahluwalia's study, which estimated a type of Kuznets curve of income distribution (shown in Figure 8.7) also produced evidence of how some variables besides per capita income impact on income distribution. Table 8.3 shows the results of two of his multiple regressions on 60 countries, mentioned earlier in this

Table 8.3 Cross-Country Regressions Explaining Income Shares

| Explanatory Variables | Dependent Variable: Percentage Income Shares | | | |
| | Top 20 Percent | | Lowest 40 Percent | |
	Direction of Influence of Variable	Equation One	Direction of Influence of Variable	Equation Two
Constant	−	9.07 (0.27)[a]	+	77.93 (4.11)
Log per capita GNP	+	50.35 (2.13)	−	47.28 (3.50)
(Log per capita GNP)^2	−	8.16 (1.98)	+	7.65 (3.35)
Growth rate of GDP	−	0.11 (0.32)	+	0.11 (0.55)
Literacy rate	−	0.09 (2.21)	+	0.06 (2.56)
Secondary school enrollment	−	0.14 (2.48)	+	0.02 (0.74)
Growth rate of population	+	3.59 (4.29)	−	1.19 (2.56)
Share of agriculture in GDP	−	0.25 (2.23)	+	0.04 (0.65)
Share of urban population	−	0.10 (1.68)	+	0.06 (1.79)
Dummy for socialist countries	−	9.41 (3.27)	+	8.57 (5.35)
R^2		.76		.69
F		22.31		6.21
SEE		4.6		2.6

Source: Ahluwalia 1976a:131.

Note: Note that on each explanatory variable the signs switch between the top 20 percent and the bottom 40 percent of the population.

[a]Values in parentheses are T ratios. For this sample, a T value of 1.68 indicates significance at the 10 percent level for a two-tailed test.

chapter. In these regressions, the variables in the left-hand column are hypothesized to impact on the relative income shares.

The numbers in the middle column (equation one) show how the variables in the left-hand column influence percentage income share among the top 20 percent of the population. The numbers in the right-hand column (equation two) show how the variables in the left-hand column influence percentage income share among the bottom 40 percent of the population.

The variables on GNP per capita and GDP per capita are included to account for the Kuznets curve. The variable at the bottom of the table, dummy for socialist countries, is included to account for the fact that, by and large, socialist countries have a more equal income distribution than nonsocialist countries. The remaining variables in the equation are included to see how they influence relative income share when the influence of the Kuznets curve and socialism are accounted for.

The signs on the numbers are of particular interest to us in examining the regression because they tell us the direction of influence that the related variable has on percentage income share when the other variables are at their average value. (Since the units of measurement of each of the variables influence the size of the regression coefficients—the numbers not in parentheses—and since we do not have these units of measurement, the size of the numbers is not of particular interest to us here. The size of the numbers in parentheses is important because they are the results of a test of significance—the bigger the number, the more likely its variable is to be of significant influence.)

First look at signs for the dummy for socialist countries. In equation one, the sign for this variable is negative, meaning that socialism tends to lower the percentage income share of the top 20 percent of the population. In equation two, the sign is positive. That is, socialism tends to raise the relative income share of the lowest 40 percent of the population.

Now examine the signs for the other variables. Increasing the literacy rate, the rate of secondary school enrollment, the share of agriculture in GDP, and the share of population that is urban all appear to increase the relative income share of the poor and reduce the relative income share of the rich.

The share of agriculture in GDP variable is not significant for the poor (T = 0.65), so we will not consider this variable important. As the percentage of the population that is urban increases, relative income share of the poor increases. This seems reasonable, because urban people generally have higher incomes than rural people, and as rural people move to the city in search of better jobs the total income distribution may become more equal. However, because of problems of crowding, pollution, crime, and so on associated with growth in Third World cities, it is hard to argue for urbanization as a means to reduce income inequality.

Literacy rate and secondary school enrollment are good indices of overall education among the poor in Third World countries. The wealthy see to it that their children get an education somehow or other. The illiterates and those without even a secondary education tend to be the poor. Increasing the rate of literacy and secondary education makes the poor potentially more productive and gives them better access to employment and better-paying jobs, thus reducing income inequality.

The influence of population growth rate on relative income share is harder to understand. It is the only one of the variables considered here for which increasing its value makes the poor worse off relative to the rich. The reasons for this are complex enough that I discuss them in their own chapter.

■ THE IMPACT OF DISTRIBUTION ON THE PACE OF DEVELOPMENT

In an attempt to find how the structure of economies change with economic development, Hollis Chenery (1971) ran a multiple regression on "about 100" countries, using 1950–1965 World Bank data. From this regression he computed values for the savings rate, school enrollment ratio (percentage of those in school versus those expected to be in school), adult literacy rate, and birth rate per thousand population at different levels of per capita income. The results give a picture of how the magnitude of these variables changes as per capita income changes (Table 8.4).

In Table 8.4 we can see that, normally, increases in the savings rate, school enrollment ratio, and adult literacy rate are associated with increases in per capita income. On the other hand, increases in the birth rate are associated with a decrease in per capita income. The educational and fertility variables in this regression are impacting on per capita income in a manner similar to the way they impacted on income distribution in the regression shown in Table 8.3.

Could it be that, by emphasizing the development of human capital through health and education programs that increase literacy and reduce fertility, countries could at the same time accelerate the pace of development and reduce income inequalities? In a collaborative effort, Ahluwalia and Chenery, joined by Carter (1979), provide data that allow us to answer this question with a tentative yes. The three researchers found 12 Third World countries where the data permitted them to examine both rate of growth of income and relative income share over a 10-year period. They sorted these countries by share of the increased income over the 10 years that went to the lowest (in terms of income) 60 percent of the population (column 5 in Table 8.5). In no case did the bottom 60 percent of the population get as much as 60 percent of the increase in income, but remember, they were not getting all that big a share in the first place. Just the same, there were substantial differences in the amount of the increase in income that went to the bottom 60 percent, ranging from 39.5 percent in the case of Taiwan to 15.5 percent in Brazil.

Since the research team were looking at their data from the point of view of performance in terms of reducing income inequalities, they ranked those coun-

Table 8.4 Normal Variations in Economic Structure with Level of Development

	Level of GNP per Capita (in 1989 US Dollars)[1]								
	200	400	800	1,200	1,600	2,400	3,200	4,000	8,000
Gross national savings, as % of GNP	9.4	12.0	14.8	16.4	17.6	19.3	20.5	21.5	24.6
School enrollment ratio	17.5	36.2	52.6	61.2	66.9	74.2	78.9	82.3	91.4
Adult literacy rate	15.3	36.5	55.2	65.0	71.5	80.0	85.4	89.4	93.0
Birth rate per thousand	46.6	41.8	36.6	33.8	31.1	28.2	25.3	22.4	17.1

Source: Chenery 1971:19.

Note: All values are computed from multiple regression for a sample of about 100 countries 1950-1965. Underlying data from the IBRD (World Bank), World Tables, December 1968.

[1]The GNP data were originally in 1964 dollars and have been converted to 1989 dollars using the consumer price index (CPI).

Table 8.5 Changes in Income and Its Distribution

Country	Income Level[1]		Percentage Income Share of Bottom 60 Percent			Growth Rates (percentage)		
	Initial year	Final year	Initial Year	Final Year	Incremental Increase	Total	Bottom 60 Percent	Ratio of Bottom 60 Percent to Total
	1	2	3	4	5	6	7	8
Good performers								
Taiwan (1964-74)	562	1,070	36.9	38.5	39.5	6.6	7.1	1.1
Yugoslavia (1963-73)	1,003	1,521	35.7	36.0	36.5	4.2	4.3	1.0
Sri Lanka (1963-73)	388	472	27.4	35.4	51.3	2.0	4.6	2.3
Korea (1965-76)	362	902	34.9	32.3	31.1	8.7	7.9	0.9
Costa Rica (1961-71)	825	1,136	23.7	28.4	33.6	3.2	5.1	1.6
Intermediate performers								
India (1954-64)	226	284	31.0	29.2	25.8	2.3	1.6	0.7
Philippines (1961-71)	336	419	24.7	24.8	25.0	2.2	2.3	1.0
Turkey (1963-73)	566	809	20.8	24.0	27.9	3.6	5.1	1.4
Colombia (1964-74)	648	880	19.0	21.2	24.0	3.1	4.3	1.4
Poor performers								
Brazil (1960-70)	615	829	24.8	20.6	15.5	3.1	1.2	0.4
Mexico (1963-75)	974	1,420	21.7	19.7	18.0	3.2	2.4	0.8
Peru (1961-71)	834	1,046	17.9	17.9	17.9	2.3	2.3	1.0

Source: Ahluwalia, Carter, and Chenery 1979:482.

[1]Measured by per capita income expressed in 1970 US dollars of constant purchasing power.

tries where over 30 percent of the increase in income went to the bottom 60 percent of the population as "good performers." Those where from 20 to 30 percent of the increase in income went to the bottom 60 percent were called "intermediate performers." And those where less than 20 percent of the increase in income went to the bottom 60 percent were called "poor performers."

Columns 6, 7, and 8 in Table 8.5 compare rate of growth of per capita income of the bottom 60 percent with rate of growth of per capita income for the economy as a whole. By and large, per capita income among the bottom 60 percent in the good performers grew more rapidly than per capita income for the economy as a whole. The average ratio (bottom 60 percent to total) of their rate of growth was 1.38. By and large, per capita income among the bottom 60 percent in the poor performers grew more slowly than did per capita income for the economy as a whole. The average ratio of their rate of growth was 0.73.

This is all very interesting, but the startling observation from this data set is that the *good performers, in terms of improving income distribution, also had higher overall rates of growth of per capita income than did the poor performers.* The good performers had an average overall annual growth rate in per capita income of 4.9 percent, while the poor performers had an average of only 2.9 percent!

Ahluwalia and his coworkers (1979) report that in Taiwan, their top performer, there was a great emphasis on education as well as on labor-intensive (as opposed to capital-intensive) manufacturing. From 1965 to 1970, a representative time period in which growth was being observed for these countries, the good performers had substantially lower birth rates than the other countries. The crude birth rate among the good performers was 33 per thousand population, while it was 41.1 and 41.5 for the intermediate and poor performers respectively (United Nations 1991; Population Reference Bureau 1970).

There is here at least the suggestion that development programs that lean toward emphasizing human capital development through programs such as primary health care, fertility control (usually part of a health program), and education improve people's productivity, especially at the bottom end of the income distribution, while programs that lean toward emphasizing physical capital investment (industrialization—the route chosen by Brazil, one of the poor performers) may lead to higher rates of underemployment and unemployment through the adoption of labor-displacing capital and technology, with an accompanying waste of human resources and slower rates of overall growth and development.

■ **THE REDISTRIBUTION/INCENTIVE PARADOX RECONSIDERED**

In Chapter 7 I argued that one of the leading causes of Third World undernutrition is lack of purchasing power among the poor, a combination of low-income and the high price of the goods and services they buy. In this chapter I argue that inequality of income *in and of itself* is a cause of Third World undernutrition, producing, as it does, Reutlinger triangles of overconsumption and underconsumption of food.

Income inequality has, at times, been dramatically reduced through draconian measures severely applied throughout the country; for example, land reform with little or no compensation to the landlords, perhaps even killing them as part of the deal; banishment of intellectuals to prison camps or forced farm labor, sometimes smashing their eyeglasses to help "keep them in their place." The collectivization experiments carried out during the revolutions of Russia in 1917, China after World War II, or more recently of the Khmer Rouge in Cambodia, are testimony to the extremes that peoples will go to, to attempt to reduce income inequality and improve the lot of the masses.

While these dramatic revolutions succeeded in reducing income inequality, and probably simultaneously reduced the size of the Reutlinger triangles, the resulting erosion of productivity incentives has left these countries struggling to keep up with their neighbors, especially in the field of agricultural output.

The theme of this chapter is that one of the ways to improve Third World nutrition is to reduce the size of the Reutlinger triangles, and that the optimal way of attempting to do this may be through sponsoring programs that put a heavy emphasis on health, fertility control, and education for all, thus simultaneously upgrading the productivity of the masses, reducing income inequality, and accelerating the pace of economic development.

□ 9

It Is Not Food Versus Population

Land, unlike people, cannot be multiplied. . . . Unlike population, land does not breed.
— Heilbroner 1953: 82 (paraphrasing Malthus)

The debate over food versus people started, you might say, with an argument between the young reverend Thomas Robert Malthus and his father. The elder Malthus was impressed by a recently published book that promised a future world devoid of "disease, anguish, melancholy, or resentment" (see Godwin 1973). Young Thomas was not similarly impressed. In fact, he was so skeptical about such a utopian future that he wrote down his objections (Malthus 1803–1826). The father was so struck with Thomas's words that he encouraged his son to publish them (Heilbroner 1953: 69–70). First issued anonymously in 1798 as *An Essay on the Principle of Population as It Affects the Future Improvement of Society*, Malthus's "essay" was never short and by its sixth edition, still claiming to be an essay, covered some 600 pages of detailed argument.

The Malthusian thesis was that the reproductive capacity of humans must put continual pressure on the "means of subsistence." Human numbers, he said, could increase by "geometric" progression: 2, 4, 8, 16, 32, 64, 128, 256 (we now call this progression exponential). Malthus did not see how subsistence could increase any faster than an "arithmetic" progression: 1, 2, 3, 4, 5, 6, 7, 8, 9 (we now call this progression linear). Unlike people, land does not breed, and Malthus thought that the potential for human numbers to increase exponentially must therefore put continuous pressure on our food supply.

Malthus enumerated a long list of checks to population growth, including war, "sickly seasons, epidemics, pestilence, and plague." Humans themselves, Malthus thought, would be unable to check their own population growth because the only way he knew to limit family size was through, as he put it, "moral restraint." (The technology of contraception was next to nonexistent at the time.) And in Malthus's view, given the "passion between the sexes," moral restraint was not strong enough to effectively limit human fertility. Therefore, lurking in the shadows, always ready to be the ultimate check on population growth, would have to be famine. "Famine stalks in the rear, and with one mighty blow, levels the population with the food of the world" (Heilbroner 1953: 83).

There was plausibility to the Malthusian argument. It was, in fact, a precursor to the now widely accepted ecological principle that any population will expand in size until it fills the ecological niche available to it. What Malthus did not foresee was that there would eventually be other checks to human population growth besides war, pestilence, and famine; that changing attitudes about family size, a kind of "small is beautiful" philosophy, could combine with a new technology in the form of effective and simple contraception to limit population growth. Nor did he foresee the enormous increases in agricultural production that would accompany the application of science to farming.

Important as Malthus's book was for the thesis that it espoused, it was more important as a stimulator of thinking among people who read it. Charles Darwin, for instance, reports that he happened to read Malthus "for amusement," yet, he says, from this reading got the theory of natural selection and survival of the fittest that would be the centerpiece of his book *The Origin of Species* (Bettany 1890; Herbert 1971).

Others were not amused. As one biographer put it, "Malthus was not ignored. For thirty years it rained refutations" (James Bonner, as quoted in Heilbroner 1953: 76). In the storm of protest that followed the publication of his essay Malthus was compared with Satan, and denounced as an immoral, revolutionary, hard-hearted, cruel atheist (Bettany 1890: ix). But the strongest refutation of the seeming inevitability of a perpetual tendency toward famine that Malthus postulated lies in what has happened since he wrote.

Since 1800 the population of the world has, in fact, grown exponentially—dramatically so (Figure 9.1). On the other hand, the growth of world population seems destined to stop eventually through a process demographers call the demographic transition.

■ THE DEMOGRAPHIC TRANSITION

The world appears to be going through a pattern of growth known as the demographic transition. Originally described by Frank Notestein (his definition is found in Box 9.1), the literature contains a number of ways of defining the term. I adopt and paraphrase from a conceptualization by Carl Haub (1987: 19) of the Population Reference Bureau in Washington, DC.

The theory of demographic transition offers a general model for the gradual evolution of a population's birth and death rates from the preindustrial to the modern pattern, which results in an S-shaped curve of population growth through time. Sweden is illustrative of the transition, which goes through four stages:

1. Preindustrial stage: Birth rates are high and fertility uncontrolled, with the birth rate exceeding the death rate and generally within the range of 25 to 45

Figure 9.1 Growth of Human Numbers

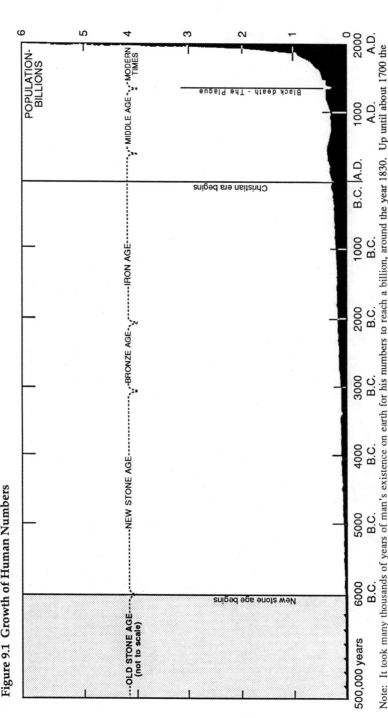

Note: It took many thousands of years of man's existence on earth for his numbers to reach a billion, around the year 1830. Up until about 1700 the human population of the earth had grown very slowly; the average rate was probably less than 0.002 percent per year. Then the growth rate began to gradually increase. In the early 1970's it rose above 2 percent, over 1,000 times the rate of growth of the ancients. In 1988 the world's current population growth rate was down to 1.7 percent. Current projections are that world population growth should approach zero around the year 2100.

Source: The 0.002 percent estimate, Frejka 1973:15; Figure adapted from Cook 1962:5; Other material, Population Reference Bureau.

Box 9.1 Terms Commonly Used by Demographers

Crude birth rate, or *birth rate:* The number of births per year per thousand individuals in the population

Crude death rate, or *death rate:* The number of deaths per year per thousand individuals in the population

Annual growth rate, or *growth rate:* Crude birth rate minus crude death rate divided by 10, which expresses the rate as a percentage

Doubling time: The number of years it takes the population to double, growing at the present annual growth rate, compounded. (You can figure out how long it will take a population to double, if it grows at a constant annual rate compounded, by dividing the number 70 by the annual, percentage, growth rate.)

Total fertility rate, or *fertility rate*: The total number of births a female has during her lifetime

Gross reproductive rate (GRR): The number of female children a newborn female will have during her lifetime if current levels of fertility by age of female continue through time

Net reproductive rate (NRR): The expected number of daughters per newborn female, after subjecting those newborn females to a given set of mortality rates (NRR is lower than GRR because some of the newborn females will die before completing their reproductive years.)

Demographic transition: A pattern of population growth experienced by Western industrialized democracies and involving an S-shaped curve of total population change through time. Frank Notestein (1945) identified three stages in the transition: (1) High growth potential: birth and death rates are high, life expectancy is short, and population growth is slow; (2) transitional growth: birth rates remain high but death rates are falling; population growth rates increase, sometimes to the point that there is said to be a population explosion; (3) incipient decline: the birth rate follows the death rate downward; population continues to grow until birth rate reaches the death rate.

Population momentum: The tendency for population growth to continue beyond the time that replacement-level fertility has been achieved; that is, even after the net reproduction rate has reached one. The momentum of a population in any given year is measured as a ratio of the ultimate stationary population to the population of that year, given the assumption that fertility remains at replacement level. Using this definition, the *World Development Report 1989* provides population momentum figures for 129 countries and an example of how the calculation is done (World Bank 1989: 214–215).

Population pyramid: A graph of the population distribution according to age and sex. Two basic kinds of pyramids are used: The first type, a numerical pyramid (such as Figure 10.2), plots numbers of people in each age and sex group; the second, a relative pyramid (such as Figure 10.3), plots the percentage distribution of people according to age and sex. The major difference between the two kinds is that the numerical pyramid increases in area as the population grows, while the relative pyramid always maintains a constant area (you can think of it as 100 percent). Thus, the two kinds of pyramids may appear to exhibit different dynamic characteristics.

Age cohort, or *cohort*: All the people in a population within a given age range (Each bar in a population pyramid represents a particular age cohort.)

Life expectancy at birth, or *life expectancy*: The average expected age of death of newborns who follow a given age-specific mortality schedule
Infant mortality rate: The number of babies who die during their first year of life per 1,000 babies born
Dependent children: (Usually) those people who are under 15 years old
Dependent adults: (Usually) those people who are 65 or over
Dependent population: Dependent children and dependent adults
Dependency ratio: The ratio of dependent to working-age adults—those from 15 to 65 (Percentage of the population dependent divided by the percentage of working age)
Child dependency ratio: The ratio of dependent children to working-age adults

per thousand. Periodic famines, plagues, and wars cause brief periods of population loss. Population grows, but slowly. In the decades just prior to 1825 Sweden was in the last phase of this stage (Figure 9.2).

2. Mortality decline prior to fertility decline: With better public health services and more-reliable food and water supplies, death rates fall and life expectancy increases. If there is no accompanying decrease in the birth rate, the population growth rate rises and population grows rapidly (in Sweden this period covers the 50 years between 1825 and 1875).

Figure 9.2 Birth and Death Rates, Sweden, 1751-1984

Rate per 1,000 population

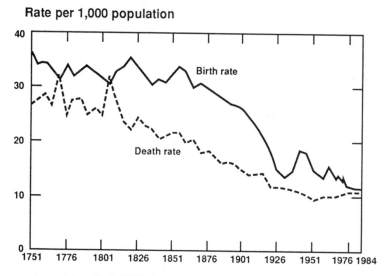

Source: Adapted from Haub 1987:20.

3. Fertility decline: At some point, usually as the country urbanizes and industrializes, the birth rate also decreases in response to desires to limit family size. Population continues to grow rapidly for a while. But eventually birth rates approach death rates, and population growth slows. The growth rate may even fall to zero or below. (The fertility decline in Sweden covers the 100-year period between 1875 and 1975.)

4. Modern stage: By this point both the birth rate and death rate are low, around 12 per thousand. After the birth rate falls as low as the death rate, population size stabilizes if the total fertility rate remains two children per woman. If the total fertility rate creeps up slightly from two, population size increases slowly, although family size remains small.

In what are today's developed countries the demographic transition is essentially finished (look at recent birth and death rates among the industrial market economies in the *World Development Report* table [e.g., World Bank 1990: 230–231] on demography and fertility). But the transition is only midway through in the Third World. Compare the demographic transition as shown in Figure 9.2 (with Sweden as representative of the developed world) and Figure 9.3 (with Mexico as representative of the Third World). The death rate decline in Sweden began shortly after 1800 and took approximately 150 years to fall from 30 to 10. The more dramatic death rate decline in Mexico did not begin until about 1915 and took only 40 years to fall to 10 per thousand. Birth rates in Mexico remained above 40 per thousand until the early

---

Figure 9.3 Birth and Death Rates, Mexico, 1895/99-1980/85

Rate per 1,000 population

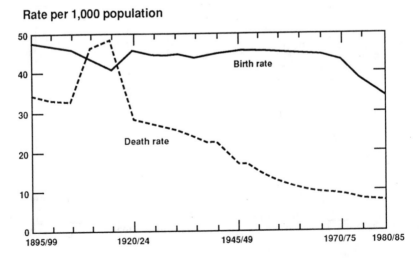

Source: Adapted from Haub 1987:20.

1970s when they began a rapid decline. Consequently by the early 1970s Mexico's population growth rate was above 3 percent, yielding a doubling time of fewer than 23 years.

The start of the rapid death rate decline in Mexico preceded that of most developing countries, which did not experience rapidly falling death rates until

---

Figure 9.4 Past and Projected World Population, A.D. 1 to 2150

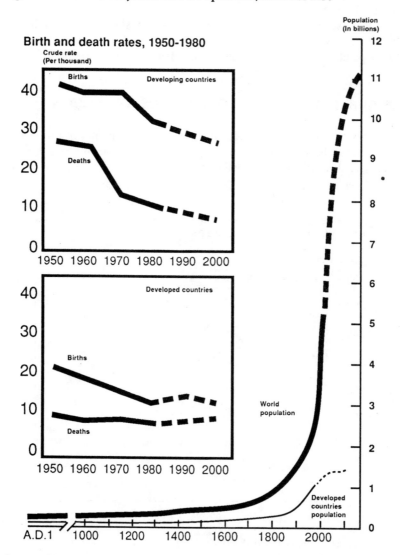

Source: Adapted from Birdsall 1984:11.

they benefited from the spread of modern medical and hygienic practices after World War II.

Despite the fact that the Third World is in the fertility decline stage of the demographic transition, its dramatic death rate decline has produced a period of rapid Third World population growth that, according to authoritative projections, will raise world population levels many billions before the numbers stabilize. Figure 9.4 shows, for both the developed world and the world as a whole (whose population numbers are dominated by the population of the Third World), the S-shaped population growth curve expected from the completion of the demographic transition.

If the world's population growth does, in fact, stop as projected, humans will have, in fact, succeeded in controlling their own numbers without resort to wars, pestilence, and famines—something Malthus did not expect.

■ CURRENT TRENDS IN FOOD VERSUS POPULATION

Not only did Malthus not expect humans to wilfully control their own population size, but he did not expect that our food supply would outpace a dramatic, exponential growth in our population. The latter half of the twentieth century ex-

Figure 9.5 World Grain Production per Capita, 1950-1988

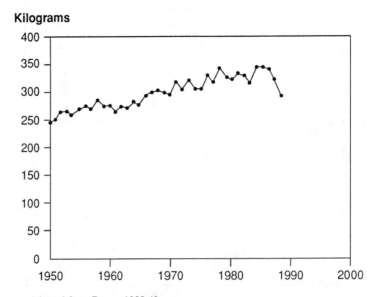

Source: Adapted from Brown 1988:43.

Table 9.1 Growth Rate of World per Capita Food Production, 1950-1990

	Growth Rate (Percentage per Year)
1950	1.4
1960	0.8
1970	0.4
1980	0.4

Source: US Department of Agriculture 1989b:3, 8.

perienced the most rapid growth of population in the entire history of the world, yet during this period of breakneck population growth per capita food production gradually increased (Figure 9.5 and Table 9.1).

The increase in food production that accompanied (and made possible) this increase in population growth was fueled largely by a chemical and biological revolution in farming. (Despite the clearing of vast acreages of tropical rain forest, from the mid-1960s to the mid-1980s, increased farm acreage in the Third World accounted for less than one-fifth of the growth in agricultural production [World Bank 1984: 90].) Although the green revolution that is raising wheat and rice yields in the Third World (see Box 8.2) has received more publicity, cereal yields in the developed world also rose dramatically during the second half of the twentieth century. Between 1950 and 1986 US wheat production more than doubled and US corn production increased almost threefold. The increase in US production came about not because of more land in use (during this time, acreage devoted to these two leading cereals actually declined by about 10 per-

Figure 9.6 Wheat Prices in 1982-1984 Dollars, United States, 1800 to 1988

Price per bushel

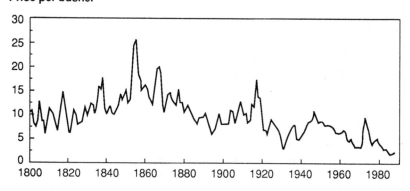

Source: Adapted from Edwards 1988.

cent) or more labor employed (farmers have been leaving agriculture) but because of better crop varieties, the application of chemicals such as commercial fertilizer and pesticides, and more-sophisticated management techniques (sources of production, acreage, and employment data for the United States can be found in US, Bureau of Census 1961, 1987).

Wheat is a major commodity in international trade and readily substitutes for other food grains. Thus it is a good indicator of the real price of food grains through time. That we are in the midst of a long-term trend of increasing abundance in food is suggested by the fact that real wheat prices in the United States, adjusted for inflation, have been declining more or less steadily since 1855 (Figure 9.6). In terms of 1982–1984 dollars the price of wheat was $25 a bushel in 1855; in 1988 it was just under $3 a bushel.

The prospects are not all rosy. Some of the increase in worldwide grain production is due to increases in irrigated acreages. And yet, in recent years both the United States and China (the world's leading food producers) have experienced unplanned declines in irrigated area. Much of the decline is due to falling water tables, drained by overpumping or the exhaustion of fossil water in largely unreplenishable underground water reserves such as the Ogallala Aquifer in the southern Great Plains of the United States (Brown 1988: 23–29).

Figure 9.7 Per Capita Grain Production, Western Europe and Africa, 1950-1987

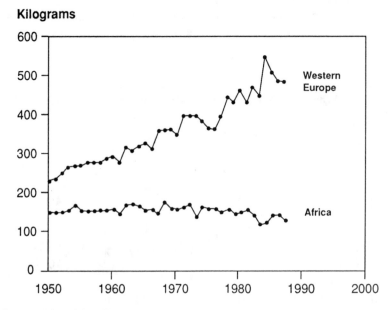

Source: Adapted from Brown 1988:16.

Some of the gains in production are due to the concentration of more and more acreage in a single crop variety. Because of the density-dependency of disease (diseases tend to spread more easily when their host population is large and packed tightly together), the worldwide trend toward monocultural farming exposes our field crops to unexpected outbreaks of disease over vast regions, such as in 1970 when a widespread blight (southern leaf blight) wiped out some 10 percent of the US crop of maize (US, Dept. of Agriculture 1970).

There is the possibility of a return of a major drought such as produced the dust bowl of the 1930s. There is the possibility that a nuclear exchange could bring on a nuclear winter resulting in widespread famine. There is that unwelcome news that there are probably more undernourished people alive today than there ever were before in the history of mankind. Furthermore there is the sad news that regions of the world that are already well fed, such as Western Europe, are experiencing rapid increases in per capita grain production, while the region of the world with the most rapid overall population growth, Africa, is suffering a gradual decline in per capita grain production (Figure 9.7).

Yet despite this unsettling information, it would appear from the history of the world since Malthus published the last edition of his essay in 1826 that famine is not inevitable. There is a good possibility that the problem of world hunger can be solved.

■ POPULATION GROWTH AS A STIMULANT TO PRODUCTIVITY

Other things being equal it would seem that a low-income family with few children would have an easier time feeding its members than a similar low-income family with many children. In fact, in Chapter 5 we examined data that supported this view. Nevertheless, there is a common feeling that farm families, at least, benefit from large numbers of children because of a labor shortage in agriculture.

In the United States, during the period of the westward movement, land was cheap and labor was scarce. Children, as soon as they could do simple chores around the farm, were a welcome addition to the work force. And in the agricultural Southeast of the United States children were often considered an agricultural asset long after the westward movement had swept by. Cotton and tobacco required long hours of stoop labor, much of which children could do perfectly well. As one sociologist (Park 1934: xix) put it in a study of black tenant farmers, emancipation imposed the necessity of making his farm pay on the newly freed but landless worker; consequently this worker, who usually had to farm a small plot of land on shares, "began to reckon his children as a personal asset."

Is labor short enough on the peasant farms of the Third World today that families with large numbers of children are better off than families with few children? There are some places where new land is being drawn into agriculture. Large acreages of tropical rain forest in Brazil and Indonesia are being cleared for farming, for instance. But most of the world's good farmland has already been located and settled. Increases in the number of farmers in the Third World commonly result in diminished farm size and fragmentation of holdings as, generation after generation, fathers split the family plots between two or more sons.

In those areas that are already under cultivation, what is the marginal productivity of labor in agriculture? That is, by how much would the addition or subtraction of one worker change farm production? Starting before World War II, a considerable literature developed that assumed that there was such a large pool of unemployed and underemployed labor in Third World agriculture that substantial amounts could be withdrawn for the industrial labor force with no diminution in agricultural production; in other words, that the marginal product of labor in agriculture was zero (e.g., Lewis 1954; Fei & Ranis 1964).

Gary Becker (1975) called that thesis into question with a powerful argument that people attach at least some value to their leisure time. If this is the case, then they will not work their fields up to the point that another minute spent farming yields no product at all. They would rather spend a few more minutes at leisure than to do this.

On the other hand there is considerable evidence that the marginal product of labor in agriculture is below the wage rate. A number of studies have shown that yields on small holdings in India, so small that all labor is supplied by the farm family, are significantly higher than yields on large farms where a substantial proportion of the labor force is hired (e.g., Berry & Cline 1979). Studies in other locations have arrived at similar results (Figure 9.8).

Farmers who hire labor are unwilling to hire so much that the product for the last hour worked by the laborer is less than the cost of hiring him for that hour. But when labor is all from the family, for those last few hours worked family members may be willing to work for something less than the going wage, since it is the family who will benefit from those last few hours and since they may have no higher-valued use for their time (Mazumdar 1965, 1975; Sen 1964, 1966).

All this argues that the marginal productivity of labor in agriculture is low, and comparisons of wages in agriculture versus nonagricultural activities in the Third World support this thesis. The ILO (International Labor Organization 1987) lists the daily wage rate for agricultural activities in the Philippines in 1985 as P 23.74 per day (just over one US dollar), but the daily rate for nonagricultural activities is P 56.48 per day, or 2.4 times the agricultural rate. ILO lists the daily rate for farm labor in India at about half a dollar and shows the manufacturing wage to be over five times that amount.

Unemployment rates for the Third World are hard to come by. The ILO (1988: 4) estimated that there were some 100 million workers unemployed and 500 million underemployed worldwide. Presumably, the majority of these people live in the Third World. ILO gives the unemployment rate for the Philip-

Figure 9.8 Farm Size and Production per Unit of Land in Less Developed Nations

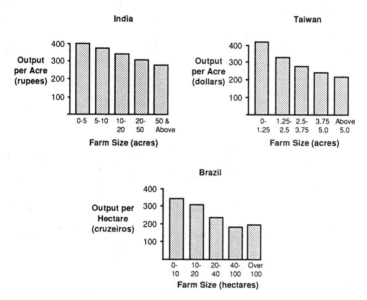

Source: Adapted from Stevens and Jabara 1988:68.

pines in 1985 as 6.1; that for Uruguay in 1986 as 11.4. It gives no estimate for India. (The ILO defines unemployment as all people above a specific age who are without work, available for work, and seeking work.)

Underemployment figures are even harder to come by. Underemployment refers to people who are employed part-time or in jobs of lower productivity than their skill levels would allow if appropriate jobs were available. Most of those who hawk cigarettes one by one on a Third World urban street corner could earn more if they could find a better job. The World Bank (1984: 88) estimates that underemployment in the Third World ranges "from 20 percent in Latin America to about 40 percent in Africa."

The unemployed, and probably also the underemployed, in the Third World are largely male and most often young men. ILO 1984 figures for Uruguay show 4.4 times as many unemployed people in the age bracket 14–24 as in the bracket 45–54. For India in 1984, ILO's figures show 73 times as many unemployed men in the 20–29-year-old age bracket as in the 40–49-year-old group.

Given the high rates of Third World unemployment, especially among young men, together with the relatively low wage rates in Third World agriculture relative to work outside of agriculture, it is hard to make a case for enough of a labor shortage in agriculture to make the typical farm family better off with many, rather than few, children. If farm productivity is the main consideration, it appears that the typical Third World farm family would be better off spending more on fertilizer for high-yielding seeds and less on raising extra children.

But we are not yet finished with the arguments about population growth as a stimulant to productivity. A number of thinkers have argued that population growth in and of itself is a stimulant to productivity. One of the writers in this school (Clark 1973) capsulized one of its chief arguments in the title of an article: "More People, More Dynamism." That is, society is better off with a large population than a small "as a result of there being more knowledge creators" in a large population (Simon 1986: 169).

Critics of this argument note that in today's high-tech world large numbers of people are no particular assurance of a high level of knowledge creation. If they were, then India and China, with over a third of the world's population between them, should account for a greater share of the world's technological development than do Germany, France, Britain, the United States, and Japan, which collectively account for only 10 percent of the world's population. In the Third World many Einsteins may be going undiscovered for want of a proper education.

Ester Boserup, in her book *Population and Technological Change* (1981: 5), argues that population growth creates a kind of crisis situation that stimulates the invention of new technology: "Shrinking supplies of land and other natural resources would provide motivation to invent better means of utilizing scarce resources or to discover substitutes for them." Note that in this "necessity is the mother of invention" argument it is population growth that drives the creation of technology, and not the creation of technology that expands the capacity of the economy to support more people.

Boserup argues that farming is most intense in the densely settled regions of the world (not that people have tended to gather in those regions of the world where soils are most productive). She argues that, since periods of technological innovation and expanding productivity have usually been accompanied by increases in population, growth of population must have caused the increase in technology and production. Critics of this thesis argue that it is just the other way around, that it is the technological innovation and expanding productivity that have, in fact, made possible the associated increase in population.

Since productivity is related to income, and income is so closely related to food consumption, those that argue that population growth, in and of itself, is a stimulant to productivity seem to imply that population growth would help alleviate the world hunger problem, or at the least be no threat to a solution. This school of thought has to contend with a series of arguments that claim that population growth has a detrimental impact on nutrition of the poor. In the next chapter we will consider four economic or demographic models that make such arguments.

☐ 10

Demographic Causes of Undernutrition

The principal determinant of whether food production per person is rising or declining in the various geographic regions is the differential rate of population growth. Where population growth is slowest, Western Europe, per capita food production is rising most rapidly. In the two regions where population growth is fastest, Africa and Latin America, it is declining.

—Brown 1988: 15

In this chapter we explore four economic-demographic models that relate population growth and undernutrition. In each case population growth is postulated to be a driving force or causal factor in undernutrition through its impact on education, capital formation, the price of grain, or equity.

■ POPULATION GROWTH, EDUCATION, AND UNDERNUTRITION

The quality of an educational system and its impact on society depend on a multitude of variables such as the resources devoted to training teachers, the level of teachers' salaries, the size and quality of school buildings and maintenance, the teacher-student ratio, and how many years of education a community provides for its children. There is, of course, more to educational quality and its impact than this. The degree of parental involvement in the process, the attitude of the parents, teachers, and children to education and educators, and the design of the curriculum, for instance, also influence the quality of education and its results. But the resources devoted to education are certainly important to the result.

A rapidly growing population is faced with an entirely different educational resource problem than a stationary one. The stationary population must spend money on training replacement teachers, refurbishing schools, improving textbooks, curriculum, and the like. The growing population must do all this and more. It is faced with constructing new classrooms as well as refurbishing old ones; training more teachers for more students, not just replacing those leaving the profession; maintaining the new schools as well as the old ones.

Figure 10.1 provides an illustration of the strain that a growing population

179

Figure 10.1 Two 50-Year Simulations of Teacher Requirements with Changing Fertility but Constant Educational Assumptions

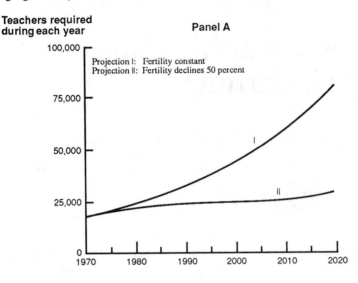

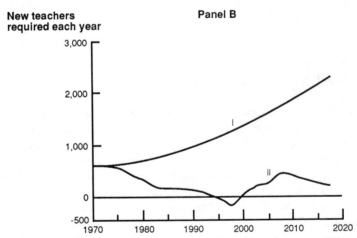

Note: In projection I the population is growing at a constant annual rate, compounded, of 3 percent.

Source: Adapted from McFarland, et al., 1974:4-6.

puts on educational resources. The projections are the results of computer simulations done on a model country with a population that has been growing at 3 percent, annual rate, compounded, for some time. Its fertility rate has been just over six during the past decades. Results from two simulation runs are shown. Simulation I allows the population to grow at its 1970 rate throughout the 50-year period. In simulation II the total fertility rate is cut in half. Both simulations assume constant class size and constant proportion of each age cohort in school.

In Panel A, with no fertility cut, the number of teachers required during each year grows from 20,000 to 80,000 during the 50-year simulation. With the cut in fertility, the number grows, but to only a little over 25,000 during the same 50 years.

Panel B shows new teachers required each year and reflects the pressure of a high fertility rate on the teacher-training system. Without the cut in fertility, the teacher-training system must expand threefold during the 50-year simulation. With the cut in fertility, the teacher training system can be reduced in size, and those resources saved can be transferred to other uses.

Most low-income, high-population-growth countries are plagued with large class sizes. In the high-population-growth countries of Malawi and Kenya, class size in the urban areas frequently exceeds 60 students. Unfortunately, large class size in the Third World often goes along with low expenditures on classroom materials. "Bolivia, El Salvador, Malawi, and the Ivory Coast, for instance, spend less than $2 a year on classroom materials for each child at primary school—compared with more than $300 per student in Scandinavian countries" (World Bank 1984: 85).

Combined with a lack of teaching materials, large class sizes can make teaching and learning difficult. Furthermore, in low-income Third World countries, typically only a fraction of the secondary school–age population is in school. In 1985 only 34 percent of this group was in school in those 39 countries where the per capita income was less than $450. On the other hand, in 18 high-income, industrial market economies, 93 percent of the secondary school–age population was in school (World Bank 1988: 278–279).

One potential use for the resources freed up over the years in simulation II of Panel B would be the training of more teachers, which would make possible a reduction in class size and the education of a greater proportion of school–age children through junior and senior high school.

☐ Population Growth, Age Structure, and Education

Conceptualizing age structure. The age composition of a population (age structure) is one of the most important features of that population. It is a reflection of the underlying demographic conditions of the preceding decades and at the same time is an important determinant of future demographic patterns.

The most convenient way to visualize the age structure of a population is through a graph of the population distribution according to age and sex, called a population pyramid. Conventionally, population pyramids represent age cohorts by five- or 10-year intervals, and place the males on the left of a vertical line and the females on the right, with the youngest cohort on the bottom. The graphic representation of the age cohorts can be either the actual numbers or the percentage distribution.

Figure 10.2 shows a numerical population pyramid for the industrialized versus the Third World in the year 1985, with projections to 2025. The horizontal lines across both sets of pyramids mark the dividing lines that are commonly, but rather arbitrarily, placed to separate the dependent age categories (in this case, below 15 years or 65 years and above) from the working-age population. Such numerical population pyramids do a nice job of making visible the differences in actual population size, Third World versus developed world, and they can also show demographic features such as the higher survival rate of older women (notice the difference between the numbers of men and women in the oldest cohort for the 2025 projection for the developed world). But to make comparisons from one country to another, or from one time period to another within a country, pyramids showing percentage distribution (relative pyramids) are usually more helpful.

Figure 10.3 shows relative pyramids for two developed countries (the United States and West Germany) and one Third World country (Morocco). The

---

Figure 10.2 Population Pyramids for Less and More Developed Countries, 1985 and Projections to 2025

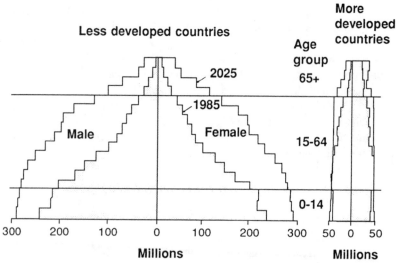

Source: Adapted from Merric 1986:19.

Figure 10.3 Age Structure in Morocco, United States, and West Germany, 1985

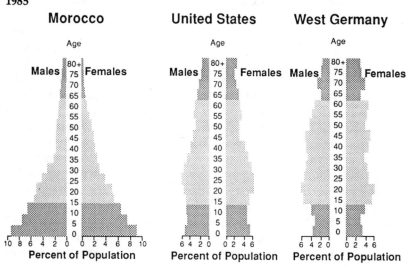

Source: Adapted from Haub 1987:21.

total area in each pyramid is exactly the same and represents 100 percent of the population of each country. The relative size of the youngest age cohort (zero to five) is reflective of the magnitude of the birth rate in the previous five years in each country. In 1972 the birth rate in Morocco was 45 per thousand; in the United States it was 16, and in West Germany it was 10.

Demographic patterns in the recent past can often be read directly from current population pyramids. For instance, during World War II and immediately afterward, birth rates in Germany declined. In 1985, the year of the pyramid shown in Figure 10.3, people born between 1945 and 1950 were between 35 and 40 years old. They are shown in the cohort labeled "35." Notice the narrowness of Germany's pyramid during that year. In contrast, the United States experienced a 15-year baby boom starting immediately after WWII, which shows up as a bulge in the 1985 pyramid extending from cohorts 25 through 35.

Age structure is of interest to demographers because, as we have noted above, it provides clues about past and future demographic patterns. It is important to policymakers because of its impact on two things we will discuss next: (1) momentum in population growth; and (2) dependency ratios.

Momentum in population growth. Over a long period of time, a population would just reproduce itself if individual couples had just the right number of children to replace themselves, allowing for some children to die before they arrive at childbearing age. In most populations this number comes to just over two children (e.g., about 2.1) per couple (or per woman). In this discussion we assume that 2.1 children, on the average, will handle replacement. If a population has remained constant for a couple of generations and then its fertility rate rises higher than 2.1, it will grow. (We are assuming no net immigration or emigration.) If, on the other hand, its fertility rate falls below 2.1, it will shrink. For that reason, a fertility rate of 2.1 is considered to be at the replacement level (Merrick et al. 1986: 6).

You might expect that when the fertility rate of a rapidly growing population falls to 2.1 births and deaths would be in balance, and population growth would stop. Such is not the case, at least not immediately. The reason for this is demographic momentum. A population that has had high fertility in the years before reaching replacement-level fertility will have a much younger age structure than a population with low fertility before crossing the replacement threshold. Consider the three countries in Figure 10.3. West Germany has a fertility rate of 1.4. It has already stopped growing, with a population growth rate of minus 0.2 percent. Notice that a substantial proportion of its population is over 35. The United States has a fertility rate of 1.9 and rate of natural increase of 0.7 percent. (It is actually growing faster than that because of immigration.) It has a more youthful population than West Germany. But an enormous proportion of the population of Morocco, which in 1982 had a fertility rate of 6.9, is below 35 years of age. Morocco's rate of natural increase was 3.2 in 1982. It has since fallen (to about 2.6 in 1989). Now suppose that Morocco's fertility rate should suddenly fall to 2.1. Would its population growth stop immediately? No, because of the large numbers of young people in the childbearing years relative to the older years. Would it stop soon? No, because of the large number of people below 15 who will be moving into the childbearing years.

As noted above, the rate of natural increase of population in the United States is 0.7 percent even though its fertility rate is 1.9, just below replacement level. This is because of momentum. To clinch your understanding of momentum in population growth, study Figure 10.4.

Dependency ratios. Once the age structure of a population is known, the dependency ratios can be easily calculated. The dependency ratio is usually defined as the ratio of dependents to working-age adults. As mentioned before, working-age adults are generally identified as those from 15 to 65 years of age. But the dependents are commonly split into groups by age, and two more ratios are then defined: The adult dependency ratio is the percentage of the population 65 and over divided by the percentage of the population between 15 and 65; the child dependency ratio is the percentage of the population below 15 divided by the percentage of the population between 15 and 65. It is the child dependency ratio that is of special importance in rearing and educating children.

In a rapidly growing population the burden of dependent children per adult is far greater than in a slowly growing population or one with zero population growth. Compare again the population pyramids in Figure 10.3, this time with regard to the child dependency ratio. In West Germany, which in 1985 had es-

Figure 10.4 A Demonstration of Momentum in Population Growth

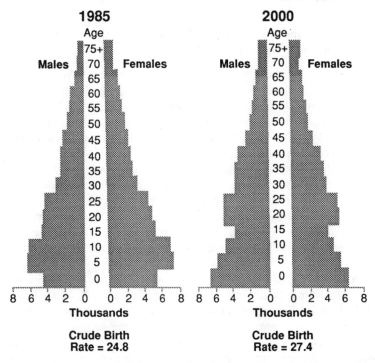

Note: The pyramids here demonstrate the effect of age structure on population change. In 1985 this population had a noticeable bulge in the age groups 5-9 and 10-14, the result of a recent baby boom. In this population about the half of all childbearing takes place in the twenties. When the bulge groups reach their twenties, the number of births will rise disproportionately. In this example the total fertility rate is held constant at 3.1, as is mortality. In 1985 the crude birth rate was 24.8 per 1,000 but by the year 2000 it had increased to 27.4, as a result of the bulge groups reaching childbearing years. The growth rate has increased from 1.65 in 1985 to 1.84 in the year 2000.

Source: Adapted from Haub 1987:14.

sentially zero population growth, 15 percent of the population was below 15 years of age, and 70 percent was in the age group 15 through 64. The child dependency ratio was thus 0.21; that is, there were 0.21 children per adult. Another way of looking at these data is to say that there were some 4.7 adults available, on the average, to raise and educate each child.

In Morocco, whose population was growing at just over 3 percent at the time the pyramid was drawn, 42 percent of the people were children and 54 percent were in the working-age group from 15 through 65. That produces a child dependency ratio of 0.77. In Morocco then, there were only 1.3 adults available, on the average, to raise and educate each child. (Raw data for calculating dependency ratios were furnished by the Population Reference Bureau.)

☐ Education and Hastening the Completion of the Demographic Transition

Other things being equal, a slow-growth population such as West Germany's will have an easier time providing many years of high-quality education for its children than will the fast-growing population of Morocco. The West Germans do not have to spend so much of their resources setting up and staffing new schools. And working adults in West Germany do not have nearly as many children to educate, per capita.

But other things are not equal. Almost all countries with population growth rates above 1 percent per year are low-income. And almost all countries with population growth rates below 1 percent per year are high-income (World Bank 1990: 274–275). The high-population-growth countries have a tough challenge to catch up with the low-population-growth countries in terms of quality and quantity of education. Hastening the completion of the demographic transition in these countries would make this task easier for them.

In Chapters 7 and 8 I argued that low incomes and high levels of income inequality are among the causes of Third World undernutrition. And in Chapter 8 I made the point that improved education in the Third World should raise productivity and thus income, and at the same time reduce income inequalities. To the extent that hastening the demographic transition in the Third World enhances education, thus improving productivity and income and reducing income inequality, such hastening should help reduce undernutrition.

■ POPULATION GROWTH, CAPITAL FORMATION, AND UNDERNUTRITION

We assumed above that a person's productivity is influenced by the quantity and quality of his or her education. In this section we assume that an individual's productivity is also influenced by the amount of capital that person has to work with. Indeed, capital has been called "the tools of labor" and the more and better tools a laborer has the more he or she can produce.

We get capital through savings and investment (see Box 10.1 for a distinction between the two). Most savings are generated by households (business and government can save too), and it would seem at first glance that families with many children would save less than families with fewer children. This is true in the developed world, and family size seems an important influencing variable. It is true also in the Third World, although the empirical evidence suggesting that family size is an important influencing variable is weak (World Bank 1984: 82). It just so happens that saving in the Third World is done heavily by the relatively few wealthy families, who happen to have fewer children than the poor.

Box 10.1 Savings and Investment

Investment occurs when you create capital—that is, when you do not consume something now so that you, or someone else, can be more productive later on. Usually investment involves spending on such things as machinery or factories that make people more productive. But it can occur in other ways. When peasants dig a channel to direct a stream around the side of a hill to their village so the village will have water, they are forgoing present consumption (probably leisure—which is a form of consumption) for future productivity and convenience. They are investing. They are creating capital.

When the wealthy Third World dowager forgoes a clothes-buying trip to Paris and instead buys bonds in the local river-valley development project, she is forgoing present consumption for future income. But she is also forgoing present consumption so as to make someone else more productive. We expect that the farmers who receive the irrigation water will be more productive than previously.

We do not create capital unless someone postpones or forgoes present consumption (e.g., leisure, trips to Paris). Postponing or forgoing present consumption is called saving. Just because someone saves does not guarantee that there is going to be a one-to-one correspondence in investment (John Maynard Keynes wrote a book on this theme). For instance, people can save gold coins, but that does not create investment or make anyone more productive. Just the same, over the long haul there tends to be a pretty close correspondence between savings and investment.

Although Third World dependency burdens and related population growth do not seem to affect the savings rate much, they do have an important impact on the need for capital. Over time and within a country there seems to be a fairly fixed ratio between the amount of capital in use and the amount of annual production. In many countries the ratio is about three units of capital to produce one unit of annual output. In other words it often takes about $3 worth of machinery, factories, railroads, trucks, irrigation ditches, fertilizer, and so forth to produce $1 worth of output (food, clothing, movies, transportation, etc.) per year. For instance, in the United States, in 1988, capital was worth $14,964 billion (domestic net worth) and output was worth $4,880 (GNP), yielding a capital-output ratio of three to one (US, Federal Reserve System 1989: 5; US, White House, Council of Economic Advisers 1989: 2).

Coale and Hoover (1958: 20) provide an illustration of the impact of population growth on necessary savings if an economy is striving to, as a minimum, maintain its current annual level of production per capita; that is, maintain its per capita income:

Assume that population A is growing at a rate of 1 percent per annum, and population B at 3 percent. If the ratio of capital stock to current annual output is 3 to 1, population A must invest 3 percent of current output to maintain its per capita income, while population B must invest 9 percent of current output. But under ordinary circumstances the supply of new capital will be no greater in B than in A. There is nothing about faster growth *per se* to lower consumption and raise savings—certainly not by such a large margin.

The expanding capital requirement just for keeping the capital per person constant while population is growing is called capital widening. The faster the population growth, the greater is the demand for capital widening and the greater is the proportion of production (and consumption) that must be forgone in order to meet this requirement. Capital widening is what is going on when growing populations build new classrooms just to maintain the same number per age cohort. In this case the physical capital widening is necessary to maintain the level of human capital. Capital widening for the maintenance of human capital must also take place throughout the economy of a growing population in order to maintain health services such as hospitals and clinics.

Box 10.2 If Capital Creates Jobs, Why Not Subsidize Loans To Entrepreneurs?

Capital is scarce in the Third World. Consequently, Third World interest rates are high. Third World moneylenders are notorious for their "usurious" rates.

If capital creates jobs, and the cost of capital (interest rate) is high, why not encourage capital use through subsidized loans to entrepreneurs? Tax monies could be used to set up low-interest loan programs for such items as tractors in agriculture, or machinery in industry.

Here is the problem with this reasoning: The point I have been making in this chapter is that increasing the stock of capital improves productivity and even creates jobs. But using nonmarket forces, such as taxation, to reallocate resources so as to bring down the cost of capital changes the relationship between the cost of an extra hour of labor and the cost of an extra dollar's worth of capital. Lowering the price of capital (interest rate) relative to the price of labor encourages the substitution of capital for labor and increases unemployment and underemployment.

Whereas a policy that increases the stock of capital per person (e.g., a policy that lowers human fertility rates) can increase productivity and wages, policies that force the price of capital to a rate substantially below the market interest rate may reduce employment and increase undernutrition.

Just as the school-age population grows when population grows, the labor force also grows. And the expanding labor force also needs capital widening in order to maintain its productivity per person. Without sufficient capital widening, unemployment and underemployment will increase and real wages will fall, not only in real terms but also relative to rents and profits. Thus income inequalities will increase.

For productivity (and thus income) to rise, investment needs to grow faster than the labor force. This process is called capital deepening. Capital deepening is different from lowering the interest rate—see Box 10.2. Rapidly growing populations find it more difficult to succeed in capital deepening than do slowly growing or nongrowing populations. The World Bank (1984: 87) gives a dramatic example of the difference in capital available to workers entering the labor force in four low-income, high-population-growth economies versus one high-income, low-population-growth economy: "If all investment in countries such as Bangladesh, Ethiopia, Nepal, and Rwanda had been allocated to potential new workers during 1980, each person would have had less than $1,700 invested on his or her behalf. . . . At the other extreme, new workers in Japan would have had about $535,000 of gross investment available."

Because rapid population growth rates both require capital widening and restrain capital deepening, they tend to limit the growth of employment and the rise of productivity and wages; indeed, they may even increase unemployment and underemployment and depress wages relative to profits and rent. The resulting lowered real income of the poor, who are largely landless workers, and the accompanying increase in income inequality are both disadvantageous to the nutrition of the poor.

■ POPULATION GROWTH, THE PRICE OF GRAIN, AND UNDERNUTRITION

In Chapter 7 I made the case that one of the causes of Third World undernutrition was lack of purchasing power among the poorest segments of the population. Purchasing power is made up of a combination of income and the price of goods and services purchased. So far in this chapter we have looked at the impact of population growth on the income of the poor and on income distribution. But population growth, of course, can have an impact on the price of food, especially on the cereal grains that loom so large in the diet of low-income people. As population grows, the demand for cereals increases, which, in turn, puts upward pressure on their price. That the real price of cereals has been generally falling during the second half of the twentieth century, when population growth was so rapid, is due to the fact that growth in cereal production has outpaced growth in population.

As I have said before, the growth in food production during this time period is attributed largely to the biological and chemical revolutions in agriculture. Because it is difficult to attribute much of the increase in cereal production to the expanding labor supply, we are led to the conclusion that slower population growth rates would have meant even lower prices for the cereals that provide so much of the nourishment for the poor. To the extent that it helps lower the price of grain, hastening the demographic transition can be expected to improve nutrition among the poor.

■ POPULATION GROWTH, EQUITY, AND UNDERNUTRITION

The American humorist Will Rogers once said, "Buy land. They ain't makin' any more of it!" Population growth tends to put upward pressure on the price of land as people compete for this limited resource for their various uses of it. To the extent that population growth has a positive impact on the price of food, it puts upward pressure on the price of land. Phipps (1984: 422) recently demonstrated that there appears to be a causal relationship between farmland prices and past levels of residual return to land.

To the extent that population growth is responsible for rising prices of other natural resources, whether renewable (such as timber) or nonrenewable (such as oil), it tends to raise the price of these resources. The owners of farmlands and other natural resources in this world are not the landless workers. The owners, in fact, tend to be among the wealthier people in the countries where these resources are found. As population growth puts upward pressure on the price of these natural resources, the wealth distance between their owners and the landless workers is increased. And to the extent that income differences between rich and poor are related to ownership of such assets as lands, forests, and oil wells, income inequality is increased as a result of population growth.

But population growth itself can put downward pressure on the price of labor relative to the price of land. An illustration of how rapid population growth can lower returns to labor at the same time that returns to land are increasing is provided by Sinaga and Sinaga (1978), who studied returns through time to factors of production in rice farming in Indonesia. They measured returns to each factor of production not in dollars but as kilograms of rice produced per hectare of rice planted (Table 10.1). During 1968/69–1973/74, when rice production per hectare was increasing significantly, the returns to land (rent) in rice farming increased 40 percent. The returns to the operator's capital and management (profits) increased by 213 percent. Because subsidies to fertilizers were increased during this period, the cost of purchased inputs such as fertilizers and pesticides decreased 23 percent. However, the startling finding was that the returns to labor, including family labor, also decreased, by 18 percent. Sinaga and Sinaga conclude that "in Indonesia the benefit from the [high-yielding, green revolution–type rice varieties] went to the operators and the landlords at the expense of the laborers, despite the fact that the labor requirement for rice production did not decline. The declining share of the laborers in Indonesia was due mainly to

Table 10.1 Average Real Earnings of Factors of Production in Rice Farming, Measured as Kilograms of Rice per Hectare, Central Java, Indonesia, 1968/69-1973/74

	1968/69	1973/74	Percentage Change
Land (landlord's return plus imputed rent)	1166	1629	40
Labor (includes family labor)	1494	1231	-18
Current inputs (cost of fertilizers, pesticides, irrigation, tractor, etc.)	530	407	-23
Operator's residual (return to operator's capital and management)	491	1535	213

Source: Sinaga and Sinaga 1978:107.

the ever decreasing real wages in the rural areas as the consequence of the continued population pressure on limited employment opportunities."

In a parallel study of shares from rice-farming earnings in the Philippines (where population growth was proceeding at an annual rate of more than 3 percent at the time they collected their data), Ranade and Herdt (1978, p. 95) found that, although the green revolution was stimulating an "increase in the amount of hired labor" in rice farming, there was, at the same time, evidence of "a declining real wage rate" in the rice paddies.

Thus there may be two aspects of population growth that tend to increase the distance between the rich and the poor: Population growth puts upward pressure on the price of land, held chiefly by the rich, while at the same time it puts downward pressure on the price of unskilled labor, the chief item that the poor have to offer for sale.

☐ 11

Health-Related Causes of Undernutrition

All infectious diseases have direct adverse metabolic effects.
—Scrimshaw, Taylor, and Gordon 1968: 12

Complex interactions among diet, disease, and physical characteristics determine the health and nutritional status of people, which in turn affects their enjoyment of life and ability to work.
—Bouis 1991: 1

■ THE SYNERGISMS BETWEEN NUTRITION AND HEALTH

A healthy person has a good appetite, likely eats a good diet, digests his food well, and makes efficient use of it in his body. A well-nourished person can keep his immune system functioning at a high level and is likely to be healthy.

A sick person is likely to lose his appetite, eat a poor diet, digest his food poorly, and must use some of his nutrients to fight infection. A poorly nourished person has a weakened immune system and is more prone to infections.

It is a positive feedback loop: Good health promotes good nutrition; good nutrition promotes good health. But when you look at it the other way around—poor health leads to poor nutrition and poor nutrition leads to poor health—you are more likely to call it a vicious circle.

There are strong synergistic relationships between health and nutrition. Put succinctly, infection exacerbates malnutrition and malnutrition exacerbates infection. The relationships are so important that the definitive review of the literature (Scrimshaw, Taylor & Gordon 1968: 267) on the relationship between nutrition and infection concludes: "Where both malnutrition and exposure to infection are serious, as they are in most tropical and developing countries, successful control of these conditions depends upon efforts directed equally against both."

■ INFECTION EXACERBATES MALNUTRITION

Infection increases the potential for and severity of malnutrition. Most common Third World infections have a heavy impact on nutritional status, in three important ways: (1) through loss of appetite or intolerance for food (e.g., vomiting); (2) through cultural factors (e.g., relatives of the sick individual substitute less-nutritious diets for the regular diet, they administer purgatives, antibiotics, or other medicines that reduce absorption of specific nutrients); and (3) through loss of body nitrogen (protein).

This last pathway to malnutrition through infection (loss of nitrogen) is complex enough that it deserves separate discussion. What happens is that protein tissue in the body is used up to fight the infection. To manufacture such disease-fighting materials such as interferon, white blood corpuscles, and mucus, the body needs amino acids, and it gets some of these amino acids by breaking down previously existing protein—chiefly from the muscles. This borrowing of muscular tissue for fighting infection is one of the reasons you feel so weak following a serious illness. It might seem reasonable to try to keep up the body's supply of protein during an illness through pushing food, but this is usually impracticable. Sick people do not usually have much of an appetite. During convalescence, with an appropriate diet, the lost body protein is usually replaced.

☐ Infection Promotes Dietary Deficiency

A reasonably healthy person who is presently on the borderline of nutritional deficiency may not show clinical signs of nutritional difficulties. But, because of the above problems associated with infection, an illness can increase his nutri-

---

Figure 11.1 Third World, Age-Specific Diarrheal Morbidity Rates

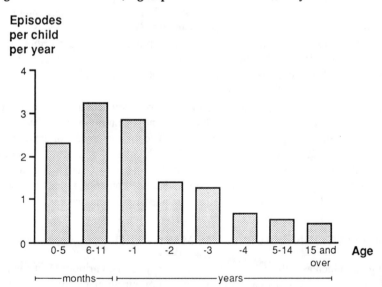

Source: Adapted from de Zoysa et al., 1985:8 using data from Synder and Merson 1982.

tional deficiency, and he can then develop any one or more of a number of conditions caused by dietary deficiency (Scrimshaw, Taylor & Gordon 1968: 265):

- Keratomalacia (a softening and ulceration of the eye's cornea) caused by shortage of vitamin A; if the shortage continues long enough and is severe enough, xerophthalmia (a dry, thickened, lusterless condition of the eyeball resulting in blindness) may ensue
- Scurvy (spongy gums, loosening of the teeth, and a bleeding into the skin and mucous membranes) caused by lack of ascorbic acid (vitamin C)
- Beriberi (inflammatory or degenerative changes of the nerves, digestive system, and heart) caused by lack of thiamine (vitamin B_1)
- Pellagra (a condition marked by dermatitis, gastrointestinal disorders, and disorders of the central nervous system) resulting from insufficient niacin (one of the B vitamins)
- Macrocytic anemia (anemia associated with exceptionally large red blood cells) caused by a deficiency of vitamin B_{12} or folic acid (one of the B vitamins)
- Microcytic anemia (anemia associated with exceptionally small red blood cells) caused by a shortage of iron

☐ Diarrhea and Nutrition

All of the above serious conditions result from a specific dietary deficiency exacerbated by infection. But the most common instance of an illness seriously affecting nutritional status is undernutrition induced by or exacerbated by a gastrointestinal infection (gastroenteritis) that causes diarrhea or, in its more extreme form, dysentery. An outstanding feature of kwashiorkor, for instance, is the frequency with which it is precipitated by an attack of acute diarrheal disease (Scrimshaw, Taylor & Gordon 1968: 27).

For the world as a whole, diarrhea is not as ubiquitous as the common cold, but in many Third World localities it comes in a close second in frequency of occurrence. Diarrhea particularly affects children under five years of age, and childhood fecal matter is a main source of the infective material. Food and water are key transmission routes. Children often make their first contact with diarrheal disease organisms through weaning foods (Martorell, pers. comm.). In fact, an outstanding feature of diarrheal disease in the Third World is the concentration of cases among children during and immediately after weaning (Durand & Pigney 1963), illustrated in Figure 11.1.

In a Third World setting the onset of diarrhea at weaning time (so common that it has sometimes been called by the special name of weanling diarrhea) is typically acute and rapidly progressive, with liquid or semiliquid stools, varying from three to as many as twenty a day. About one-fourth of the patients have blood or mucus in the stools and, frequently, pus. Fever may be absent, but low-grade fever is usual, along with malaise, toxemia (build-up of toxic substances in the blood), intestinal cramps, and tenesmus (a distressing but ineffectual urge to evacuate the rectum or bladder). The usual clinical course is four to five days. Repeated episodes can result in a month or more total time spent fighting diarrhea during a year's time (Figure 11.2). In malnourished children a low-grade indisposition often continues for a month or more, sometimes as long as three months, with irregularly recurring loose stools, a progressively depleted nutritional state, and occasional recurrent acute episodes (Scrimshaw, Taylor & Gordon 1968: 220).

Although there are some 25 different organisms (bacteria, viruses, and parasites) that can cause diarrhea, all cases result in a shortage of water and salts (electrolytes) in the body. This dehydration of the body can be the most serious consequence of diarrhea. By the time a weanling child is seriously dehydrated from diarrhea it is lethargic; its eyes are dulled and when it cries there are no tears; its skin is wrinkled up like an old man's; it stops urinating; the fontanel (soft spot at the top of an infant's skull) is sunken. If you pinch the child's skin, it only slowly returns to the normal conformation (Goodall 1984). At best this dehydration stands in the way of a quick recovery from the diarrhea. At worst

Figure 11.2 Diarrheal Illness, Developing Regions and Selected US Sample

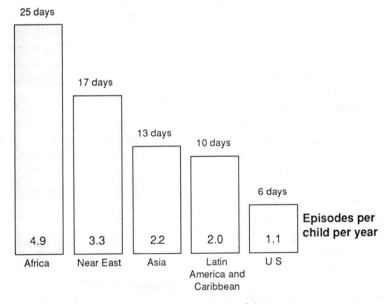

Average number of days per year with diarrhea

25 days				
	17 days			
		13 days	10 days	
				6 days
				Episodes per child per year
4.9	3.3	2.2	2.0	1.1
Africa	Near East	Asia	Latin America and Caribbean	U S

Note: An average episode of diarrhea is expected to last 5 days.

Source: Adapted from de Zoysa et al., 1985:11.

Box 11.1   Oral Rehydration Therapy (ORT)
Roger M. Goodall

The discovery that sodium transport and glucose transport are coupled in the small intestine so that glucose accelerates absorption of solute and water was potentially the most important medical advance this century.
—*Lancet* 1978, no. 2: 300

In the normal healthy intestine, there is a continuous exchange of water through the intestinal wall. Every 24 hours, up to 20 liters of water is secreted and very nearly as much is reabsorbed. This mechanism allows the absorption into the bloodstream of the soluble breakdown products of digestion.

In a state of diarrheal disease, this balance is upset and much more water is secreted than is reabsorbed, causing a net loss to the body that can be as high as several liters in a day. If more than 15 percent of the body's fluid is lost, death occurs.

In addition to water, sodium is lost. The body's store of sodium is almost entirely in solution in body fluids and plasma. By contrast, 98 percent of the body's total potassium is held within cells.

For the proper functioning of the body, the concentration of sodium in the blood has to be held to within close limits (which perhaps correspond with the salinity of the archaic seas from which our evolutionary ancestors emerged eons ago). This sodium concentration is normally precisely controlled by the kidneys. However, in a state of dehydration water is conserved by the reduction or even complete absence of urination, and the kidneys cannot do their normal job of regulating sodium concentration. Continued diarrhea causes rapid depletion of water and sodium.

Simply giving a saltwater solution by mouth has no beneficial effect because, in the diarrheal state, the normal mechanism by which sodium ions are absorbed by the healthy intestinal wall is impaired, and if the sodium is not absorbed, the water cannot be absorbed either. In fact, excess salt in the intestinal cavity causes increased secretion of water into the intestine (through osmotic pressure), and the diarrhea worsens!

If glucose (also called dextrose) is added to a saline solution, a new mechanism comes into play. The glucose molecules are absorbed through the intestinal wall—unaffected by the diarrheal disease state—and in a process called cotransport coupling, carries sodium through the wall at the same time. This occurs in a one-to-one ratio; one molecule of glucose cotransporting one sodium ion. Glucose does not cotransport water. Rather it is the now increased relative concentration of sodium across the intestinal wall that pulls water through.

It was the discovery of the mechanism of cotransport of sodium and glucose that Doctor Kathleen Elliott, in an editorial in the prestigious British medical journal *Lancet*, described as potentially the most important medical advance of this century. *ORT is, in fact, the practical realization of this potential.*

While common table salt and ordinary white sugar are the dominant constituents of the recipe for oral rehydration salts (ORS) recommended jointly

(continued on next page)

Box 11.1 continued

by WHO and UNICEF, two other constituents are included: potassium chloride and sodium citrate.

Although 98 percent of the body's potassium is held within the cells, prolonged diarrhea will result in a loss of potassium. The loss of potassium from repeated diarrheal attacks over a period of time causes muscular weakness, lethargy, and anorexia. The typical distended abdomen of a chronically undernourished child is caused by loss of muscle tone in the abdominal wall largely attributable to chronic depletion of potassium.

Potassium is not involved in any way in the sodium-glucose cotransport mechanism. But restoring a potassium deficit promotes a feeling of well-being and stimulates the appetite. Although potassium is not absorbed as dramatically as is sodium during ORT, the effectiveness of the recipe is enhanced by its inclusion, especially for a child who has suffered repeated diarrheal attacks.

The loss of body salts and fluid leads to an inappropriate pH level in the blood, called acidosis, that is corrected by the addition of a base such as sodium citrate to the recipe. When account is taken of the different molecular weights of glucose and sodium and the needs of the body for the depleted salts, the completed recipe typically comes out as:

Sodium chloride	3.5 grams
Sodium citrate	2.5 grams
Potassium chloride	1.5 grams
Glucose	20.0 grams

The above to be dissolved in one liter of clean drinking water.

Research is going on at many centers around the world to develop new and improved versions of ORS. Other effective recipes are now in use. Some, for instance, substitute starch for sugar. In the intestine, starch is metabolized to glucose and therefore has the same properties of enhancing sodium adsorption. However it has the added advantage that it has less osmotic effect (through this process sugar has some limited tendency to pull water back into the cavity of the intestine).

Although diarrhea always produces at least some dehydration, some of the more than 25 pathogens that cause it may strip the tips of the villi from large patches of the intestinal wall, leaving the inside of the intestine looking rather like a piece of velvet that has lost its nap. This decreases the surface area and can lower by more than 50 percent the specific absorptive capacities of the intestine. The result is malabsorption, which can cause or exacerbate undernutrition, most especially in a child already nutritionally compromised by repeated previous attacks of diarrhea.

Withholding food, even for one or two days, greatly exacerbates the undernutrition. This, coupled with anorexia, caused partly by chronic potassium depletion, results in a vicious circle: diarrhea causing undernutrition and undernutrition causing ever more frequent and severe diarrhea.

More detail on this subject is available in Goodall 1984. Roger Goodall was formerly senior advisor on oral rehydration therapy and essential drugs to UNICEF. He is currently an independent consultant.

(if the individual loses more than 15 percent of his body fluids) it is fatal. A baby may well die within 24 hours of the arrival of these signs of serious dehydration. Some 60 to 70 percent of the 5 million annual diarrheal deaths are caused by this associated dehydration (WHO 1985c: 6).

For generations it was thought that the only way to replace these electrolytes was through intravenous injection (IV). Oral replacement using the salts alone simply did not work. In the late 1960s researchers in India and what is now Bangladesh found that merely adding common cane sugar to the missing salts produced a formula that worked by mouth. Called oral rehydration therapy (ORT), this simple technology was first used to fight cholera (the most virulent form of dysentery) in an epidemic in India in 1971. Since then it has become a Third World public health mainstay and is being vigorously promoted by both the United Nations Children's Fund and WHO. UNICEF (1987: 8) has called ORT the cheapest and most effective health intervention that can be implemented in the home to decrease childhood mortality. A brief explanation of how it works is provided in Box 11.1.

■ MALNUTRITION EXACERBATES INFECTION

Malnutrition often amplifies the impact of infection. An example from the Philippines is illustrative. Severely undernourished children admitted to a hospital for acute respiratory infection are found to be 13 times as likely to die from the disease as children whose nutrition is normal (see Figure 11.3).

Malnutrition is almost always synergistic with intestinal diseases caused by worms or protozoa and with any disease caused by bacteria (Scrimshaw, Taylor & Gordon 1968: 263–264). That is, malnutrition aggravates the course of the disease, and the disease, in turn, intensifies the malnutrition.

A wide variety of nutrients have been demonstrated to have an impact on the competency of the body's immune system (Gershwin et al. 1985: 2; Phillips & Baetz 1980). The impact of nutrition on infection begins at birth and lasts throughout life. Not only is breast milk loaded with the appropriate nutrients for an infant's diet, but it carries with it a load of substances that help protect the infant against disease: immunoglobulins; macrophages; lymphocytes; neutrophils; components of the complement system, and so on (Rivera & Martorell 1988). (The complement system involves a set of more than 11 proteins normally found in the bloodstream. These proteins act in conjunction with the blood's antibody system in fighting infection, complementing the work of the antibodies.) Undernutrition increases the duration of infections, especially diarrhea. There is unequivocal evidence that the immune response is reduced in severe undernutrition, and some evidence suggesting a diminished immune response in moderate undernutrition, particularly in wasted children (Rivera & Martorell 1988).

Worldwide, malnutrition is the most common cause of deficiencies of the immune system, even among adults. Two examples will help to illustrate this

Figure 11.3 Acute Respiratory Infection Mortality by Nutritional Status, Philippine Hospital Cases

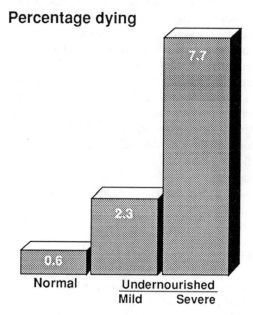

Source: Adapted from Galway et al., 1987:23 using data from Tupasi 1985.

point. Nutritional supplements given to the elderly have been found to improve their response to the influenza virus vaccine. And among individuals given the BCG vaccine to protect them from tuberculosis there was a positive correlation between better nutrition and resistance to the disease (Chandra 1988). Malnutrition interferes with various bodily mechanisms that attempt to block the multiplication or progress of infectious agents (Figure 11.4). The list of ways it can do this is long, but significant among them are a decrease in the response and activity of white blood corpuscles; a reduction in the production of interferon; a decrease in the integrity of the skin, the mucous membrane, and other tissues that serve to bar the entrance of infection; and interference with normal tissue replacement and repair (Scrimshaw, Taylor & Gordon 1968: 263–264).

The exploration of the mechanisms of how undernutrition impacts on the immune system has only just begun, but already we have enough information to provide interesting clues as to what is going on. For instance, the mucous membrane not only provides a physical barrier against the entrance of foreign particles that might cause infection (bacteria, viruses) but provides a chemical barrier as well. Mucus contains a variety of biochemical and immunological disease fighters, one of which is an enzyme called lysozyme, which has the ca-

Figure 11.4 Protective Factors Instrumental in Health Maintenance

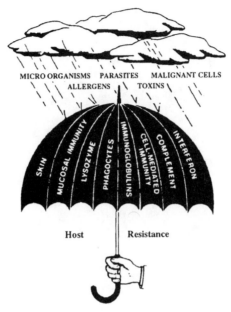

Source: Adapted from Chandra 1980.

pacity to attack the cell walls of invading bacteria. Colombian children suffering from protein-energy malnutrition (PEM) were found to be producing reduced levels of lysozyme. In a process called cell-mediated immunity, T lymphocytes play a key role attacking disease-causing microbes. Children with PEM are also likely to have an atrophied thymus, the organ that is primarily responsible for the "education" and proliferation of T lymphocytes, and at the same time to produce fewer of these lymphocytes than expected when their body is challenged with invading disease organisms (Sherman 1986).

A final point we must remember: Not only does malnutrition reduce resistance to infection, but it decreases stamina, decreases the capacity to cope with life and to perform on the job, making it more difficult to earn money to pay for transportation to health care centers, to pay for the services themselves, and to pay for appropriate drugs for combating infection.

■ Part III

POLICY APPROACHES TO UNDERNUTRITION

In Part II we looked at the main causes of undernutrition—the vehicles by which undernutrition is delivered to families—and attributed these causes mainly to economic, demographic, and health variables. A number of models were introduced to help in understanding how economic, demographic, and health variables deliver undernutrition. The central activity of Part III is to explore applications of the above-mentioned models as tools for the formulation and evaluation of public policy alternatives of interest to nutrition planners. Another model, supply, is introduced to provide a better understanding of the importance of price in motivating production.

This last part is introduced with a section that tells how failure to account for conflicting worldviews of the hunger problem can erode the efforts of activists who would seek to improve Third World undernutrition and ends with a set of recommendations on how to achieve policy reform.

Philosophical Approaches to Undernutrition

In 1988, 12 of every 13 children born (92%) [could expect to] survive to age one ... an important advance ... Many international organizations, and some governments, continue to place almost exclusive emphasis in their program-ming on further reducing mortality, with little attention to the development and welfare of the survivors.

What will happen to the twelve who survive? Many of the same living conditions that previously put them at risk to die now put them at risk of im-paired mental, social, and emotional development in their earliest months and years.

Delayed or debilitated development can affect all of later life. It can also be prevented and, because children are amazingly resilient, it can be over-come. But that requires more effort than most places have been willing to spend up to now. As a result, millions of children will fail to live up to their po-tential and will be further thwarted in their attempt to escape from the persis-tent cycle of poverty. Many of these survivors will lead lethargic, unproductive, unrewarding, and dependent lives.

As more infants survive, the moral and social imperative grows to re-spond to the question: Survival for what?

—Myers (forthcoming)

■ THREE APPROACHES TO WORLD HUNGER

Our first chapter opened with a reference to starving Ethiopian babies—babies with bloated bellies, spindly arms and legs, and bodies too weak to sit up. The device is a standard technique for grabbing the attention of people attuned to Western culture and making them stop and think about the world food problem.

Those who live in the Western industrialized democracies are exposed to repeated appeals to conscience to join in the battle to end hunger. In 1980 the Presidential Commission on World Hunger urged that the United States "make the elimination of hunger the primary focus of its relations with the developing world." Commenting on this in a paper written for a religious audience, M. McLaughlin (1984) wrote: "The moral and humanitarian reasons for such a pol-icy seem self-evident." Barbara Huddleston (1984a), writing in a CARE brochure, refers to the "Right to Food" and states that "providing food security for the individual means guaranteeing for every child, woman and man the right to freedom from hunger." An undated fund-raising letter from UNICEF, sent out during the late 1980s and signed by Hugh Downs, appeals for money to sponsor Third World childhood immunizations, ORT, and breast-feeding promotional programs in a "massive educational campaign needed to teach parents these basic ways of preventing malnutrition." Downs says, "I can't think of a single cause more important than the life of a child."

Yet increasingly people are beginning to ask tough questions about programs that concentrate on keeping children alive without adequate additional programs to see that they live a good life as they mature and live their adult lives. Robert Myers raises the issue of what happens later in life to those undernourished Third World children who are coaxed through a childhood of marginal nutrition through Western-sponsored aid programs: "Many of the same living conditions that previously put them at risk to die now put them at risk of impaired mental, social, and emotional development." To those who would save lives through intervention programs, Myers asks, with reference to the surviving at-risk children, some difficult questions: "Who is caring for these children? How is that care given? What is their early life like? What can be done to enhance their growth and development and to help them realize their individual and social potential?"

We live in a world of resource scarcity. Even if we knew the exact amount of food required for reasonably minimal nutrition for each individual (remember the rather inconclusive results of our explorations on this issue in Chapter 3), the costs of supplementing the diet of all nutritionally at-risk people in the world today would undoubtedly be very high. And there are a host of other needs competing for public dollars to be spent on the welfare of the world's poor. If we lived in a world of perfect knowledge, perhaps we could make a number of comparisons between costs and benefits from various welfare programs and come up with an allocation where the last dollar spent on one program gave just as much return as the last dollar spent on any other program.

We do not live in a world of perfect knowledge, but the concept is useful in thinking about how to allocate public resources among competing programs (such as, say, highway construction, rural electrification, nutrition intervention, education, and family planning). Let us first look at how benefits and costs change as food consumption increases in one Third World low-income household. In our model we will use energy intake as a proxy for food consumption or nutritional status. For this one household, the cost of each extra unit of energy purchased is the same. (Variations in the small amounts they purchase do not affect the price of food.) In Figure 12.1 the cost per unit of energy is shown as constant as food purchases increase.

The benefits from additional calories are more complex to model. Without a certain minimal level of food, there is no life. Thus the benefits from food first show up some distance across the horizontal axis of Figure 12.1. Once there is enough food for life, benefits from small additions are great: preventing disease; enabling increasing amounts of work to be done; satisfying hunger. But as food

Figure 12.1 Marginal Benefit and Marginal Cost of Energy Intake for One Household

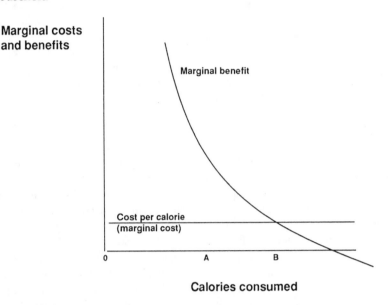

Calories consumed

intake increases, the benefits from additional amounts decline. The additional energy will be allocated to activities with lower benefits, such as recreation and social interaction, and if the process continues far enough, eventually additional energy will end up as excess fat, which can be detrimental to health (a negative benefit). (For a fuller discussion of this see Reutlinger 1984.)

At first glance it might seem that our household would purchase enough calories so that the marginal benefit from the last calorie purchased just equaled the cost of that calorie (amount OB in Figure 12.1). But remember we said we were modeling a Third World low-income household. With its very limited income and the competing demands for clothing, housing, medicine, and so forth, the limited household budget constrains spending on food. Instead of spending up to the point where marginal benefit just equals marginal cost, food expenditure will be held at some lower level, say amount OA in Figure 12.1. Spending more than this amount will require a greater sacrifice of other expenditures (on clothing, etc.) than the household is willing to make.

What I have just said ties in with our earlier discussion of income elasticity of demand for food. Remember that Gray found the income elasticity of demand for calories (percentage change in consumption of calories with a 1 percent change in income) in low-income, rural Brazil to be 0.46 (Table 7.3). And Ho found the income elasticity of demand for calories in a low-income region of Indonesia to be 0.58. That is, when these consumers experience an increase in income, they spend only part of it on food, and in fact, spend a greater part of the increase on nonfood items. (You may want to review the section on quantifying income elasticities in Chapter 7.)

In Third World low-income households food is a fungible item. That is, it is interchangeable with money. In fact, it is not hard to find villages where, even today, children may be sent to the local store with a small bag of rice to trade for a bit of spice. So when such families receive a food handout from some welfare agency, they treat it as an increase in income. They spend part of it on food and part of it on other items, either by trading part of it directly for nonfood items today or by reducing food expenditures tomorrow. This phenomenon explains why, in case after case around the world, food subsidy programs have been found to increase nutritional status by considerably less than was expected, given the amount of the food subsidy (Beaton & Ghassemi 1982).

The elasticity figure is important because it enables you to estimate what fraction of a given food supplement will be consumed as food within a given community. And the declining value of income elasticity of demand as income is increased means that it will take a greater subsidy to increase consumption by the second 100 calories than it does to increase consumption by the first 100 calories. Reutlinger offers an illustration of this concept in Box 12.1.

As the marginal costs of a food supplementation program rise, they not only have to be compared to the declining marginal benefits as shown in Figure 12.1, but they have to be compared to the benefits from spending on other public activities (the highway construction, rural electrification, education, etc., that I mentioned earlier).

So far we have looked briefly at two philosophical approaches to undernutrition. The first, the altruistic or moralistic approach (a sort of "food is a basic human right" idea) tends to stress the pathos of children suffering and dying from insufficient food. The second is the benefit-cost approach that the economist would use to examine activities to alleviate undernutrition in a political environment where there are competing uses for public expenditures. The latter approach would count as a benefit the reduction in any losses associated with the adverse effects of undernutrition on intellect, education, the capacity to do work, and health (including the waste of resources invested when a child dies prematurely from undernutrition). But it would also take into account the opportunity costs of dollars diverted from nonnutrition programs (such as road building or education) when increased expenditures on nutrition intervention projects reduce resources available for these nonnutrition programs.

A third philosophical approach to undernutrition considers the benefits associated with it. I already mentioned in passing in Chapter 2 that lean women are less prone to cancer because their lower levels of estrogen may reduce the growth of cells that can start tumors. I also mentioned that women who have fewer ovarian cycles (a phenomenon associated with late menarche and early menopause, which, in turn, can be associated with undernutrition) are at reduced risk for breast cancer. When menarche occurs late, menopause commonly occurs early, thus also shortening the woman's reproductive life. Shortening the number of years a female is fertile tends to reduce the total fertility rate, with all the accompanying benefits that reduced fertility has for rapidly growing Third World populations. There are other benefits to undernutrition; for example, undernourished populations are less subject to cardiovascular disease.

Box 12.1 The Increasing Cost of Increasing Food Consumption Through a Subsidy

Shlomo Reutlinger

If households allocate only an increasingly smaller share of additional income to the augmentation of their energy intake, then the marginal cost of inducing energy augmentation through public intervention rises sharply as higher levels of intake are sought.

As an illustration, consider a nation in which 5 million people have average daily energy intakes of 1,500 calories, 15 million of 1,600 calories, 10 million of 1,700 calories and the remainder of 1,800 calories and more. Let's further assume that, with declining income elasticity of demand as income rises, the additional (annual) income required to increase daily energy intake by 100 calories is $10, $15 and $25, respectively, at the level of intake of 1,500, 1,600 and 1,700 calories. If the goal of the public intervention is to assure the entire population a minimum energy intake of 1,600 calories, 5 million people at very low levels of intake would have to get a total cash transfer of 50 million dollars. If the goal were to assure a minimum of 1,700 calories in the population, an additional 15 dollars per capita would have to be provided to the 5 million people with the lowest energy intake as well as to 15 million more people. The additional cost would be 300 million more dollars. If a minimum energy intake of 1,800 calories were to be assured, the additional cost would be 1,000 million dollars. The marginal cost of raising minimum energy intakes from 1,700 to 1,800 calories is 20 times the marginal cost of raising minimum intakes from 1,500 to 1,600 calories.

The above calculations are illustrative, but not unrealistic, given what we know about the declining marginal propensities of households, at different levels of energy intake and income, to allocate additional income to energy intake. The marginal cost of public interventions to increase energy intake rises sharply as higher levels of intake are sought.

Source: Extracted from Reutlinger 1984.

We might also look at the selective effects of undernutrition. In many Third World communities boy babies are preferred over girl babies. In these communities girls are more likely to be underfed than boys and are more likely to succumb to infection, undernutrition, or accident (Cassidy 1987: 309). This social selection for boys reduces the number of girls in the population, with the accompanying demographic benefits. (In communities where girl babies are preferred over boys, of course, the demographic benefits are negligible.) In a population that is so short of food that death rates from undernutrition are elevated, it is undoubtedly the less fit children, by and large, who die off. Those who survive to grow up are tough. Furthermore, they tend to be stunted. And small people need less food. In a food-short economy, this is an advantage. David Seckler (1982) has gone so far as to propose that Third World children who are "stunted but not wasted," to use the Waterlow classification described in Chapter 3, have probably not been particularly stressed, but rather are "small but healthy," although his argument has met with considerable criticism among nutritionists (Martorell 1989).

Finally, there is evidence that mild undernourishment during youth may prolong adult life, at least in rats. Early studies on the relationship between starvation and longevity indicated that slower growth in rats was associated with delayed menarche and senescence as well as greater longevity. A recent study (Masoro, Yu & Bertrand 1982) reported that rats living on severely limited quantities of a well-balanced diet lived substantially longer than those who consumed enough to satisfy their appetite (1,047 days vs. 714 days). Could it be that mild underfeeding of humans could prolong life? Furthermore, could it be that delaying the onset of sexual maturity would save educational resources, as it would prolong the period of time that youngsters are relatively pliable (that is, before they become interested primarily in each other) and thus make education more efficient during those extra years gained before the onset of puberty?

■ FIVE WORLDVIEWS ON THE WORLD FOOD PROBLEM

From the above discussion it is evident that there are a number of ways that the world food problem can be approached. In two seminal papers on toddler malnutrition, anthropologist Claire Cassidy (1980, 1987) brings order and clarity to this subject by identifying and describing various worldviews of the hunger problem. Cassidy begins her classification by postulating three general interpretations of the universally observed fretfulness, crying, frequent illnesses, and even deaths that are associated with Third World weaning children who are at risk for undernutrition: (1) the activist position; (2) the adaptor position; and (3) the acceptor position. These interpretations lead to five worldviews of the hunger problem: (1) altruism; (2) intervention economics; (3) bioecology; (4) social cohesion; and (5) status quo. Her scheme is shown in condensed form in Figure 12.2.

The activist believes that there is a problem. Children are undernourished and something should be done about it. The activist has difficulty seeing any benefits to undernourished children. Activists come in two categories, the altruist, who would like to see every child in the world nourished properly but who is less conscious of economic cost of programs that would accomplish this goal than the economist, who would intervene in the socioeconomic system in such a way that the last dollar spent in each of the alternative social welfare programs yields an equal return.

The adaptor is not so sure that there is a problem. He notes that benefits accrue from adapting persons to the existing situation. The adaptor is fully aware of scarce resources. He knows that there are times when, for the benefit of the group, it makes sense to feed adequately the more productive members of the

---

Figure 12.2 Five Worldviews Relevant to the World Food Problem

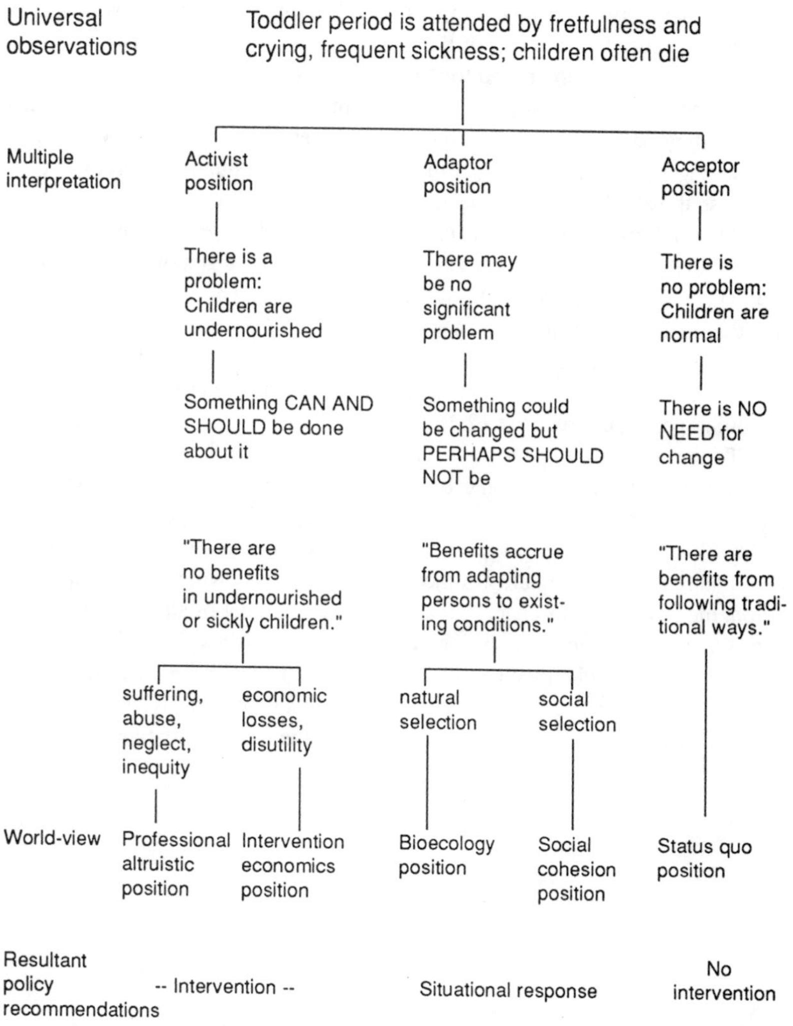

Universal observations	Toddler period is attended by fretfulness and crying, frequent sickness; children often die		
Multiple interpretation	Activist position	Adaptor position	Acceptor position
	There is a problem: Children are undernourished	There may be no significant problem	There is no problem: Children are normal
	Something CAN AND SHOULD be done about it	Something could be changed but PERHAPS SHOULD NOT be	There is NO NEED for change
	"There are no benefits in undernourished or sickly children."	"Benefits accrue from adapting persons to existing conditions."	"There are benefits from following traditional ways."
	suffering, abuse, neglect, inequity — economic losses, disutility	natural selection — social selection	
World-view	Professional altruistic position — Intervention economics position	Bioecology position — Social cohesion position	Status quo position
Resultant policy recommendations	-- Intervention --	Situational response	No intervention

Source: Adapted from Cassidy 1987:297.

family (the working adults) and to slight the less productive (the children and old people), even if in the process, some must die. Those who note that the natural selection taking place through this sorting process tends to adapt the genetic material of the group to the harsh conditions under which they live are said to be taking the bioecologist's position. Those who note the benefits to society from lower birth rates from preferences shown boy babies over girl babies, or who note the economic savings (food savings) to society from a stunted population are said to be taking the social cohesionist's position.

The acceptor does not think there is a problem. To him, children who show symptoms that biomedical specialists call undernutrition are behaving normally. Children have always behaved in this way. Following traditional ways has, in the past, assured the survival of the group, and therefore there is no need for change now. The acceptor therefore takes a status quo position.

To the activist, intervention in the system is required. To the adaptor, intervention may be required, depending on the situation. The adaptor would question saving infants' lives without the assurance of adequate resources to properly raise the children saved. The acceptor sees no need for any intervention.

Although most people will find value in more than one of the above positions, most of us tend to side more heavily with one or the other. Westerners (and I) tend to take the activist position. Low-income Third World people tend toward the adaptor position, or in some cases even the acceptor position. These differences in worldview can, at the least, lead to difficulties in communication between aid givers and aid recipients and at worst can lead to rejection and failure of aid programs (see Box 12.2).

To the reader, the latter part of this book will seem heavily freighted with the attitudes of the intervention economist. We will be examining and evaluating policies to improve health and reduce fertility rates. We will also be examining and evaluating policies and programs designed to increase the income of the poor and reduce the inequality of income and wealth (of which food supplementation, mentioned in this chapter, is only one of a number of alternatives). But in addition to the above intervention economist approaches, I will borrow from other worldviews when we examine programs for famine relief (altruism) and when we stress the existence of Third World resource scarcity and the importance of taking a long-term view of the good of the community (adaptor).

Box 12.2 Worldview Conflicts and Change Agent Dilemmas
Claire Monod Cassidy

Western humanitarian philosophy focuses on the individual, views the child as of prime importance, and uses activism to solve problems. In contrast, many nonindustrialized peoples focus on the importance of the group, view the productive adult as of prime importance, and use consensus to address problems. These philosophical differences mean that customs Westerners interpret as damaging are, to many non-Westerners, plausible, reasonable, acceptable, normal, or even benevolent.

Persons holding such different perspectives use different decision modes and, in a nutrition intervention setting, may have considerable difficulty communicating. The stage is set for conflict—and for intervention failure—if these differences are not understood and adjusted for.

The intervention economist, typically Western-trained, sees the societal costs of hunger and sickness as measured mainly in material terms of money and goods, and is concerned with the disutility or inefficiency of the systems that foster malnutrition. Solutions tend to be activist and material, emphasizing, for example, improved commodity exchange or production, or income generation and redistribution.

In contrast, the intervention altruist, also typically Western-trained, sees costs mainly in terms of the social-spiritual quality of individual human lives (especially those of infants and children) and worries about suffering and social inequity. For him or her, solutions are still activist but tend to emphasize food distribution programs for the needy, and educational and outreach (nonmaterial) aids that are intended to change behavior and decrease inequity.

Of these two activist positions, the intervention altruism approach focuses primarily on the individual, while the intervention economics approach focuses on impersonal abstractions such as the sector, region, or market. Neither focuses on the society, and thus both effectually, if unintentionally, deemphasize the importance of the community or familial context in which suffering occurs. However, it is precisely this social context that has value for most of the activists' target populations.

The activist child-survival focus is a short-range type of future orientation; some present lives are saved, but little emphasis is placed on providing long-term supportive social, educational, or economic contexts for those lives. For example, ORT is popular because it can both cheaply and relatively easily prevent toddler and infant deaths from diarrhea. Most often, however, its use is not linked to efforts to maintain the child once it survives diarrhea, or to prevent recurrent bouts. UNICEF's four-part plan to save 20 million preschool lives a year by encouraging use of vaccinations, breast-feeding, growth charts, and ORT does provide a larger context for ORT. But it is not a maintenance context, for the plan does not address the linked, long-term problems of underemployment, poverty, inequity, lack of educational facilities, or rapid population growth.

In their enthusiasm for the position, altruists may be tempted to assign pejorative labels to nonaltruists: "ignorant" if circumstances suggest that the nonaltruist has not had the opportunity to learn altruistic behaviors, and perhaps "inhumane," "abusive," "racist," or "neglectful" to those who have apparently rejected components of the altruistic worldview.

(continued on next page)

Box 12.2 continued

Additionally, activists, frustrated by being unable to promote change as fast as they would like to, summarize their perceptions of the "traditional" client populations' attitudes as if they were a mirror image of the activist position. Thus, where the activist finds abnormality, this traditional "acceptor" is assumed to find normality; where the activist loves change, the acceptor is supposed to abhor it; and where the activist recommends intervention, the acceptor wants none.

Although there is no doubt that individual villagers sometimes think in this rigid acceptor manner, I do not know of modern ethnographic sources that describe any groups of people whose thinking would conform to this model. Rather, most Third World villagers tend to think like adaptors.

There are two adaptor positions, the bioecology and social cohesion positions. The first summarizes a position of evolutionary and ecological biologists, few of whom are directly involved in delivering development aid. The second represents the position of many Third World rural and poor urban populations. Both adaptor positions emphasize the context in which an organism finds itself, and both ask how an individual organism relates to the larger context. Thus questions of "good" are typically phrased in terms of group continuity rather than of individual life, and it is often recognized that what damages an individual organism may paradoxically help maintain the larger group. Also, adaptors measure time in years or generations rather than in the months characteristic of activist thinkers. Thus adaptors find that short-term individual survival is relatively unimportant unless those who survive grow to adulthood and take their proper places as productive members of the community.

Another reason adaptors tend not to think in utopian terms is that they assume that scarcity exists and that there is never enough to provide an ideal environment for all organisms. Consequently, some competition for resources is inevitable and "normal." Together, these values mean that adaptors measure the desirability of change against their own twin realities of scarcity and competition, and express good in terms of long-term group continuity.

The social cohesionist realizes that one means of coping with scarcity is to maintain a high ratio of producers to nonproducers, and one way to do this is to deny resources—at least in a relative sense—to those perceived as less productive. The most productive members of such societies are adults. Among the less productive members are children. Many customs and behaviors that activist interveners have associated with poor child health and lowered chances for survival can be interpreted as societal efforts to decrease the resources devoted to child rearing. This approach might not make sense where food is abundant or most children live to school age, but where food is scarce it does.

It is important to note at once, however, that societal efforts to be frugal are typically unrelated to whether or not parents love their children. Numerous ethnographic studies show that, with few exceptions, poor and village parents do love their children and that the quality of their love is no different from that which altruistic parents may offer their children.

Children who survive resource competition in a family of extreme scarcity enjoy steadily increasing social value as they mature and become productive. A four-year-old who can carry and look after a younger sibling is already productive and proportionately more valued. In asking the young child to work, its parent is perhaps acting out of economic necessity but is also, and more importantly, drawing the child closer to valued adult groups and expressing approval and trust.

The worldview differences contrasted here can lead to miscommunication in intervention settings. Where the altruist focuses on individuals, physical health, and longevity, the social cohesionist focuses on group robustness. Where the social cohesionist fears scarcity, the altruist hopes it is not true, and the activist claims we can change the world so as to eliminate what we fear. Where the activist orients toward children, the social cohesionist orients toward adults. Worse, when both focus on children they want to raise them quite differently. Consider again the case of the four-year-old toting its younger sibling. An altruistic thinker might find that requiring such a child to work devalues it and might attempt to re-rig the system so as to eliminate this custom. Yet in the village context, relieving the child of its physical burden is equivalent to relieving it of some part of its social value and of its sense of belonging.

Worldview conflicts like those summarized here have seriously eroded the effectiveness of the well-meant programs of donor activists. How can we resolve the dilemma that worldview differences weaken the effectiveness of donor programs? It is obvious that interveners have three basic choices:

1. They can see the activist and adaptor positions as mutually exclusive and withdraw from further intervention work, feeling it to be useless.

2. They can see the two positions as mutually exclusive and be so convinced of the superiority of their own ethic that they interpret their mission as one of replacing the worldview of their clients.

3. They can recognize the validity and cogency of both positions and seek commonalities that will permit true communication between intervener and client. The aim is to help clients to engage in ameliorative redesign (by their definition) of their own cultures.

Based on my assumption that most interveners are impelled by a sincere desire to help, and can recognize the rights of others to believe and behave differently from themselves, I suggest that most professional interveners will aspire to the third of the three possibilities.

For a more in-depth treatment of worldview conflicts and change agents see Cassidy 1980, 1987.

□ 13

Policies Aimed at Health-Related Causes of Undernutrition

If we could increase the health spending in the developing countries by only $2 per head, we could immunize all their children, eradicate polio, and provide the drugs to cure all their cases of diarrheal disease, acute respiratory infection, tuberculosis, malaria, schistosomiasis and sexually transmitted diseases.
—Hiroshi Nakajima, director-general of WHO, in WHO 1989: 1

■ THE ECONOMIC EFFICIENCY OF PUBLIC HEALTH PROGRAMS

In Chapter 11 I noted the positive feedback loop between good health and good nutrition. Good health promotes good nutrition; good nutrition promotes good health. In recent years there has been a lot of talk about the fact that, by and large, it is cheaper to maintain good health than it is to make people well after they get sick. This idea is coloring a lot of the present developments in Third World health care, where there is a new emphasis on low-cost delivery of health services to the poor. There are "barefoot doctors" in China, "nutrition huts" in the Philippines, and "health huts" in Haiti.

Actually, we have known of the economic efficiency of public health programs for a long time, and, despite the emphasis in many Western countries on private health care, governments have been sponsoring public health services in the West for many years. Modern engineering principles were applied to waterborne sewage disposal systems in the West during the 1840s. By the early 1900s it was common for local governments in the Western world to consider the supply of drinking water to be properly within their purview. In this century public programs promoting the iodization of salt and the fortification of flour with vitamins have become routine in the West. (The history of such programs in the United States is outlined in Box 13.1.) Third World countries now have parallel public programs for drinking water, sewage, food fortification, and salt iodization (see Box 13.2).

The present emphasis on publicly sponsored, low-cost primary health care for the poor is relatively recent. Most common Third World illnesses can be successfully treated in the field by paramedical workers using simple equipment and a limited range of medicines. Thus there is a strong argument for placing increased emphasis on preventive medicine carried out by lower-level technicians in clinics close to people's homes, contrasted with curative medicine carried out by highly trained physicians surrounded by a hierarchy of staff in expensive urban hospitals.

Box 13.1 A Brief History of Food Fortification in the United States

Richard Ahrens

The leading cause of draft deferment in the United States during World War I was the swelling of the thyroid gland called goiter. One problem associated with goiter was that boys who had the condition could not fit into the tight collars of the military uniforms. In 1923 the Harding Commission, appointed by President Warren Harding, recommended a voluntary program for the iodization of salt to combat goiter. A gentlemen's agreement was worked out between the salt companies and the executive branch of the government that there would be no price difference charged between the iodized and uniodized product.

During World War II a bill was introduced into Congress that would have made it mandatory that all table salt be iodized, but the bill was defeated in committee when a number of medical doctors testified that there were probably some people in the United States who were sensitive to iodine and who would have skin problems as a result of being unable to obtain iodine-free salt.

Fortification of flour arose at the start of World War II, after President Franklin Roosevelt asked the NAS to evaluate the nation's readiness for war. As one of their recommendations, the NAS came up with a proposal to ask flour millers to fortify wheat flour with iron, thiamin, riboflavin, and niacin. The flour fortification program became policy in 1940 and was looked after by the US War Department. Later it became the province of the US Department of Health, Education and Welfare, and now it is the province of the US Food and Drug Administration.

A recommendation to increase substantially the iron fortification of enriched flour and bread came out of the 1969 White House Conference on Food, Nutrition and Health, and in 1973 the Food and Drug Administration proposed to triple the iron-enrichment level in flour. Several experts recommended against this proposal because doing so would exacerbate a problem of iron toxicity (hemochromatosis) among some 100,000 people, and by 1977 the idea of upping the iron level in flour was dropped.

Richard Ahrens is professor of nutrition at the University of Maryland and teaches a course on the history of nutrition.

Toward the end of Chapter 8 I suggested that development programs that lean towards emphasizing human capital development (which would include primary health care and public health programs) not only serve to improve people's productivity, especially at the bottom end of the income distribution, but may also raise per capita income faster than programs that emphasize physical capital investment (industrialization). So although we are now discussing policies aimed at health-related causes of undernutrition, keep in mind that these

---

Box 13.2 Food Fortification in the Third World
Eileen T. Kennedy, et al.

Countries in which a single grain product supplies a disproportionate share of the total dietary intake consistently show a higher prevalence of micronutrient deficiencies. Fortification intervention schemes have been put into effect in order to alleviate this problem.

Fortification is a process whereby nutrients are added to a food to maintain or improve its quality; protein, amino acids, vitamins, minerals, and fat are all fortificants that can be added to a food. In order for fortification to be feasible and effective, a carrier for a particular fortificant must be consumed regularly and in sufficient quantity. As such, staples such as grains, sugar, salt, monosodium glutamate (MSG), and other condiments have been used as carriers in fortification interventions.

To serve as carriers, however, these staples must pass through the market. Thus, fortification of staples produced for consumption on the farm is not usually feasible, and malnourished members of semisubsistence farm households cannot usually be reached by this approach.

Microlevel fortification interventions have been regarded as a relatively easy method of alleviating some forms of malnutrition among food-purchasing households, since micronutrients can be added to food with a minimum of change in the diet and at a relatively low cost.

Vitamin A, iodine, and iron-folate are the three most common micronutrient deficiencies in developing countries. As a result, fortification programs have been focused on these three nutrients.

The most dramatic results have been obtained by the addition of iodine to salt. Iodization of salt has almost completely eliminated goiter and cretinism in the United States and some parts of Latin America and Asia.

The results of vitamin A and iron-folate fortification programs are less clear-cut. Results from a sugar fortification project in Guatemala and an MSG fortification program in the Philippines indicated that serum vitamin A levels were increased as a result of these interventions. The MSG fortification also showed a reduction in the clinical signs of vitamin A deficiency.

A limited number of iron-folate supplementation programs have been successful in improving hematological status in pregnant women. Results of iron-folate supplementation for preschoolers, however, has been less successful. In Tanzania, iron supplementation of the diets of children 5–14 years old failed to improve hematological status; the prevalence of malaria was then diagnosed as the primary cause of the anemia rather than simply dietary iron deficiency.

Source: Extracted from Kennedy et al. 1983: 42–46.

policies not only serve to simultaneously improve health and nutritional status, but they also serve to accelerate income growth among the poor and help to reduce income inequality, both of which, in turn, help to reduce Third World undernutrition.

One highly effective means of delivering primary health services where costs are very low relative to the benefits is through maternal and child health care centers.

■ SUBSIDIZING MATERNAL AND CHILD HEALTH SERVICES

Providing public subsidies for expanding and improving maternal and child health services is entirely consistent with promoting better nutrition in the Third World and can be done within the framework of modestly trained field health technicians working outside of the hospital environment. Immunization services are an obvious candidate for expansion in such low-cost field activities.

Box 13.3 The Difficulties of Preparing Baby Formula in a Third World Low-Income Household
Michael Latham

The reasons for the contamination of baby formula, or milk, in a baby bottle are numerous. Milk is a good vehicle and culture medium for pathogenic organisms. It is incredibly difficult to provide a clean formula, let alone a sterile one when:

1. The family water supply is a ditch or a well, contaminated with human excrement (and few households in developing countries have their own safe supply of running water).
2. Household hygiene is poor and the home environment is characterized by flies and feces.
3. There is no refrigerator or other safe storage place for a mixed formula.
4. There is no turn-on stove and in order to sterilize the bottle or boil some water, someone has to gather fuel and light a fire on each occasion.
5. There is no suitable equipment for cleaning the bottle between feeds or when the bottle used may be a cracked and almost uncleanable soda bottle.
6. The mother, with little access to education, lives in the pre-Pasteur era, having little knowledge of hygiene and no knowledge of the germ concept of disease.

Source: Extracted from Latham 1984:60.

About 46 million infants per year are not fully immunized against six common, vaccine-preventable childhood killers—measles, tetanus, diptheria, pertussis, tuberculosis and polio. About 2.8 million children die from these diseases annually, according to recent WHO (1989: 2) calculations.

Of these, measles presents the greatest hazard. By itself, measles is rarely a killer. However, it has a devastating effect on the nutritional and immune status of its victims. With the body's defenses down, the child suffering from measles is vulnerable to a cascade of complicating infections, most commonly diarrhea or pneumonia. Measles frequently precipitates severe protein-calorie malnutrition, and as many as one-fourth of infected children are left with a formidable 10 percent weight loss. This single vaccine-preventable disease, together with its complications, is estimated to account for more than 2 million deaths annually (Galway et al. 1987: 16).

In areas where the childhood diet is short on vitamin A, a program for its distribution would be an appropriate activity for maternal and child health centers. This idea is supported by an interesting controlled experiment that was conducted in Ache province in northern Sumatra, where vitamin A deficiency may well be the most severe in the world. During a one-year time period, some preschoolers in Ache were given one capsule containing 200,000 International Units of vitamin A every six months. Others were given no vitamin A supplement. The vitamin A supplement was shown to dramatically reduce both the risk of xerophthalmia and the death rate (Sommer et al. 1986; Gopalan 1986). Vitamin A pills such as those used in this experiment can be manufactured for less than 5 cents (US) each. The cost of distribution far exceeds the cost of the pills. The presence of an ongoing maternal and child health care center permits the cost of a vitamin A supplementation program to be shared among the costs of other health delivery programs.

Such other health delivery programs appropriate to maternal and child health care centers include promoting growth monitoring of preschoolers, providing family-planning services, and promoting the use of oral rehydration salts for the control of diarrhea.

And, of course, maternal and child health care centers are logical vehicles for gaining health and nutrition benefits through promoting breast-feeding. As was pointed out in Chapter 4, and as is here amplified in Box 13.3, the sanitary and educational conditions prevalent in low-income Third World homes can easily lead to a diarrhea disaster for a bottle-fed infant. But there are other problems when low-income Third World mothers substitute the bottle for the breast. To such mothers, commercial infant bottle-feeding formula can seem exorbitantly expensive. So there is a tendency to overdilute the mixture with water or even to mix it with white flour or sugar (after all, it looks very much the same). These practices can lead to marasmus. Even in relatively well-off Third World households, the knowledge situation can be such that substituting the bottle for the breast can lead to marasmus (see Box 13.4). Breast milk also contains anti-

---

Box 13.4 Marasmus in a Newly Rich Urbanized Society
Peter Pellett

I was long of the opinion that infantile marasmus would be essentially eliminated when social and political changes were accomplished such that abject poverty no longer existed. However, recent experience in Libya, a rich but still developing nation, has caused me to reconsider somewhat this view.

The Libyan Arab Republic was formed in 1969 by a coup d'état led by Colonel Muamar al-Qaddafi against the king. During the eight years between then and 1977, real incomes for ordinary workers in Libya increased fourfold. In 1977 the major food items (flour, rice, tomato paste, meat, olive oil, coffee, tea, and sugar) were subsidized by the government, and baby foods were tax-free. Both gross poverty and inadequate housing were largely eliminated and phenomenal social progress was accomplished.

Despite this, in 1977 infantile marasmus in Libya remained a widespread problem. As elsewhere in the developing world, breast-feeding had declined.

In a study in Tripoli, the capital city of Libya, we compared the family backgrounds of 50 marasmic infants with the backgrounds of 50 essentially healthy infants of similar age. Total income was similar in both sets of families, and major consumer items such as TV sets, cars, and refrigerators were widely present in both groups. However, families with marasmic infants had less-literate mothers who tended to breast-feed for shorter periods and to feed purchased pureed baby foods more frequently. We concluded that the causal factor for marasmus in most of these instances was probably unhygienic infant feeding, despite the availability of clean water and modern kitchen facilities.

Although there were no statistical studies to back them up, some local hospital staff members were of the opinion that the rapid decline in breast-feeding and the accompanying rapid increase in bottle-feeding and in the use of purchased pureed baby foods had combined to increase mortality rates for children during the early period of the very rapid rise in per capita income!

For more information on this topic see Pellett 1977 and Mamarbachi et al. 1980.

---

infective properties not present in infant formula. Furthermore, lactation prolongs postpartum amenorrhea (the lack of menstruation that reduces fertility following birth). The contraceptive protection from lactation declines with each month of breast-feeding following birth, and about 7 percent of women conceive during this period without having resumed menstruation (World Bank 1984: 116). Nevertheless this lower fertility during lactation does reduce the chance of another pregnancy following too closely upon the recent birth, and increases the physical, emotional, and economic resources the mother has available for care of her preschooler.

■ PUBLIC HEALTH MEASURES TO INTERRUPT THE TRANSMISSION OF DIARRHEA

Programs to interrupt the transmission of diarrhea are among the important activities that public health services can do to promote better Third World nutrition. Leading measures to take here are better handling of fecal wastes, especially those of children; programs to teach cleanliness, especially washing of hands before cooking or eating; improving case management, especially through promoting ORT; promoting breast-feeding; increasing the rate of measles immunization; and improving the local water supply.

Not only do breast-fed infants have a lower morbidity rate from diarrhea, but breast-feeding protects against death from diarrhea. Infants who receive no breast milk were found to be about 25 times more likely to die of diarrhea than those who were exclusively breast-fed (Feacham & Koblinsky 1984).

Measles associated diarrhea is more severe and is more likely to lead to death than other diarrheas. One estimate suggests that up to a quarter of diarrheal death among preschoolers could be prevented by an effective measles immunization program (Feacham & Koblinsky 1983).

Improving the local water supply in rural areas can involve something as simple and effective as technical assistance and encouragement for the construction and use of rainwater-gathering vats. Use of such vats provides not only a clean, but convenient source of household water. When a mother does not have to walk so far to get her household supply of water she has more time available for other activities, including child care.

Providing an ample supply of clean water to the poor in a Third World city can be a political as well as an engineering problem. The city of Port-au-Prince in Haiti during 1976 provides an extreme example. In this case a shortage of water outlets gave rise to a rather substantial and profitable private market for what was, ostensibly, a publicly provided city service (see Box 13.5).

Box 13.5 The Political Economics of Drinking Water
Simon M. Fass

An in-depth examination of one small segment of the public service sector in Haiti, specifically water distribution management in Port-au-Prince, highlights the severe consequences which deficient administration can bring to bear upon a relatively large number of people.

In Port-au-Prince, in 1976, about 50 percent of the water input leaked out of the municipal water system. For the most part the loss was due to breaks and leaks in pipes, but much of it occurred because connections to reservoirs in homes and establishments were not equipped with automatic shut-off valves, or sometimes any valves at all. When such reservoirs, including swimming pools, were full, the overflow spilled into the streets. Since there were no metering devices or enforced penalties for not having valves, and the water tariff was on a flat-rate basis, subscribers had little incentive to invest in appropriate valves. The United Nations estimated that control mechanisms at private connections could have reduced losses to a more reasonable rate of 30 to 35 percent.

Individuals installed reservoirs because of irregular distribution and pressure of water flows. Heavy demand fluctuations, variations in rainfall, limited public storage capacity, and high distribution losses caused the irregularities. Subscribers had to be prepared for periods of several days, sometimes weeks, between deliveries through the pipes.

The 30,000 legal and clandestine private connections in 1976 provided direct service to only about 150,000 residents. The remaining 490,000 residents were in theory serviced by the 36 officially designated standpipes [public water outlets employing multiple spigots] that were supposed to exist at the time. In reality only 27 standpipes functioned. The others had long since been destroyed. The total outflow from the operating standpipes on any given day did not exceed 1.4 million liters. Thus under the best of circumstances their total supply could not provide more than 2.8 liters per person each day for the 490,000 residents presumably dependent on them. To put this in perspective, a single flush of a modern toilet facility requires 19 liters.

The extreme scarcity caused by the municipal distribution system led the city's population to adapt in a number of ways. There were a number, something on the order of 40,000, who relied on leaks and breaks in the pipes. It was common to knock a hole in a pipe, if necessary digging into the street to find one, plugging it with a wooden spike when not in use, and attaching a short rubber hose from the hole to a bucket when drawing water from it. Since penalties for this practice could be quite severe, this method of obtaining water was not widespread.

A more common practice, providing water to some 95,000 residents, was sharing among neighbors. In a number of areas, high, middle, and low income homes are located side by side. In such neighborhoods, the proportion of families with connections tend to be relatively high, and so the number of individuals requesting water from a particular subscriber on any given day, usually in the form of a request to a household servant, is low, typically less than 10 or 12.

The majority of nonsubscribers, however, some 300,000 low income residents who lived in downtown areas with relatively few private connections, were obliged to buy water from fixed and mobile vendors. The shortage of water outlets had in effect given rise to a rather substantial private market for a publicly-provided service.

The Private Water Market, 1976

The private water market in 1976 contained three principal sets of vendors. The first set were tanker truck operators who drew water from fire hydrants and transported it to industrial and commercial establishments and to about 1,200 higher income homes located in areas without piped service or with very irregular service. Charges for truck supply varied between U.S. $3.00 and U.S. $6.00 per m³. The gross revenues of truckers, who paid nothing for water, either in the form of user charges or in the form of license fees, amounted from these consumers alone to an average or $2,700 per day, $980,000 per year, and an annual return of $39,000 per truck.

There were substantial profits to be made, and often truckers were known to break pipes in order to create demand for transported water over the extended periods required to locate the breaks and repair them.

The second set of vendors consisted of some 2,000 households which had connections to the system and sold water in lower income areas to neighboring consumers and/or to mobile sellers who would transport it further afield. The common method was to sell water by the bucketful (about 18 liters per bucket).

The minimum price, in effect during the rainy season if water was flowing in the pipes, was two cents a bucket, or about $1.10 per m³. In the dry season the typical price would be ten cents, equivalent to $5.60 per m³. During drought periods, as happened in 1975 and 1977, unit prices could reach anywhere from $10.00 to $20.00 per m³ for several months at a stretch.

The third set of vendors were mobile vendors who bought water from connected households and transported it to consumers. They numbered 14,000 or about 4.5 percent of the urban labor force.

The margin charged by the vendors in ordinary circumstances was one cent per bucket, or two if the transport distance was long. These were margins on top of whatever the vendors themselves paid to connected families. For 1976, the aggregate net earnings of mobile vendors came to $930,000, or approximately $5.50 a month for each vendor.

Total expenditures by consumers in the private water market thus amounted to about $3.8 million a year, a quarter being paid largely by a very small group of high income residents and the balance by some 300,000 low income families. By contrast, [the municipal water authority's] total annual revenue from the sale of water was $650,000 during the same period.

Impacts on Low Income Families

At a price of $2.30/m³ a typical family of five would have to spend about $4.00 a month in order to consume 11 liters of water per day. In 1976 about 40 percent of urban families had incomes of $20 per month or less.

Given all the various daily demands placed on the use of money, many of these families found it impossible to spend a fifth of their income on water. They responded in a number of ways.

The poorest of them, with incomes of less than $10 per month, used purchased water only for cooking and drinking. They used surface run-off for cleaning themselves. They might also launder and wash less often. A major hazard was that of illness caused by contaminated water or by residence in areas with

(continued on next page)

Box 13.5 continued

disastrous sanitary conditions, susceptibility to which was aggravated by the extra energy expended by already malnourished bodies to trudge 20 kilogram buckets of water several kilometers each day. With the risk of illness came the possibility of seriously compromising the capacity to generate income streams. Curative medical services would require such families to curtail other expenditures further, to dig into savings, or to incur heavy debts.

Source: Extracted from Fass 1982.

□ 14

Policies Aimed at the Demographic Causes of Undernutrition

One result of [population/resource] projections and their use in public discussion of population policy has been a shift in concern toward future generations. In China, as in most traditional societies, childbearing decisions were shaped by a desire by parents to be looked after in old age. By emphasizing future population/resource relationships in shaping family planning programs, government officials have shifted the focus of childbearing from the well-being of parents to the well-being of children.

—Brown 1983: 38–39

In Chapter 10 we noted that rapid population growth makes the task of education more difficult, thins out the supply of capital per person, puts upward pressure on the price of grain, and tends to decrease equity, all of which exacerbate Third World undernutrition. But remember also how, in the section on family factors predisposing undernutrition in Chapter 5, we found that undernutrition tends to be concentrated among the youngest children of large families. Thus we have both indirect and direct ways through which reducing the tendency toward large family size will improve Third World nutrition.

The theme of this chapter is to examine policy alternatives for lowering the fertility rate. I should note at the outset that, worldwide, fertility rates are already falling. The demographic policy problem for the nutrition planner in countries with high fertility and high undernutrition rates, then, is how to accelerate the downtrend, or to put it in other words, how to hasten the demographic transition.

We begin with a review of the causes for the downtrend in fertility rates, which has proceeded furthest, of course, in those countries that have completed or almost completed the demographic transition. Those variables that have contributed to the slow but substantial fertility decline in the high-income, industrial countries provide, at the least, interesting prospecting ground for policies to reduce fertility in the Third World.

■ ONGOING REASONS FOR THE FALL IN FERTILITY RATES

Over the years, research has produced increasingly reliable and convenient methods of contraception, thus making it easier to limit fertility. But at the same time many other things have been happening that have lowered human fertility rates (Caldwell 1983; Pullum 1983). It is a widely observed phenomenon, for example, that high income yields lower fertility, at least after the initial stages of extreme poverty are overcome. In Figure 14.1 this relationship is illustrated.

When very poor families experience an increase in income their initial reaction is often to have more children. (The increased income, for instance, may enable earlier marriage when marriage otherwise might have been postponed for want of adequate dowry. Or the increased income might motivate the substitution of bottle-feeding for breast-feeding, with its consequent increase in fertility.) But as incomes rise, other factors mitigate to reduce fertility. Higher income is usually associated with better education, and with more education parents tend to trade off child numbers for child quality. They spend a greater proportion of their child-rearing resources on their children's health and education, with correspondingly smaller resources left over for raising large numbers

Figure 14.1 Relationship Between Fertility and per Capita Income

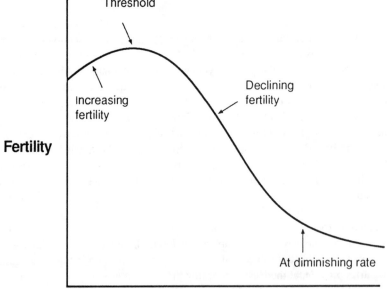

Source: Adapted from World Bank 1984:109.

Figure 14.2 Total Fertility Rate by Education of Wife, Selected Countries

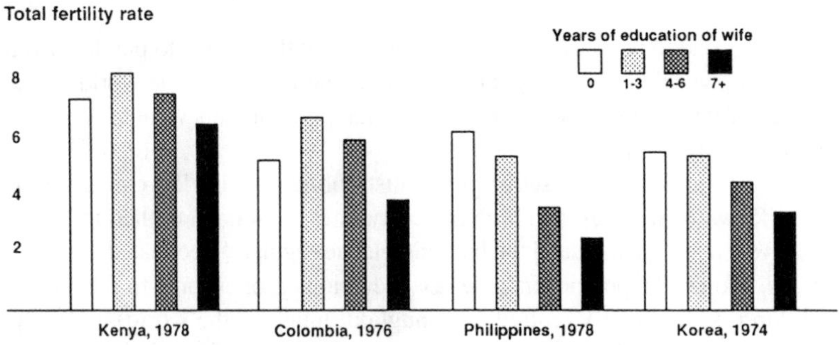

Source: Adapted from World Bank 1984:110.

of children. As income continues to rise, alternative uses of family resources open up: travel, more education, more leisure time activities, for example. These, in turn, further compete with child-rearing resources in family decision-making, putting further downward pressure on fertility.

As education, income, and health improve, there is normally a decline in infant and child mortality rates. After one or two generations of low infant and child mortality rates, people are less prone to have large numbers of children as insurance that at least some offspring will survive to maturity. Very high levels of income lead to a proliferation of private pension programs, or even government-sponsored social security programs, all of which lessen the pressure to have children to assure there is someone to take care of you in your old age.

The education of women is particularly significant in reducing fertility. Educated women are more likely to put off marriage in order to enter the work force, more likely to delay having children in order to remain in the work force, and are more likely to know about and use contraception than are uneducated women (Anon. 1988). The relationship between education and fertility for selected countries is shown in Figure 14.2.

Increased employment of women in paying jobs outside the home not only lessens their dependence on men (who sometimes have less motivation to limit family size than do women) and thus increases their tendency to make decisions favorable to the use of contraception, but tends to change women's images of themselves. As women more and more gain equality with men in the work force and elsewhere in society (gaining the right to vote, to inherit property, to own land, to participate in the choice of a husband, etc.) they tend to move away from thinking of themselves primarily as wives and mothers and toward thinking of themselves as playing a multiplicity of roles in life. And as they do this, they tend to have fewer children.

■ PUBLIC MEASURES TO ACCELERATE THE DEMOGRAPHIC TRANSITION

The various phenomena we have been discussing will continue to put downward pressure on worldwide fertility rates. But in some regions of the world the advantages of lower fertility rates are so great that governments want to accelerate the downward movement.

Most countries have a set of pronatalist public policies left over from the days when wars, famines, and high mortality rates from uncontrolled infectious diseases such as smallpox and the bubonic plague regularly decimated their populations. Pronatalist policies include tax deductions proportional to the number of children in the family (common throughout much of the world), unlimited subsidized maternity leaves sponsored by government or private industry (again common throughout the world), and child care subsidies during the first several years of a child's life (found only in certain high-income countries, e.g., Canada, France, Australia). For countries with such policies, a first task in the direction of reducing fertility is to modify these policies so that they favor small families.

☐ Economic Incentives and Disincentives

Both economic incentives to reward low fertility and economic disincentives to discourage high fertility can be used to motivate lower fertility.

One of the more imaginative incentive schemes was set up on three tea estates in India. By law, the tea estates are required to provide substantial maternity and child care benefits for their workers (tea pickers are largely women). The benefits include hospitalization and medical care for the mother and infant as well as long-term food, clothing, schooling, and medical care for the child. The tea estates set up a "savings account for family planning." Each woman employee of childbearing age is offered a savings account, the proceeds of which are available to her on retirement, and into which the firm will pay the equivalent of one day's wages for each month that she is not pregnant. If a woman becomes pregnant, the company suspends payments for a year. For third and higher-order pregnancies, the company not only suspends payment for a year, but also reclaims part of its past payments into her account in order to help pay for its legally mandated maternal and child care expenses. Women thus get a choice: maternity and child care benefits for more children, or a better retirement program. Many women are opting for fewer children and more retirement benefits (Brown 1974: 169; World Bank 1984: 126).

Economic incentives for lower fertility are attractive, but they have the disadvantage of being expensive. In Bangladesh a program was proposed that would provide a 12-year bond with a maturity value of around $350 for individuals of childbearing age who had only two or three children and who underwent sterilization. Attached to the proposal was a scheme whereby couples who signed certificates to delay their first birth for three years after marriage, or who delayed their second and third births for at least five years, would be given $20 on presentation of their certificates after the agreed time, provided they had kept their pledge. It was estimated that to cover the entire population with both schemes would require about 10 percent of the annual government budget (World Bank 1984: 126).

Not only are incentive payments for low fertility expensive, but they involve a certain amount of waste of public resources, as people who would have had fewer children despite the program go ahead and claim its benefits.

While economic incentives involve payments provided to delay or limit childbearing, economic disincentives usually involve the withholding of social benefits from those couples who have more than some targeted number of children.

In the early 1980s a series of economic disincentives to large families was in use in Singapore. The system (which was dropped subsequent to a decline in birth rates) included incentives to have two children but disincentives for more than two. The system was summarized by a Draper Fund report (Salaff & Wong 1983: 16) as follows:

- Paid maternity leave for the first two children, but not for third and subsequent children
- Preference in the choice of primary school given only to the first two children, with highest preference to the two children of a parent who has undergone sterilization before age 40
- Removal of the large-family priority in the allocation of subsidized housing; only families with three or fewer children are allowed to rent rooms in public housing units
- Escalating delivery fees in public hospitals for higher-order births, as well as fees for prenatal care (fees are remitted if sterilization follows delivery)
- Full tax relief only for the first two children, and none for fourth or subsequent children

During this same time period a somewhat more Draconian set of rewards and punishments, using Glory Certificates to promote the one-child family, was in place in China (see Box 14.1).

☐ Moral Suasion and Regulations

The average age at marriage for women in Bangladesh is 16. Half the women in South Asia and sub-Saharan Africa are or have been married by the time they are 19. The younger a woman is when she marries, the longer she is exposed to the risk of conception. So, to reduce fertility it seems reasonable to try to persuade people to postpone the age of marriage. Minimum marriageable age legislation is commonly used to attempt to encourage support for later marriage. Of those countries that have tried it, China seems to have been most successful. In

1980 the government of China raised the legal minimum age at marriage to 20 for women and 22 for men.

Box 14.1 The Chinese Glory Certificate System
Lynn Landman

To stimulate acceptance of the one-child family, the Chinese have instituted a system of incentives. Those who contract to limit their families to one child receive "Glory Certificates." Such couples are widely publicized and held up as models for their countrymen, as are the rewards they earn. In general, these may include free and priority medical care for the child; priority admission to nurseries, kindergartens, and primary schools; allotment of larger housing accommodations; bonuses for city workers and increased work points, as well as large private plots and larger housing, for peasants. All these benefits remain in effect until the child reaches 14.

If holders of "Glory Certificates" renege on their commitment, they must return all the benefits and, in addition, their annual income may be reduced by 5 to 15 percent for varying lengths of time. Those who already have two children and go on to have a third must pay all the expenses associated with childbearing, and will not be entitled to paid maternity leave. Salaries are reduced and the usual subsidized grain allotment is not provided for the third child, obliging parents to purchase it on the open market at higher prices. Job promotions may be withheld for a time and mothers sometimes are fired from their jobs.

In a country where per capita annual income is only about $235, where housing is in short supply and schooling and jobs are not guaranteed, these incentives and disincentives may be presumed to carry considerable clout.

Note: The 1989 World Population Data Sheet of the Population Reference Bureau gives the total fertility rate for China as 2.4. While this is remarkably low for a Third World country, it is more than double China's target total fertility rate of one.

Source: Landman 1983:9.

India has long carried on a vigorous advertising campaign to promote the small family, with government-sponsored advertisements appearing on billboards, buses, at movie theaters, in magazines and newspapers, and on radio and television. (India's total fertility rate in 1986 was 4.4.)

Some countries have tried intense community pressure on couples of childbearing age to limit their family size. Examples of such efforts in Indonesia and China are described briefly in Box 14.2.

☐ Subsidizing Family-Planning Services

Use of contraceptives among married women of childbearing age varies widely in the Third World, from less than 10 percent in sub-Saharan Africa to around 40 percent in Latin America to as high as 70 percent or more in China and Singapore (World Bank 1984: 128). Controlled experiments conducted in Mexico,

Box 14.2 Community Pressures to Lower Fertility
Rodolfo A. Bulatao

Pressures can be exerted by the community, or by major sections of it, to promote lowered fertility. Two cases will illustrate group pressures: *banjars* in Bali
and production teams in China.

Banjars—traditional units of local self-government, which serve as centers
for mutual aid and cooperative work—consist of all the male household heads in
a hamlet or subvillage. The form is centuries old. The traditional head of a banjar
is democratically elected but has no official standing. Instead, the banjar also has
a second, official head, who may be appointed and may have charge of more
than one banjar (Hull 1978).

Banjar meetings may be held every month (or 35 days), usually with perfect attendance (there is a system of fines for absence or lateness) and typically
discuss development of the community and religious affairs (Astawa 1979).

Since 1974 these meetings have also included discussion of the family-
planning status of each family. Each member is asked what he and his wife are
doing about family planning. A register is kept, and a color-coded map of the
community indicating eligible couples and their contraceptive status is promi-
nently displayed in the banjar hall (Meier 1979).

The decline in marital fertility in Bali of about 30 percent in less than a
decade has been dramatic enough to be labeled a "demographic miracle" (Hull
et al. 1977). How much of the change has been due to the community pressures
exerted through the 3,700 banjars is a difficult and probably unanswerable question. Other elements of the Balinese situation, such as acute pressures on the
land, the penetration of modern influences (through such means as consumer
goods, communication, and transportation systems, Western-style schooling and
tourism), and cultural factors like the relative independence of young couples—
which may facilitate contraceptive decisions—may encourage the decline in fertility. Furthermore, the effective logistical system of the family-planning program and creative uses of native art forms to communicate family-planning
messages, and a stable, supportive government, may be influential.

Production teams in China, which are usually the effective unit in rural areas for production and income sharing, consist of 30 to 40 households in a small
village, within which kinship ties may be strong. Production teams assume important responsibility for the fertility of their members. As part of the national
wan xi shao campaign (named for the reproductive norms of later marriage,
longer birth spacing, and fewer births), the production teams were responsible
for deciding which couples could have births, in line with the reproductive
norms and with team quotas set from above (Chen & Kols 1982). The team
birth-planning leadership group (the leaders all being local residents) might call
all eligible couples to a meeting, at which their individual birth plans could be
scrutinized and allocations made. Under the one-child campaign, which replaced
the wan xi shao campaign in 1979, community birth planning still takes place,
although allocation of birth quotas follows different norms. As couples become
familiar with the system, the time-consuming meeting to adjust birth plans may
be dispensed with, and the leaders may simply notify couples of their decisions.
Adherence is in theory voluntary, resting on persuasion and education. Such elements as adult study groups and visits from birth-planning delegations maintain
the peer pressure (Chen 1981).

(continued on next page)

> **Box 14.2 continued**
> As with the Balinese banjars, it is not possible to determine the specific im-
> pact of the social pressures exerted through production teams, which are only
> one element in the Chinese population program.
>
> For greater detail on local control of fertility see Bulatao 1984a.

India, Bangladesh, Korea, and the Philippines have all demonstrated that the
provision of family-planning advice, technology, and materials significantly reduces fertility.

In a 31-country study, Bongaarts (1982) looked at determinants of fertility
decline as it proceeds from rates well above six to rates close to two. The difference in total fertility was almost five children. He found that, in the countries
studied, higher age at marriage reduced total fertility by 1.4 children. Increased
use of contraception reduced fertility by 4.5 children. More induced abortion accounted for a reduction of 0.5 children, for a total reduction of 6.4 children. Re-

**Table 14.1 Accounting for Fertility Decline in Selected Third World
Countries**

Selected Countries and Years	Total Fertility Rate Initial	Total Fertility Rate Final	Total Fertility Rate Differ- ence	Higher Age at Marriage	Reduced Breast- Feeding	More Use of Contra- ception	More Induced Abortion	All Other Factors
India (1972-78)	5.6	5.2	.5	41	-58	114	--	3
Indonesia (1970-80)	5.5	4.6	.9	41	-77	134	--	2
Korea (1960-70)	6.1	4.0	2.2	50	-38	53	30	4
Thailand (1968-78)	6.1	3.4	2.7	11	-17	86	16	4
Composite of 31 countries (long term)	>6	<3	5	28	-29	90	10	1

The columns under "Percentage of Reduction by Contributing Factor" are: Higher Age at Marriage, Reduced Breast-Feeding, More Use of Contraception, More Induced Abortion, All Other Factors.

Sources: Composite of 31 countries: Bongaarts 1982; all other data: Bulatao 1984b:38.

Note: -- = not available. The composite of 31 countries' data account for the decline in
total fertility typical of countries that started their fertility decline with rates above six (the
predecline phase of fertility rates) and ended rates below three (the postdecline countries). The
difference in pre- to postdecline rates among these countries amounts to almost five
children.

Table 14.2 Percentage of Married Women, Age 15-44, Who Do Not Want to Become Pregnant and Who and Use Contraception

Region, Country, and Year of Survey	Percentage Who Do Not Want a Birth During the Next Year	Percentage Who Do Not Want Any More Births	Percentage Who Use a Modern Contraceptive Method
Africa			
Benin 1981-82	70*	8	1
Botswana 1984	76	31	19
Cameroon 1978	--	--	1
Ghana 1979-80	65*	11	6
Ivory Coast 1980-81	41*	4	1
Kenya 1984	77*	35	10
Lesotho 1977	--	14	3
Mauritania 1981	54*	14	0
Nigeria 1981-82	33*	4	1
Senegal (rural) 1982	78	7	0
Sudan (north) 1978-79	--	18	4
Zimbabwe 1984	76	22	28
Near East			
Egypt 1980	74*	53	23
Jordan 1983	86	42	21
Morocco 1983-84	--	41	22
Syria 1978	--	36	15
Tunisia 1983	86	67	35
Yemen, Arab Republic 1979	27*	19	1
Asia			
Bangladesh 1979-80	71*	48	9
Fiji 1974	84*	51	36
Java and Bali 1976	--	42	24
Republic of Korea 1979	81*	76	43
Malaysia 1974	90*	43	26
Nepal 1981	55	42	7
Pakistan 1975	--	42	4
Philippines 1978	--	58	17
Sri Lanka 1982	91	65	32
Thailand 1981	89	66	56
Latin America and Caribbean			
Barbados 1980-81	--	52	45
Bolivia 1983	89	74	11
Brazil (northeast) 1980	90	58	29
Brazil (south) 1981	87	49	52
Colombia 1980	84	69	43
Costa Rica 1981	84	53	57
Dominican Republic 1983	88	72	43
Ecuador 1979	91	59	27
El Salvador 1978	93	53	32

Table 14.2 *(continued)*

Region, Country, and Year of Survey	Percentage Who Do Not Want a Birth During the Next Year	Percentage Who Do Not Want Any More Births	Percentage Who Use a Modern Contraceptive Method
Guatemala 1983	79	40	21
Guyana 1975	--	62	32
Haiti 1983	78	59	4
Honduras 1981	92	76	24
Jamaica 1983	97	54	49
Mexico 1979	88	65	34
Panama 1979-80	90	63	57
Paraguay 1979	84*	31	25
Peru 1981	92*	74	18
Trinidad and Tobago 1977	--	56	49
Venezuela 1977	--	57	38

Source: Galway et al. 1987:43.

Note: Percentages not wanting a birth are adjusted to exclude the percentage undecided or not stated. Modern methods of contraception include voluntary sterilization, oral contraceptives, intrauterine devices (IUDs), condoms, injectables, and vaginal methods (spermicides, diaphragms, and caps).

*Only fecund married women are included.

duced breast-feeding, of course, works the other way around, and accounted for an increase in fertility of about 1.5 children. On the bottom line of Table 14.1, these data are expressed as percentage contribution to reduction in fertility decline. Data for selected individual countries are also shown in Table 14.1.

In most Third World countries there is a substantial gap between the number of women who would like to limit their fertility and their access to modern contraceptive methods (Table 14.2). In the conclusion to a major National Research Council survey of how specific program elements contribute to the effectiveness of Third World family-planning programs, Simmons and Lapham (1987) note that family-planning programs increase the availability of contraception and the level of contraceptive use and that they lower fertility, but that their impact varies with programmatic and environmental factors. For instance, the availability of multiple public and private channels for the delivery of services increases the effectiveness of national programs. A wide variety of choice of methods is more effective than a narrow choice, since diverse groups of clients have different needs. Good leadership and positive political support also increase the effectiveness of such programs.

■ THE COMPLEMENTARITY OF FERTILITY REDUCTION POLICIES

Fertility reduction policies often complement each other. For instance, providing subsidized family-planning services not only makes the technology available for reducing fertility but sends a message to the community that government supports the idea of fertility regulation.

However, fertility reduction policies are often also complementary with other programs that help to reduce undernutrition. For instance, successful promotion of prolonged breast-feeding not only reduces fertility but improves childhood nutrition and health. Persuading couples to marry later in life not only reduces fertility but, as women remain in the work force longer as a result, raises per capita income, improving nutrition. Increasing the educational level of women not only decreases fertility but increases their future productivity and undoubtedly improves the quality of the child care they deliver.

☐ 15

Policies Aimed at Reducing Inequalities and Raising the Income of the Poor

The advent of high-yielding varieties, increased reliance on chemical pesticides and fertilizers, control over irrigation water, and the multitude of ways in which urban-dominated agricultural policy can countermand any nominal gains from better land-use opportunities, all combine to render—in many instances—land ownership quite irrelevant. There are so many factors that impinge upon the economic environment of a newly landed peasant that the legal and/or economic relations of that person to the land resource may be quite beside the point. Land cannot be considered important in either a policy or a political context when it is often so irrelevant in the ultimate reckoning of a peasant's economic position.

—Bromley 1981: 399

In Chapter 8 I argued that inequality of income, in and of itself, contributes to undernutrition. Programs that reduce the income gap (and therefore reduce the size of the Reutlinger triangles) will reduce the tendency of the rich to bid food away from the poor, and thus improve the nutrition of both groups.

In this chapter we examine a set of policies and programs that are commonly advocated for reducing income inequality, either by increasing the income of the poor or by transferring income or wealth from the rich to the poor.

One technique for transferring income from the rich to the poor, food-linked income transfer programs, will be left for discussion in the next chapter, when we examine policies aimed at lowering the price of food. Food-linked income transfer programs include famine relief programs, food consumption subsidies, and selling in the Third World at below-market prices, food obtained on concessional terms from the developed countries (e.g., the PL 480 Food for Peace Program). Such programs are usually intended to effectively lower the domestic price of food. It therefore seems appropriate to consider them, together with other policies aimed at lowering food prices, in a separate chapter.

■ LAND REFORM

Land reform is one of the most common ways of attempting to redistribute wealth and the income associated with it. Since 1960 virtually every country in the world has passed land reform laws (De Janvry 1981: 385). Land reform can mean many things, but typically it means at least one of the following:

1. *Redistributing the ownership of private or public land in order to change the pattern of land distribution and size of holding:* At the one extreme this might mean creating small plots from large blocks of land and allocating these small plots to the poor. At the other extreme it might mean nationalizing all agricultural land and assigning it to large, state-owned farms.

2. *Changing the rights associated with land:* For instance, tenant farmers or sharecroppers can be made owners of the land they work. Or lenders can be prohibited from taking land from smallholders for lack of payment of debt.

Land reform can mean other things, such as consolidation of individual holdings, that is, regrouping fragmented holdings into contiguous blocks of land (World Bank 1975: 20–21). In this case there is no wealth redistribution objective, but only productivity considerations. In most cases of land reform the hope is that the twin objectives of accelerated growth and increased equity can be accomplished.

□ The Hope for Land Reform

The land reform program carried out by the US military government in Japan following World War II is widely credited with helping significantly with the re-

Table 15.1 Acres of Land Owned, by Ownership Group, Bagbana Village Households, 1968 and 1981

| | Land Owned | | | |
| | 1968 | | 1981 | |
Quintile	Land Owned	Percentage of Total	Land Owned	Percentage of Total
Highest	202.6	73	192.0	76
Second	54.2	19	43.8	17
Third	19.6	7	15.6	6
Fourth	1.5	1	1.3	1
Lowest	0	0	0	0
	277.9	100	252.7	100
Gini ratio	.7142		.7388	

Source: Fishstein 1985:74.

construction of Japanese agriculture at the time. Similarly, a land reform program in Taiwan at about the same time is credited with stimulating greater productivity in Taiwanese agriculture.

Given the tendency for land distribution to be skewed in such a manner that relatively few owners control very large shares of this valuable productive resource, land reform presents an attractive tool for redistributing wealth.

In Figure 8.4 we saw the Lorenz curve for the skewed land distribution in 1968 and 1981 for the Indian village we have looked at from time to time in this book. In Table 15.1 the same data are presented in a different form. In 1981, 20 percent of the households owned 76 percent of the land. This, by the way, was after a land reform program that limited farm size to a maximum of 50 acres in India (De Janvry 1981: 386). The situation in this village is representative of much of the agriculture of the Third World, where typically landownership is concentrated and where a third of the families, more or less, typically own no land. But in places, concentration of ownership is more intense.

Before Algerian independence from the French in 1962, the good farmland in that country had become concentrated into large estates. In 1960, 6,000 French colonists owned one-third of all the agricultural land (the best land) while 2 million Algerian peasants owned the other two-thirds (the marginal land) (Aron et al. 1962). In other words, 0.3 percent of the farmers owned one-third of the land. This situation was certainly one of the most dramatic instances of a skewed landownership pattern. (The French-owned farms were nationalized in a land reform program initiated in 1962.)

Today, Latin America in general is notorious for concentration of landownership in the hands of the few. In Colombia the top 10 percent of owners control more than 80 percent of the total farmland (Stevens & Jabara 1988: 272–273). Gini coefficients for land concentration in Latin America run very high. A 1975 collection of such coefficients listed Colombia at 0.86 and Peru, the highest, at 0.95 (World Bank 1975: 26).

In Figure 15.1 land distribution in Wisconsin is compared to that in Brazil. Over half of the farmers, and over half of the farmland, in Wisconsin are on farms of between 100 and 500 acres. In Brazil, on the other hand, over three-fourths of the farmers are on holdings of less than 100 acres whereas almost half of the farmland is in holdings greater than 2,000 acres in size.

Not only is land reform attractive as a means of wealth redistribution, but it has compelling logic in terms of productivity. Remember in Chapter 9 I pointed out that production per unit of land in the Third World is typically higher on smaller farms (Figure 9.8). This suggests that dividing up large landholdings in and of itself should result in increases in productivity.

But there is another compelling productivity argument. Farmers with limited capital typically operate their farm on shares, splitting a share of the harvest (50 percent, more or less) with the landlord. A share tenant who receives only half of the returns from his last hour of labor on the farm is presumably less motivated to work long hours than would an owner. Since tenant farmers normally

Figure 15.1 Agrarian Ownership Structure in Wisconsin and Brazil, 1980

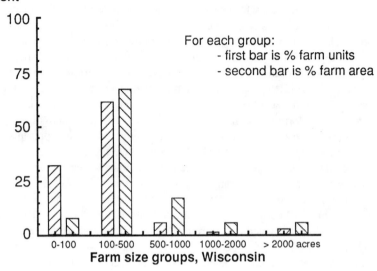

Percent

For each group:
- first bar is % farm units
- second bar is % farm area

Farm size groups, Wisconsin

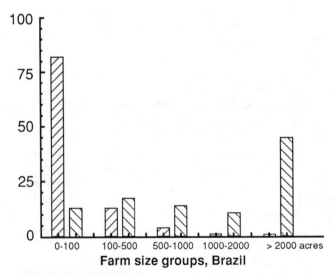

Percent

Farm size groups, Brazil

Source: Adapted from Carter 1989:1.

operate on a short-term lease, often on a year-to-year basis, the insecurity of tenure discourages them from spending on land-associated capital investments like fences, irrigation, or fruit trees (Herring 1983: 253). It is because of these issues that the argument is usually made for transferring landownership from the landlord to the tiller.

☐ The Disillusionment About Land Reform

Despite the compelling nature of the equity and productivity arguments for land reform, there is a growing disillusionment with the idea. The history of the twentieth century is replete with instances where land reform failed to live up to its promise. As of this writing two of the greatest land reform experiments in world history, those of the USSR and China, are being seriously questioned from within and are apparently in the process of being restructured.

But it is not only the grand socialist experiments with collectivized agriculture that have experienced major disappointments. Various other types of reform have produced unforeseen consequences, some of which made the supposed beneficiaries worse off that they might have been without the reform. A few examples will illustrate some of the common difficulties.

One of the most pressing goals of the 1962 Algerian land reform was to provide employment for as many workers as possible. Yet it did not take the self-management committees on the newly nationalized large estates long to realize that fewer workers on their farm meant more returns per worker, and an early study of the situation showed employment on the farms actually decreasing after reform (Foster & Steiner 1964). A later study of the ongoing land reform process in Algeria (Pfeifer 1985: 81) concluded that the reform "promoted, rather than curtailed, the class differentiation of agricultural producers into successful commercial farmers and propertyless wage workers." Pfeifer goes on to observe rather caustically that "in this, the 'agrarian revolution' in Algeria in the 1970s seems to have completed the historic task begun by the French intruders in 1830."

An agrarian reform law passed in Peru in 1969 was intended to do something about the skewed landownership in that country. An important principle of the reform legislation was "land to the tiller." By late 1978 ownership of 8.6 million hectares had been transferred, and some 370,000 families had benefited from the reform (Alberts 1983). But the benefits went largely to those already in the richer strata in Peru. Reforms carried out on the sugar estates, for instance, mainly benefited the permanent workers. The families living outside the sugar plantations received no benefits at all. In a detailed study of the reform, Alberts (1983: 47, 49, 141–142, 175, 226) concluded that "the poor majority of Peruvian peasants has only received land, credit and technical assistance to a minor extent." According to Alberts, "the agrarian reform did not accomplish a radical and lasting improvement in the degree of equity within the agricultural sector. The economic policies implemented by the military government were not conducive to agricultural growth nor did they accomplish anything toward reducing the urban-rural income gap."

In the early 1950s Burma undertook an economic development program that included a land reform component designed to provide land to the tiller. All agricultural landholdings in excess of 50 acres were subject to confiscation, and those up to 50 acres in size were also subject to confiscation unless the entire 50 acres were worked by the owner and his family. In order to retain their lands, absentee owners began working the land themselves, forcing their former tenant farmers off the land and making landless laborers of them. The former tenants usually stayed on as laborers, but they no longer enjoyed some of the benefits that had been theirs as tenants (Walinsky 1962: 137, 294).

This same Burmese economic development program undertook to protect farmers from losing their land to banks and moneylenders when they defaulted on their loans by making it illegal to foreclose on mortgages on agricultural land. This not only denied landowners the opportunity to use their land as collateral to raise capital for farm investments, but the diminished security for the lender meant that the farmer-borrower had to pay higher interest rates for his money. Thus the protection afforded the cultivator came at a high cost (Walinsky 1962: 504–505).

In 1972 a land reform law in the Philippines gave permanent tenure rights to those who had sharecropped a piece of land for three or more years. Sharecropping had traditionally been a way for the young landless worker to get started in farming, but after passage of this law it became next to impossible for a landless worker to gain access to land through sharecropping. Landowners were too worried about becoming disenfranchised again.

The disillusionment with land reform comes not only from the multiplicity of disappointments in real-world attempts to implement it, but from a growing realization that who owns a piece of land is only one, and sometimes only a minor one, of the variables that affect the productivity of the workers and of the land they work. After all, some form of tenant farming (renting, sharerenting, sharecropping) in the highly productive US corn belt is, in places, the predominant pattern. As was noted by Bromley (1981) availability of low-cost purchased inputs, attractive farm-gate prices for farm produce, appropriate technical assistance, paved farm-to-market roads, and so on often turn out to be more important in determining farm productivity than who owns the land.

With so many botched cases of land reform on the record, people are asking whether land reform can even be expected to do a creditable job of redistribution. De Janvry (1981: 389) makes this observation: "With agriculture well advanced on the road to modernization . . . any drastic land redistribution is likely to nullify past technological achievements and imply shortfalls in production, at least in the short run. Where the population is increasingly landless and urbanized, the social cost of higher food prices [because of the inefficiencies resulting from land reform] may be more widespread than the welfare gains of land redistribution."

Critics of land reform ask if the inequality in the ownership of land is any greater than the inequality in the ownership of oil wells, or ships, or factories, or radio stations, or automobile plants. And if concentration in these sources of wealth turns out to be greater than that in land, they ask, why should these sorts of concentration not be shared out among the people along with the land?

An important problem associated with land reform, or even the threat of land reform, is the chilling effect it may have on investment in agriculture relative to investment in other productive activities. Landowners who fear that land reform may be in the offing are understandably hesitant to invest heavily in productive improvements for their farms. In this view, land reform is part of a number of antiagricultural policies collectively referred to as urban bias, about which I will have more to say in the next chapter.

■ PROGRESSIVE TAXATION

Taxes that take a greater percentage of income or wealth from the rich than they do from the poor are called progressive. Progressive taxation is one way of transferring income or wealth from the rich to the poor. In developed countries the income tax is usually designed to be progressive, and the same features can be incorporated into the tax structure of the Third World, as they often are.

Taxes that take a greater percentage of income or wealth from the poor than they do from the rich are called regressive. Sales taxes have a reputation for being regressive. In the developed world the poor spend a greater proportion of their income; in contrast to the rich, who save a greater proportion of theirs. However, in the Third World the poor are not generally as well integrated into the market economy as are the rich. The poor are much more likely to barter and exchange goods and services and to raise some of their own food. All these activities escape the sales tax. So in the Third World a sales tax is generally progressive and can therefore be recommended as another method of reducing income disparity.

Income and sales taxes are attractive alternatives to land reform because they transfer income from the rich to the poor across all sectors of society. We must bear in mind, however, that the method of spending the money in the government tax till can have distributive effects just as surely as does the method of collecting it. Spending public money on programs to increase agricultural production can do much to improve the nutritional status of the poor through the impact of such expenditures on lowering the price of food and increasing employment (see Chapter 18). On the other hand, a mere transfer of purchasing power from the rich to the poor may prove less effective as a way of improving the nutrition of the poor. For example:

> To take a simple case within a developing country, say India. If one rupee of purchasing power is taken away from a person in the top 5% of the income

distribution, that will cause a reduction, in constant prices, of 0.03 rupee in foodgrain consumption. That same rupee provided to a person in the bottom 20% of the income distribution will provide increased demand for 0.58 rupee of food grains. The one-to-one equality of financial transfers is matched by a 19-to-one inequality in the material transfers. Thus, a marginal redistribution of income is profoundly inflationary in driving up food prices. In this case, what the left hand of society gives to the poor, the right hand of the market takes away (Mellor 1988: 1003).

Taxing land according to use-value is another attractive alternative to land reform. Through a properly done land-use survey, farmland can be classified according to its value associated with its use potential. Often Third World land taxes on good farming land are so low that large landholders can afford to keep their holdings while farming them inefficiently. By raising taxes and keeping them proportionate to land use-value, farmers who are making poor or inefficient use of their land will be forced to sell out to those who would farm the land better. The beauty of this system is that it readjusts resource use by weeding out the bad farmers without forcing out the good farmers who may be doing a fine job for society.

■ SUBSIDIES FOR MECHANIZATION

When citizens of high-income, industrialized nations drive through their countryside they expect to see farmers sitting on big tractors pulling complex machinery in large fields. It is a short (if erroneous) step from there to equating large farms and agricultural mechanization inevitably with economic efficiency, and they then wonder why Third World farmers are still using animal-powered equipment, or worse yet, hand tools, for their farming operations. Why are peasant farmers, they wonder, seemingly condemned to a life of drudgery? Why not accelerate the rate of agricultural mechanization by subsidizing it? Would not this improve the lot of the poor in the Third World?

The problem that faces Third World agricultural policymakers is not so much whether to mechanize, but rather how to do so in a way that advances a country's development objectives. Third World agricultural economies are in a very different state than those of the developed world. In contrast with the developed world, the Third World finds itself with abundant supplies of labor but with scarce capital.

In a high-wage nation where the relative cost of capital is low, it makes sense to farm with a very limited supply of labor and an abundant use of capital. But in a Third World economy, finding ways to stretch the limited supplies of capital among millions of underemployed laborers is a salient problem. The risk that mechanization will displace labor warrants very careful consideration in a labor-surplus economy.

☐ Methods of Subsidy

Unfortunately most developing countries pursue a mix of policies that tend to accelerate mechanization beyond the pace that is appropriate for their labor force (Binswanger, Donovan et al. 1987: 1). They do this in a variety of ways.

Often there is preferential tariff treatment for machinery, and especially low tariffs for agricultural machinery. Farmers are sometimes given a tax shelter through tax deductions for farm machinery set at levels greater than the cost of the machinery. Brazil, for instance, has allowed a deduction for farm machinery of six times the value of the machine in the first year of operation. Other farm investments are treated less favorably, and labor costs enjoy no preferential tax treatment at all (World Bank 1986: 97).

Countries often set the official exchange rate for their domestic currency higher than the market value. The market value for a rupee in India, for example, might be 10 (US) cents, but the Indian government might declare a rupee to be worth more, say 15 cents. The upshot of this artificially inflated exchange rate is that, if you can get dollars from the government at the official rate, you can buy goods, like machinery or food, from abroad at bargain prices. When this happens, there is immediately competition for these cheap dollars, and government has to ration them among competing uses. Commonly agricultural machinery imports get a substantial allocation. Cheap foreign currency plus low tariffs make for a substantial subsidy to imported machinery.

Subsidized credit makes capital cheaper than it otherwise would be and is another way that Third World governments often foster the acceleration of machinery use.

☐ Effects of Subsidy

The benefits of machinery subsidies typically go to the large farms. Thus they provide the wealthy farmers with a competitive advantage relative to their poorer neighbors.

If mechanization increases production, resulting lower prices will be shared by all, rich and poor alike. In some circumstances increased mechanization does result in production increases: Mechanization may make possible more timely preparation of land for planting and thus increases the growing season and the resulting harvest; mechanization may speed postharvest operations and reduce losses of grain through shattering or spoilage; and in agricultural regions with good rainfall or good irrigation systems tractorization can break labor bottlenecks that may occur at the time of harvest and before the next planting, resulting in more crops per year than would otherwise be the case (Stevens & Jabara 1988: 236–237).

But mechanization does not necessarily increase yields. Binswanger (1978: 73), in a careful review of the studies of impact of tractorization on yields in

South Asia, found that the surveys failed "to provide evidence that tractors are responsible for substantial increases in intensity, yields, timeliness, and gross returns on farms in India, Pakistan, and Nepal." It seems that, by and large, an acre of land tilled with hand or animal power does not yield less than an acre of land tilled by a tractor (Campbell 1984: 47). When mechanization does not increase output, it usually merely redistributes income, typically to the disadvantage of the poor, as machinery is substituted for, and collects the earnings that formerly went to, them (see Box 15.1).

Box 15.1 Who Gains from Mechanization?
Robert W. Herdt

In the absence of increased output, machinery adoption may shift earnings from one group to another. That is, a machine which replaces labor will receive the wage formerly paid to the laborers. In such an event, the machine owner receives the earnings formerly paid to laborers.

There is an inherent difference in the ownership pattern of capital and labor. In the absence of slavery, labor can only be owned at a rate of 1 unit per person, or at most 5 to 10 units per household. On the other hand, ownership of capital can be and, in most economies, is concentrated in the hands of relatively few, usually through inheritance, political power, or business acumen. Concentrated capital ownership means that income earned by capital is also concentrated.

The introduction of machinery has redistributing effects which, when it also leads to increased output, will add to the welfare of low income consumers and technology adopters. When machinery has no output effect, it simply redistributes income.

Source: Extracted from Herdt 1983:12.

From the point of view of improving Third World nutrition, there is no justification for a machinery subsidy. When machinery is profitable, farmers will buy it and society will benefit from it. If the machinery is available only in fairly large units, small farmers can benefit from using rental machinery.

Subsidizing agricultural mechanization denies funding for alternative investments that are at least as productive as the machinery and that do not reduce labor demand as much as the subsidized machinery (Binswanger, Donovan et al. 1987: 1).

Stevens and Jabara (1988: 272–273) list four undesirable effects from premature acceleration of agricultural mechanization resulting from subsidies: (1) reduced employment; (2) greater income disparities; (3) attempts by those with tractors and other machines to increase farm size; and (4) increased incentives to inventors and manufacturers to develop and produce even more labor-saving agricultural machinery.

■ CREDIT SUBSIDIES

☐ Rationale for Subsidizing Credit

To the extent that credit can remove existing financial constraints, it can accelerate the adoption of new technology. Third World governments commonly feel that a scarcity of credit is constraining the development of their low-income farm sector and see subsidized credit as a way of transferring income to the poor, who will then benefit by becoming more productive through the use of this cheap credit. Furthermore, these same governments often engage in policies that result in farm-gate prices below what the market would normally pay, and look at subsidized credit, with its below-market interest rates, as a way of compensating low-income farmers for their losses from these pricing policies (Adams et al. 1984).

Billions of dollars have been spent on subsidized credit programs in the Third World. These programs have arisen because of a number of assumptions about peasant farmers as savers and borrowers and about the credit sources that are commonly available to them. For instance, it is commonly assumed that, despite their ability to repay a loan, small farmers have difficulty obtaining loans because of a lack of collateral or the feeling among rural lenders that small farmers present too great a risk to bother with.

Dale Adams and others, having reviewed these assumptions, concluded that many of them are erroneous (see Box 15.2). To take only one example, the assumption about collateral and small farmers presenting too great a risk: an innovative bank in Bangladesh has had reasonable success with loans to poor families who put up no other collateral than joining and meeting regularly with a support group that promises to see to it that its members do, in fact, pay back their loans (Hossain 1988: 25–26).

As we will see below, subsidized credit is not an effective instrument for transferring income to the poor. Furthermore, subsidized credit turns out to have harmful side effects on financial institutions and other segments of the economy, particularly the poor.

☐ Methods of Providing Cheap Credit

There are two common ways that governments provide low-interest loans. One is directly through a government bank or quasi–government bank that simply loans out the money to preferred borrowers at below-market interest rates. For instance, in Jamaica during the 1970s the parastatal development bank supplied loans at less than half of the commercial bank rate.

The other common way of providing low-interest loans is for the government to require commercial banks to supply a given amount of money to preferred borrowers at below-market rates. In Nigeria, for example, banks must devote 8 percent of their loans to the agricultural sector at approximately half the going commercial interest rate (Bale 1985: 17).

Box 15.2 Common Assumptions about Lenders and Borrowers

Dale Adams and Douglas Graham

Common assumptions about saver-borrower behavior are that the rural poor cannot save and therefore will not respond to incentives or opportunities to save, that most farmers need cheap loans and supervision before they will adopt new technologies and make major farm investments, and that loans in kind are used in the form granted.

Common assumptions about lender behavior are that most informal lenders are exploitative and charge borrowers rates of interest that result in large monopoly profits, that the rural poor do not receive formal loans because formal lenders are overly risk-averse, that nationalized lenders can be forced to ignore their own profits and losses to serve risky customers and the rural poor, and that all formal lenders can be induced to follow government regulations in allocating financial services.

At a national level it is commonly assumed that cheap credit is an efficient way of offsetting production disincentives caused by low farm product prices or high farm input prices, that loan quotas established in the capital city are efficient ways of allocating loans in the countryside, that loans should be a part of a package of inputs, that only production loans should be made, and that rural financial market vitality is not related to projects and policies.

Research is showing that many of these assumptions are either unsubstantiated, weak, or incorrect.

Source: Extracted from Adams and Graham 1981.

Beginning in 1965 in Brazil, the law required commercial banks to lend at least 50 percent of their demand deposits to farmers at 17 percent interest per year. At that time the annual inflation rate was ranging from 20 to 40 percent per year so these loans were very profitable for the borrowers. In 1971 the mandated rural interest rate was lowered to 15 percent, even though high rates of inflation continued (Sicat 1983: 381).

☐ Problems Associated with Subsidized Credit

When the credit subsidy is paid for directly by government, the costs can run very high, so high that governments often use deficit financing to pay for the programs. The deficit financing, in turn, leads to inflation, which discourages saving, the basis of capital formation. The question must be asked if the resources devoted to providing cheap credit might better be used in other government programs—more agricultural research, better rural roads, or improved educational services.

When the credit program is paid for implicitly, as happens when you force commercial credit institutions to give low-interest loans to priority borrowers, the costs of this hidden subsidy must be borne by the less preferred borrowers.

They get less credit or pay higher interest rates for their loans, both of which are a constraint on development.

Sometimes governments attempt to limit the possibility that someone will make a profit by obtaining cheap credit and then depositing the money right back in the bank at the (higher) commercial rate by putting a ceiling on the commercial interest rate. Forcing down the interest rate in this way lessens the rewards from saving, discouraging some people from saving and motivating others to send their savings (and thus their capital) out of the country where they can get a better return.

From the point of view of income distribution, the worst aspect of subsidized credit is that it discriminates against the poor. The subsidized credit almost always goes to those in the community who are better prepared to receive it. In rural areas this means the rural elite, those well connected politically. Seldom does it go to the poorest of the poor.

The impact of a credit subsidy is thus regressive. Loans are seldom all the same size, and the size of the subsidy is directly proportional to the size of the loan. The larger farmers get larger loans and more subsidy. Medium and small farmers get proportionally smaller subsidies. The smallest farmers and landless laborers get no subsidy at all (González-Vega 1983: 371).

☐ An Alternative to Subsidized Credit

There is evidence to show that the availability of credit in the countryside can be greatly expanded merely by rigging the system so as to encourage rural financial markets to serve as intermediaries between savers and borrowers. This seems to be the appropriate alternative to subsidized credit.

Contrary to the commonly held assumption, Third World low-income farmers do save. In a review of the available data on savings among rural households in Taiwan, Japan, South Korea, Malaysia, and India, Dale Adams found positive average propensities to save to be the norm. (The average propensity to save is the percentage of income that is not spent for consumption or taxes.) Furthermore, rural households' savings are responsive to changes in the real interest rate. (The real interest rate is the difference between the nominal interest rate and the inflation rate.) In 1965 South Korea allowed the interest rate paid on time deposits and applied to loans to almost double. This resulted in real interest rates of over 8 percent per year. During the ensuing four years, total time and savings deposits in all banks increased fourteenfold. The number of savings accounts also increased sharply during this period (Adams 1983: 401–405). The average propensity to save among Korean farm households steadily increased during the 10 years following the credit reform (Table 15.2). Interestingly, the rate of increase in propensity to save was greatest among those farm households with the smallest landholdings.

Mere convenience can be a factor in attracting rural savings. In India, when banks were encouraged to open up rural branches for the primary purpose of

Table 15.2 Average Propensity to Save, South Korean Farm Households, by Farm Size, 1962-1974

Farm Size (in Cheongboa)	1962	1965	1966	1968	1970	1972	1974
0.5 or less	0.05	-0.05	0.01	0.06	0.03	0.02	0.22
0.5-1.0	0.12	0.01	0.09	0.11	0.13	0.21	0.29
1.0-1.5	0.16	0.06	0.10	0.20	0.16	0.34	0.35
1.5-2.0	0.15	0.12	0.13	0.23	0.26	0.30	0.43
2.0 or more	0.22	0.13	0.23	0.24	0.19	0.30	0.40
Average all households	0.15	0.04	0.11	0.16	0.15	0.24	0.33
Total number of households	1,163	1,172	1,180	1,181	1,180	1,182	2,515

Source: Adams 1983:404.

Note: One cheongbo equals 0.992 hectares or 2.45 acres. In this table average propensity to save was calculated as follows: (net income after taxes - consumption)/net income after taxes.

disbursing agricultural loans, but at the same time offered a positive real interest rate on deposits, the response was so substantial that some authorities were concerned about the drain of funds from rural areas (World Bank 1986: 101).

When rural people are offered convenient, secure savings institutions providing financially attractive real rates of return on savings, they seem to flock to make deposits. This increases the supply of lendable funds, eventually reducing the cost of credit through market mechanisms. Abundant credit at reasonable commercial rates eliminates the need for the capital rationing associated with subsidized credit, with its tendency to favor rural elites, and makes credit more readily available to the rural poor.

■ SUBSIDIZING FARM-TO-MARKET ROADS

The construction and maintenance of the roads and highways of a nation is almost always the responsibility of the government. While improving the rural transportation network is not usually the first thing that policymakers think of when wondering about how to reduce income inequalities, it turns out to be one of the better policies for this purpose.

Building a new road into a region that formerly was reached only by human or animal transport can have an important impact on that region's economy. Because it dramatically reduces the cost of transporting farm products out of the region, it raises the farm-gate price of what farmers sell to country marketing agents who buy and transport food to the city. And because it simultaneously reduces the cost of transporting materials into the region, it reduces the cost of purchased farm inputs such as fertilizer. Higher farm-gate prices and lower input costs increase farm income, stimulate greater farm production, increase the demand for farm labor, and raise local wage rates.

In a study of the impact of new roads on 46 Philippine rural communities, Santos-Villanueva (1966) found a decrease in transportation costs of from 17 to 60 percent per kilometer and a substantial increase in the amount of agricultural products sold off the farm (see Table 15.3).

In a study of 16 villages in rural Bangladesh it was found that villages with a good infrastructure, including good all-weather, hard-surfaced roads, used 92 percent more fertilizer per hectare than villages with poor infrastructure. They used 4 percent more labor per hectare, and they paid their agricultural laborers 12 percent more per day than did villages with poor infrastructure (Ahmed & Hossain 1990).

Higher local wage rates reduce the pressure for out-migration. In other words, good roads help keep people home! Good roads stimulate private entrepreneurs to start bus services, often with very small vehicles ranging from large three-wheeled motorcycles to minibuses, and thus make it possible for rural people who live within reasonable commuting distances to get a job in town but continue living in their home in the country. Good roads enlarge employment opportunities outside the home neighborhood.

As roads lower the cost of transportation to and from the countryside, the annual fluctuation in the price of food is reduced. Remote communities find it cheaper to export food in good crop years and import food in poor crop years, thus reducing price swings between the bad and the good harvests. Reducing these price swings reduces the probability that low-income families will face undernutrition during the years of bad harvest.

Table 15.3 Average Increases in Volume of Sales of Selected Farm Products After the Construction of a Nearby Road from Farm to Market, Philippines

	Percentage Increase
Corn	104
Chicken	69
Swine	47
Coconuts	30
Rice	24
Bananas	12

Source: Santos-Villanueva 1966.

As a good road network reduces the cost of transporting agricultural commodities around the country, increased agricultural specialization by region can take place. For instance, perishable fruits and vegetables can be grown farther from urban markets than previously, making possible a higher-valued use of land far from market, reducing the income disparity between remote areas and the major cities.

The same sorts of advantages that accrue with new roads into a formerly remote territory apply to improvements in old roads. Putting a hard surface on a dirt road, or mending potholes on a worn-out older all-weather road, has benefits of the same nature, albeit less dramatic, as the benefits from putting in a new road.

■ MINIMUM-WAGE LAWS

It is frequently, and often emotionally, argued that minimum-wage laws are an effective way to improve the income of the poor. There is no question that, for those workers covered by minimum-wage legislation whose wages are higher than they would otherwise be, minimum-wage laws yield a higher level of living. However, effective minimum-wage legislation, as it raises wages at the bottom end of the scale, motivates entrepreneurs to substitute capital for labor. This drives labor out of the sector of the economy covered by the minimum wage and increases unemployment in the economy generally (Mincer 1976). If credit subsidies are available, the motivation to substitute capital for labor is even greater.

Minimum-wage laws are more easily enforced in urban than in rural areas. So one result of effective minimum-wage laws is an increase in the wage differential between the country and the city. In the Third World the difference in wage rates between farm and city has resulted in masses of rural population migrating to the city in search of jobs. Although the probability of an unskilled rural migrant obtaining an urban job may be small, the decision to migrate may be rational since some, in fact, do get good urban jobs (Todaro 1980). The waiting period may take months, years, or even go on for a lifetime, but if enough get jobs, then by and large for most people the wait seems worth it.

Effective minimum-wage legislation increases the ultimate reward from waiting for an urban job. It simultaneously increases the number of people in the queue, increases urban unemployment, wastes labor resources, and increases the number of family members accompanying unemployed migrants who may be subjected to undernutrition.

■ EMPLOYMENT CREATION

Unquestionably, the creation of a large number of jobs for the vast numbers of urban and rural underemployed and unemployed would do much to raise the income of the poor and reduce overall income inequalities in the Third World.

Governments do not create jobs very efficiently, but there are times when governments engage in public works projects that can employ substantial amounts of labor—roads, irrigation projects, rural electrification, to name a few.

Box 15.3 Machines Versus Labor

Under conditions of full employment, if it is cheaper to do a job using machinery than by hiring labor, there is no question but that it makes sense to use the machinery. But there are times, under conditions of widespread unemployment, when using machinery on a job may appear cheaper than hiring labor, but society would be better off using the more expensive hired labor. The following hypothetical example will illustrate the point.

The government of Kenya has decided to widen the road from Nairobi to the international airport some miles outside of town. The first step is to build up the shoulders. A local construction firm that has an inventory of trucks, bulldozers, and backhoes has bid 30,000 Kenya shillings to do the job. A labor contractor has also bid for the job and says he can do it for Sh 50,000 using 100 presently unemployed laborers at a cost of about Sh 500 per laborer.

If they do not get the job, the unemployed laborers actually will be producing something for society. They will spend their time producing handicrafts at home and raising vegetables in their back yards and will make some Sh 6,000 on these activities. These activities are the opportunity costs of hiring the laborers; the opportunity to make Sh 6,000 is lost if they go to work on the road.

But if the workers go to work on the road they will have other costs associated with employment. They will spend some Sh 4,000 on transportation to and from the job and on the extra food they will have to consume because they are engaged in heavy construction work. These are the associated costs of employment.

The true cost to society of hiring the earth-moving equipment is the Sh 30,000 bid by the machinery contractor. This money is needed to maintain the equipment, hire skilled workmen to operate it, and amortize the foreign exchange costs of purchasing it. If the machinery contractor does not win the bid, he will use his resources elsewhere in the economy in an equally productive activity (carrying gravel for construction of a downtown skyscraper, for instance). The contract cost of using the equipment is the same as the opportunity cost, which in this case is the true cost to society.

But the true cost to society of hiring the unemployed laborers is not the Sh 50,000 in salary. It is the opportunity cost of the laborers' time plus the associated costs of their employment—Sh 6,000 plus Sh 4,000, or Sh 10,000 total.

With a true cost to society of Sh 30,000 for the machinery contractor and Sh 10,000 for the labor contractor, society saves Sh 20,000 by going with the (apparently) more expensive labor contractor.

Note that, if the labor contractor had to withdraw his 100 laborers from a fully employed labor pool, and assuming he paid the same wage as they were making elsewhere in the economy, the opportunity cost of their labor would have been exactly the same as his costs in hiring them, or Sh 50,000. In this case, using labor would have cost society Sh 20,000 more than using machinery.

There is a strong tendency for governments to want to be "modern" in their public works construction projects and to use the latest in modern machinery. There are times when using expensive heavy equipment will both massage the ego of the country's leaders and be the most socially efficient construction technique. On the other hand, when there are large numbers of unemployed and underemployed laborers, it may be socially beneficial to use laborers instead of machinery (see Box 15.3).

One of the most important things that can be done to increase employment in a Third World economy dominated by its agricultural sector is to stimulate increased agricultural production. This is important not only because increased agricultural production increases farm employment but because increasing the quantity of food supplied lowers its price.

Food is a wage good (Mellor & Johnston 1984: 550). That is, the cost of food can substantially affect the wage rate. Consider two Third World countries competing in the international marketplace to sell a labor-intensive product such as shoes. In country A the price of food is high, and in country B it is low. Even though a shoe manufacturer in country B pays lower wages than his competitor in country A, the workers in the shoe factory in country B can live as well as those in country A because they can buy food more cheaply. Low food prices stimulate employment.

As low food prices make possible low wage rates, employment is stimulated not only in the export sector but in the domestic sector of the economy. Local manufacturers can compete more successfully with importers to manufacture goods. Low food prices reduce the proportion of the household budget that all people, middle- and upper-income people as well as low-income people, must allocate to food, and thus release purchasing power for nonfood items. This stimulates the demand for nonfood goods and services and further stimulates employment.

Stimulating Third World agricultural production will involve making policy shifts away from the large number of production disincentives now in place and toward production incentives. There are other aspects of stimulating increased agricultural production, such as government sponsorship of agricultural research and educational services. The main policy alternatives available here are outlined in the second half of Chapter 18.

■ HUMAN CAPITAL–INTENSIVE PROGRAMS FOR REDUCING INEQUALITY

Government spending on education can do much to improve the productivity and thus the income of the poor, and simultaneously reduce the distance between the rich and the poor. The rich in the Third World do fairly well at seeing to it that their children get a good education. But the poor must depend on government-sponsored educational programs, and improving both the quality and quantity of these programs, especially at the primary and secondary levels where so many of the poor presently drop out, is important for reducing inequalities.

In designing increased educational opportunities for the poor it is important to take into account the special importance for nutrition of providing equal educational opportunities for girls. Women with some education are more likely to be employed in a wage job than those with no education, and women with more education are likely to have higher wages than those with less. And the relative earnings of the husband and wife have been found to influence the allocation of resources within the family. A higher wage rate of the wife and mother has a positive impact on the allocation of calories to her and her children and a negative effect on the husband's calorie allocation (Senauer et al. 1988: 179).

Methods of improving the income potential of the low-income segment of a population through health care and fertility control programs, already discussed in Chapters 13 and 14, are also important in increasing income of the poor and reducing income inequalities.

■ A SCORECARD FOR POLICY ALTERNATIVES

Because of the widely different consequences of the several policy alternatives outlined in this chapter, a recapitulation is perhaps in order to sort out those that promise to do the best job of increasing the income of the poor and reducing income inequalities.

Several popular proposals have been called into question. The results of land reform, as commonly worked out, have generally proved to be disappointing both from the point of view of income redistribution and wealth generation among the poorest of the poor. Land reform tends to have a chilling effect on investment in agriculture, with adverse production consequences. Subsidies for mechanization and credit, as well as the passage of minimum-wage laws, can be particularly damaging to the poor because of their tendency to benefit middle-class elites, to encourage the substitution of capital for labor, and to increase unemployment among the poor.

On the other hand, several policies have been found to have considerable promise in improving income of the poor or reducing income inequalities. Among them are progressive taxation; transportation subsidies; stimulating increased employment, especially through increased agricultural productivity; and human capital–intensive programs including health care, fertility control, and education—especially at the primary and secondary levels.

□ 16

Policies Aimed at Lowering the Price of Food Through Explicit Subsidized Consumption

In developing countries . . . direct government intervention in the production, pricing, and distribution of foods on a massive scale is common. There is a profound distrust of the ability of the market to value and allocate resources. . . . Government intervention gives rise to price distortions in the domestic economy that have serious allocative and efficiency effects. In order to defend domestic controls, it becomes necessary for governments also to control border trade. This type of policymaking, thus, has a lock-step nature to it where the implementation of certain policies necessarily requires further controls on other parts of the economy. . . .

The policies of intervention are rooted in a model of development where it is thought desirable, in the interests of growth and development, to skim excess resources from agriculture and direct them toward industrialization; the assumption being that such a diversion of agricultural surpluses does not reduce agricultural output. . . . Only recently have the self-defeating nature of these interventions, in the longer run, and the extent of their generally negative effect on agricultural output been fully understood.

—Bale 1985: abstract and 10–11

In Chapter 7 I argued that lack of purchasing power is one of the leading causes of undernutrition. Purchasing power is a function of both income and the price of the goods and services purchased (see Box 7.1). In Chapter 15 we surveyed policies to increase the income of the poor. Food is a major component in the budget of the low-income people most at risk for undernutrition, so in this chapter, and in the next two, we survey policies aimed at lowering the price of food.

Food-linked income transfer programs properly belong in the previous chapter, because they are a way of transferring income from one group to another. They are included here and in the next chapter because they have an impact on the price of food. Indeed, legislation for food-linked income transfer programs often attempts to reduce the price of food through intervention in the marketing system (for instance, legislating ceiling prices) or by offering subsi-

259

dized food to people at below the market price, sometimes as a gift. As I pointed out in Chapter 1, because food-linked income transfer programs intervene in the marketplace and attempt to reallocate the food resource so that those in most need have more of it, they are often called nutrition intervention programs.

The alternative to lowering prices through subsidized consumption is to increase the quantity of food supplied to the marketplace through subsidizing food production. In this and the next chapter, we consider policies for subsidizing food consumption. In Chapter 18 we consider policies for subsidizing food production.

Food-linked income transfer programs may involve explicit subsidies, perhaps paid for by the domestic government out of the general tax till, but often paid for by some foreign donor agency that supplies food at below-market prices. Often the costs of an explicit food consumption subsidy are shared by a developed world surplus food producer, which supplies the food, and a Third World government, which pays for at least part of the food distribution costs and may pay some nominal part of the cost of the food itself.

On the other hand, the cost of the food subsidy may be implicit, that is, hidden from view through programs that assign the burden of the subsidy, by subtle or not so subtle means, to the agricultural sector of the domestic economy. Let us look first at explicit subsidies.

■ RATIONALE FOR EXPLICIT FOOD SUBSIDIES

There are a number of reasons why explicit food consumption subsidies are so popular. Developed countries have generally followed farm production policies that have led to burdensome agricultural surpluses. Furthermore, large numbers of people are hungry now and it would therefore seem logical to feed people today rather than to sponsor programs, such as enhanced agricultural production research, that may take months or years before benefits will become obvious. Finally, the famines that pop up periodically dramatize human hunger and make the logic of transferring surplus food from the developed world to the Third World seem inescapable.

There are other reasons for the popularity of explicit food consumption subsidies. By and large, rich people prefer to give hungry people food rather than cash. But more important, perhaps, are the benefits that particular groups of rich people get from the food distribution programs. In the developed world a number of groups have a financial interest in the creation or continuance of such programs: farmers who see the demand increased for their already abundant production; farm input suppliers who see the market enhanced for their farm machinery, fertilizer, and agricultural chemicals; food processors who hope to win the contracts to powder the milk, grind the flour, and crush the soybeans for shipment overseas; the grain elevators that hope to store the food before shipment; the sea-freight shippers; and finally the private voluntary agencies such as

CARE and Catholic Relief Services that have grown up to service the disposal of surplus food through overseas food distribution programs.

In the Third World, political leaders have an interest in the creation or continuance of such programs. Political leaders derive benefits from instituting such programs and may incur losses from their discontinuation. In the Third World the groups that are most likely to influence political power are the military, the civil servants, urban labor, and industrial interests. All of these groups are happy to be the recipients of cheap food, and political leaders are generally happy to curry favor among them, even at the expense of the country's rural sector (Hopkins 1988).

■ COST OF EXPLICIT FOOD SUBSIDIES

During the past few decades, as the size of the agricultural surplus in the developed world diminished, the magnitude of explicit food subsidies to the Third World shrunk. Nevertheless, the magnitude of food aid to the Third World remains significant. In 1981, for instance, the share of food aid among total food imports of developing countries was 8 percent (Huddleston 1984b: 22). Since 1946, PL 480 food assistance (the US Food for Peace Program) has averaged about 12 percent of the US foreign assistance budget. (Military assistance has accounted for about a third of this budget.) During the 1980s the rate of expenditure for PL 480 ran something over a billion dollars a year (US, Dept. of Agriculture 1990). Countries of the developed world pledged $1.4 billion to the FAO World Food Program (WFP) for food assistance to the Third World during fiscal 1987/88 (World Food Program 1989: 12). (The United States is one of the contributors to the WFP.) Food aid constitutes approximately 15 percent of all official development assistance (Maxwell & Singer 1979).

Explicit food subsidies can be an effective way of improving nutrition of the poor. One of the advantages of such programs is that the cost is accounted for in the program. Governments enter the marketplace and purchase food at market value for use in the subsidized food distribution program. This is in contrast to implicit food subsidies where the costs are not only hidden, but are almost impossible to estimate reliably.

But at the same time explicit food subsidization is an expensive way of improving nutritional status. Since the food is typically purchased in the developed world it must be shipped to Third World countries. OXFAM, one of the leading voluntary agencies involved in distributing surplus food to Third World countries, commissioned a report on food aid for such purposes as disaster relief, food-for-work, mother and child health, and school feeding programs. Jackson and Eade found that the cost of the sea-freight to the US food aid program came to 53 percent of the value of the food. When the food arrives at a Third World port, there are other costs—warehousing, transportation, and administration as the food is distributed to the needy. The OXFAM report's authors found that the sea-freight plus within-country costs of the US food aid program in one country, Guatemala, ran to 89 percent of the original cost of the food (Jackson & Eade 1982: 65).

Jackson and Eade cite a number of disturbing studies that suggest that there are sometimes ways to improve Third World nutrition more cheaply than by explicit food subsidies. To cite one example, a study in India found that it cost 1.5 times as much to prevent a child's death through supplementary feeding as it would to provide basic medical services, and that, "for children aged 1–3 years, nutrition supplementation was up to 11 times more expensive in terms of lives saved than medical services." The study concluded that, "even where it has been nutritionally effective, supplementary feeding has not proved to be cost-effective" (Maxwell 1978b: 295 fn. 36, 297).

Despite their costliness, these programs can provide a solution to the most immediate of Third World nutritional needs, such as famine relief. It must be remembered, however, that, to be effective they must be well administered, and this in itself is expensive. Furthermore, it must be remembered that these programs do not become self-sustaining. Long-term, self-sustaining solutions to the hunger problem will have to involve such things as changes in population growth rates, purchasing power of the poor, income distribution, and health.

■ FAMINE AND DISASTER RELIEF

Natural disasters such as earthquakes, drought, or flooding adversely affect local food availability and provide circumstances for strong arguments for explicit food consumption subsidies. The aftermath of war can provide similar circumstances. Although shortage of food can contribute to famine conditions, contrary to popular conception this is usually not the leading cause of famine. The more likely cause of famine following natural disaster or war is lack of purchasing power (Sen 1981). The farm family whose crops have failed, or the landless worker who is now out of a job, are the types who starve during a famine. Reutlinger and his colleagues (1986: 27) list the types of groups most likely to fall victim to famine:

- Small-scale farmers or tenants whose crops have failed and who cannot find other employment in agriculture (the Wollo in Ethiopia in 1973)
- Landless agricultural workers who lose their jobs when agricultural production declines (Bangladesh in 1974) or who face rapidly rising food prices and constant or declining wages (the Great Bengal famine of 1943)
- Other rural people, including destitutes and beggars, who are affected by a decline in real income in the famine regions (almost all famines)
- Pastoralists who get most of their food by [trading] animals for foodgrains; their herds may be ravaged by the drought, or animal prices may collapse relative to foodgrain prices (the Harerghe region of Ethiopia in 1974 and the drought-stricken Sahel in 1973)

The authors of the well-documented and detailed OXFAM report (Jackson & Eade 1982) warn that poorly supervised or uncontrolled distribution of food aid can do more harm than good. To quote one example, a field worker helping out in a drought-relief food aid program (where the food handouts were supposed to be free of charge to the recipients) wrote: "In Haiti we had . . . a problem of theft and mishandling. In [a] town . . . fairly near to us and very badly hit by drought, the magistrate (appointed mayor) was known to sell PL480 food for $7.00 a 50 lb. bag. At other times the CARE food distributors were so desperate that they would just throw bags of food off the truck and drive on so that the food would go to the strong and the swift" (p. 9).

When a disaster has created the need for assistance, but the local food supplies are adequate, supplying emergency food relief can be counterproductive. It depresses the local price of food, in turn depressing the income of the local farming community, and may lead to other socially undesirable results (see Box 16.1).

Sometimes famines are basically the result of political forces operating within a society where those in power attempt to gain control of resources or subdue opposition through programs that result in starvation. The Soviet famine of 1932–1934 provides one such example. During its first five-year plan the Soviet government felt that, in order to carry out its program of rapid industrialization, it needed to gain control over agriculture. The policy instrument it used for this purpose was collectivization of the peasants' farms. The disruptions growing out of collectivization and the heavy food procurement requirements of central government led to a famine that resulted in the death of some 5 million people in the Ukraine and nearby regions. The peasants were not interested in joining socialized agriculture, and government used the famine to drive the last of the peasant diehards onto the state or collective farms, or simply out of existence (Dalrymple 1964).

The Ethiopian famine of 1984/85 is a more recent example of government-induced starvation. In the Western countries that supplied over $1.2 billion for food aid to Ethiopia during the crisis, the commonly accepted explanation for the famine was that a record-breaking drought was the chief cause. Journalists covering the famine cited official Ethiopian government explanations of the cause of the famine as a disastrous failure of rain, and their reports were backed up by official reports from UN representatives and other dignitaries who likewise accepted the Ethiopian government position.

In retrospect, we find that rainfall was down during and preceding the famine, but that the drought was not much worse than Ethiopian farmers had come to expect as their lot. A study by Clay and Holcomb (1986: 192) found that the main causes of the famine were government policies that had been implemented in order to accomplish "massive collectivization of agricultural production and to secure central government control over productive regions of the country where indigenous peoples have developed strong antigovernment resistance." The Clay and Holcomb study in Ethiopia involved hundreds of inter-

Box 16.1 When Food Aid Is Not Needed

Tony Jackson and Deborah Eade

Imported food may not be necessary at all, despite a major disaster, and its arrival may do more harm than good. The classic example of this comes from Guatemala where the earthquake in 1976 killed an estimated 23,000 people, injured over three times as many and left a million and a quarter homeless. The earthquake occurred in the middle of a record harvest. Local grain was plentiful and the crops were not destroyed but left standing in the fields or buried under the rubble but easy to recover.

During the first few weeks, small consumer items—salt, sugar, soap etc.—were in short supply and temporarily unavailable in the shops. Some of these small items, such as salt, were lost when the houses collapsed. People expressed a need for these food items in the short period before commercial supplies were resumed. However, during that year, about 25,400 tons of basic grains and blends were brought in as food aid from the US. A further 5,000 tons of US food aid already stored in Guatemala were released and supplies were also sent in from elsewhere in the region.

Catholic Relief Services (CRS) and CARE both received reports from their field staff saying food aid was not needed. The Director of CARE's housing reconstruction program visited the disaster area soon after the earthquake. In a US Government report he stated:

> Another thing I was really concerned with was whether there was any need to import food or seed. But I saw no indication of that whatsoever. First of all, the earth was not damaged, and there was no reason why the crops couldn't be harvested on time, and I believe it was a good crop that year. Also, in a few places I visited, I asked people if they could pull the food they had in their houses out of the rubble, and they said they certainly could.

CRS field staff objected to the importing of food aid but they were overruled by their headquarters in New York. Two weeks after the disaster, the League of Red Cross Societies asked national Red Cross Societies to stop sending food. As early as February (the same month as the earthquake), the Co-ordinator of the National Emergency Committee of the Government of Guatemala asked voluntary agencies to stop imports of food aid. On 4 March, the Assistant Administrator for the Latin America Bureau of the United States Agency for International Development (AID), the Hon. Herman Kleine, testified before a House of Representatives Sub-Committee. "I should like to add here, Mr. Chairman, that the Guatemalan Government has requested officially to all donors that further contributions not be of food and medicine but roofing and building materials."

Finally, the Government of Guatemala invoked a presidential decree to prohibit imports of basic grains from May 1976 onwards. Yet after this decree, quantities of food aid were still imported in the form of blended foodstuffs. One article refers to these blends as "basic grains in disguise".

Field staff and local leaders identified three negative results. Firstly, they considered that food aid contributed to a drop in the price of local grain that occurred soon after the earthquake and continued throughout 1976. As to the need for basic grains, a peasant farmer explained: "There was no shortage. There was no need to bring food from outside. On the contrary, our problem was to sell what we had."

After an extensive survey of towns and villages in the worst-hit area six weeks after the earthquake, an OXFAM-World Neighbors official reported: "Virtually everyone in the area is selling more grain this year than he does normally. Furthermore, emergency food shipments have drastically curtailed demand for grains. Thus the prices of the farmers' produce have plummeted."

Later, the then Director of CRS in Guatemala was to tell the *New York Times*: "The general effect was that we knocked the bottom out of the grain market in the country for nine to twelve months."

This last view may be overstated as other factors, such as the excellent grain harvest, would usually have led to a fall in prices anyway. Nonetheless, the basic fact remains: $8 million of food aid was sent into a country with plentiful food-stocks of its own. Any food that it was necessary to distribute to earthquake victims could have been bought in Guatemala (as WFP did).

The second negative effect of the continuing supply of free food was to encourage the survivors to queue for rations instead of engaging in reconstruction or normal agricultural work.

Thirdly, it brought about a change in the quality and motivation of local leadership. The OXFAM-World Neighbors official, quoted above, noted:

Immediately after the earthquake, we tended to see the same leaders whom we'd seen before the earthquake—people [with] a high degree of honesty and personal commitment to the villages. But gradually . . . I began seeing fellas who I knew were totally dishonest. They'd go into the different agencies and . . . say that theirs was the most affected village in the Highlands, and they'd get more food. So largely because of the giveaways, the villages started to turn more to leaders who could produce free things like this, whether they were honest or dishonest, rather than to the leaders they'd been putting their trust in for years.

With larger and larger quantities of free food coming in, there are increased incentives to corruption. . . . Groups that had worked together previously became enemies over the question of recipients for free food.

Source: Extracted from Jackson and Eade 1982:9–11. (Consult the source for copious documentation.)

views, including both farm families and representatives of public and private agencies delivering famine assistance. The explanations of Oromo farm families of the decline in productivity in their area is particularly revealing. All respondents reported a decline in agricultural production since 1976. Their average yield in the 1975/76 crop year was 4,600 kilograms, while their average yield on the same land in the 1984/85 crop year was only 900 kilograms. When asked the reason for the decline, none of the farmers reported lack of rain. They cited a host of other reasons, all of which had to do with government policies (Table 16.1).

Clay and Holcomb concluded that, in the case of the 1984/85 Ethiopian famine, foreign food aid was distributed with very little monitoring by the aid

Table 16.1　Causes of Agricultural Production Declines as Reported by a Sample of 45 Oromo Farmers, Ethiopia, 1985 (Interviewed in Yabuus, Sudan, Factors Mentioned in Combination)

	Percentage Responding
Lack of rain	0.0
Government programs interfere with food production	
Work required four to five days a week on peasant association collective plots	95.4
Other peasant association obligations	27.2
Required attendance at peasant association meetings and literacy programs	73.4
Disarming populations	63.6
Military conscription	15.6
Imprisonment prevents farm work	86.3
Government policies force redistribution of assets	
Land redistribution	52.2
Forced sale of oxen to pay taxes and "voluntary contributions"	41.0
All products confiscated for taxes (including seed grain)	36.3
Oxen and tools confiscated for collectivization or resettlement	13.6
Oxen given to others in peasant association	6.8
Government "improvement" programs destroy crops	
Government "experts" untrained in farming	13.6
Grass, for erosion control, overtook crops	9.0

Source: Clay and Holcomb 1986:124.

donors and was, in fact, used mainly by the central government to help suppress resistance groups within the country, and probably increased the rate of death through starvation (see Box 16.2).

■ MARKETWIDE EXPLICIT SUBSIDIES

In an attempt to reduce food prices, some countries have adopted marketwide food subsidies, that is, subsidies that are available to all, not just to the needy. Such subsidies have become especially significant in countries where people have come to regard cheap food as a right; for example, China, Sri Lanka, and Egypt.

Third World countries receiving food contributions, whether as outright gifts or at prices reduced from international market prices, have the option of selling the food on the open market at the market price and spending the revenue generated for whatever purpose suits them. The increased quantity supplied through the foreign assistance lowers the market price and thus provides a food subsidy to all purchasers. Donor countries sometimes specify that revenue generated through such sales be spent only with their approval, but their control over these funds, often called counterpart funds, is tenuous. After all, money within government can be easily transferred from program to program, and the program preferred by the donor government can easily be funded from the counterpart funds, allowing funds generated by domestic taxes to be concentrated on other types of expenditures.

Box 16.2 Politics and the Ethiopian Famine 1984–1985
Jason W. Clay and Bonnie K. Holcomb

Governments as well as humanitarian assistance agencies have not attempted to systematically understand the causes of the present famine. While their assistance, they claim, feeds the hungry, they fail to address the issue of whether their assistance will eradicate or exacerbate the conditions that led to the present famine. If the West is willing to feed starving Ethiopians without asking how they came to be in that condition or evaluate whether Western assistance programs alleviate those conditions, then they will face a monumental task in the future. The government of Ethiopia is establishing a social and economic system that will produce starving people for generations to come.

Assistance to the government, unless scrupulously monitored:

• Facilitates the uprooting of distinct peoples in one region of the country and the displacement of self-sufficient food producers in another, primarily through the resettlement program.

• Gives hostile Ethiopian government forces access to areas that had successfully withdrawn from the reach of the state and re-established efficient, autonomous agricultural production systems.

• Reinforces transport and communication lines of obvious strategic military importance in areas that the government has not been able to control militarily.

• Supports programs designed by a tiny minority of the region's inhabitants while simultaneously undermining programs that have broad popular support.

• Allows the government to reinforce the programs that lead to the famine as well as intensify programs, such as resettlement and villagization, that will spread the famine to previously productive and fertile regions.

According to our own research and the efforts of numerous other individuals and organizations, Ethiopian government policies have become the major cause of death in the country. The provision of "humanitarian" assistance, with no questions asked, helps the Ethiopian government get away with murder.

Source: Clay and Holcomb 1986:192–193.

When a general food subsidy is substantial, demand for the subsidized food becomes so great that it is necessary to limit access through a system of rationing. For instance, during 1954–1966 everyone in Sri Lanka could buy rice at prices substantially below the market price, but, through rationing, access was restricted to four pounds per week, which provided just under 1,000 Calories of subsidized food per capita per day (Edirisinghe 1987: 12–13).

Third World countries sometimes pay for part or all of their food subsidy. China and Brazil have borne most of the costs of their food subsidies themselves. India and Egypt have shared the costs with foreign donors.

We will look at experiences with marketwide food subsidies in three Third World countries: Brazil, an upper-middle-income country that bore most of the costs itself; Egypt, a middle-income country that shared the costs with foreign donors; and Sri Lanka, a low-income country that shared a small part of the costs with foreign donors and eventually decided to shift from a marketwide food subsidy to a subsidy targeted at the needy.

During 1966 to 1982 the government of Brazil attempted to achieve self-sufficiency in wheat production and at the same time provide cheap wheat to its consumers. As part of its attempt to achieve these goals, the government became the sole seller and buyer of both domestically produced and imported wheat. The prices of wheat and wheat products were rigidly controlled throughout the economy. Farmers were encouraged to increase wheat production through a price-support subsidy, and millers were provided with wheat at a price substantially below that paid to the producer, with the government making up the difference out of the general tax till.

In their study of the Brazilian wheat policy, Calegar and Schuh (1988: 9–10, 43–45) determined that 86 percent of the subsidy went to consumers. That is, only 14 percent of the subsidy costs went to administration or were lost through slippages such as manipulations by the millers. On the other hand, only 19 percent of the total subsidy went to the true target group, the low-income consumers. Furthermore, gains in consumer welfare were slightly biased toward the high-income population groups (they bought more bread per capita than did the low-income groups). Calegar and Schuh conclude that the marketwide wheat consumption subsidy was not an effective policy for redistributing income and suggest that a preferred policy would be to target the food subsidy specifically at low-income groups.

The Egyptian government has a history of intervening in the food-marketing system that dates back to Biblical times when Joseph, interpreting the pharaoh's dream, recommended storing grain during seven fat years to prepare for the seven lean years that he prophesied were to come (Genesis 41). Since the mid-1970s, the Egyptian government has taken on a substantial burden of public expenditures for food subsidies, with the share of the government expenditures for this purpose running as high as 17 percent (Alderman & von Braun 1984: 12).

Additional costs of the Egyptian food subsidy have been borne by North American and European governments, which have provided substantial quantities of food at below-market prices. Indeed, the availability of such programs may be one of the reasons that Egyptians embarked on such an ambitious explicit marketwide food subsidy.

Table 16.2 Farm-Gate and Retail Price of Selected Agricultural Commodities, Egypt, 1982

	Price as Percentage of World Price	
	Farm-Gate	Retail
Wheat	64.5	36.8
Rice	26.6	17.7
Sugar	46.0	27.3
Beans	75.4	49.0
Cotton	27.2	41.3

Source: Rountree 1985.

As of the late 1980s the Egyptian government was handling the major share of the sales of bread, flour, pulses, sugar, tea, and cooking oil in the country, making these commodities available to householders at prices significantly below world prices. Farm-gate prices deviated less from world prices than did retail prices (Table 16.2), but both sets of prices demonstrated a priority goal of Egyptian policy: cheap food for all.

The policy is widely credited with keeping the Egyptian rate of undernutrition to a minimum. Average calorie consumption was found to be above standard even among the poorest 12 percent of the population as a whole (US, Dept. of Agriculture 1984: 9), although significant numbers of urban households in the lowest-income quartile were found to be calorie-deficient (Alderman & von Braun 1984).

Despite the apparent success of the Egyptian food subsidy, it has come under severe criticism for its costliness. Besides the annual cost to the budget mentioned above, there are a variety of efficiency costs, among them

- *Wastage:* When food is cheap, there is less incentive to store it carefully to preserve its value. With bread as cheap as it is in Egypt, farmers purchase significant quantities of it for livestock feed. The livestock products are eventually eaten by humans, but the benefits from this cheap feed accrue largely to the wealthy who consume the livestock products. Furthermore the resources spent processing the wheat into bread are a dead loss to society when the bread is fed to livestock.
- *Underinvestment in industry:* Industrial investment, and output, are responsive to the availability of foreign exchange. The more foreign exchange that is spent on a food subsidy the less is available for industrial investment. One study suggested that reducing the volume of food imports would therefore increase the level of industrial output; specifically, a 10 percent increase in foreign exchange was estimated to increase industrial investment by 6 percent and industrial output by 4 percent (Sco-

bie 1983). High rates of government spending on imported food could adversely affect industrial employment among the poor.

- *Consumption inefficiencies:* Because of the depressed price of wheat, Egyptians eat more wheat than they would if they were paying the world price. The Egyptian government buys much of its wheat on the world market at the world price. There is a loss to Egyptian society associated with this overconsumption because government paid more for the last tons of wheat it bought at world market prices than Egyptian citizens would have been willing to pay for them. The amount of this cost above worth is represented by triangle 1 of Figure 16.1.
- *Production losses:* Because the domestic price of wheat is depressed below the world market price, farmers produce less than they would if they were offered the world market price. This loss of production is a loss to the Egyptian economy, represented by triangle 2 in Figure 16.1.

The same sorts of consumption inefficiencies and production losses for wheat can be found in other subsidized commodities also.

The substantial budgetary costs, combined with the substantial efficiency costs of the Egyptian food subsidy, suggest that a shift in the direction of a targeted food subsidy might be in order in Egypt as well as in Brazil.

Sri Lanka's food subsidy dates back to 1942. At that time, rice supplies were limited because of World War II. Therefore subsidized rice was offered to the general public through a rationing program designed to distribute supplies equitably (Edirisinghe & Poleman 1983). The rice subsidy has operated continuously ever since, albeit with some ups and downs.

In 1953 the government found itself with budgetary problems, in part because of spending on the rice subsidy, and proposed an austerity program that would have resulted in a price rise of nearly 300 percent on rice rations. There were to be simultaneous increases in the price of postal, telegraph, railway, and electricity rates, but the proposed rice price rise was particularly unpopular. A massive protest stopped the price increases and forced both an increase in the rice ration (at the old price) and the resignation of the prime minister. In the next election the ruling party was defeated.

The rice subsidy was such a sensitive political issue that no significant change in the program was attempted for 12 years. Then, in 1966, the basic weekly ration was cut in half but issued free of charge. Two things were significant here: (1) Since government did not need to purchase so much rice overseas, substantial foreign exchange savings accrued; and (2) there were no food riots. Government had found a successful compromise to reduce the cost of the food subsidy.

Four years later, subsidized rationed rice was made available in addition to the free rice. Eight years after that, in 1978, the ration system was targeted to the lower end of the income range through a means test. A year and a half later, food stamps were substituted for the ration cards. Since the food stamps carry a

Figure 16.1   Cost Above Worth and Producer's Surplus Lost Due to a Market-Wide Explicit Subsidy

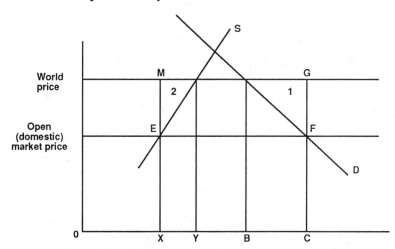

Cost above worth: Suppose that D represents the demand curve for wheat, and that amount OC represents the wheat consumed, given the domestic market price. If BC quantity of wheat is imported, then the area of the triangle 1 is a loss to society since government paid more for this wheat than it was worth to consumers.

Producer's surplus lost: Now suppose that S represents the supply curve for wheat, assuming no concessionary sales were available. Quantity OX represents wheat produced in Egypt given a depressed, domestic market price. Quantity XY represents wheat imported which would have been produced locally had the local price of wheat been equal to the world price. The area of triangle 2 is a loss to the Egyptian farmer because it is a producer's surplus he could capture were he getting the world price, but which he now misses out on. Notice that the consumer would not care whether he paid the world price to the farmer or to a foreigner. But the Egyptian farmer cares because he can produce that quantity of wheat with fewer resources than can the foreigner. And the economy cares, too. Triangle 2 is a loss to the Egyptian economy.

fixed rupee value, their purchasing power declines with inflation, resulting in an automatic reduction of the costs of the food subsidy with no further government action. In 1985 policy reforms were instituted to target the food stamps more intensely at the poor by doubling the entitlement and by attempting to reserve them for the bottom quartile of the income distribution (Sahn & Edirisinghe, forthcoming).

That the cost of the subsidy to government has been declining is documented by some figures from the World Bank. In 1970 food subsidies amounted to 23 percent of government expenditures. In 1978 they were 19 percent, and by 1984 they were only 4 percent of government expenditures.

The subsidy is difficult to target precisely. The 1978 means test mentioned above was designed to limit subsidized food to those households with annual incomes below Rs 3,600 ($240). A 1978/79 household survey indicated that only 7.1 percent of the population lived in such households, yet almost half of the population managed to pass the means test for inclusion in the program (World Bank 1986: 93).

■ SUBSIDIES TARGETED TO THE CHRONICALLY NEEDY

There are a number of ways of targeting food-linked income transfers to the chronically undernourished. One of the most obvious methods involves geography: Limit the program to, or provide special emphasis in, regions where large numbers of undernourished are thought to exist. Food aid donor countries presumably have this as a common consideration in allocating their resources among recipient nations.

Within geographic regions subsidies can be self-targeting or aimed at groups that pass some sort of means test. The common means tests involve either the anthropometric measurements used in the growth monitoring of children or some method of assessing family economic status (through gathering data on family income or assets such as landholdings). Of these two, the anthropometric measurements are far cheaper to assess with reasonable accuracy. But in either case the assessment must be redone periodically to keep the targeting focused on the needy (Rogers 1988a).

The authors of a study that examined a price subsidy scheme in the Philippines concluded that a two-step procedure based on anthropometry would be advisable: (1) Identify target villages with high concentrations of underweight preschoolers; and (2) within the selected villages, target households containing preschoolers whose measurements indicate that they are at high risk for undernutrition (García & Pinstrup-Andersen 1987: 78).

In the sections below we first examine self-targeting methods for limiting food-linked income transfers to the needy. Then we examine those requiring some sort of means test, namely direct distribution, rationing, food stamps, and food-for-work.

☐ Self-targeting

The easiest way to target a food subsidy is to subsidize foods with negative income elasticities of demand; the inferior goods, to use the economist's jargon that we adopted in Chapter 7. Inferior foods vary from culture to culture but are typically starchy staples such as cassava, yams, maize, sorghum, or millet. (Note that, of this list, cassava is the only food that has less protein than rice. Maize, sorghum, and millet all score higher on protein content than rice. Yams, on a dry-weight basis, are competitive with rice in protein content.) As income increases, people usually eat less of these products (review Figures 7.2c and d).

The government of Bangladesh experimented with this idea in one area by subsidizing sorghum consumption, but the experiment, although supposedly successful, was not implemented countrywide (Karim, Majid & Levinson 1984; Ahmed 1988: 226).

☐ Direct Distribution

Affluent countries are familiar with direct food distribution programs carried out through school lunch programs or by soup kitchens set up in low-income urban areas. In the Third World, direct distribution of food is more likely to take the form of supplemental feeding programs targeted at the groups most vulnerable to undernutrition: pregnant and lactating women, infants, and preschoolers. Despite the popularity of such programs, the results have been disappointing (Kennedy & Knudsen 1985).

Beaton and Ghassemi (1982) found that in the eight supervised feeding programs and 13 take-home food programs for which they had data, the net increase in food intake by the target recipients ranged from 45 to 70 percent of the food distributed, with one program showing a net effect of only 10 to 15 percent. Some of the reasons for these disappointing results are discussed in Box 16.3.

☐ Rationing

A subsidized food-rationing system allows a consumer who holds a ration card to purchase a specific amount of some food or foods in a given time period at a price lower than the market value. In Sri Lanka, from 1966 to 1979, some food was available free with the ration card.

A subsidized food-rationing system requires either that the government set up a marketing system of its own, which it operates or licenses to operate parallel to the regular market (which may be declared illegal and is then called a black market); or that the government set up a system for reimbursing commercial retail outlets for the discounts that they give for the rationed food. In either case government must employ auditors to monitor the system so as to minimize cheating.

When government sets up or licenses its own distribution system and sells food at below-market prices through ration cards, the resulting retail outlets are often called "fair-price" shops, although farmers would generally be willing to debate the accuracy of the term.

A 1983/84 experiment in the Philippines provides a case study of costs and benefits from a real-world subsidized food ration scheme. The experiment was set up so that all households in seven villages, known for a high incidence of undernutrition and poverty, were provided subsidized food. These villages were matched with seven control villages. The program did increase food consumption among the target villages. Although distribution of the extra food within the household favored adults, preschool children also consumed more and showed improvements in their nutritional status. If only weight gains among the undernourished were counted as benefits, the cost of adding one kilogram to the weight of an undernourished preschooler was estimated at $101 per year.

Box 16.3 Supplementary Feeding
Eileen T. Kennedy and Per Pinstrup-Andersen

Supplementary feeding programs distribute foods through noncommercial channels to pregnant and lactating women, infants, and preschoolers. These programs are the most common form of nutrition intervention in developing countries.

There are three common forms of delivery: 1) On-site feeding, 2) take-home feeding, and 3) nutrition rehabilitation centers (NRC's). NRC's include both residential facilities and programs in which children are cared for during the day but return home at night.

Data from more than 200 supplementary feeding projects indicate that many supplementary feeding programs have had a significant and positive effect on prenatal and child participants (Anderson et al. 1981; Beaton and Ghassemi 1982). Despite the significant, positive effect, however, the benefits are usually small. Increments in birth weights attributed to the supplementary feeding programs are typically in the range of 40–60 grams. Similarly, the increases in growth seen in preschoolers, although significant, are small.

Several reasons are given for these small but significant effects. First, it appears that only a part of the food given is actually consumed by the target population. "Leakages" occur when the food is shared by nontarget family members or when the food is substituted for other food that normally would be consumed. Other factors, such as the timing of supplementation, duration of participation, nutritional status of recipients, and related services available, all influence the effectiveness of supplemental feeding.

Timing of supplement. Pregnancy and the period from six months to three years of age are the most nutritionally vulnerable times. Studies indicate that it is the last trimester of pregnancy that is the most critical for supplementation. Preschoolers below the age of three are also at special risk. Inappropriate weaning practices, delayed introduction of solid foods, food taboos, and infection all contribute to a higher prevalence of second- and third-degree malnutrition in this group.

Duration. For prenatal women, there appears to be a minimum participation of 13–15 weeks needed to produce significant changes in birth weight. For infants and children, the minimum level of participation needed to affect growth depends heavily on the type of delivery system used.

Nutritional status of participants. Children with second- or third-degree malnutrition exhibit greater benefits from supplemental feeding than do marginally undernourished children. The same is true for pregnant women.

Other services. Inadequate intake of food is only one of several factors that contribute to undernutrition. Undernutrition and infection often occur simultaneously. It is not surprising, therefore, that the most successful supplementation activities have been those with strong ties to primary health care programs.

Source: Extracted from Kennedy and Pinstrup-Andersen et al. 1983:35–40.

(Edirisinghe [1987: 70], in his study of food subsidies in Sri Lanka, found that discrimination against younger family members diminished when the more productive members of the household had at least 80 percent of their energy requirements met.)

The researchers in the Philippine experiment estimated that the cost-effectiveness of the program compared favorably with other programs. Costs were kept low through careful targeting, the cooperation of the local bureaucratic structure in administering the program, and by using existing retail outlets instead of a parallel, government-operated marketing system (García & Pinstrup-Andersen 1987: 9, 78–79).

Although the Philippine effort was targeted at rural villages, it has been found that nationwide subsidized ration schemes generally show an urban bias. For instance, the subsidized wheat ration system in use in Pakistan was found to contribute about 11 percent of household income for urban households with incomes below the median. Rural households gained less than 1 percent of their income from the system. The difference was accounted for by the facts that rural households are less likely to participate in the program, smaller quantities of rationed food are available there, and wheat is not sold in many rural areas (Rogers 1988c: 247).

☐ **Food Stamps**

Food stamps are somewhat different from ration coupons for purchasing subsidized food. Food stamps have a face value that can be used in any food store to purchase food at the market value. Another difference is that people are usually expected to purchase their food stamps. Since a food stamp plan does not require government to set up a parallel marketing system for the subsidized food, the system may be cheaper than rationing.

The first food stamp plan ever was introduced in the United States just before World War II, but it is the 1961 revision of the plan that economists like to talk about. In this version eligible families got stamps with a cash value depending on household needs for food. They paid varying amounts for the stamps depending on their income level. This arrangement made it possible to vary the food-linked income transfer according to need and therefore extend the limited government food welfare expenditures to a broader segment of the population.

In his study of the food stamp program in Sri Lanka, Edirisinghe (1987: 55) found that the caloric intake response to an additional rupee from food stamps was exactly the same as from an additional rupee of income. Because of decreasing income elasticity of demand as income rises, the cost of providing 100 additional calories through food stamps increases as income increases. Despite this finding, food stamp programs will probably stay around simply because they are more acceptable politically than straight cash transfers.

☐ **Food-for-Work**

Adding the requirement that recipients of food aid work in exchange for the food-linked income transfer is an interesting twist. Food-for-work (FFW) has the potential to increase the productivity of the region in which it is applied and, at the same time, provide productive activities for recipients who would otherwise be unemployed or underemployed (Mellor 1988: 1004). FFW projects typically improve rural infrastructure through building farm-to-market roads, constructing irrigation canals, and so forth. They have also been used in improving squatter settlements or in erecting community buildings (Jackson & Eade 1982: 24).

During the early 1980s an FFW project in the Rift Valley of Kenya employed low-income farmers on local public works projects, particularly for erosion control and water-harvesting devices. The project had two positive economic outcomes: A good deal of farmland was improved and its access to irrigation water enhanced; the participating farmers used some of their food-linked income transfers for capital investments on their farms and thus increased their own productivity. In fact, during the second year of the program the farmers devoted fewer hours to FFW activities, apparently in part because of a greater need to tend their own farms (Bezuneh, Deaton & Norton 1988).

This success story is heartwarming, yet at the same time it introduces one of the problems with FFW. The benefits tend to go mainly to those who possess land. Typically, the recipients of FFW food are not landowners but the landless unemployed and underemployed. If their projects end up improving the productivity of land owned by others, the inequality of asset distribution in the area could increase. In one FFW tree-planting project in Ethiopia the workers became so resentful of the fact that their work was enhancing the private property of already powerful landed people that they planted all the trees upside down (Maxwell 1978a: 40).

Another problem stems from the fact that a growing number of FFW laborers are women. The extra time they put into FFW programs may detract from the quantity and quality of child care services that they deliver to their children. Typically they leave their infants and preschoolers to be cared for by older siblings (Kennedy, Pinstrup-Andersen et al. 1983: 28).

■ EFFECTS OF EXPLICIT FOOD SUBSIDIES

Explicit food subsidies succeed in transferring income, but they are expensive. Third World governments seldom have the resources to sponsor explicit food subsidies on their own. Therefore, the direction of income transfer through these programs has been mainly from the developed to the underdeveloped world, chiefly through PL 480 and the WFP.

These subsidies increase food consumption. Because of the fungibility of the food transferred (commonly grains or grain products) in the Third World setting, the food received is usually treated as the equivalent of cash. Therefore some of the resulting increased purchasing power is spent on nonfood items.

Marketwide subsidies usually benefit urban consumers far more than rural consumers. This is due in part to the difficulty of running a subsidy program in rural areas and in part to the greater political clout of urban special interest groups. In these untargeted subsidies the rich get a greater income transfer than the poor because the rich purchase more food. On the other hand, the poor may well get a greater percentage increase in income from the subsidy.

In very low–income households the lion's share of the increased food consumed may go to the productive adults unless the subsidy is sufficient to approach food adequacy among those adults.

Even with foreign assistance, explicit subsidies can be costly to Third World governments, often claiming more than 10 percent of their annual budget expenditures. The question must be raised whether the same amount spent on other programs would accomplish more for the poor. Careful targeting of the subsidy can save considerably on costs.

Food subsidies put downward pressure on wages. This partially offsets the real income transfer. On the other hand, lower wages may increase employment among the poor.

If the food for an explicit food subsidy is purchased in the same country where it is dispensed, the demand for food is increased, since the poor are now eating more than they otherwise would. This results in higher food prices, which work as an incentive to agricultural production. The US food stamp and school lunch programs thus provide an incentive to US agriculture.

On the other hand, if the subsidized food is purchased in a developed country and dispensed in a Third World country, the effect is to raise farm prices in the developed country and lower them in the Third World country. The program thus acts as an incentive to agriculture in the developed country but as a disincentive to agriculture in the Third World country. In the developed world, special interest groups who benefit from food surplus disposal programs are prone to insist that their donated food does not depress Third World farm prices. It is hard to see how they can claim the incentives to the developed world's agriculture without recognizing the corresponding disincentives to agriculture in the Third World.

If Third World farmers bear some of the costs of explicit food subsidies through the price disincentives described above, those costs are small beside the costs they may incur from implicit food-linked income transfer programs, which are the subject of the next chapter.

☐ 17

Policies Aimed at Lowering the Price of Food Through Implicit Subsidized Consumption

The most important class conflict in the poor countries of the world today is not between labor and capital. Nor is it between foreign and national interests. It is between the rural classes and the urban classes.

—Lipton 1977: 13

As pointed out in Box 17.1, it is one of the surprising anomalies of the world food problem that developed countries (where agriculture is already highly productive and food supplies are abundant) generally stimulate farm production by engaging in agricultural policies that result in high farm prices, while Third World countries (where agricultural production is often marginal and food supplies are scarce) generally discourage farm production by engaging in agricultural policies that result in low farm prices. A central idea underlying Third World policies that result in low farm prices is that such policies represent an easy way to transfer income. In this chapter we see that, popular as they are, such pricing policies are not an efficient way of transferring income to the poor.

■ IMPLICIT SUBSIDIES

Third World government activities that result in low (that is, below–world market) farm prices include: noncompetitive procurement of grain from farmers; below-market food prices set by law; foreign trade controls; support of an overvalued domestic currency; and limits on cash cropping. All these activities are carried out in the name of lower food prices, and all of them, in turn, amount to implicit food subsidies. In contrast to explicit food subsidies, implicit food subsidies are food-linked income transfer programs whose costs are, at least to some extent, obscured and difficult to estimate.

Third World implicit food subsidies are almost always paid for by the farm

279

sector through the below-market food prices that result from these food-linked income transfers. The difference between the depressed price the producer gets for his food (depressed because of an implicit subsidy program in operation) and the international price for that food is a hidden cost to the farmer. It is his contribution to the food subsidy and represents an income transfer from him to the recipient of the subsidized food.

Box 17.1 Pricing Policies in World Agriculture
Anandarup Ray

Even a casual look at agricultural policies around the world reveals many surprising anomalies. In the United States, for example, the government pays farmers not to grow cereals; in the European Community (EC), farmers are paid to grow more. In Japan, rice farmers receive three times the world price for their crop. In 1985, farmers in the EC received 18 cents a pound (US) for sugar that was then sold on the world markets for 5 cents a pound; at the same time, the EC imported sugar at 18 cents a pound. Canadian farmers pay up to eight times the price of a cow for the right to sell that cow's milk at the government's support price.

In contrast to industrial market economies, developing countries tend to tax agriculture—even those low-income countries that depend critically on agriculture for their economic growth. Some pay their producers no more than half the world price for grains and then spend scarce foreign exchange to import food. Many subsidize consumption to help the poor, but end up reducing the incomes of farmers who are much poorer than many of the urban consumers who benefit from the subsidies.

Most developing countries pronounce self-sufficiency in food as an important objective, while taxing farmers and subsidizing consumers and thus increasing their dependence upon imported food. And in periods of economic adjustment, when shortages of foreign exchange make export promotion urgent, many have increased taxes on agricultural exports and cut producer support programs, while relying on unrestricted food imports to satisfy urban consumers.

Source: Extracted from Ray 1986:2.

In this way, farmers have sometimes ended up paying the lion's share of the cost of a food subsidy. In Table 17.1 we see data on the distribution of costs of food subsidy systems in three south Asian countries, Sri Lanka, India, and Pakistan, during the 1970s. During the years cited, rationed food in these countries was available at about half the market price. In all three countries, but particularly in India and Pakistan (where producers were picking up the tab on over half the cost of the subsidy), part of the heavy burden of price subsidization was shifted to farmers through the use of forced government procurement at below-market prices. Marketing regulations such as administered prices also helped to keep producer prices below world levels. India and Pakistan set prices in their

Table 17.1 Extent and Cost of Food Subsidy Systems for Sri Lanka, India, and Pakistan, 1970s

	Ration Price as Percentage of Open Market Price	Quantity Rationed as Percentage of Total Consumption	Per Capita Cost (US Dollars)	Fiscal Cost of Subsidy to the Economy		
				Government's Share of Cost	Producer's Share of Cost	Budgetary Cost as Percentage of Total Expenditure
	1	2	3	4	5	6
Sri Lanka 1974	48	46	15.01	68	32	17
1975	60	54	10.14	87	13	16
1976	65	53	7.02	89	11	–
India 1974	47	15	7.88	10	90	–
1975	47	18	4.22	20	80	–
1976	60	13	3.54	10	90	–
Pakistan 1974-75[a]	44	32	7.19	24	76	13
1975-76	55	27	7.34	45	55	11
1976-77	51	33	5.03	36	64	–

Sources: Ration price as percentage of open market price in Sri Lanka: Edirisinghe 1987:12; all other data: Scandizzo and Tsakok 1985:64.

[a]For Pakistan the cost estimate refers to the calendar year; for example, the 1974 estimate appears under 1974-75.

fair-price ration shops at a high enough level to cover most of their procurement costs, administrative expenses, and possible losses on imports, leaving the rest of the cost of the subsidy to be borne by the farm population (Scandizzo & Tsakok 1985: 60–76).

Because of their nature, most implicit food-linked income transfers are marketwide, but some can be and are, occasionally, targeted to low-income groups. We will now examine several commonly practiced programs which result in implicit, food-linked, income transfers from farmers to the recipients of subsidized food.

☐ Non-competitive Procurement

A number of countries use compulsory procurement methods to obtain grain from farmers at below-market prices. In India, for instance, the Food Corporation of India (FCI) is empowered to obtain grain from farmers through compulsory means. State corporations often act as agents for the FCI for both procurement and later distribution through the fair-price shops. In 1981 in India there were about 280,000 fair-price shops distributing subsidized grain through a rationing program available to some 660 million people. During the 1980/81 agricultural year about 35 percent of the rice and 60 percent of the wheat sold in the market in India was procured by government agencies (George 1988).

Compulsory procurement amounts to a tax on the growers of the commodities procured. One problem with it is that it may motivate some farmers who have the opportunity, because of climate, soil, and topography, to switch from producing grain to producing nontaxed alternative crops, such as vegetables and fruits. Increasing the quantity supplied and thus lowering the price of vegetables and fruits benefits chiefly the high-income consumer. Low-income consumers do not spend much on these foods.

☐ Administered Prices

In many Third World countries, farm-gate and retail food prices are administered. An administered price may be fixed substantially below the international price. This ceiling price becomes the highest price that can legally be offered to farmers. When this price is below the market price it may be necessary to dissuade farmers from selling their crop on the black market by making it illegal for anyone but government representatives to purchase or transport the commodities covered by the ceiling price. This requires that government enter the marketing system as an active participant or at least license certain firms to do so.

Malcolm Bale (1985: 13) describes how such a system of below-market ceiling prices worked in Pakistan in the decade prior to 1981, after which the administered prices were allowed to rise:

> The government sets a price at which it will buy wheat. Farmers may sell to government agents or private traders. The government buyers resell to ration

shops at a fixed (low) price, which essentially sets the upper limit of the open market price. Private middlemen typically pay producers less than the government price, because they provide extra services such as credit or transportation to growers. Wheat procured by the government is milled and sold by privately owned ration shops to ration card holders at the same price at which the government sells the flour to them. The ration shop covers costs and profits by selling the gunny bags in which flour is delivered. Until 1981, the government price of wheat was as much as 60 percent below the border price.

Pakistani wheat farmers were implicitly taxed, and Pakistani consumers were implicitly subsidized, by the support prices. A similar program kept the price of Pakistani rice at an average of 35 percent below the border price during 1973–1983 (Bale 1985).

In Tanzania, where the government controls most aspects of agricultural marketing, government-controlled farm prices were lowered between 1970 and 1984 so that the average of official producer prices declined 46 percent. Rising export taxes and the costs of the government marketing program reduced the farmers' share of final sales value of export crops to 41 percent in 1980. Output of some export crops (cashews, cotton, and pyrethrum) fell drastically in the 1970s. By 1984 the tonnage of export crops moving through the government marketing boards was 30 percent less than it had been in 1970 (World Bank 1986: 74–75). The implicit tax on agriculture was a substantial disincentive to agricultural production.

A common aspect of administered prices is pan-pricing, that is, the practice of maintaining identical prices across time and place within the economy. The policy discourages private traders from storing food just after harvest and shifts the burden of storage, together with its costs, to the government. Jamaica practiced pan-pricing when, for several years prior to 1980, it placed a ceiling price on the retail price of wheat flour, all of which was imported. Most of the flour imported into Jamaica is landed at Kingston, and the administered ceiling price made it just barely profitable for supermarket operators in the city and suburbs to stock flour. But the cost of transporting the flour to remote markets in the mountains some distance from the port was greater than the legally allowed marketing margin. In time, the only flour available in many remote locations was black market flour, which sold at a considerable premium. Thus the rural poor ended up paying more for their flour than they would have without the government policy, while the urban rich found flour available at reasonable prices in their supermarkets.

☐ **Export Taxes**

Third World governments frequently place a tax on the export of agricultural commodities. This not only generates revenue for the government but lowers the domestic price of the commodity, since exporters can pay farmers only the world price minus the export tax that they have to pay to the government. The lower price can be a substantial disincentive to production. The government of

Ghana set up its own Cocoa Marketing Board and gave it a monopoly on buying, transporting, and exporting cocoa. Then it undertook to raise significant tax revenue from cocoa exports. This combined with exchange rate manipulations to raise the effective export duty on cocoa from a high of 54 percent in the last half of the 1960s to 90 percent in the last half of the 1970s. Domestic cocoa prices fell to levels far below those in competing cocoa-exporting countries, and Ghana's share of world cocoa exports fell from 40 percent in 1961–1963 to 18 percent in 1980–1982 (World Bank 1986: 76).

From 1940 to 1972 the government of Argentina generally maintained a policy to keep agricultural prices low relative to the prices of nonagricultural goods. This was accomplished through a variety of measures that, in general, added up to a high tax on agricultural exports and a tariff on nonagricultural imports. This resulted in an implicit tax on agriculture that is estimated to have amounted to 50 percent of total agricultural output during the period. Among the consequences of this policy were that employment in agriculture declined, agriculture lost resources to nonagriculture, and agricultural productivity grew more slowly. In fact, per capita agricultural production in the 1970s was less than it was before World War II. And this happened in a country that is well known for its excellent agricultural soils and climate and during a period when per capita world agricultural production was growing (Cavallo & Mundalk 1982: 13–14).

☐ Overvalued Domestic Currency

At the same time that Third World governments are attempting to skim resources from the agricultural sector through export taxes on farm products, they are commonly engaged in activities that further tax agriculture through an overvalued exchange rate (Schuh 1988). Here is what typically happens: As economic development proceeds in a Third World country, local demand for attractive foreign goods usually becomes so great that a foreign currency deficit develops. People want lots of foreign currency so they can buy foreign-made goods that, ultimately, have to be paid for in foreign currency. (To simplify the discussion I will refer to local currency as rupees, a common Third World currency denominator, and to foreign currency as US dollars, the standard currency of world trade.)

As the dollar deficit develops, the value of the rupee falls relative to the dollar. That is, you have to spend more and more rupees to buy one dollar. As the value of the rupee falls, the cost (in terms of rupees) of imported goods rises. Government frequently attempts to stop this progression by fixing into local law the price of rupees relative to the dollar. This fixed ratio becomes the official exchange rate. As the free-market value of the rupee continues to fall, government usually defends the exchange rate by discouraging the purchase of foreign goods. It does this by such measures as requiring that approved buyers obtain a license to obtain dollars, issued at the official exchange rate, from the central bank; placing quotas on imports; and placing high tariffs on imports. The limitations on imports serve to protect domestic industry by cutting back on foreign competition and by raising the local price for industrial products. (For the level of protection afforded to industry in selected countries see Table 17.2.) One thing that this means, of course, is that prices rise on the inputs that farmers use for increasing their production, such as fertilizers, irrigation pumps, and pesticides, whether foreign or produced domestically. But perhaps more important to farm profitability is what it does to the prices of farm products that are exported.

Let us assume that rice costs $0.25 per pound on the world market. And let us assume that the official exchange rate is Rs 6 to $1. A dollar will buy four pounds of rice on the world market, and Rs 6 will buy four pounds. The local farmer therefore can export his rice at Rs 1.50 a pound (assuming no export tax).

But let us also assume that, because of the continued deterioration in the free-market value of the rupee, it now takes Rs 10 to buy a dollar on the unofficial market. The value of a pound of rice on the international market is really Rs 2.50 (Rs 10 equals $1, so four pounds of rice are really worth Rs 2.50 a pound at the market rate). The farmer who exports his rice at Rs 1.50 a pound because he gets only the official exchange rate for his rice is being taxed Rp 1 per pound for his exports. Since the export price sets the domestic price, the farmer who sells on the domestic market is also being taxed Rp 1 per pound for his sales. The domestic consumer receives the benefit of the tax when he purchases the rice at Rs 1.50 rather than at the world price of Rs 2.50.

When you combine the implicit tax resulting from the overvalued domestic currency with an explicit export tax and thus force farm prices well below the international market, and when, in addition to this, you throw in the condition

Table 17.2 Protection of Agriculture Compared with Manufacturing in Selected Developing Countries

	Year	Relative Protection Ratio[a]
Philippines	1974	0.76
Colombia	1978	0.49
Mexico	1980	0.88
Nigeria	1980	0.35
Egypt	1981	0.57
Turkey	1981	0.77
Ecuador	1983	0.65

Source: World Bank 1986:62.

Note: A ratio of 1.00 indicates that effective protection is equal in both sectors; a ratio greater than 1.00 means that protection is in favor of agriculture.

[a]Calculated as $(1 + EPR_a)/(1 + EPR_m)$, where EPR_a and EPR_m are the effective rates of protection for agriculture and the manufacturing sector, respectively.

that the farmer is required to pay more than the world price for his modern purchased inputs, you have a recipe for a substantial disincentive to agricultural production.

Malcolm Bale (1985: 24) studied five developing countries from the point of view of the impact of overvalued domestic currency on agricultural production. He found that

> The extent to which currencies are misaligned in most developing countries is not widely recognized, and certainly its effect on output is not generally appreciated by their policy makers. For example, in the Philippines during most of the 1970s, the exchange rate was overvalued by an estimated 25–30 percent; in Jamaica during the early 1980s by 35 percent; in Colombia in the early 1980s by about 25 percent; and in Nigeria during the past five years by 44 percent. When margins of less than ten percent determine the outcome of a sale or a profit, the effect of implicit taxes of these dimensions on domestic agriculture can be devastating.
>
> The results of these World Bank studies show that misaligned exchange rates have played the prime role in inhibiting agricultural performance.

In a study of the impact of trade and exchange-rate policies on agricultural production incentives in the Philippines, it was found that a 10 percent rise in the domestic price of imported goods (caused by tariffs, for example) results in a 6.6 percent decline in the domestic price of agricultural export products relative to home goods (Bautista 1987: 9).

Thirty-one countries of sub-Saharan Africa, for which data on changes in the degree of overvaluation of domestic currency were available, were examined for the relationship between these changes and agricultural productivity. The countries fell into two groups of approximately equal size, those whose degree of overvaluation was lessening and those whose degree of overvaluation was increasing. Those countries found to be lessening the degree of overvaluation of their domestic currency were found to be increasing their agricultural production, on the average, at 2.4 times the rate of those who were increasing the degree of overvaluation of their currency (Cleaver 1985: 18–19).

☐ Limits on Cash Cropping

A cash crop is one that is produced for sale. It is this commercial orientation of the crop, and not whether it is a food or a nonfood crop, that identifies it as a cash crop. An export crop is, of course, a particular kind of cash crop: one that is ultimately exported from a country (von Braun & Kennedy 1986: 1). In contrast with cash crops, those that are grown for home consumption are called subsistence crops.

It is often argued that the growing of cash crops, and in particular, the growing of cash crops for export, limits the local food supply and therefore raises local food prices. So limits on growing cash crops for export from Third

World countries are often proposed as a means of forcing a shift in cultivation to food crops, thereby lowering the local price of food.

Lappe and Collins (1977), proponents of this point of view, quote a Colombian government economist as estimating that, in Colombia, "one hectare planted with carnations brings in a million pesos a year; planted with wheat or corn, the same hectare would bring only 12,500." In other words the gross returns from a field of carnations in this situation are 80 times the gross returns from grain. These authors assume that growing carnations for export will automatically raise local food prices through limiting the local food supply, and observe, rather sarcastically, that, "if the local peasants cannot afford chicken or eggs, perhaps they can brighten their shacks with cut flowers" (p. 266).

The argument that growing cut flowers in Colombia deprives the local peasants of their food supply misses a couple of important points: (1) Colombians can purchase a lot more grain from the United States (the recipient of the cut flowers) in exchange for a field of carnations than they can raise on that field themselves; (2) the cut flower industry is highly labor-intensive. Regardless of who owns or manages the field of carnations, many more peasants are going to be employed to produce an acre of cut flowers than to produce an acre of grain.

What happens when Third World farmers do, in fact, expand their production of cash crops? Let us look at the evidence from some recent studies.

Kennedy and Cogill (1987) studied smallholders in a low-income farming region in southern Kenya. These farmers were reducing their activities in subsistence agriculture and increasing their commercial sugarcane production activities. As sugarcane acreage expanded it did replace maize acreage. However, the return to labor for sugar was three times the daily agricultural wage rate and significantly higher than the return to maize. Incomes of the farmers who had joined the cane-growing scheme were significantly higher than those of non-sugar farmers, and the increased income positively affected household calorie consumption. For each 1 percent increase in sugarcane income, household energy intake was found to increase by 24 calories (p. 9). The increase in household calorie intake translated into modest increases in calorie intake among the children (Kennedy 1989: 54). The expansion of the sugar industry in the area was also increasing employment opportunities. Typically the sugar mill hired labor and supplied it to the sugar farmer for such activities as weeding and cutting the cane and transporting the cut cane to the mill (Kennedy & Cogill 1987: 9).

Bouis and Haddad (1990) studied families in an area of Mindanao, the Philippines, where a sugar mill had been introduced seven years earlier. Among those who had access to land, all households grew corn but some had switched part of their acreage from corn to sugar. Women were found to be more involved in corn production than in sugar production, contributing 23 percent of the total labor going into corn production, but only 11 percent of the total labor going into sugar production. During breast-feeding, wives in households that grew some sugar spent less time away from home, more time in child care, and less time in field work. The youngest children in sugar households were found to be significantly taller than the same age group in corn households.

In a study that looked at the household-level effects of cash cropping in rural Guatemala, von Braun and his colleagues (1989) surveyed 400 households, about half of whom had recently started raising nontraditional vegetable crops for export. The nontraditional export crops were substantially more profitable than traditional crops and were adopted by even the smallest farmers. Net returns per acre from one of the export crops, snow peas, averaged 15 times those of maize, the most important traditional crop. Returns per unit of family labor for the new crops in general were about twice as high as for maize and 60 percent higher than those for traditional vegetables.

Because the export crop producers had yields for their subsistence food crops some 30 percent higher than their nonexport crop neighbors, the export crop producers tended to have higher amounts of maize and beans available, per capita, for home consumption. Among the reasons that they had higher yields was the fact that they were using some of their increased income to purchase fertilizer to enhance yields on their subsistence crops. Nontraditional export crops enhance local employment, not only on the farm (see Figure 17.1) but

Figure 17.1 Labor Inputs for Traditional Crops (Maize and Traditional Vegetables) and New Export Vegetables (Broccoli, Cauliflower, and Snow Peas), Guatemala, 1985

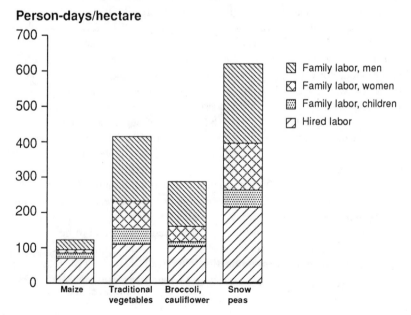

Source: Adapted from Von Braun et al., 1989:49.

also, through backward and forward linkages, off the farm. The farmers purchase locally manufactured sticks and ropes for tying the snow pea plants, for instance. And the marketing of the vegetables for export is labor-intensive, requiring activities such as selection, grading, and packing of the produce (pp. 11–12, 48).

In a statistical analysis of 78 developing countries that devoted at least part of their farmland to cash crops, von Braun and Kennedy (1986: 2) found that the hypothesis that the expansion of cash cropping is at the cost of staple food production was not generally supported. Growth in area allocated to cash crops positively correlates with growth in staple food production. Furthermore, growth in share of cropland allocated to cash crops is generally positively associated with per capita staple food production.

Box 17.2 Export Crops and Food Crops
Uma J. Lele

Development debates and government and donor policies have not stressed the critical role of agriculture for the development of the rest of the economy. Instead of promoting policies that support balanced development of the agricultural sector as a whole, they have tended to emphasize the conflict between food and export crop production.

The attainment of food security is of fundamental importance in the farming decisions of small rural households. Assured food crop production releases land and labor for diversification into other higher-value production for domestic use or export. Export crop production, however, helps raise and stabilize household and national income, thereby increasing food security.

Due to labor intensity, export crops tend to generate greater employment than food cropping. Moreover, the production of most export crops tends to be scale-neutral and therefore can be undertaken by farmers with holdings of any size. Despite these features, export crops were neglected by both governments and donors in the 1970's.

Source: Extracted from Lele, n.d

The case can reasonably be made that limiting cash crop production may, in fact, limit rural incomes and have adverse affects on nutrition. Unfortunately, the advantages of export crop production in the Third World are often neglected by policymakers (see Box 17.2).

■ FARM TAXATION VERSUS IMPLICIT FOOD SUBSIDIES

Government must be financed. And the taxation system that finances government should not only be fair, it should be economically efficient. For efficiency and fairness, all sectors of the economy must bear a portion of the total tax burden, and the tax incidence should fall proportionally across all sectors. There is no question that agriculture should be taxed. The problem in the Third World is how to avoid the excessive taxation of agriculture.

We have seen that it is not uncommon for producers to be taxed as much as 50 percent or more on the value of their farm commodities that are involved in implicit food subsidy programs (see India data, columns 1 and 5 of Table 17.1). Rates of export taxation on the order of 50–75 percent for farm products have not been unusual (World Bank 1986: 64).

It is not equitable to place such a heavy tax burden on the agricultural sector when other sectors are taxed at a lighter rate or even subsidized with protective import measures. Nor is it efficient. Placing an unduly heavy tax burden on agriculture steers productive resources away from this sector and slows productivity within agriculture. The resources lost to agriculture would have yielded a higher return to society in agriculture than they will at the margin in a protected industrial sector. The rate of growth of per capita income slows, and to the extent that such policies exacerbate unemployment, the poor suffer more than do the rich.

There are explicit tax alternatives to the implicit taxes on agriculture that were described above: taxing agricultural land; taxing agricultural income; and taxing agricultural commodities at the point of consumption rather than lowering farm-gate prices. Since these explicit taxes are readily identifiable, they are more likely to be applied equitably relative to other sectors of the economy than are implicit taxes. And because they are not commodity-specific, they do not favor the production of one agricultural commodity over another. For both of these reasons they have a higher degree of economic efficiency than do implicit taxes.

Complaints about the high administrative costs of taxing agricultural land have been used to explain why this method of taxing agriculture has fallen out of favor. Such complaints are hard to justify. It is, after all, fairly easy to determine who has an interest in farming the land; the sort of title search that may be necessary during the transfer of landownership is unnecessary for tax purposes. Market prices can be a ready guide to the value of the land, and satellite imagery now provides a cheap means of sorting out which regions have access to irrigation water, or are growing which crops. Setting up an equitable system of land taxation today is technically feasible and not unduly costly.

It is possible to tax agricultural income, especially on the large agricultural holdings. In Latin America 1 percent of the population controls over 50 percent of the land, and the operations of these landholders account for more than one-sixth of the GNP for the area (World Bank 1986: 83). The income of these large landholders would be fairly easy to identify for taxation. For large agricultural corporations, the personal income tax can be used to tax employees and the corporation profits tax can be used to tax the business itself. As the tax collection system improves it can be extended downward toward the smaller farmers, as appropriate.

Taxing agricultural commodities at the retail level instead of at the farm gate puts a greater burden on the wealthy than on the poor, since the wealthy are more likely to purchase their food in a retail outlet where the tax is collected.

Shifting from implicit taxes on agriculture to explicit taxes does not have to mean the demise of all food-linked income transfer programs. Such programs can be financed by explicit means using money in the public tax till. This type of financing has the advantage of providing considerable motivation to the framers of the food subsidy to target it carefully toward the most needy.

■ THE COSTS OF URBAN BIAS

When Third World governments adopt policies that lower the price of farm outputs and raise the price of industrial products, they are demonstrating a preference for industrial development over agricultural development. This preference for industry or, more broadly, for the people and resources that are concentrated in the cities is sometimes called urban bias.

Societies pay a heavy price for urban bias. As governments encourage the substitution of locally made industrial goods for imported goods (the policy is sometimes called import substitution for short), the rate of growth of the whole economy is inhibited. In a worldwide study of the effects of such policies, Chenery, Robinson, and Syrquin (1986: 356–358) found that "economies which pursued export led growth—as opposed to a strategy of import substitution—grew faster, industrialized sooner, had higher rates of total factor productivity growth, and tended to achieve the input-output structure of an advanced economy faster." These researchers showed that shifting away from a tariff-induced import substitution trade policy to a neutral trade policy can account for an increase of as much as one percentage point in annual rate of growth of the entire economy. They found furthermore that export-led economies are more likely to attract capital inflows. This helps to explain the success of such export-oriented economies as Korea and Taiwan.

A common aspect of Third World urban bias is the implicit taxation of grain, which is often the leading agricultural product. Taxing one commodity or set of commodities to the exclusion of others shifts resource use in the direction of the untaxed commodities. When the taxed commodity is grain, the diet of the poor, the tax encourages the production of nongrain foods such as livestock products (livestock can eat the grain before it is taxed), fruits, and vegetables. These items are favorites of the rich. It is hard to make a case that there is any nutritional gain to lowering the price of foods for the rich while limiting the production of the chief foods of the poor.

But perhaps the ultimate problem with urban bias is that, as it slows the growth of the entire economy, it deprives the poorest not only of job opportunities but of possible income transfers from the rich to programs that would improve the welfare of the poorest.

Urban bias and its accompanying discrimination against the poor has been widely and loudly criticized, but never more eloquently than by Michael Lipton (see Box 17.3).

Box 17.3 Urban Bias in World Development
Michael Lipton

The most important class conflict in the poor countries of the world today is not between labor and capital. Nor is it between foreign and national interests. It is between the rural classes and the urban classes. The rural sector contains most of the poverty, and most of the low-cost sources of potential advance; but the urban sector contains most of the articulateness, organization and power.

So the urban classes have been able to "win" most of the rounds of the struggle with the countryside; but in so doing they have made the development process needlessly slow and unfair. Scarce investment, instead of going into water-pumps to grow rice, is wasted on urban super-highways. Scarce human skills design and administer not clean village wells and agricultural extension services, but world boxing championships in showpiece stadia.

The poor—between one-quarter and one-fifth of the people of the world—are overwhelmingly rural: landless laborers, or farmers with no more than an acre or two, who must supplement their income by wage labor.

The disparity between urban and rural welfare is much greater in poor countries now than it was in rich countries during their early development. This huge welfare gap is demonstrably inefficient, as well as inequitable. It persists mainly because less than 20 per cent of investment for development has gone to the agricultural sector, although over 65 per cent of the people of Third World countries, and over 80 per cent of the really poor who live on $1 a week each or less, depend for a living on agriculture.

In most Third World countries, governments have undertaken numerous measures with the unhappy side-effect of accentuating rural-urban disparities: their own allocation of public expenditure and taxation; measures raising the price of industrial products relative to farm products, thus encouraging private rural saving to flow into industrial investment because the value of industrial output has been artificially boosted; and educational facilities encouraging bright villagers to train in cities for urban jobs.

Such processes have been extremely inefficient. For instance, the impact on output of $1 of carefully selected investment is, in most countries, two to three times as high in agriculture as elsewhere, yet public policy and private market power have combined to push domestic savings and foreign aid into non-agricultural uses.

Urban bias also increases inefficiency and inequity *within* the sectors. Poor farmers have little land and much under-used family labor. Hence they tend to complement any extra developmental resources received—pumpsets, fertilizers, virgin land—with much more extra labor than do large farmers. Poor farmers thus tend to get the most output from such extra resources (as well as needing the extra income most). But rich farmers (because they sell their extra output to the cities instead of eating it themselves, and because they are likely to use much of their extra income to support urban investment) are naturally favored by urban-biased policies. It is they, not the efficient small farmers, who get the cheap loans and the fertilizer subsidies.

But am I not hammering at an open door? Certainly the persiflage of allocation has changed recently, under the impact of patently damaging deficiencies in rural output. Development plans are nowadays full of "top priority for agriculture." This is reminiscent of the pseudo-egalitarian school where, at mealtimes, Class B children get priority, while Class A children get food.

It is *not* my wish to *overstate* the case for reducing urban bias. Such a reduction is not the *only* thing necessary. But a shift of resources to the rural sector, and within it to the efficient rural poor even if they do very little for urban development is often, perhaps usually, the *overriding* developmental task.

Urban bias does not rest on a conspiracy, but on convergent interests. Industrialists, urban workers, even big farmers, *all* benefit if agriculture gets squeezed, provided its few resources are steered, heavily subsidized, to the big farmer, to produce cheap food and raw materials for the cities. Nobody conspires; all the powerful are satisfied; the labor-intensive small farmer stays efficient, poor and powerless, and had better shut up. Meanwhile, the economist, often in the blinkers of industrial determinism, congratulates all concerned on resolutely extracting an agricultural surplus to finance industrialization.

Source: Reprinted by permission of the publishers from *Why Poor People Stay Poor: Urban Bias in World Development* by Michael Lipton, Cambridge, Mass.: Harvard University Press, copyright © 1976 by Michael Lipton.

☐ 18

Policies Aimed at Lowering the Price of Food Through Subsidized Production

While the most important reasons for inadequate agricultural output are diffi-cult to ascertain, T. W. Schultz, in the first Elmhurst Memorial Lecture to the International Association of Agricultural Economists, left no doubt as to his ranking of the causes. He stated that the level of agricultural production de-pends not so much on technical considerations, but in large measure, "on what governments do to agriculture."

—Bale and Lutz 1981: 8

Lack of purchasing power is one of the leading causes of undernutrition (see Chapter 7). In Chapters 16 and 17 we reviewed policies aimed at increasing pur-chasing power through food-linked income transfers, that is, through subsidiz-ing consumption. In this chapter we examine policies designed to increase pur-chasing power by lowering food prices through increased agricultural production. Flooding Third World markets with locally grown food would not only bring down the local price of food but would reduce dependence on food imports, allow these countries to build up reserve stocks of food against future bad crop years, and enhance their opportunities for food exports.

■ MOTIVATING INCREASED PRODUCTION: SOME PRELIMINARY CONSIDERATIONS

The task here is to persuade farmers to raise production. Raising production is important not only as a means of lowering the price of food but because, as John Mellor (1985a), former director of the International Food Policy Research Insti-tute, puts it, "the single most important element in reducing rural poverty is in-creased agricultural production."

Higher farm production increases the demand for labor and increases the income of landless rural workers. Local off-farm activities rise as crop produc-tion goes up. Increased agricultural production tends to decrease food prices, which benefits the rural poor. Lower-cost food releases capital and public-sector resources for industrial and commercial development and increases the demand for labor in the urban sector, thus providing jobs for some of the surplus labor that agriculture is continually plagued with (Mellor 1985a).

It must be kept in mind, however, that the farm sector of an economy is vastly different than the nonfarm sector. There may be millions of farm firms, but only a few steel plants. Farmers operate dispersed across the landscape rather than in a few concentrated locations. They are subjected to high levels of risk and uncertainty. Their production is, of necessity, seasonal. (For a fuller discussion of the uniqueness of the farm sector in the Third World, see Box 18.1.) Because of the enormous differences between the farm sector and nonfarm sectors of the economy, persuading the farm sector to raise production may be vastly different from persuading some sector of the nonfarm economy to raise production. To persuade the farm sector to increase production, the typical Third World government must make it in the self-interest of millions of farmers to want to increase production.

To be more specific, in order to stimulate increased agricultural productivity, governments have to rig the system to motivate farmers to want to do such things as invest more in their farms, adopt new technology, and learn better management techniques. How all three of these activities are important to increasing agricultural production is illustrated in Figure 18.1, using data from India, where

Figure 18.1 Greater Response of Modern Rice Varieties to Nitrogen Fertilizer (Experiment Station Yields in the United States and India, 1964)

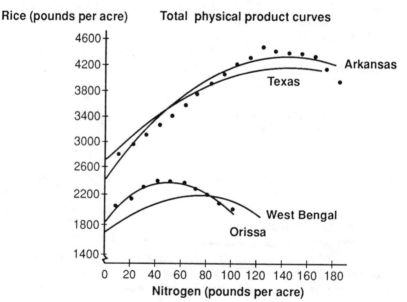

Source: Adapted from Herdt and Mellor 1964:150-160.

Box 18.1 The Agricultural Sector is Different
C. Peter Timmer, Walter P. Falcon, and Scott R. Pearson

A number of features set the agricultural sector of an economy apart from the other productive sectors. Three of the most important of these features are: 1) Agriculture's large contribution to national income, 2) The large number of participants in agriculture, and 3) The peculiarities of the agricultural production process.

The Relatively Large Size of the Agriculture Sector
In most Third World countries, a large proportion of economic activity is provided by agriculture. The percent of the labor force in agriculture in most Third World countries runs over 50 percent, while the percent of the labor force in agriculture in most industrial market economies runs less than 15 percent (World Bank 1988, p. 282–283).

In a few countries just emerging from centuries of traditional economic organization, the agricultural sector contributes as much as 70 percent of the gross national product. Half the output in many developing countries is still produced in agriculture. If agriculturally related industries are also counted in (these develop rapidly in the course of modernizing agriculture), the share of this broader "agribusiness" sector seldom declines to less than one-quarter of national economic output, even in advanced industrial societies. When agriculture contributes half or more of the gross national product, rapid growth in per capita income is difficult to achieve unless rural income is rising.

The Large Number of Participants in Agriculture
In many countries, 60 to 80 percent of the population still lives in rural areas, earning a livelihood directly or indirectly from agriculture. In nearly all developing countries a majority of the population lives in the countryside. In addition to the fact that much of the world's poverty is found in rural areas, the overwhelming predominance of the rural population has two important consequences for understanding agricultural policy making: 1) Most farms are small because large numbers of people must share the arable land, and 2) Millions of individuals each behave according to their particular decision making environments.

Small size of operation. In most countries, if the available arable land were divided equally among the farm population, the resulting average farm size would be small by comparison with U.S. or European standards. Farms of less than a hectare would characterize China, Bangladesh, and Java. Even Japanese farms average only slightly more than a hectare. The average in India would be about 1 to 2 hectares, and in Africa and Latin America farms would tend to be less than 20 hectares. Average farm size is well over 100 hectares in the United States and well over 50 hectares in the United Kingdom.

Decentralized decision making. Growing food is a decision-intensive undertaking. What crops to plant, what inputs to use, when to plow, to seed, to cultivate, to irrigate, to harvest, how much to keep for home consumption, how much to sell and how much to store for later sale are decisions that constantly confront farmers. Agriculture is truly unique in that literally *millions* of individuals and households are making these decisions themselves or in consultation with relatively small numbers of neighbors, friends, or partners. In Brazil, India, Indonesia, Nigeria, and even in China, influencing agricultural production decisions to increase food output is an entirely different process from changing decisions
(continued on next page)

Box 18.1 continued
about how much steel or cement to produce. In each of the countries—indeed, in most countries—a dozen or so individuals could take direct action which would lead to a 10 percent increase in steel output in a year or so. Their decisions would be decisive.

Nowhere, not even in socialist countries, can a similar small group of individuals decide to raise food production by 10 percent. To increase food production by 10 percent, Third World governments must convince the *millions of farmers* in their country to *want* to increase food production by 10 percent, and *make it in their self-interest to do so.*

Here is the true importance of the vast number of agricultural decision-makers. There are simply too many of them to reach directly either with pleas for cooperation or with police power.

Farmers' decisions are likely to be altered only when they perceive the *incentives* to be favorable to the change.

The Peculiarities of the Agricultural Production Process
In farming, management skill is frequently combined with the farm household's own labor power. Several other features contribute to the uniqueness of the agricultural production process. The most important of these are 1) Seasonality of production, 2) Geographical dispersion of production, 3) High levels of risk and uncertainty, and 4) Off farm sources of technical change.

Seasonality of production. No agricultural region of the world has an absolutely constant climate, year-round. Winter and summer create distinct growing seasons in the temperate zones. In the tropics, wet and dry seasons and monsoons create conditions in which planting is appropriate, harvesting is difficult, or some crops simply do not thrive.

Seasonality is important to farmers because it is generally cheaper to let Mother Nature provide many of the essential inputs for agricultural production—solar energy, water, carbon dioxide, temperature control, and essential nutrients from natural soils—than to do so artificially.

Seasonality also tends to place high premiums on the timely performance of such critical agricultural tasks as plowing, planting, cultivating, and harvesting. Even though the available labor pool may seem more than adequate to provide the required number of man-days per hectare over an entire year for all the crops being grown, significant labor bottlenecks may occur if certain tasks must be performed very quickly at specific times to ensure maximum yields. Such bottlenecks may induce individual farmers to mechanize specific tasks—plowing or harvesting—even when much rural unemployment exists over the course of the year.

There are often very high private economic returns to eliminating seasonal bottlenecks in production. When these private returns are generated at least partly by higher and more stable yields of agricultural products, society is also likely to gain. But if the private gains come from displacing hired labor that has few alternative jobs, the social gains may be small or even negative.

Geographical dispersion of production. Agriculture is the only major sector that uses the land surface as an essential input into its production function. Like seasonality, this widespread use of land is due to the largess of nature. It is simply cheaper to let farms capture the free solar energy and rain than to stack a hundred hydroponic "fields" on top of each other and provide the light, nutrients, and water from industrial sources. This wide geographical dispersion of agricultural production has an important economic consequence: Transportation becomes essential if any output is going to leave the farm for consumption by others or if purchased inputs, such as modern seeds, fertilizer, pesticides, or machinery, are to be used on the farm to raise output.

In combination, seasonality and geographical dispersion create the need for a marketing system that can store the product from a short harvest period to the much longer consumption period, and can move the commodity from the farm where it was grown to the many households where it will be consumed.

High levels of risk and uncertainty. Farmers the world over talk primarily about two topics: the weather and prices. On these two variables ride the rewards for the whole year's effort in farming. A failed monsoon, a flood, or a hailstorm can wipe out the crop. A bumper harvest can cause large losses if the price falls too low. No other industry depends on the whims of nature and volatile markets as much as farming does.

Fluctuations in aggregate production are magnified at the level of marketings (produce available for consumption by nonfarm households) because farm household consumption tends to vary somewhat less than production. Consequently, in economies where a significant share of food production is consumed directly by the farm household, marketings vary more than production.

Off farm sources of technical change. In the long run, technical change is the source of most productivity growth. Very few farmers, even in the United States, have the resources to carry out significant agricultural research, and most of it is now conducted by publicly funded agricultural research centers and by a handful of large agribusiness concerns, which are involved primarily in developing hybrid seed technology, chemical technology (herbicides and insecticides), and agricultural machinery. The small scale of most farms and their limited financial resources mean little important agricultural research is conducted by farmers.

Source: Extracted from Timmer, Falcon, and Pearson 1983: 79–91.

Note: As pointed out by Timmer, Falcon, and Pearson, there are high levels of risk and uncertainty involved in agricultural production. Farmers can be encouraged to increase production through farm price and income support programs and through other risk-reducing policies such as subsidized crop insurance programs. Furthermore, price fluctuations in agriculture can be reduced through government-sponsored programs wherein large quantities of grain or other farm commodities are purchased and held in government stockpiles and then offered to the market during periods of scarcity, or increased in size during periods of abundance.

Because of their enormous expense, these production-increasing subsidies are, for all practical purposes, a luxury that can be afforded only by governments of the affluent Western industrialized democracies. (Gardner [1979, 1987] details agricultural policies typical of high-income industrialized democracies.) Governments of low-income, Third World countries are more likely to spend their scarce money on the higher-payoff, production-increasing subsidies outlined in the second half of Chapter 18.

modern (green revolution) rice varieties were not generally available in 1964, the year of the study, and the United States, where modern high-yielding varieties were the norm. In both countries rice was responsive to the application of nitrogen fertilizer (a capital investment), although in the United States it required considerably more investment in fertilizer to reach full production potential than it did in India. In the United States rice was more productive per acre than in India at all levels of fertilization. US farmers were using a higher level of technology—modern rice varieties. To be fully effective, modern rice varieties call for an appropriate package of inputs, including not only the high-yielding seed, but water as well as fertilizer and perhaps pesticides. This involves a higher level of farm management.

Helping farmers to increase investment, adopt new technology, and learn better management techniques requires government spending on things such as rural infrastructure, agricultural research, and agricultural education. This kind of government spending, of course, amounts to a subsidy to agricultural production.

But experience has shown that governments can do all of the above and still find that agricultural production grows far more slowly than expected. Farmers are simply not going to be persuaded to increase production much if the prices they get for their products are too low.

☐ Farmers Are Price-Responsive

In the last chapter I noted that antifarm policies such as noncompetitive government buying of food, low administered farm prices, agricultural export taxes, overvalued domestic currency and protection to industrial production are common in Third World countries, and that singly or in combination they can result in terms of trade that are disadvantageous to agriculture. That is, they can result in lower-than-world-market prices for the things that farmers sell and higher-than-world-market prices for the things that farmers buy.

So the first task for governments that would subsidize agricultural production to motivate increased food production is to rig the price system so that farmers do not face serious price disincentives to production. In most Third World countries this will mean shifting away from an urban bias and toward a more neutral stance regarding agriculture versus industry—in other words—providing a more level playing field on which the agricultural and industrial sectors compete.

During the midtwentieth century it was fashionable to believe that peasant farmers were not responsive to changes in market prices. After all, so the argument went, peasant farmers consumed what they produced and marketed only small amounts in exchange for a few necessities. Their basic behavior was governed by tradition; they worked small plots; they used very little money; there were only a few goods available in their remote village markets. How could price affect their production?

Experience has shown that this position is not supportable. Even though peasant farmers sell only small amounts off their farm, they are responsive to the price ratio between their purchased farm inputs and their marketable surpluses. In fact, in Africa, where farmers are more isolated from market effects than elsewhere because, by and large, they are thinly scattered over the landscape and must make do with a poor system of farm-to-market roads, farm production has been found to be as responsive to increases in price as in other Third World regions. That is, the short-run supply elasticity for farm products in Africa is found to be as high as in other developing regions (World Bank 1986: 68).

☐ Third World Supply Elasticities

Elasticity of supply with respect to price is the percentage change in quantity supplied to the market given a 1 percent change in price. In contrast with demand elasticities with respect to price, supply elasticities are positive; as price increases, quantity supplied increases. In Table 18.1 we see some short-run supply elasticities for several farm products in African countries. (The short run, in this case, refers to the fact that land and other fixed inputs such as tube wells are not allowed to vary in the elasticity analysis.)

Although the evidence is not conclusive, it appears that agricultural supply elasticities are somewhat higher in the developed than in the Third World (Askari & Cummings 1976; Herdt 1970: 518–519), indicating that Third World farmers are somewhat less responsive to changes in prices than are farmers in the developed world. If this is the case, it is most likely explained by the three characteristics of Third World farmers: (1) They are less involved in the market economy—they sell a smaller percentage of their production and therefore are less impressed by swings in market prices; (2) they use lower quantities of purchased inputs relative to output sold and are therefore less able to adjust their production to variations in market prices; (3) they are more risk-averse than farmers in the developed world—they do not like spending large amounts on purchased inputs when there is a chance that, because of low prices, the investment may not pay off. Nevertheless, the fact is that hundreds of estimates of supply response to price among Third World farmers have generally shown a positive relationship between price and production (Askari & Cummings 1976).

Table 18.1 Short-Run Supply Elasticities, Selected Crops, African Countries

	Elasticity
Wheat	.31
Maize	.23
Sorghum	.10
Groundnuts	.24
Cotton	.23
Tobacco	.48
Cocoa	.15
Coffee	.14
Rubber	.14

Source: World Bank 1986:68; data are derived from Askari and Cummings 1976 and Scandizzo and Bruce 1980.

Similar results are obtained for long-run aggregate supply elasticities, that is, the percentage that aggregate farm output changes with a 1 percent change in real farm prices. (Aggregate supply elasticities are called long-run because all inputs, including land and major capital items, are allowed to vary with price changes. Because all inputs are allowed to vary, long-run supply elasticities are generally higher than short-run supply elasticities.) In the Third World the aggregate supply elasticity of agriculture with respect to price appears to range between 0.3 and 0.9. More-advanced Third World countries tend to have aggregate supply elasticities in the 0.6 to 0.9 range while the less-advanced countries, with poorer infrastructure, tend to fall in the range around 0.3 to 0.5 (Chhibber 1988).

Policymakers must face the fact that the relationship between agricultural production and price is positive. No amount of legislation will change this. The upward slope to the supply curve is due to physical and cost relationships involved in production (Box 18.2).

☐ Is Getting Prices Right a Precondition for Effective Subsidized Production?

The fact that the supply curve slopes upward presents policymakers concerned with the world food problem with their thorniest dilemma: Low food prices make it easier for the poor to purchase food, yet they discourage food production and have other adverse social costs, some of which are borne by the poor.

Urban-biased policies have, unquestionably, succeeded in battering down Third World farm prices. Peterson (1979) measured real farm prices in various countries in terms of the amount of fertilizer that 100 kilograms of wheat would purchase. Using this measure, he found that, during 1968–1970, real farm prices in the top 10 countries in terms of prices (mostly high-income industrialized democracies) averaged 3.7 times those of the bottom 10 countries (all Third World countries).

Unfortunately, as I mentioned earlier, the poor have often paid a price for this cheap food. Bale and Lutz (1981) attempted to quantify some of the costs to the poor of low farm prices. In all five countries they studied, with policies that had depressed prices of the leading food grains, they found reductions in production resulting from these price policies. One of the most important consequences of these policies, however, was increased levels of unemployment among the rural poor. Bale and Lutz found, for instance, that the below-world-market prices for food in Egypt led to a reduction in agricultural employment of 1.15 million workers, or around 5 percent of the rural population. This reduction in employment opportunity in the countryside adds to rural underemployment, increases the rate of migration to already overcrowded cities, and increases unemployment in those cities. These authors conclude that "the conventional lay wisdom that if prices for farm products were to be increased in developing countries, poor people would be hurt, needs to be scrutinized" (p. 17). Policy-

Box 18.2 Why the Supply Curve Slopes Upward

There is a physical and a cost basis for the relationship between price and the amount that a farmer will try to produce. Let us start with the underlying physical relationship, using as our example the relationship between the amount of seed planted in one field (say a hectare of land) and crop yield. The raw data we assume are given in Table a and plotted in Figure a. The top curve in Figure a represents the total yield from varying amounts of fertilizer (total physical product or production function). The bottom curve represents the yield added by each successive increment of 10 units of seed (marginal physical product).

What we have in Figure a is a graphic representation of the fact that, as we increase the amount of an input used, holding other inputs constant, we experience diminishing returns to successive inputs (thus the downward-sloping marginal physical product curve — which is often called diminishing marginal returns). (Notice the similarity between the hypothetical total physical product

Table a Hypothetical Yield Response to Varying Amounts of Seed

Seed	Yield	Marginal Product
0	0	
10	39	39
20	52	13
30	61	9
40	66	5
50	66	0
60	64	-2

Figure a Hypothetical Total Physical Product and Marginal Product from Use of Seed on a Fixed Quantity of Land

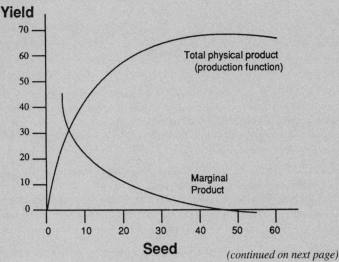

(continued on next page)

Box 18.2 continued
curve in Figure a and the real-world total physical product curves shown in Figure 18.1. The functional relationships we are talking about here are based on observations that have been made in the real world, like those in Figure 18.1.)

Now let us combine the variable inputs commonly used to increase production on our hypothetical one hectare of land. As we increase production we not only add more seed, but more fertilizer, more labor, and maybe other inputs such as irrigation water and pesticides. These things cost money. As we increase production, we could, at various amounts produced, add up the costs of the things we are using to increase production and plot these sums to get a cost curve.

The cost curve would say very much the same thing that Figure a says, except that it would measure costs, instead of seed, along the horizontal input. (The relation between cost and production is based on the underlying physical relationships between inputs and production.) We diagram our cost curve in Figure b. Because the fixed cost of land is not included in our set of costs, we identify the costs in this diagram as variable costs.

Figure b As Variable Costs Increase, the Rate of Increase in Yield Decreases

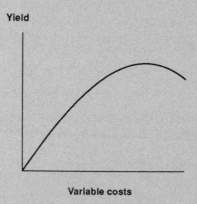

Notice in Figure b that, although not specifically diagrammed, as yield increases there are diminishing marginal returns to costs, just as there were diminishing marginal returns to seed in Figure a.

It is a convention of economics to draw cost curves with the cost on the vertical axis and the yield on the horizontal axis. So let us redraw Figure b in the conventional way, namely as shown in Figure c. (To see what happens to the cost curve when this is done, you might want to trace Figure b and then flip it over and look at it from the back side so as to get Figure c.)

With Figure c, instead of thinking about what happens to yield as we increase costs by one unit, we can think about what happens to costs as we increase yield by one unit. If you examine Figure c you will see that we produce under conditions of increasing marginal cost. For each additional unit of yield from our hectare of land, we have to spend somewhat more on our bundle of variable costs.

These increasing marginal costs are diagrammed on Figure d.

Figure c As Yield Increases, Variable Costs Increase at an Increasing Rate

Variable costs

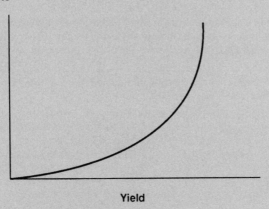

Yield

Figure d As Yield Increases, Marginal Cost Increases

**Marginal cost
(vertical scale is
expanded from
the scale in
Figure c)**

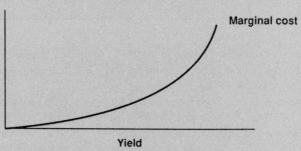

Marginal cost

Yield

Thus we see that we produce under diminishing marginal returns, which results in producing with increasing marginal costs. The two are based on the same underlying physical relationship.

For an individual producer, the marginal cost curve (Figure d) is the price schedule at which he is willing to produce various amounts of goods for the market. He is willing to produce up to the point where the price equals his marginal

(continued on next page)

Box 18.2 continued

cost of production. If he is producing at this point and we want to motivate him to produce more, barring a shift in technology or a reduction in the costs of some of his inputs, we will have to pay him more. This is represented in Figure e as shifting production from A to B, which is motivated by an increase in price from P_1 to P_2.

Adding up the marginal cost curves (individuals' supply curves) for all the individual producers yields the supply curve for the industry. Increasing the price of the product will motivate the industry to produce more.

Figure e Increasing the Price of a Product Makes Possible Increased Production

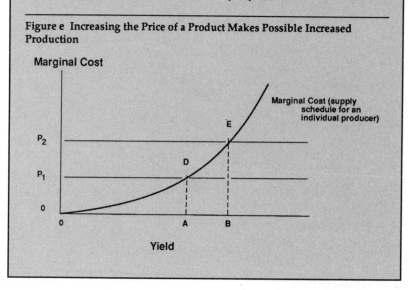

makers would be well advised to bear in mind that "the price paid for cheap food today is food import dependence and a lethargic agricultural performance tomorrow" (Bale 1984).

Earlier in this chapter we saw that long-run supply elasticities in agriculture are higher than short-run supply elasticities. Farm families can eat less, for a while, in response to a sudden rise in the price of food, and thus market more of their production. And they can make minor changes in the amounts of labor and fertilizer they are using, in response to what they perceive as a short-run change in price. But if price changes last long enough, and if farmers perceive the price change to be long-lasting, they can adjust their major capital investments and even the amount of land that they devote to agriculture. That is why farmers are more responsive to price changes over the long run than they are over the short run.

Farmers are often reluctant to adopt new technology because of the risk and uncertainty associated with it. Higher prices to farmers may counterbalance the risk and uncertainty associated with such change and thus encourage technology adoption (Mellor 1984: 165).

Figure 18.2 Effect of Improved Technology on the Supply Curve

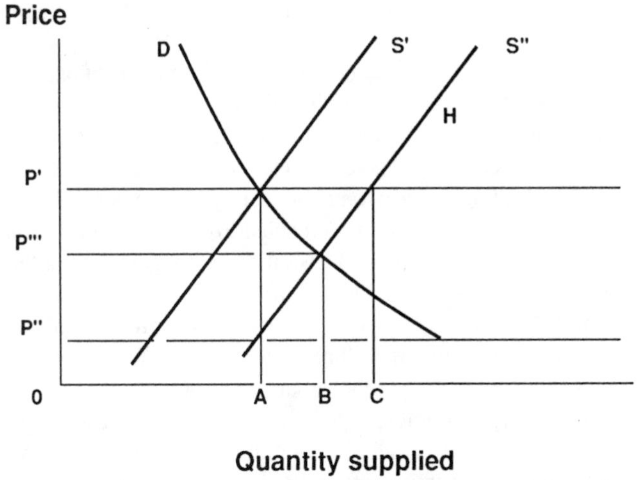

Price

Quantity supplied

Note: When the supply curve shifts from S' to S'', farmers are willing to furnish to the market: (1) an increase quantity (OC rather than OA) at the same old price (P'); (2) the same old quantity (OA) at a new price (P''); or (3) some other combination of quantity and price: for instance, the quantity and price represented by point H on the diagram. In the absence of a shift in demand, the new price will be P''' and the new quantity supplied will be OB. That is, consumers will have more food at a lower price.

Once farmers have invested in new capital, adopted new technology, and learned the more complex management techniques necessary to go along with these changes, they are not likely to abandon them in the face of the lower prices that accompany generally increased production. That is, farmers will be willing to supply more food to the market at all price levels than they were prior to making the changes described above. In other words, they will have shifted their supply curve to the right (Figure 18.2). What I am saying here is that higher prices, combined with the expectation of continued high prices, may provide the conditions for a permanent shift in the supply curve for agriculture to the right. Once this has happened, and in the absence of a shift in demand, farmers will be supplying more food to consumers and at a lower price.

Let us now review the arguments for allowing Third World domestic farm prices to rise to international levels. This action would stimulate farm production and reduce reliance on imported food, thus saving scarce foreign exchange; stimulate rural employment and reduce the pressure for migration to the city, thus reducing urban unemployment; and help provide conditions under which the supply curve for agriculture shifts permanently to the right, resulting in a permanent reduction of the cost of food.

■ SUBSIDIZING PRODUCTION

I have been arguing that allowing farm prices to rise to international levels and ending pricing policies that favor industry over agriculture are important, not only to stimulate agricultural production, but to provide the preconditions for a permanent shift in the supply curve to the right. While getting prices right will not, in and of itself, solve the hunger problem, it will help to make possible its solution. As one economist has quipped, "getting prices right" is not the end of economic development, but "getting prices wrong" frequently is (Timmer 1984: 188).

Lowering the price of food through subsidized production is what we set out to discuss in this chapter. The discussion so far suggests that, although subsidizing production may shift the supply curve to the right, thus simultaneously increasing food production and lowering food prices, production subsidies, in the absence of appropriate prices, will be only partially effective. In other words, getting prices right seems to be a necessary but not a sufficient condition for rapidly accelerating agricultural production. Just the same, subsidizing food production, or government investment in agriculture, as it is sometimes more euphemistically called, is an important method for stimulating increases in farm production. (See Box 18.3 for a discussion of the way the word *subsidy* is used in this book.)

Elias (1985) looked at government expenditures on agriculture in nine Latin American countries between 1950 and 1980. He found a positive correlation between public.inputs to agriculture and growth in agricultural production. The higher the rate of such expenditure, the higher was the rate of growth of agriculture. Spending on irrigation and on agricultural research and extension had a higher payoff than the other expenditure components studied. Furthermore, stimulating agricultural productivity stimulates industrial productivity (Haggblade & Hazell 1989). A study in India, for instance, suggests that a 1 percent addition to the agricultural growth rate stimulates a further 0.5 percentage point increase in the growth rate of industrial output (Rangarajan 1982: 5).

I said earlier that, to stimulate increased agricultural productivity, governments have to rig the system to motivate farmers to want to do such things as invest more in their farms, adopt new technology, and learn better management techniques. Besides getting prices right, what are the sorts of expenditures that governments can make to motivate the above changes? That is, how can government spend in ways that will shift the supply curve for agriculture to the right? Subsidies to do this are commonly proposed for agricultural research; diffusion and adoption of technology, including training in better management techniques; purchased inputs; and rural infrastructure.

☐ Subsidizing Agricultural Research

Technological change is one of the primary driving forces behind increasing production. Improved technology (e.g., a higher-yielding variety of rice) can in-

Box 18.3 Subsidies, Public Goods, and Public Investment

A subsidy, to quote a Merriam-Webster dictionary, is a grant or gift of money as, for instance, money granted by one state to another or a grant by a government to a private person or company to assist an enterprise deemed advantageous to the public.

Subsidies are usually granted because of a failure of the market to provide certain public goods. A small public park, a downtown sidewalk, national defense, and free public education are examples of public goods. Public goods have two critical properties: (1.) It is impossible to exclude individuals from enjoying the benefits from them; and, (2.) it is undesirable to exclude individuals from enjoying the benefits from them, since such enjoyment does not detract from that of others (Stiglitz 1986: 119).

No one wants to produce a public good because, once produced, it is available to all. The producer cannot sell it and capture his costs. Therefore government needs to give an incentive (the subsidy) to someone to provide the public good.

Because we think of investment as an expenditure that will provide production or income on into the future, the distinction between subsidy and public investment may be blurred or fuzzy. For instance, we can think of expenditure on the education of our children not only as a subsidy spent for a public good, but as investing in human capital, because educated children will be more productive later on in life than uneducated children.

Some subsidies are not available to all, but only to a particular class of people. For instance, the US government has, at times, subsidized farmers by paying them to put lime on their fields, or homeowners by giving them a tax break for insulating their homes. These subsidies were available, respectively, only to farmers and homeowners. The subsides were provided, however, because it was thought that they would improve welfare for all. The lime was to increase food production, thus lowering the price of food for all, and the home insulation was to lessen US dependence on overseas sources of oil.

Because the word *subsidy* carries negative connotations for many people, we often use the phrase *public investment* when a subsidy results in increased benefits to society through time. Thus when a consortium of governments pays a public agricultural experiment station for research to develop high-yielding varieties of rice, we may want to call it a public investment. All rice farmers can benefit from the new rice varieties, and of course the public benefits from the lower market price of rice after the higher-yielding rice varieties are put into use. We could also call the rice research and the resulting high-yielding varieties a public good. So it is with many other public expenditures for enhancing agricultural production, such as research on irrigation machinery or agricultural extension programs—they are pitched at the farm sector but they benefit the public.

The word *subsidy* is used here in a nonpejorative sense to indicate government expenditures deemed advantageous to the public, whether to another government, an institution, a company, or a person. In many cases the phrase *public investment* could be substituted for the word *subsidy*. The important thing is that you understand what happens with, what are the impacts of, the various types of expenditures governments make as they allocate their scarce resources among alternative ends in order to minimize undernutrition.

crease the productivity of every item of the set of resources that a farmer uses—land, labor, management, and capital. Yet the agricultural researcher intent on developing new technology for agriculture faces an extraordinarily intricate range of scientific challenges. One recent analysis of technological change (Lele, Kinsey & Obeya 1989: 42) listed these areas as important to researchers in improved crop varieties in Third World agriculture:

- Yield potential and responsiveness to available chemical fertilizers and pesticides
- Adaptation to the growing period and drought tolerance
- Disease and pest resistance
- Improvements in quality, palatability, and consumer acceptance
- Storage, transport, and other handling qualities (including processing) with available technology
- Changes in labor requirements in production and processing in relation to the available mechanical technology, in view of other requirements for household labor and incentives for labor use
- Compatibility with other social, cultural, and economic norms

Not only is the range of challenge complex, but the disciplines brought to bear on agricultural research are varied. Advancing agricultural technology involves research in biology, chemistry, and engineering, as well as in the social sciences, which are crucial to the appropriate integration of the new technology into the production system.

Despite the challenging nature of agricultural research, the payoff has been nothing short of spectacular. Agricultural research has been instrumental in dramatic increases in crop yields per acre (Box 18.4) as well as in livestock productivity. And when the costs of agricultural research are compared to the benefits to society, agricultural research turns out to be a real bargain.

On Table 18.2 studies of payoffs to research done at agricultural experiment stations around the world are listed. The last column, annual internal rate of return, is of particular interest. The internal rate of return represents the average earning power of the resources used in a project during the project period. For an agricultural research project, it is the equivalent of the interest rate you would have to get from a savings account to have the same return on your savings as the public got from the agricultural research project.

Take the first item on the list in Table 18.2, returns to research on hybrid corn (maize) in the United States, calculated by the economist Griliches (1958). (The corn breeding research was done by many people.) The internal rate of return to hybrid corn research in the United States is calculated at 35–40 percent. That means that for every dollar the US public paid for agricultural research on hybrid corn, up until 1955, it collects $0.35 to $0.40 every year in benefits (mostly through lower prices for corn).

Box 18.4 Increases in Yield per Hectare — A Personal View
Theodore W. Schultz

Agricultural research, along with complementary inputs, has been very success-ful in developing substitutes for cropland (some call this land augmentation). Actual increases in yield per hectare have held and may well continue to hold the key to increases in crop production.

For example, during my first year at Iowa State College, 1931, the U.S. yield of maize was 1,500 kg/ha, a normal crop. In 1978 this yield came to 6,300 kg/ha. Although the maize area harvested in 1978 was 16 million hectares less than in 1931, total production was over 175 million metric tons, compared with 65 million tons in 1931. No wonder the estimated rates of return on maize re-search in the United States are exceedingly high.

The achievement with sorghum is even more dramatic. Taking 1929 as a normal year, the yield of sorghum grain rose from 870 kg/ha to 2,800 kg/ha in 1978, despite the fact that the area devoted to this crop [only] increased from 1.8 to 6.7 million hectares. Total production in 1978 was 19 million tons, which is over 15 times as much as that in 1929.

Source: Extracted from Schultz 1979.

Of the 62 studies collected in Table 18.2, only four showed internal rates of return below 20 percent. Interestingly, rates of return to agricultural research run about the same for Third World countries as for developed countries. It would be hard to find another set of investments that pay off as well as agricultural research.

If agricultural research has such a spectacular payoff, why do farmers them-selves not pay for it? There are two reasons why it is not appropriate to ask farmers to pay: (1) Most farmers have far too small an operation to sponsor and benefit from agricultural research; and (2) because the elasticity of demand for most farm products is less than one, the majority of the benefits from agricul-tural research go to consumers. Farmers generally lose out when the new tech-nology is widely adopted because they see their farm-gate prices fall faster than they can increase production. Long-term data from the United States, with a his-tory of public sponsorship of agricultural research dating back to the 1870s is illustrative:

> The decline in the real price of food has been dramatic. Available data for the period 1888 to 1891 indicate that consumers spent an average of about 40 per-cent of their income for food. From 1930 to 1960, the food expenditure pro-portion of consumer incomes ranged from 20 to 24 percent. In the seventies, the proportion of total disposable personal income spent for food dropped to a range of 16–17 percent. By the mid-eighties, that proportion for the average family had dropped to a record low of 15 percent (Lee & Taylor 1986).

Table 18.2 Internal Rate of Return from Agricultural Research Projects

Study	Country	Commodity	Time Period	Annual Internal Rate of Return (Percentage)
Griliches 1958	USA	Hybrid corn	1940-55	35-40
Griliches 1958	USA	Hybrid sorghum	1940-57	20
Peterson 1967	USA	Poultry	1915-60	21-25
Evenson 1969	South Africa	Sugarcane	1945-62	40
Ardito Barletta 1970	Mexico	Wheat	1943-63	90
Ardito Barletta 1970	Mexico	Maize	1943-63	35
Ayer 1970	Brazil	Cotton	1924-67	77+
Schmitz and Seckler 1970	USA	Tomato harvester	1958-69	
		With no compensation to displaced workers		37-46
		Assuming compensation of displaced workers for 50 percent of earnings lost		16-28
Ayer and Schuh 1972	Brazil	Cotton	1924-67	77-110
Hines 1972	Peru	Maize	1954-67	35-40[a] 50-55[b]
Hyami and Akino 1977	Japan	Rice	1915-50	25-27
Hayami and Akino 1977	Japan	Rice	1930-61	73-75
Hertford, Ardila,	Colombia	Rice	1957-72	60-82
Rocha, Trujillo	Colombia	Soybeans	1960-71	79-96
1977	Colombia	Wheat	1953-73	11-12
	Colombia	Cotton	1953-72	0
Pee 1977	Malaysia	Rubber	1932-73	24
Peterson and Fitzharris	USA	Aggregate	1937-42	50
1977			1947-52	51
			1957-62	49
			1957-72	34
Wennergren and Whitaker 1977	Bolivia	Sheep, wheat	1966-75	44.1-47.5
Pray 1978	Punjab (Br. India)	Agricultural research and extension	1906-56	34-44
	Punjab (Pakistan)	Agricultural research and extension	1948-63	23-37
Scobie and Posada 1978	Colombia	Rice	1957-74	79-96
Tang 1963	Japan	Aggregate	1880-1938	35
Griliches 1964	USA	Aggregate	1949-59	35-40
Latimer 1964	USA	Aggregate	1949-59	Not significant
Peterson 1967	USA	Poultry	1915-60	21
Evenson 1968	USA	Aggregate	1949-59	47
Evenson 1969	South Africa	Sugarcane	1945-58	40

Table 18.2 *(continued)*

Study	Country	Commodity	Time Period	Annual Internal Rate of Return (Percentage)
Ardito Barletta 1970	Mexico	Crops	1943-63	45-93
Duncan 1972	Australia	Pasture improvement	1948-69	58-68
Evenson and Jha 1973	India	Aggregate	1953-71	40
Kahlon, Bal, Saxena, and Jha 1977	India	Aggregate	1960-61	63
Lu and Cline 1977	USA	Aggregate	1938-48	30.5
			1949-59	27.5
			1959-69	25.5
			1969-72	23.5
Bredahl and Peterson	USA	Cash grains	1969	36[c]
1976		Poultry	1969	37[c]
		Dairy	1969	43[c]
		Livestock	1969	47[c]
Evenson and Flores	Asia (national)	Rice	1950-65	32-39
1978	Asia	Rice	1966-75	73-78
	(international)	Rice	1966-75	74-102
Flores, Evenson and	Tropics	Rice	1966-75	46-71
Hayami 1978	Philippines	Rice	1966-75	75
Nagy and Furton 1978	Canada	Rapeseed	1960-75	95-110
Davis 1979	USA	Aggregate	1949-59	66-110
			1964-74	37
Evenson 1979	USA	Aggregate	1868-1926	65
	USA	Technology-oriented	1927-50	95
	USA (south)	Technology-oriented	1948-71	93
	USA (north)	Technology-oriented	1948-71	95
	USA (west)	Technology-oriented	1948-71	45
	USA	Science-oriented	1927-50	110
			1948-71	45
	USA	Farm management research and agricultural extension	1948-71	110

Source: Evenson 1981:358-360. (See the source for the studies from which these data are derived.)

[a]Returns to maize research only.
[b]Returns to maize research, plus cultivation "package."
[c]Lagged marginal product of 1969 research on output discounted for an estimated mean lag of five years for cash grains, six years for poultry and dairy, and seven years for livestock.

Patent laws protect mechanical and chemical innovations more effectively than biological innovations. For this reason, some agroindustrial firms have been able to sponsor research in farm machinery or agricultural chemicals and capture the benefits from that research. Hybrid seeds are protectable by patents and, since they do not breed true, farmers must purchase new supplies each year. So after government-sponsored research led the way, hybrid seed companies set up their own research and are developing their own varieties. But by and large, biological innovations in agriculture have to be paid for by government. Thus animal breeding, animal nutrition, plant breeding, plant pathology, entomology, agronomy, soil science, and so on are, by and large, government-sponsored (Judd, Boyce & Evenson 1987: 7).

Some governments are too small to sponsor agricultural research. Their funds are best spent on adaptive agricultural research—finding out which of the innovations discovered elsewhere are most adaptable to their own situation. The Consultative Group on International Agricultural Research stations are helping to fill in the research gap felt by the smaller countries. As of 1989 there were 12 international agricultural research stations belonging to this group and sponsored by a variety of sources. The group includes the International Rice Research Institute in the Philippines and the International Maize and Wheat Improvement Center in Mexico, both of which were mentioned in Box 8.2, as well as a number of other centers whose activities range from plant and animal breeding to food policy. On Table 18.3 all of the centers, with their location and their program focus, are listed.

Modern-day challenges to agricultural research are legion. The techniques of recombinant DNA and cell fusion are making it possible for biotechnologists to engage in investigations with very high reward opportunities, developing highly productive organisms that might not ever have arisen in nature (US, Congress, Office of Technology Assessment 1986).

Innovative research sometimes can take unusual directions, such as the simultaneous cultivation of fish and rice in one rice paddy. Such a practice has been shown to increase the yield of rice and at the same time provide a high-protein supplement to the regular rice crop (Table 18.4). Alternatively, a tiny water fern called *azolla* can be grown with the rice in the paddy. "Azolla plays host to a blue-green alga, *Anabaena azollae*, that can convert or 'fix' atmospheric nitrogen into a form that plants can use. Azolla floats on the water between the rice plants. When it dies and is incorporated into the soil, decomposition frees the nitrogen. A rice crop fertilized only with azolla can yield about 1.5 tons more per hectare than an unfertilized crop" (International Rice Research Institute 1989: 1).

Low-income rural householders could benefit from research on hardy but efficient scavenging animals. High-yielding, disease-resistant breeds of chickens, ducks, goats, pigs, cattle, bees, or fish that can utilize garbage or other food that may be locally available but is not fit for human consumption would be of considerable benefit to the Third World's poor.

Table 18.3 International Agricultural Research Centers Supported by the Consultative Group on International Agricultural Research (CGIAR), 1986

Acronym (Year established)	Center	Location	Research program, geographic focus	1986 Budget[a] (Millions of US Dollars)
IRRI (1960)	International Rice Research Institute	Los Baños, Philippines	Rice, global Rice-based cropping systems, Asia	21.6
CIMMYT (1966)	Centro Internacional de Mejoramiento Maíz y Trigo	Mexico City, Mexico	Maize, global Bread wheat, global Durum wheat, global Barley, global Triticale, global	21.9
IITA (1967)	International Institute of Tropical Agriculture	Ibadan, Nigeria	Farming systems, tropical Africa Maize, tropical Africa Rice, tropical Africa Sweet potato, yams, global Cassava, tropical Africa Cowpea, tropical Africa Soybean, tropical Africa	22.0
CIAT (1968)	Centro Internacional de Agricultura Tropical	Cali, Colombia	Cassava, global Field beans, global Rice, Latin America Tropical pastures, Latin America	21.4
CIP (1971)	Centro Internacional de la Papa	Lima, Peru	Potato, global	10.9
WARDA (1971)	West African Rice Development Association	Monrovia, Liberia	Rice, West Africa	2.1
ICRISAT (1972)	International Crops Research Institute for the Semi-Arid Tropics	Hyderabad, India	Chickpea, global Pigeonpea, global Pearl millet, global Sorghum, global Groundnut, global Farming systems, semiarid tropics	21.1
ILRAD (1973)	International Laboratory for Research on Animal Diseases	Nairobi, Kenya	Trypanosomiasis, global Theileriosis, global	10.4
IBPGR (1974)	International Board for Plant Genetic Resources	Rome, Italy	Plant genetic resources, global	4.5
ILCA (1974)	International Livestock Center for Africa	Addis Ababa, Ethiopia	Ruminant livestock production systems, Africa	14.4

Table 18.3 *(continued)*

Acronym (Year established)	Center	Location	Research program, geographic focus	1986 Budget[a] (Millions of US Dollars)
IFPRI (1975)	International Food Policy Research Institute	Washington, DC, USA	Food policy, global	4.3
ICARDA (1976)	International Center for Agricultural Research in the Dry Areas of West Asia and North Africa	Aleppo, Syria	Farming systems, wheat, barley triticale, broad bean, lentil, chickpea, forage crops, dry areas	18.1
ISNAR (1980)	International Service for National Agricultural Research	The Hague, Netherlands	National agricultural research, global	3.8

Source: Herdt and Anderson 1987:40-41.

[a]CGIAR-supported core budget, net of capital (December 12, 1985), estimate of the Secretariat.

Africa poses a particular challenge to agricultural research. Its soils are more diverse, its climate more varied, its pest and disease hazards more pronounced, and its farming systems more complex than those of monsoon Asia where the green revolution has been such a success (Lele & Goldsmith 1989; Lipton & Longhurst 1990). African agriculture is characterized by mixed cropping (more than one crop at a time is grown in a field), which occupies over 90 percent of the cropped area in most countries on the continent. Mixed cropping falls into three main categories:

1. Intercropping: more than one crop on a given area at one time, arranged in a geometric pattern
2. Relay cropping: a form of intercropping where not all the crops are planted at the same time
3. Sequential cropping: more than one crop (or intercrop) on a given area in the same year, the second crop being planted after the first is harvested

A special challenge for the agricultural research community working in Africa is to intensify agricultural production within this complex farm management system while maintaining its flexibility and its proven sustainability (Dommen 1988). One production innovation that holds promise for sustainability in the semiarid tropics that cover so much of Africa is agroforestry, a system of strip-cropping rows of trees between narrow strips of crops. The trees help conserve water, pro-

Table 18.4 Growth and Yield of Rice with and Without Fish at Barddhaman, West Bengal, 1987 Wet Season

Characteristic	Rice Without Fish	Rice with Fish
Rice		
Plant height (cm)	133.21	120.8
Effective tillers/plant	12.0	15.2
Panicle length (cm)	26.4	26.8
Grains/panicle	158.21	178.4
Grain yield (t/ha)	4.1	4.9
Straw yield (t/ha)	5.2	6.0
Fish		
Recovery (%)	--	81.3
Increase in length (cm)	--	8.2
Increase in weight (g)	--	96.4
Fish yield (t/ha)	--	0.7

Source: Datta, Ghosh, and Bairagya 1988.

vide a ready source of organic matter, and reduce erosion. On Figure 18.3 some of the advantages of combining forestry with agriculture are suggested.

☐ Subsidizing Technology Diffusion and Adoption

Profitable technology will spread from farmer to farmer all by itself. But the rate of adoption can be accelerated by government-sponsored educational programs. Such programs are often called "extension" because they were originally conceived to extend the knowledge developed in the US land-grant college system directly to the farmer. Programs that provide education and advice to farmers are now in place in most countries with a significant agricultural economy.

A classic study of Iowa farmers illustrates the typical growth curve of knowledge that an agricultural community goes through as its farmers gradually first become aware of a new technology, then try it out, and finally adopt it as part of their regular farming activities. In this case, a new chemical weed control called 2,4-D had come on the market. It took approximately 11 years between the time that a few farmers (4 percent) had even heard of it until all of them were, in fact, using it. Notice in Figure 18.4 how awareness precedes trial, which precedes adoption. In 1949, for instance, about midway through the process, 74 percent of the farmers were aware of the existence of the new weedicide, but only 40 percent had adopted it. By 1955 all farmers in the area were using it. Without the vigorous extension program carried on by Iowa State University, the new technology undoubtedly would have spread, but whether it would have spread as fast is open to question. It is the charge of the extension service to accelerate the adoption of new technology, whether it be new agricul-

Figure 18.3   Schematic Representation of Nutrient Relations in a Forest Ecosystem, an Agricultural System, and an Agroforestry System

A. Forest Ecosystem

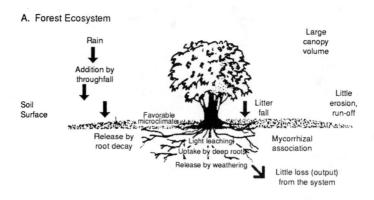

B. Agricultural System

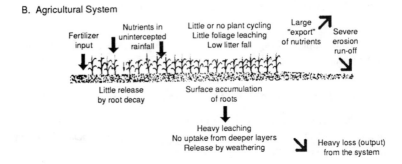

C. Agroforestry System

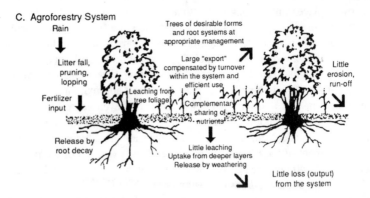

Source: Adapted from Dover and Talbot 1987:44.

Figure 18.4 Cumulative Percentage of Farm Operators at the Awareness, Trial, and Adoption Stages for 2, 4-D Weed Spray, by Year, Iowa, 1944-1955

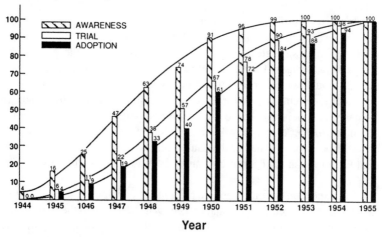

Source: Adapted from Beal and Rogers 1960:8.

tural chemicals, better plant and animal varieties, or better farm management practices.

Accelerating the spread of technology begins with government sponsorship of agricultural training institutions—places where technicians learn the skills necessary for backstopping agriculture in the field—plant and animal sciences, farm management and finance, for example. Not only do government-sponsored farm advisors need to know agricultural technology, but rural banks need farm appraisers, and rural tax collectors need to know about the economics of farming. Sponsoring the training of these technicians is an important subsidy to agricultural production. The success of an agricultural extension service depends not only on the quality of training that the farm advisors get at their local colleges of agriculture but perhaps more importantly on the quality of the technology that they have to extend. Building up an array of extension agents without providing them with a set of technologies appropriate to the region where they are working does not endear them to farmers and weakens the future effectiveness of their organization.

☐ Subsidizing Purchased Inputs

Publicly sponsored irrigation systems date back some 6,000 years, to when vast irrigation works were developed for the floodplain of the Tigris and Euphrates rivers in Mesopotamia. In modern times huge dams thrown across major rivers throughout the world (Nile, Indus, and Colorado, for example) have furnished low-cost irrigation water to millions of farmers. Cost-benefit analysis has shown substantial gains to society from such projects, which are usually promoted for their multiplicity of benefits—flood control, electrical generation, and irrigation water for agriculture.

In most countries government subsidizes irrigation water. In Egypt it is free. In the Philippines, during 1980/81, the subsidy amounted to 90 percent of the marginal cost (Bale 1985: 17). It can be argued that there is no need to charge the water users for the cost of the dam. Without government sponsorship, the dam would not have been built. There is no efficiency gain to society in asking water recipients to pay for the dam. Once the resources are sunk into the dam, they cannot be moved, so charging users for the dam does not alter the decision on whether or not to make the investment. (This discussion does not address the question of whether the dam should have been built in the first place. That is a question for benefit-cost analysis and is outside of the scope of this book.)

Once the dam is built, there are a couple of conditions that render it illogical to charge for even the marginal costs of water delivery to the farmer: (1) The water supply is so abundant that there is no allocation problem; (2) monitoring use may be more expensive than the marginal cost of the water. In most other situations economic efficiency would be improved through charging farmers the full cost of irrigation water. For instance, in areas where the underground aquifer is close to the surface and is rapidly recharged, such as on the Ganges plain in India, tube wells have a high payoff. In this sort of situation farmers might as well pay the full cost of the water. This will make it more likely that resources are being allocated to their highest-valued use for society.

Concerns that the introduction of irrigation and the modern technologies that go with it will lead to increased inequalities in income distribution have proved unfounded. Irrigation was found to substantially increase the income of all factors of production, although the increases to land, fixed capital, and purchased inputs appear to be higher than those to labor and management. Just the same, the poor benefit substantially from irrigation. Gains in labor income resulting from irrigation ranged from 12 percent in the Philippines to over 400 percent in Thailand (where dry-season irrigation doubles the cropping intensity, and wet-season labor use is higher in irrigated than in unirrigated areas; Rosegrant 1986).

Fertilizer subsidies are common in the Third World. During the 1980s, for example, urea sold at 56 percent below cost in Sir Lanka and at 60 percent below cost in Gambia. There is a long list of arguments in favor of subsidies to fertilizer, for instance: to encourage learning by doing; to overcome risk aversion and credit constraints; to help poor farmers; to offset disincentives caused by taxing or pricing policies; and to maintain soil fertility (World Bank 1986: 95). Let us look briefly at each of these arguments.

• When fertilizer was a new idea, it made sense to provide it to farmers at below cost as an incentive to them to try it out. But knowledge of fertilizer is widespread now.

• As we discussed in Chapter 15, encouraging rural financial markets is the most appropriate way to deal with rural credit constraints.

• Fertilizer subsidies are a poor way to help poor farmers. Farmers with large operations, and those on better land, are likely to reap benefits more intensively than the poor farmers. Examine Table 18.5 with a view to the distribution of benefits from a fertilizer subsidy among soybean farmers in Brazil.

• The best way to cope with production disincentives caused by antifarm taxing or pricing policies is to eliminate urban bias. Subsidizing the price of fertilizer is an inequitable way to transfer income to the the farm sector because it provides the greatest subsidy to the biggest farmers.

• Subsidizing fertilizer use to maintain soil fertility is a questionable practice, especially when making fertilizer cheap encourages farmers to substitute it for naturally occurring organic fertilizers that have better moisture-retaining properties.

Similarly, making pesticides cheap through subsidization encourages farmers to use more of the chemicals than they would if they paid the full costs. The subsidies undermine efforts to promote integrated pest management—a method

Table 18.5 Soybean Producers and Production in Brazil, 1975

Size of Farm (Hectares)	Number of Farms	Total Production in Thousand Metric Tons
0-10	162,859	594
10-20	149,288	1,134
20-50	127,331	1,976
50-100	26,709	1,127
100-200	10,301	1,042
200-500	6,552	1,284
500-1,000	2,286	794
1,000-10,000	1,518	650
10,000-100,000	25	16
Total	486,872	8,721

Source: Leclercq 1988:Annex I, Table 6.

Note: As can be seen from this table, of the nearly half million soybean farmers in Brazil in 1975, barely 10,000 with control over the largest landholdings accounted for almost one-third of the total output.

of pest control that stresses biological control of insects and weeds and minimizes the use of chemical pesticides (Repetto 1985; US, Dept. of Agriculture 1989a).

As fertilizer use increases, scarcities often develop as the government-subsidized distribution falls behind demand. Furthermore, the cost of the fertilizer subsidy can become a major concern to government. Concern over the budgetary costs of the fertilizer subsidy in Bangladesh prompted a study of the production impact of removing the subsidy. It was found that eliminating the subsidy would result in an increase in the domestic price of fertilizer some 34 percent over what it would have been during 1983/84, and that this increase in price would result in a decrease in fertilizer use. On the other hand, several factors were found to be of even greater importance than the fertilizer subsidy in stimulating fertilizer use and farm production in Bangladesh. Many of these factors were related to the fact that, because of the subsidy to fertilizer, government had gotten involved in the distribution of fertilizer, with its attendant bureaucratic inefficiencies. In Box 18.5 four factors are discussed that were found to be of greater importance to fertilizer use and resulting farm production than the fertilizer subsidy.

Subsidizing farm machinery and agricultural credit were discussed in Chapter 15 and therefore will not be discussed again here.

☐ Subsidizing Rural Infrastructure

Rural infrastructure can be defined as including a host of publicly owned capital items from roads through the courthouse. The effect of this infrastructure on agricultural production, rural employment, and so forth, is proving to be much more profound than previously recognized. A recent study in Bangladesh found that the rate of diffusion of agricultural technology in villages with developed infrastructure is about twice that of villages with poor infrastructure (Ahmed 1989).

Without government sponsorship or subsidy, the rural infrastructure, whose quality is strategic to agricultural productivity, will develop only poorly. The parts of rural infrastructure that probably have the most bearing on agricultural production are the road network, the communication network, the marketing system and financial institutions, as well as the electrical, water, educational, and health care systems. The advantages to subsidizing some of these parts were discussed earlier in this book. The production benefits of subsidizing rural roads were discussed in Chapter 15, and the importance of quality water, educational, and health care systems to productivity was discussed in earlier chapters. So I here confine the discussion to electricity, communications, and marketing. The three have important interrelations but each has important functions separately.

Rural electrification makes possible the powering of a host of time-saving and production-enhancing devices. Small irrigation pumps and power tools are efficiently driven by electricity. They are easy to start and easy to maintain.

**Box 18.5 Fertilizer Pricing Policy and Food Grain
Production Strategy**
Bruce Stone

During 1984/85, the International Food Policy Research Institute (IFPRI) collaborated with the Bangladesh Institute of Development Studies in examining fertilizer subsidies for the Bangladesh Ministry of Agriculture. The study identified several areas of greater importance than fertilizer subsidy in boosting the growth of fertilizer use and farm output. Four of these are introduced below:

1) Although national procurement of fertilizers was usually sufficient, acute and widespread shortages occurred in a few years. These shortages so reduced farm output and incomes that maintenance of somewhat larger fertilizer buffer stocks can be justified. Examination of a recent shortage revealed weaknesses in the procedures under which sales forecasts and targets are made. It also pinpointed several difficulties with procurement and highlighted the need to streamline procedures for promptly identifying and responding to acute shortages.
2) Weaknesses in the transport and distribution system at the local level can cause supply back-ups and delay the arrival of adequate quantities beyond optimal application periods, reducing fertilizer sales and effectiveness. Studies examining these and other supply- and demand-related difficulties in specific localities, especially those experiencing either rapid growth or chronically stagnant fertilizer sales, are now important research priorities.
3) The response of yield to fertilizer use on Bangladesh farms can be improved considerably. This is partly because application techniques are currently poor and the balance of major nutrients applied is inappropriate, despite a dense extension network. Deficiencies of zinc and sulfur are also common, so that providing micronutrients to such areas and conducting more extensive soil analyses to detect local nutrient imbalances are, respectively, short- and medium-term priorities. Longer-term research to improve the effectiveness of fertilizers under various Bangladesh conditions and strengthening links between research organizations, extension workers, and farmers are critically important.
4) Changes in water control, changes in cropping patterns, and varietal improvement are determinants of greater importance than fertilizer price in explaining past growth of fertilizer use in Bangladesh. For example, even under the standard estimating procedures, the fertilizer subsidy is shown to be less effective in generating growth in food output than is irrigation investment, if capacity utilization rates are satisfactory.

Source: Extracted from Stone 1985.

Rural electrification makes communications easier in the countryside, for example by making a modern telephone switching system possible. Access to a telephone, even if there is only one per village, can be useful in a medical emergency. But efficient communications are also important in marketing farm products as well as in gaining access to purchased farm inputs.

One of the important functions of a marketing system is to reflect back to producers the wants and preferences of consumers. As economic development brings changes in food demand patterns, a good marketing system will efficiently transmit this information to farmers, who can then reallocate their resource use to take advantage of the new production opportunities.

And as the sophistication of agricultural production increases with the adoption of new technology and improved management, a good marketing system for agricultural inputs will reflect farmers' preferences back to the farm suppliers. Bureaucratic, government-sponsored fertilizer distribution schemes usually supply only a limited choice of plant nutrient mixes. But if allowed to function in an appropriate institutional framework, a private-enterprise marketing system will make available a wide variety of fertilizers, allowing farmers to choose those which are most efficient for their particular situation.

Government support can supply radio stations and newspapers with price information of interest to farmers. This activity is especially important for small farmers who, because of lack of information about market prices, might otherwise be discriminated against in comparison with the larger farmers who can afford to get such information on their own.

Government-sponsored terminal markets, where buyers can assemble farm products from the countryside and distribute them to retailers in the city, can increase the efficiency of the marketing system. Increasing the efficiency of the marketing system lowers prices to consumers and increases prices to producers, thus improving nutrition and stimulating increases in production. Appropriate government subsidies are important to an efficiently functioning agricultural marketing system.

◻ 19

Policy Concepts and Policymaking

Governments . . . have an interest in keeping the exchange rate overvalued (one of the principal tools of depressing the incomes of small farmers) because the resulting need for rationing and allocating foreign exchange gives politically established groups extra money and power. The power of these groups is one of the strongest sources of resistance to changing exchange rates in many countries. Rents caused by economically inefficient interventions present political resources which can be used to organize political support.

Farming interests are opposed by urban workers who want low-priced food; urban industrialists, who want low wages and low prices for raw materials; bureaucrats and white collar workers who want higher salaries and lower food prices; and politicians who run governments which need taxes and which are major employers and industrialists in their own right.

—Streeten 1987: 77

Part III of this book is about policy approaches to undernutrition. We have examined and evaluated a number of policy alternatives that have been proposed for the alleviation of Third World hunger. In this chapter we look formally at policy concepts, policy conflicts, the types of policy instruments available, the modes of policy formulation, and finally, at an action framework for policy reform.

■ POLICY OBJECTIVES AND POLICY INSTRUMENTS

A public policy can be defined as course or direction taken by government, selected from among various alternatives in light of given conditions and designed to guide and determine present and future decisions.

Public policies almost always motivate a particular type of behavior or affect distribution of income, wealth, education, health care, and so on. You can usually break a public policy down into one or more policy objectives and one or more policy instruments. The policy objective is the desired result. The policy instrument is the specific technique used to motivate the desired behavior or to affect distribution.

Some examples will help to make this clear. Let us start with some simple automobile traffic policies:

Policy objective: Improve efficiency of traffic flow at major intersections
Policy instrument: Install traffic lights

Policy objective: Reduce traffic deaths caused by excessive speed
Policy instrument: Establish and enforce low speed limits

Tax policy takes a multitude of forms. Here is one designed to affect distribution:
Policy objective: Have rich people pay more tax per dollar earned
Policy instrument: Progressive income tax structure

Taxes are often used to promote certain types of human behavior; for example:
Policy objective: Promote human fertility
Policy instrument: Provide a tax break for each dependent child in the family

There are public health policies:
Policy objective: Promote better health through a reduction of cigarette smoking
Policy instrument: Publish a health warning on the side of each cigarette package

Policy objective: Promote better health through reduction in marijuana smoking
Policy instrument: Make possession of marijuana illegal

One US agricultural policy began with a law signed by Abraham Lincoln in 1862:
Policy objective: Promote the production of food
Policy instrument: In every state set up a college that teaches and conducts research and extension in agriculture and the mechanical arts (the land-grant college system)

US policy toward the Third World can be defined in the same terms; for example:
Policy objective: Promote economic development in the Third World
Policy instrument: Pay for projects in economic development administered through the Agency for International Development (AID)—the US foreign assistance agency

■ TYPES OF PUBLIC POLICY INSTRUMENTS

Government has available to it six broad categories of policy instruments: (1) moral suasion; (2) the tort system; (3) regulations; (4) charges; (5) subsidies; and

(6) markets in rights. We will examine briefly each of these categories and, when possible, mention examples of specific nutrition policy instruments advocated under each category.

☐ Moral Suasion

When governments engage in admonitions, advertising, or education as a means to persuade people to behave in certain ways, they are using moral suasion. The health warning on a cigarette package is an example. In the nutrition field, campaigns to promote breast-feeding or oral rehydration therapy fit within this category, as do campaigns to persuade people to eat less fat or less salt or to have smaller families.

☐ The Tort System

An old principle from Roman law is that you should, at all times, conduct yourself in such a way so as to not damage someone else, and that if you do damage him, you must compensate him for it. It is this principle that allows people to sue for damages. Lawyers call the whole process the tort system. It is a cumbersome way to motivate people to behave rightly, because it involves lots of time and money in court. But it does influence people's behavior. One reason you drive carefully is to avoid having to pay for the damage to someone else's car should you be found to be at fault in an accident.

The tort system is not much used to promote better nutrition. However, it was used recently in one well-publicized case in the United States in an effort to improve infant nutrition. In a New York State court the Beech-Nut company was found guilty of cutting costs by cutting apples from its apple juice. It had sold millions of bottles of baby food labeled "apple juice" but containing little or no apple juice at all—only sugar, water, flavoring, and coloring. As a result of the lawsuit, Beech-Nut paid a $250,000 fine to the State of New York and a $2 million fine to the US government. Two Beech-Nut executives each paid $100,000 fines and were sentenced to prison terms of a year and a day (Traub 1988).

☐ Regulations

Regulations backed up by police power, as in "There ought to be a law!" are the most commonly thought-of method for changing behavior. A host of regulations have been advocated and tried out in attempts to reduce Third World undernutrition. Among them are raising the legal marriage age, land reform (which commonly places a ceiling on the amount of land an individual may own), minimum-wage laws, food rationing, low administered prices for food, overvalued domestic currency, and limits on cash cropping. The last three regulations mentioned are examples of regulations that result in an implicit tax on agriculture. No money is collected directly by government, as is done in explicit taxation, which is next on our list.

☐ Charges

Fees, taxes, and other charges are not only a way for government to gain purchasing power; they also direct people to behave in particular ways. The high tax on gasoline in Europe has persuaded most Europeans to purchase small, fuel-efficient cars.

Third World tax policy commonly results in disincentives to agricultural production. For instance, noncompetitive procurement of food from farmers acts like a commodity tax levied at the farm gate and discourages farm production. In a rice-exporting country an export tax on rice lowers the price to the producer and acts as a disincentive to production.

Tax policy can also be used to modify distribution. Progressive taxation is a policy instrument designed to redistribute income and wealth from the rich to the poor.

☐ Subsidies

Subsidies pay people or institutions for behaving in a particular way. They can be very expensive. They can also result in paying people for behavior that they would have engaged in anyway. For instance, it has been advocated that we pay high school students who have dropped out of school a bonus for going back and finishing. If such a policy were instituted, every student worth his salt would drop out and reenter whether or not he would even have thought of it in the absence of the subsidy.

Sometimes subsidies and tax policies overlap. Providing a tax break to those couples that have children or a tax write-off of more than 100 percent for purchasing a tractor are examples of tax policies that result in subsidies. In the name of better nutrition, subsidies have been advocated and tried out for farm mechanization, farm credit, and direct distribution of food to the needy, to name a few. From the point of view of improving nutrition of the poor in the Third World, some of the most beneficial subsidies that government can engage in are those to education, agricultural research, mother and child health centers, family-planning services, and sanitary water and sewage facilities.

☐ Markets in Rights

Governments can establish a market in rights to behave in a certain way, or to engage in a particular activity. You might, for instance, bid for the right to pasture your livestock on public rangeland, or for the right to add a certain amount of pollutant to a stream.

The concept of markets in rights is relatively new on the public policy scene, but proposals abound. Few have to do with improving nutrition, but one proposal, advanced by the economist Kenneth Boulding (1964: 135–136), albeit humorously, was to establish markets in rights to have babies. Marketable rights for babies, claimed Boulding, would combine the efficiency of the marketplace with controls necessary to slow or halt population growth.

Each girl on approaching maturity would be presented with a certificate which will entitle its owner to have, say 2.2 children, or whatever number would ensure a reproductive rate of one. The unit of these certificates might be the "deci-child" and accumulation of ten of these units by purchase, inheritance, or gift would permit a woman in maturity to have one legal child. We would then set up a market in these units in which the rich and the philoprogenitive would purchase them from the poor, the nuns, the maiden aunts, and so on. The men perhaps could be left out of these arrangements, as it is only the fertility of women which is strictly relevant to population control.

Boulding points out that his plan would have the

advantage of developing a long-run tendency toward equality in income, for the rich would have many children and become poor and the poor would have few children and become rich. The price of the certificate would of course reflect the general desire in a society to have children. Where the desire is very high the price would be bid up; where it was low the price would also be low. Perhaps the ideal situation would be found when the price was naturally zero, in which case those who wanted children would have them without extra cost.

If, sometime in the future, you are trying to create a new public policy, you may want to refer back to the above checklist of alternative policy instruments. By and large, the last four in the above set have been found to be stronger and more efficient than the first two.

■ POLICY CONFLICTS AND POLICY DILEMMAS

Whether in a dictatorship or a democracy, public policy is made and revised in the hot crucible of competing and conflicting interests. As was highlighted by Streeten (1987), Third World farm and nonfarm interests are frequent competitors. Urban bias is commonplace in the Third World and repeatedly leads to policies that have an adverse impact on the poor, such as industrial protectionist policies (import substitution) instead of export-led growth policies.

But even in the absence of urban bias, nutrition policy planners continually grapple with the dilemma that low administered food prices make it easier for the poor to purchase food, yet they discourage food production and have other social costs, such as increased unemployment, that adversely affect the poor.

A common policy conflict affecting Third World nutrition is between the goals of food self-sufficiency and economic efficiency. Food self-sufficiency is a politically attractive slogan and conjures up images of independence, Henry David Thoreau, Robinson Crusoe, and all that. But food self-sufficiency requires policies that raise the domestic price of food, as when more-expensive domestically produced food must be substituted for cheaper foreign-produced food. This may be one of the consequences of policies that limits the production of export crops in favor of the production of food crops. The poor suffer from a food self-sufficiency policy as the price of their food rises.

Whether to promote more vigorously increased grain or increased livestock production is a thorny problem frequently faced by Third World planners. Because of the lower demand elasticities for grain, promoting grain production benefits farmers less and lower-income consumers more than does promoting livestock production. Promoting livestock production increases the demand for grain and raises its price, as livestock consume increasing amounts of grain, which may adversely affect the nutrition of the poor while lowering the price of livestock products that are consumed largely by the already overfed rich. On the other hand, livestock production is more labor-intensive than grain production, and promoting livestock production does increase demand for rural labor.

Just the same, if we are to improve the nutritional status of the Third World's poor, decisions on policy reform must be made. As John Mellor (1985b) put it, "in allocating a government's resources, it is not enough to inventory the things that must be done to facilitate agricultural development: the next step of dividing the tasks between the private and the public sectors and setting priorities must also be taken." In this context the importance of increasing agricultural production should not be overlooked. Again, John Mellor (1986a): "In developing countries, rising incomes of low-income people, derived from employment growth, are converted by remarkably high demand elasticities to increased effective demand for food: 60 to 80 percent of incremental income is so spent. Thus in developing countries, increased food supplies and increased employment are two sides of the same coin; one cannot proceed long without the other."

■ MODES OF POLICY FORMULATION

Policy formulation always involves choice among alternatives. We would like to think that all choices that decisionmakers in government make are rational. Unfortunately, such is not the case. Sometimes, choice making in policy formulation is far from rational, but let us begin this discussion with the assumption that governmental decisionmaking regarding policy alternatives is rational. In this case, how does it go?

☐ Rational Choice Using the Alternatives-Consequences Model

Let us take an idealized situation. Government policymakers identify a problem of strategic importance—say the fact that 27 percent of the preschoolers in the country classify as moderately to severely undernourished (the rate quoted for the Philippines in Chapter 3). The next step is to identify goals and objectives relative to the problem. Say that the policymaking group takes as its goal to cut the rate of moderately to severely undernourished preschoolers by 50 percent during the next 10 years.

Once the goal has been agreed upon, the policy options must be considered. There are already in place a set of programs and policies that influence preschool nutrition, so examination of policy options is largely a matter of considering changes in the present policy structure. The range of policy objectives and policy instruments relative to the above goal must be laid out. These can be called the public policy alternatives. Each alternative will generate a set of consequences. Examination of the consequences of each proposed policy alternative will, in turn, lead the policymakers back to the most appropriate set of policy alternatives for achieving their policy goal. In Figure 19.1 the alternatives-consequences model is diagrammed.

In this system the quality of policy analysis is crucial. Bad analysis of the consequences of policy alternatives will lead to bad policy. Good analysis, combined with rational choice makers, will result in good policy.

Figure 19.1 The Rational Alternatives-Consequences Model in Policy Decisionmaking

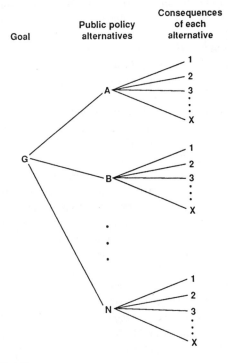

Source: Foster 1972:149.

☐ Applying the Alternatives-Consequences Model

I have attempted to furnish a framework for the application of the rational alternatives–consequences model in choosing policy objectives and policy instruments for alleviating Third World undernutrition. It is the thesis of this book that it is particular economic, demographic, and health variables that deliver undernutrition to millions of people in the Third World. A corollary of this thesis is that alleviation of hunger requires changes in policies so as to adjust these variables. Since it is these variables that deliver undernutrition, I have called them nutrition impact vehicles.

We have examined policy instruments, grouped by policy objectives, designed to adjust these variables in such a way as to reduce undernutrition by improving health, lowering high population growth rates, reducing income and wealth inequalities and raising income of the poor, lowering the price of food through explicit subsidized consumption, lowering the price of food through implicit subsidized consumption, and lowering the price of food through subsidized production. Our policy objectives, plus sample policy instruments commonly proposed in association with these objectives, are listed and organized in Table 19.1.

A real-world complexity that we must deal with in choosing a set of policies to alleviate undernutrition is the fact that a policy instrument proposed to improve nutrition through adjusting one nutrition impact vehicle often affects one or more of the other nutrition impact vehicles. Improving health, for instance, may be supposed to have a positive impact on nutrition and yet it can simultaneously lead to negative nutrition impacts if it leads to increased population growth rates. Solving the world food problem will require the use of a multiplicity of policy instruments. There is no "single-bullet" solution to this complex problem.

As we evaluate alternative policy instruments proposed to reduce undernutrition, we must, therefore, examine the impact of each proposed instrument on each nutrition impact vehicle, at least to the extent that it affects it significantly. I attempted to do this in Chapters 13 through 18; the discussion in these chapters is capsulized in Table 19.2, where policy instruments, grouped by policy objectives, are listed in the left-hand column. Across the top are listed the nutrition impact vehicles. Because production incentives in agriculture are so important to agricultural production, which, in turn, influences both employment and the price of food, production incentive to agriculture is included as a nutrition impact vehicle in column 6.

On occasion in Chapters 13 through 18, the question of the impact of a particular policy instrument on overall economic efficiency was discussed. This is because polices that lessen overall economic efficiency reduce total income available for taxation and thus reduce the resources available for programs to alleviate undernutrition. Policies that lessen overall economic efficiency also reduce employment opportunities, overall economic growth, and so on, which, in

Table 19.1 Commonly Proposed Policy Alternatives for Reducing Third World Undernutrition

Policy Objective	Generalized Policy Instrument	Specific Policy Instrument
Improve health	Food fortification	Iodized salt Iron, vitamins in grain
	Mother and child health centers	Immunization Oral rehydration therapy education Vitamin A distribution Promotion of breast-feeding Family planning
	Interrupt transmission of diarrhea	Improved sewage handling Hygiene education Sanitary water supply
Reduce high population growth rates	Eliminate pronatalist policies	
	Upgrade the status of women	Equal educational opportunities for both sexes Equal employment opportunities for both sexes
	Adopt antinatalist policies	Contraceptive research Economic incentives for small families Economic disincentives for large families Moral suasion Raise legal marriage age Legal regulation of fertility Subsidize family-planning services
Reduce income and wealth inequalities and raise income of the poor	Land reform Progressive taxation Subsidies for mechanization Credit subsidies Encourage rural financial markets Rural roads subsidies Minimum wage laws Employment creation	Tax shelter Preferential tariffs on machine imports
	Human capital intensive programs for reducing inequality	Provide public education, especially primary and secondary Reduce human fertility Improve health care Famine, disaster relief Marketwide explicit food subsidies

Table 19.1 *(continued)*

Policy Objective	Generalized Policy Instrument	Specific Policy Instrument
Lower the price of food	Explicit subsidized consumption	Famine, disaster relief Marketwide explicit food subsidies Subsidies targeted to the needy: 　Self-targeting 　Direct distribution 　Rationing 　Food stamps 　Food-for-work
	Implicit subsidized consumption	
		Noncompetitive procurement Administered prices Export taxes Overvalued domestic currency Limits on cash cropping
	Subsidized production	
		Subsidize: 　Technology creation 　Technology diffusion 　　and adoption 　Purchased inputs: 　　Irrigation water 　　Fertilizer 　　Pesticides 　Rural infrastructure: 　　Electrification 　　Communication 　　Marketing system 　　Other, mentioned above

Note: The distinction between policy goals and instruments is not always clear-cut. For instance, improved health is the first policy goal listed, yet improved health care is listed as a specific policy instrument for reducing income and wealth inequalities and raising income of the poor.

turn, affect nutrition. Because of its importance, improving overall economic efficiency is also listed as a nutrition impact vehicle (column 7).

We have the opportunity in Table 19.2 to examine and compare the impact of various nutrition policy instruments on the various nutrition impact vehicles as an aid in selecting an appropriate set of policy instruments for solving the hunger problem. Pluses and minuses have been assigned where data or logic seem to lend strong support to such a relationship. The table is constructed in such a way that a plus indicates a relationship that will result in an improvement in nutritional status; a minus indicates a relationship that will result in a worsening of nutritional status. Where the relationship is virtually nonexistent, weak, or highly debatable, the cells in the table have been left blank.

For instance, vitamin A distribution is expected to improve health through a reduction in xerophthalmia and at the same time cut down on the incidence of deaths from diarrhea, thus increasing the population growth rate. The impact of vitamin A distribution on the variables listed in columns 3 through 7 was not deemed clear enough or strong enough to categorize.

Successful promotion of breast-feeding will improve infant health (a plus in column 1), but the reduction in births attributable to the contraceptive effects may be great enough to reduce the birth rate more than the death rate is reduced by the positive health effects. The plus in column 2 is therefore plausible, but debatable.

A reduction in high population growth rates will probably improve mother and child health, decrease the population growth rate, increase equality of income and wealth (review Table 8.3), reduce the rate of unemployment, and decrease rate of increase in the demand for food, thus helping to lower the price of food. Thus, programs that successfully reduce the birth rate get a plus in columns 2–5.

Land reform has been shown to have positive or negative impacts on distribution, depending on the situation. It gets both a plus and a minus in column 3 to suggest this. On the other hand, since such programs seldom increase the level of food productivity and frequently reduce it, it gets a minus in column 5. And since the threat of land reform may reduce investment in agriculture, it ranks a minus in column 6.

In some cases the direction of influence will depend on the assumptions you make. For instance, in Table 19.2 it is assumed that explicit subsidized consumption will be supported in greater measure by donor countries than by Third World countries, and that therefore the price effect of the food purchases for sale at discount prices will act as a production incentive in the donor countries, but that the price effect of the sale of surpluses from overseas will act as a production disincentive to agriculture in the recipient country. Therefore, explicit food subsidies get a minus in column 6.

Look through the table and see if the assignment of pluses and minuses makes sense to you. In cases where it does not, go back to the chapter in which the relationship is discussed and review the data or the reasoning process (the numbers of the related chapters are given in parentheses after each major subhead in the table).

After you have worked through the consequences of the various proposed policy instruments, you will not necessarily be a nutrition policy expert, but you will have a better feel for the types of policy adjustments that will have to be made in order to reduce Third World undernutrition.

☐ Nonrational Policymaking

So far in this section we have examined policy formulation in the rational decisionmaking framework. But government policymaking is not always rational.

Graham Allison (1971), a perspicacious observer of government decision-

Table 19.2 Direction of Probable Effect of Selected Policy Instruments on Nutrition Impact Vehicles

Policy Objective (Related Chapter) or Policy Instrument	Nutrition Impact Vehicle						
	1 Improve health of the poor	2 Decrease population growth rate	3 Increase equality of income and wealth	4 Increase income and/or employment of the poor	5 Lower price of food for the poor	6 Production incentive to Third World agriculture	7 Improve overall economic efficiency
Improve Health (13)							
Food fortification	+						
Immunization	+	−					
Oral rehydration therapy education	+	−					
Vitamin A distribution	+	−					
Promotion of breast-feeding	+	+	+	+	+		
Improved sewage handling	+	−					
Hygiene education	+	−					
Sanitary water supply	+	−					
Lower high population growth rates (14)							
Elimination of pronatalist policies		+	+	+	+		
Equal educational opportunities for both sexes		+	+	+	+		
Equal employment opportunities for both sexes		+	+	+	+		
Contraceptive research		+	+	+	+		
Economic incentives for small families		+	+	+	+		
Economic disincentives for large families		+	+	+	+		
Moral suasion		+	+	+	+		
Raising legal marriage age		+	+	+	+		
Legal regulation of fertility		+	+	+	+		
Subsidizing family planning services		+	+	+	+		

Table 19.2 *(continued)*

Policy Objective (Related Chapter) or Policy Instrument	Nutrition Impact Vehicle						
	1 Improve health of the poor	2 Decrease population growth rate	3 Increase equality of income and wealth	4 Increase income and/or employment of the poor	5 Lower price of food for the poor	6 Production incentive to Third World agriculture	7 Improve overall economic efficiency
Reduce and wealth inequalities and raise income of the poor (15)							
Land reform			+/−			−	−
Progressive taxation			+				
Subsidies for mechanization			−	−		+	
Credit subsidies			−	−			
Encouraging rural financial markets			+	+		+	+
Rural roads subsidies			+	+	+	+	+
Minimum-wage laws			−	−		−	−
Employment creation			+	+		+	+
Providing public education, especially primary and secondary	+	+	+	+	+	+	+
Reducing human fertility	+	+	+	+	+		
Improving health care	+	−	+	+			
Lower the price of food through explicit subsidization consumption (16)							
Famine, disaster relief	+	−	+		+		−
Marketwide explicit food subsidies	+	−	−		+		−
Subsidies targeted to the needy							
Self-targeting	+	−	+		+		−
Direct distribution	+	−	+		+		−
Rationing	+	−	+		+		−
Food stamps	+	−	+		+		−
Food-for-work	+	−			+		−

Table 19.2 Direction of Probable Effect of Selected Policy Instruments on Nutrition Impact Vehicles *(continued)*

Policy Objective (Related Chapter) or Policy Instrument	Nutrition Impact Vehicle						
	1	2	3	4	5	6	7
	Improve health of the poor	Decrease population growth rate	Increase equality of income and wealth	Increase income and/or employment of the poor	Lower price of food for the poor	Production incentive to Third World agriculture	Improve overall economic efficiency
Lower the price of food through implicit subsidization consumption (17)							
Noncompetitive procurement			−	−	+	−	−
Low administered prices			−	−	+	−	−
Export taxes on farm products			−	−	+	−	
Overvalued domestic currency			−	−	+	−	−
Limits on cash cropping			−	−	+	−	−
Lower the price of food through subsidized production (18)							
Subsidization of							
Technology creation				+	+	+	+
Technology diffusion and adoption:							
High-yielding grains				+	+	+	+
Grain-fed livestock				+	−	+	+
Purchased inputs							
Irrigation water				+	+	+	
Fertilizer			−	+	+	+	−
Pesticides			−	+	+	+	−
Rural infrastructure							
Electrification			+	+	+	+	+
Communication			+	+	+	+	+
Marketing system			+	+	+	+	+

making, postulates three modes of policy formulation. The first is the mode of the rational actor, working with the alternatives-consequences model, which we assumed above. The second mode he calls that of organizational process. The third he calls governmental politics. Because these latter two modes are important in the policymaking process, let us look at them briefly.

Organizational process. In Allison's view, "government consists of a conglomerate of semi-feudal, loosely allied organizations, each with a substantial life of its own" (p. 67). These individual organizations carry weighty names such as Ministry of Agriculture, or Ministry of Defense, or Ministry of Health. In the United States they are called departments. These organizations develop their own bureaucracies, each with its own institutionalized way of doing things—the standard operating procedures.

In the short run, decisionmaking within the organization is limited by the standard operating procedures. (That is why we often find bureaucracies so frustrating to deal with.) In the long run, decision outputs can be influenced by gradually changing organizational goals, still modified by the entrenched standard operating procedures. Top government leaders can influence the bureaucracies, but only with some difficulty and much effort.

Governmental politics. Top government leaders are, of course, not always absolute paragons of virtue, with no interests at heart except the welfare of the population. They got to the top in a competitive struggle, and each one has his or her own agenda, his or her own strategic objectives, his or her own personal goals. As Allison puts it, "the name of the game is politics: bargaining along regularized circuits among players positioned hierarchically within the government" (p. 144).

Sometimes one individual or group will succeed in putting its pet policy in place unscathed by the bargaining process. More likely, in this mode, policy choices are the result of bargains and compromises representing a mixture of conflicting preferences and the unequal power of various groups and individuals holding diverse stakes and stands. In this mode, what finally motivates the policy choice is not rational decisionmaking, not the routines of government organizations, but "the power and skill of proponents and opponents of the action in question" (p. 145).

■ AN ACTION FRAMEWORK FOR POLICY REFORM

If you want to do something significant about the problem of Third World hunger, you will, ultimately, have to exert some influence in the adjustment of the nutrition impact vehicles so that less undernutrition is delivered to the Third World's poor. This will involve not only supporting careful policy analysis for the use of rational decisionmakers, but coping with the less-than-rational modes of the policymaking process, described above. You will have to become involved in power struggles, such as the one alluded to by Streeten (1987). This is the stuff of which policy reform is made.

Achieving changes in policies is a process of social action. Two sociologists at Iowa State University (Beal & Hobbs 1969) studied this process and described a model for successfully, and nonviolently, achieving social change. The essence of their model is presented below.

Establish convergence of interest. If you play an active role in achieving nutrition policies, and if you help to instigate the changed policies yourself, you are a change agent. A change agent must realize that all social action takes place within the context of social systems. And any social action must begin with a convergence of interest, a common definition of need, on the part of two or more people. In other words, to motivate social change, you have to work with groups, and you have to find or create allies who will work with you.

Analyze the social system. After you have found some allies in your cause, it would pay to take a careful look at the social system you must deal with. There are all kinds of groups in the social system. Try to figure out which ones of these subsystems, as these groups are called, are relevant to your cause. That is, determine which ones are likely to give you support, and also which ones may give you opposition.

Establish initiating sets. Your original small group should now undertake to contact key leaders in the organizations and groups. You will be seeking support from some groups and trying to find ways to neutralize the potential opposition from others.

Legitimize. The more people you can get to support your cause the better. But it is especially important to seek out and try to gain the support of people of status who have the power to make or break your action program—the "legitimizers." Legitimizers may be formal; for example, the official heads of the relevant groups. Or legitimizers may be informal, in which case they may not be so easy to identify. In either case they are important. A relevant legitimizer may not lift a finger to help your cause. But if you fail to contact him or if you somehow antagonize him somewhere along the line, his opposition could spell delay or even disaster for your cause.

Find and use diffusion sets. If everything is going well so far in your campaign and if the legitimizers are on your side, support for your cause should be growing. Then it is time to spread the word about your ideas more broadly. Here you need people who can be instrumental in diffusing information throughout the community, region, or nation, whatever is the eventual target of your social action program. Newspaper editors can help here, as well as others associated with the mass media. So can other communicators, such as teachers, school administrators, farm advisors, or religious leaders.

Generalize the movement. Now your objective is to get the general population, or at least a majority of the decisionmakers, to favor your stand. As the diffusion of the information goes on through the mass media, you can assist in developing a general "felt need" for your program by promoting discussions, carrying out surveys, doing anything you can to make your cause a "people's problem."

Use personal contact. Observers of social change feel that people are made aware by impersonal methods of communication (newspapers, postcards, and so on), but they are only persuaded or convinced by face-to-face contact. Of course, you or your original allies cannot possibly make all the necessary personal contacts at this time. That is why it is important to bring together as many groups as possible in the service of your cause. Keep in mind throughout your whole effort that social action takes place within the context of social systems. You must work with groups.

Move toward action. After the relevant groups agree that the problem really exists, and after a general feeling of support for your cause has been built up, it is time to move toward a specific action program. Perhaps the original goals that your initial allies had in mind will turn out to be too vague for this stage of the game. More-specific goals may have to be set. So the process of looking at alternative public policies and their consequences must begin again, this time with rather more specific policy alternatives in mind.

With lots of hard work, and probably after a long period of time, you and the others who began work on the program together may well be able to participate in the final stages of the social action process, setting up the plan of work and carrying out the action program. Perhaps this will be worked out in some government agency, maybe in the legislature. The important thing, of course, is that your efforts ultimately yield a change in public policy in the right direction.

Evaluate throughout. Throughout the social action process, it is important that you continually evaluate progress so far, decide whether progress is satisfactory, and plan for the next step. Continual evaluation will help you avoid the mistake of moving too fast or too far and thus jeopardizing the chances of your next step's being a success.

> *It is for us, the living, to be dedicated to the unfinished task.*
> —Abraham Lincoln, Gettysburg Address

References

Adams, Dale W. 1983. Mobilizing household savings through rural financial markets. In *Rural financial markets in developing countries, their use and abuse*, ed. J. D. Von Pischke et al. Baltimore, MD: Johns Hopkins University Press.

———, and Douglas H. Graham. 1981. A critique of traditional agricultural credit projects and policies. *Journal of Development Economics* 8:347–366.

———, et al., ed. 1984. *Undermining rural development with cheap credit*. Boulder, CO: Westview Press.

Adelman, I., and C. T. Morris. 1973. Economic growth and social equity in developing countries. Stanford, CA: Stanford University Press.

Ahluwalia, Montek S. 1976a. Income distribution and development: Some stylized facts. *American Economic Review* 66 (May):128–135.

———. 1976b. Inequality, poverty and development. *Journal of Development Economics* 3 (September):307–342.

———, N. Carter, and H. Chenery. 1979. Growth and poverty in developing countries. In *Structural change and development policy*, ed. H. Chenery. Oxford: Oxford University Press (also available in *Journal of Development Economics* 6 [September]: 299–341).

Ahmed, Raisuddin. 1988. Structure, costs, and benefits of food subsidies in Bangladesh. In *Food subsidies in developing countries*, ed. Per Pinstrup-Andersen. Baltimore, MD: Johns Hopkins University Press.

———. 1989. Making rural infrastructure a priority. *IFPRI Report* 11, no. 1:1, 4.

———, and Mahabub Hossain. 1990. *Developmental impact of rural infrastructures: Bangladesh*. IFPRI Research Report no. 83. Washington, DC: International Food Policy Research Institute.

Alberts, Tom. 1983. *Agrarian reform and rural poverty: A case study of Peru*. Boulder, CO: Westview Press.

Alderman, Harold. 1986. The effect of food price and income changes on the acquisition of food by low-income households. Washington, DC: International Food Policy Research Institute.

———, and Joachim von Braun. 1984. *The effects of the Egyptian food ration and subsidy system on income distribution and consumption*. IFPRI Research Report no. 45. Washington, DC: International Food Policy Research Institute.

Allison, Graham T. 1971. *Essence of decision: Explaining the Cuban missile crisis*. Boston: Little, Brown.

Anderson, Jock, and J. A. Roumasset. 1985. Microeconomics of food insecurity: The stochastic side of poverty. Unpublished ms. available through the Department of Economics, University of Hawaii, Manoa.

———, et al. 1985. *International agricultural research centers: A study of achievements and potential; Summary*. Washington, DC: World Bank Consultative Group on International Agricultural Research.

Anderson, Mary Ann, et al. 1981. *Nutrition intervention in developing countries, study I: Supplementary feeding*. Cambridge, MA: Oelgeschlager, Gunn & Hain.

343

Angel, J. Lawrence. 1984. Health as a crucial factor in the changes from hunting to developed farming in the Eastern Mediterranean. In *Paleopathology at the Origins of Agriculture*, ed. M. N. Cohen and G. J. Armelagos. New York: Academic Press.

Anonymous. 1974. How hunger kills. *Time*, November 11:68.

———. 1988. Women and development: Education and fertility. *Finance and Development* (September):43.

Arnold, Jesse C., R. W. Engel, D. B. Aguillon, and M. Caedo. 1981. Utilization of family characteristics in nutritional classification of preschool children. *American Journal of Clinical Nutrition* 34 (November):2546–2550.

Aron, Robert, et al. 1962. *Les origines de la guerre d'Algérie*. Paris: Fayard.

Askari, Hossein, and John T. Cummings. 1976. *Agricultural supply response: A survey of the econometric evidence*. New York: Praeger.

Astawa, I. B. 1979. Using the local community: Bali, Indonesia. In *Birth control: An international assessment*, ed. M. Potts and P. Bhiwandiwala. Baltimore, MD: University Park Press.

Bale, Malcolm D. 1984. Opening of the discussion on plenary paper 5, proceedings of the fourth congress of the E.A.A.E., agricultural markets and prices. *European Review of Agricultural Economics* 12:82–83.

———. 1985. *Agricultural trade and food policy: The experience of five developing countries*. Staff Working Paper no. 724. Washington, DC: World Bank.

———, and Ernst Lutz. 1981. Price distortions in agriculture and their effects: An international comparison. *American Journal of Agricultural Economics* 63 (February):8–22.

Bautista, Romeo M. 1987. *Production incentives in Philippine agriculture: Effects of trade and exchange rate policies*. IFPRI Research Report no. 59. Washington, DC: International Food Policy Research Institute.

Beal, George M., and D. J. Hobbs. 1969. *Social action: The process in community and area development*. Ames: Iowa State University Cooperative Extension Service, Soc-16 (August).

Beal, George M., and Everett M. Rogers. 1960. *The adoption of two farm practices in a central Iowa community*. Special Report no. 26. Ames: Iowa State University Agricultural and Home Economics Experiment Station.

Beaton, George H., and Hossein Ghassemi. 1982. Supplementary feeding programs for young children in developing countries. *American Journal of Clinical Nutrition* 35 (April):864–916.

Becker, Gary. 1975. *Human capital*. New York: Columbia University Press.

Belmont, Lillian, and Francis A. Marolla. 1973. Birth order, family size, and intelligence—A study of a total population of 19-year-old men born in the Netherlands. *Science* 182, no. 4117, (December):1096–1101.

Bengoa, J. M. 1972. Nutritional significance of mortality statistics. In *Proceedings of the Third Western Hemisphere Nutrition Congress*. New York: Futura.

Berg, Alan. 1973. *The nutrition factor—Its role in national development*. Washington, DC: Brookings Institute.

———. 1987. *Malnutrition—What Can Be Done?* Baltimore, MD: Johns Hopkins University Press.

Berry, A. R., and W. R. Cline. 1979. *Agrarian structure and productivity in developing countries*. Baltimore, MD: Johns Hopkins University Press.

Bettany, G. T. 1890. Introduction. In T. R. Malthus, *An Essay on . . . population*. London: Ward.

Bezuneh, Mesfin, Brady J. Deaton, and George W. Norton. 1988. Food aid impacts in rural Kenya. *American Journal of Agricultural Economics* 70 (February):181–191.

Binswanger, Hans. 1978. *The economics of tractors in South Asia: An analytical review*. New York and Hyderabad, India: Agricultural Development Council and Interna-

tional Crops Research Institute for the Semi–Arid Tropics.
——, Graeme Donovan et al. 1987. *Agricultural mechanization, issues and options.* Policy Study. Washington, DC: World Bank.
Birdsall, Nancy. 1984. Population growth: Its magnitude and implications for development. *Finance and Development* 21 (September):10–13.
Blake, Judith. 1989. *Family size and achievement.* Berkeley: University of California Press.
Bliss, C. J., and N. Y. Stern. 1982. *Palanpur: The economy of an Indian village.* Oxford: Clarendon Press.
Boediono. 1978. Elastisitas permintaan untuk berbagai barang di Indonesia; Penerapan metode Frisch. *Ekonomi dan Keuangan Indonesia* 26 (September):362.
Bongaarts, John. 1982. The fertility-inhibiting effects of the intermediate fertility variables. *Studies in Family Planning* 13:179–189.
Boserup, Ester. 1981. *Population and technological change: A study of long-term trends.* Chicago: University of Chicago Press.
Bouis, Howarth E. 1991. The changing focus of economic research on nutrition. *IFPRI Report* 13, no. 2:1, 4.
——, and Lawrence Haddad. 1990. *The effects of agricutlrual commercialization on land tenure, household resource allocation, and nutrition in the Philippines.* IFPRI Research Report no. 79. Washington, DC: International Food Policy Research Institute.
Boulding, Kenneth. 1964. *The meaning of the 20th Century.* New York: Harper & Row.
Briscoe, J. 1979. The qualitative effect of infection on the use of food by young children in poor countries. *American Journal of Clinical Nutrition* 32 (March):648–676.
Bromley, Daniel. 1981. The role of land reform in economic development, policies and politics: Discussion. *American Journal of Agricultural Economics* 63 (May): 399–400.
Brown, Lester R. 1970. *Seeds of change: The green revolution and development in the 1970's.* New York: Praeger.
——. 1974. *In the human interest—A strategy to stabilize world population.* New York: Norton.
——. 1983. *Population policies for a new economic era.* Paper no. 53. Washington, DC: Worldwatch.
——. 1988. *The changing world food prospect: The nineties and beyond.* Paper no. 85. Washington, DC: Worldwatch.
Bulatao, Rodolfo A. 1984a. Fertility control at the community level: A review of research and community programs. In *Rural Development and Human Fertility,* ed. W. Schutjer and C. Stokes. New York: Macmillan.
——. 1984b. *Reducing fertility in developing countries: A review of determinants and policy levers.* Staff Working Paper no. 680, Population and Development Series no. 5. Washington, DC: World Bank.
Burki S., and Robert Ayres. 1986. A fresh look at development aid. *Finance and Development* 23 (March):6.
Caldwell, John C., 1983. Direct economic costs and benefits of children. In *Determinants of fertility in developing countries, Vol. 1: Supply and demand for children,* ed. Rudolfo A. Bulatao et al. New York: Academic Press.
Calegar, Geraldo M., and G. Edward Schuh. 1988. *The Brazilian wheat policy: Its costs, benefits, and effects on food consumption.* IFPRI Research Report no. 66. Washington, DC: International Food Policy Research Institute.
Campbell, Joseph K. 1984. Machines and food production. In *World food issues,* ed. Matthew Drosdoff. Ithaca, NY: Cornell University College of Agriculture.
Carner, George. 1984. Survival, interdependence, and competition among the Philippine rural poor. In *People-centered development,* ed. David Korten and Rudi Klauss.

West Hartford, CT: Kumarian Press.

Carter, Michael. 1989. *U.S. farm exports and third world agricultural development.* Economic Issues no. 111. Madison: University of Wisconsin, Department of Agricultural Economics.

Cassidy, Claire. 1980. Benign neglect and toddler malnutrition. In *Social and biological predictors of nutritional status, physical growth, and neurological development,* ed. Lawrence S. Greene. New York: Academic Press.

———. 1987. World–view conflict and toddler malnutrition: Change agent dilemmas. In *Child survival: Anthropological perspectives on the treatment and maltreatment of children,* ed. Nancy Scheper-Hughes. Norwell, MA: Reidel.

Cavallo, Domingo, and Yair Mundalk. 1982. *Agriculture and economic growth in an open economy: The case of Argentina.* IFPRI Research Report no. 36. Washington, DC: International Food Policy Research Institute.

Chambers, Robert, Richard Longhurst, David Bradley, and Richard Feacham. 1979. *Seasonal dimensions to rural poverty: Analysis and practical implications.* Discussion paper no. 142. Brighton, Eng.: University of Sussex Institute of Development Studies.

Champakam, S., S. C. Srikantia, and C. Gopalan. 1968. Kwashiorkor and mental development. *American Journal of Clinical Nutrition* 21 (August):844–852.

Chandra, Ranjit K., 1980. Immunocompetence in undernutrition and overnutrition. *Nutrition Review* 39:225–231.

———. 1988. Nutritional regulation of immunity: An introduction. In *Nutrition and Immunology,* ed. Ranjit Chandra. New York: Alan R. Liss.

Chávez, Adolfo, and Celia Martínez. 1982. *Growing up in a developing community—A bio-ecological study of the development of children from poor peasant families in Mexico.* Mexico City: Instituto Nacional de la Nutrición (translated from the Spanish).

Chen, P. C. 1981. China's birth planning program. In National Research Council Committee on Population and Demography, *Research on the population in China: Proceedings of a workshop.* Washington, DC: National Academy Press.

———, and A. Kols. 1982. Population and birth planning in the People's Republic of China. *Population Reports* Series J, number 25, January–February, Volume X, Number 1:577–618.

Chenery, Hollis B. 1971. Growth and structural change. *Finance and Development Quarterly* 3:16–27.

———, Sherman Robinson, and Moshe Syrquin. 1986. *Industrialization and growth: A comparative study.* New York: Oxford University Press.

Chhibber, Ajay. 1988. Raising agricultural output: Price and nonprice factors. *Finance and Development* (June):44–47.

Chisholm, Anthony H., and Rodney Tyers, eds. 1982. *Food security: Theory, policy, and perspectives from Asia and the Pacific Rim.* Lexington, MA: Lexington Books.

Chu, Yung-Peng. 1982. Growth and distribution in a small, open economy. Ph.D. diss., University of Maryland, College Park.

Clark, Colin G. 1973. More people, more dynamism. *CERES* (Rome: FAO), (November–December).

Clay, Jason W., and Bonnie K. Holcomb. 1986. *Politics and the Ethiopian famine 1984–1985.* Cambridge, MA: Cultural Survival.

Cleaver, Kevin M. 1985. *The impact of price and exchange rate policies on agriculture in Sub-Saharan Africa.* Staff Working Paper no. 728. Washington, DC: World Bank.

Coale, Ansley J., and Edgar M. Hoover. 1958. *Population growth and economic development in low-income countries: A case study of India's prospects.* Princeton, NJ: Princeton University Press.

Cohen, Mark N. 1989. *Health and the rise of civilization.* New Haven, CT: Yale University Press.

Cook, Robert C., 1962. How many people have ever lived on Earth? *Population Bulletin* 18:(February).

Cowell, F. A. 1977. *Measuring inequality: Techniques for the social sciences.* New York: John Wiley.

Dagum, Camilo. 1987. Gini ratio. In *The new Palgrave, A dictionary of economics,* Vol. 2, ed. John Eatwell et al. New York: Stockton Press.

Dalrymple, Dana G. 1964. The Soviet famine of 1932–1934. *Soviet Studies* 15 (January):250–284.

———. 1979. The adoption of high-yielding grain varieties in developing countries. *Agricultural History* 53 (October):704–726.

———. 1985. The development and adoption of high-yielding varieties of wheat and rice in developing countries. *American Journal of Agricultural Economics* 67 (December):1067–1073.

Dam, Marjory. 1989. *Report of World Health.* (September). Geneva: WHO.

Das Gupta, Monica. 1988. Selective discrimination against female children in rural Punjab, India. *Population and Development Review* 13:77–100.

Datta, S. K., S. H. Ghosh, and C. N. Bairagya. 1988. Growth and yield of wet season rice with *Tilapia* fish. *International Rice Research Newsletter* 13 (August):46.

Deaton, Angus, and John Muellbauer. 1980. *Economics and consumer behavior.* Cambridge: Cambridge University Press.

De Janvry, Alain. 1981. The role of land reform in economic development: Policies and politics. *American Journal of Agricultural Economics* 63:384–392.

Dever, James R. 1983. Determinants of nutritional status in a North Indian village: An economic analysis. Master's thesis, University of Maryland, College Park.

De Zoysa, Isabelle, et al. 1985. *Focus on diarrhoea.* London: Ross Institute, London School of Hygiene and Tropical Medicine; for Save the Children Fund (UK).

Dixon, John A. 1982. *Food consumption patterns and related demand parameters in Indonesia: A review of available evidence.* Working Paper no. 6. Washington DC: International Food Policy Research Institute, International Fertilizer Development Center, and the International Rice Research Institute.

Dommen, Arthur J. 1988. *Innovation in African agriculture.* Boulder, CO: Westview Press.

Dover, Michael, and Lee M. Talbot. 1987. *To feed the earth: Agro-ecology for sustainable development.* Washington, DC: World Resources Institute.

Durand, C. H., and J. P. Pigney. 1963. Revue de 410 cas de diarrhées aqueuses infectieuses chez le nourrisson et l'enfant de moins de deux ans, traites pendant quatre ans dan les même service hospitalier. *Ann. Pediat.* 39:1386.

Edirisinghe, Neville. 1987. *The food stamp scheme in Sri Lanka: Costs, benefits, and options for modification.* Washington, DC: International Food Policy Research Institute.

———, and Thomas T. Poleman. 1983. *Behavioral thresholds as indicators of perceived dietary adequacy or inadequacy.* International Agricultural Economics Study no. 17. Ithaca, NY: Cornell University.

Edwards, Clark. 1988. Real prices received by farmers keep falling. *Choices* (4th quarter):22–23.

Elias, Victor J. 1985. *Government expenditures on agriculture and agricultural growth in Latin America.* IFPRI Research Report no. 50. Washington, DC: International Food Policy Research Institute.

Elliott, Kathleen. 1978. Editorial. *Lancet* 2:300.

Evelth, P. G., and J. M. Tanner. 1967. *Worldwide variation in human growth.* Cambridge: Cambridge University Press.

Evenson, Robert E. 1984. Benefits and obstacles to appropriate agricultural technology. In *Agricultural development in the third world,* ed. Carl K. Eicher and John M. Staatz. Baltimore, MD: Johns Hopkins University Press (also available in Annals of the American Academy of Political and Social Science 458 [1981]:54–67).

———, and P. M. Flores. 1978. Social returns to rice research. In *Economic consequences of the new rice technology*, ed. R. Barker and Y. Hayami. Los Baños, Philippines: International Rice Research Institute.

FAO (Food and Agricultural Organization of the United Nations) 1974. *FAO/WHO Handbook on human nutritional requirements*. FAO Nutritional Studies no. 28. Rome: FAO.

———. 1984. *Food Balance Sheets, 1979–81 average*. Rome: FAO.

———. 1989. *Food Outlook* (May).

———. 1991. *Food balance Sheets, 1984–86 average*. Rome: FAO.

Fass, Simon M. 1982. Water and politics: The process of meeting a basic need in Haiti. *Development and Change* 13:347–364.

Feacham, R. G., and M. A. Koblinsky. 1983. Interventions for the control of diarrhoeal diseases among young children: Measles immunization. *Bulletin of the World Health Organization* 61, no. 4:641–652.

———. 1984. Interventions for the control of diarrhoeal diseases among young children: Promotion of breast–feeding. *Bulletin of the World Health Organization* 62, no. 2:271–291.

Fei, John C. H., and Gustav Ranis. 1964. *Development of the labor surplus economy: Theory and policy*. New Haven, CT: Yale University Press.

Finch, V. C. and O. E. Baker. 1971. *See* U. S. Department of Agriculture. 1917.

Fishstein, Paul. 1985. Pre and post green revolution income distribution in a North Indian village. Master's thesis, University of Maryland, College Park.

Foster, Phillips. 1972. *Introduction to environmental science*. Homewood, IL: Richard D. Irwin.

———. 1991. Malnutrition, starvation, and death. In *Horrendous death, health and well-being*, ed. Dan Leviton. New York: Hemisphere.

———, and Herbert Steiner. 1964. *The structure of Algerian socialized agriculture*. Agricultural Experiment Station MP no. 527. College Park: University of Maryland.

Frejka, Thomas. 1973. The prospects for a stationary world population. *Scientific American* 228 (March):15.

Frisancho, A. Roberto. 1981. New norms of upper limb fat and muscle areas for the assessment of nutritional status. *American Journal of Clinical Nutrition* 34: 2540–2545.

———. 1989. *Anthropometric standards for the evaluation of nutritional status of children and adults*. Ann Arbor: University of Michigan Press.

Galler, Janina R. 1986. Malnutrition—A neglected cause of learning failure. *Journal of Postgraduate Medicine* 80 (October):225–230.

Galway, Katrina, et al. 1987. *Child survival: Risks and the road to health*. Columbia, MD: Westinghouse Institute for Resource Development Demographic Data for Development Project.

García, Marito, and Per Pinstrup-Andersen. 1987. *The pilot food price subsidy scheme in the Philippines: Its impact on income, food consumption, and nutritional status*. IFPRI Research Report no. 61. Washington, DC: International Food Policy Research Institute.

Gardner, Bruce L. 1979. *Optimal stockpiling of grain*. Lexington, MA: Heath.

———. 1987. *The economics of agricultural policies*. New York: Macmillan.

George, P. S. 1988. Costs and benefits of food subsidies in India. In *Food subsidies in developing countries*, ed. Per Pinstrup-Andersen. Baltimore, MD: Johns Hopkins University Press.

Gershwin, M. Eric, et al. 1985. *Nutrition and immunity*. New York: Academic Press.

Gilmore, Richard, and Barbara Huddleston. 1983. The food security challenge. *Food Policy* 8 (February):31–45.

Godwin, William. 1793. Political justice. In *A reprint of the essay on "Property"*, ed. H.

S. Salt. London: Allen & Unwin, 1949.

Gómez, F., R. Galvan, S. Frank, R. Chávez, and J. Vázquez. 1956. Mortality in third degree malnutrition. *Journal of Tropical Pediatrics* 2:77+.

González–Vega, Claudio. 1983. Arguments for interest rate reform. In *Rural financial markets in developing countries, their use and abuse*, ed. J. D. Von Pischke et. al. Baltimore, MD: Johns Hopkins University Press.

Goodall, Roger M. 1984. CDD Information Papers no. 1 and 2. New York: UNICEF (United Nations Children's Fund).

Gopalan, C. 1970. Some recent studies in the nutrition research laboratories: Hyderabad. *Journal of Clinical Nutrition* (January):35–53.

———. 1986. Vitamin A deficiency and child mortality. *Nutrition Foundation of India Bulletin (NFI Bulletin)* 7, no. 3.

———, and K. S. Rao. 1979. Nutrient needs. In *Human nutrition: A comprehensive treatise. Vol. 2: Nutrition and growth*, ed. D. Jelliffe and E. Jelliffe. New York: Plenum Press.

Gray, Cheryl W. 1982. *Food consumption parameters for Brazil and their application to food policy*. IFPRI Research Report no. 32. Washington, DC: International Food Policy Research Institute.

Griffiths, Marcia. 1985. *Growth monitoring of preschool children: Practical considerations for primary health care projects*. Geneva: World Federation of Public Health Associations.

Griliches, Zvi. 1958. Research costs and social returns: Hybrid corn and related innovations. *Journal of Political Economy* 66:419–431.

Guggenheim, Karl Y. 1981. *Nutrition and nutritional diseases: The evolution of concepts*. Lexington, MA: Heath.

Haggblade, Steven, and Peter Hazell. 1989. Agricultural technology and farm-nonfarm growth linkages. *Agricultural Economics: The Journal of the International Association of Agricultural Economists* 3:345–364.

Hancock, G. 1985. *Ethiopia: The challenge of hunger*. London: Victor Gollancz.

Harlan, Jack R. 1975. *Crops and man*. Madison, WI: American Society of Agronomy.

Haub, Carl. 1987. Understanding population projections. *Population Bulletin* 42, no. 4.

Hayami, Yujiro, and Robert Herdt. 1977. Market price effects of technological change on income distribution in semisubsistence agriculture. *American Journal of Agricultural Economics* 69:245–256.

Heilbroner, Robert L. 1953. *The worldly philosophers*. New York: Simon & Schuster.

Herbert, Sandra. 1971. Darwin, Malthus and selection. *Journal of History of Biology* 4:209–217.

Herdt, Robert W. 1970. A disaggregate approach to aggregate supply. *American Journal of Agricultural Economics* 52:512–520.

———. 1983. Mechanization of rice production in developing Asian countries. In *Consequences of small–farm mechanization*. Manila: International Rice Research Institute.

———, and Jock R. Anderson. 1987. The contribution of the CGIAR Centers to world agricultural research. In *Policy for agricultural research*, ed. Vernon W. Ruttan and Carl E. Pray. Boulder, CO: Westview Press.

Herdt, Robert W., and John W. Mellor. 1964. The contrasting response of rice to nitrogen—India and United States. *Journal of Farm Economics* 46:150–160.

Herring, Ronald J. 1983. *Land to the tiller: The political economy of agrarian reform in South Asia*. New Haven, CT: Yale University Press.

Ho, T. J. 1984. Economic status and nutrition in East Java. World Bank Working Paper in manuscript. Data from The East Java Nutrition Study sponsored by the University of Airlangga, Surabaya, the Provincial Health Services of East Java, and the Royal Tropical Institute of Amsterdam.

Hopkins, Raymond F. 1988. Political calculations in subsidizing food. In *Food subsidies in developing countries*, ed. Per Pinstrup-Andersen. Baltimore, MD: Johns Hopkins University Press.

Hossain, Mahabub. 1988a. *Credit for alleviation of rural poverty: The Grameen Bank in Bangladesh.* IFPRI Research Report no. 65. Washington, DC: International Food Policy Research Institute.

———. 1988b. *Nature and impact of the green revolution in Bangladesh.* IFPRI Research Report no. 67. Washington, DC: International Food Policy Research Institute.

Huang, Kuo W. 1985. *U.S. demand for food: A complete system of price and income effects.* Technical Bulletin no. 1714. Washington, DC: USDA.

Huddleston, Barbara. 1984a. *Briefs.* New York: CARE.

———. 1984b. *Closing the cereals gap with trade and food aid.* IFPRI Research Report no. 43. Washington, DC: International Food Policy Research Institute.

Hull, T. H. 1978. Where credit is due: Policy implications of the recent rapid fertility decline in Bali. Paper presented at the annual meeting of the Population Association of America, Atlanta.

———, et al. 1977. Indonesia's family planning story: Success and challenge. *Population Bulletin* 32, no. 6.

Hutabarat, Pos M. 1990. Proyeksi distribusi konsumsi kalorie menurut kelompok–kelompok pendapatan di Indonesia tahun 1990. [Projections of the distribution of caloric consumption by income groups in Indonesia in 1990]. Master's thesis, Bogor Agricultural University Agricultural School.

Imam, Izzedin I. 1979. *Peasant perceptions: Famine.* Dacca, Bangaladesh: Bangladesh Rural Advancement Committee. In *People centered development—contributions toward theory and planning frameworks*, ed. David C. Korten and Rudi Klauss. West Hartford, CT: Kumarian Press.

ILO (International Labor Organization). 1987. *Yearbook of labor statistics 1987.* Geneva: International Labor Office of the ILO.

———. 1988. *I.L.O. Information* 16, no. 3 (August).

Indonesia Oleh Direktorat Gizi Departemen Kesehatan R. I. 1979. *Daftar Komposisi Bahan Makanan.* Jakarta: Bhratara Karya Askara.

Indonesia. Diro Pusat Statik. 1981. *Statistik harga yan diterima dan yan dibayar pentani untuk biaya produksi pertanian dan Kebutuhan Rumah Tangga Tani.* Jawa: Madura dan beberapa Propinsi Luar Jawa. (December).

International Rice Research Institute. 1989. Azolla helps organic farmer earn more. *The IRRI Reporter* (June). Manila: International Food Policy Research Institute.

Jackson, Tony, with Deborah Eade. 1982. *Against the grain, the dilemma of project food aid.* Oxford: OXFAM.

Jelliffe, D. B. 1966. *The assessment of the nutritional status of the community.* Monograph Series no. 53. Geneva: WHO.

Johnson, Stanley R., Zuhair A. Hassan, and Richard D. Green. 1984. *Demand systems estimation methods and applicaitons.* Ames: Iowa State University Press.

Joy, Leonard. 1973. Food and nutrition planning. *Journal of Agricultural Economics* 24:166–197.

Judd, M. Ann, James K. Boyce, and Robert E. Evenson. 1987. Investment in agricultural research and extension. In *Policy for agricultural research*, ed. Vernon Ruttan and Carl E. Pray. Boulder, CO: Westview Press.

Kakwani, Nanak 1987. Lorenz curve. In *The new Palgrave, a dictionary of economics*, vol. 3., ed. John Eatwell et al. New York: Stockton Press.

Karim, Rezaul, Manjur Majid, and F. James Levinson. 1984. The Bangladesh sorghum experiment. *Food Policy* 5:61–63.

Kates, Robert W., et al. 1988. *The hunger report: 1988.* Providence, RI: Brown University World Hunger Program.

Keilmann, A. A., and C. McCord. 1978. Weight-for-age as an index of death in children. *Lancet* (June):1247–1250.

Kennedy, Eileen T. 1989. *The effects of sugar cane production on food security, health and nutrition in Kenya: A longitudinal study.* IFPRI Research Report no. 78. Washington, DC: International Food Policy Research Institute.

———, and Bruce Cogill. 1987. *Income and nutritional effects of the commercialization of agriculture in southwestern Kenya.* IFPRI Research Report no. 63. Washington, DC: International Food Policy Research Institute.

———, and Odin Knudsen. 1985. A review of supplementary feeding programmes and recommendations on their design. In *Nutrition and Development*, ed. Margaret Biswas and Per Pinstrup-Andersen. Oxford: Oxford University Press.

———, Per Pinstrup-Andersen et al. 1983. *Nutrition–related policies and programs: Past performance and research needs.* Washington, DC: International Food Policy Research Institute.

Kenya. Ministry of Planning and National Development. 1984. *Kenya contraceptive prevalence survey.* Nairobi: Central Bureau of Statistics.

Keys, Ancel, et al. 1950. *The biology of human starvation.* Minneapolis: University of Minnesota Press.

Krick, Jackie. 1988. Using the Z score as a descriptor of discrete changes in growth. *Nutritional Support Services* 6, no. 8 (August).

Kuznets, Simon. 1955. Economic growth and income inequality. *American Economic Review* 65:1–28.

Landman, Lynn. 1983. China's one-child families—Girls need not apply. *RF Illustrated* (New York: The Rockefeller Foundation) (December):8–9.

Lappe, Frances Moore. 1971. *Diet for a small planet.* New York: Ballantine.

———, and Joseph Collins. 1977. *Food first.* Boston: Houghton Mifflin.

Latham, Michael C. 1984. International nutrition problems and policies. In *World food issues*, ed. Matthew Drosdoff. Ithaca, NY: Cornell University Center for the Analysis of World Food Issues, Program in International Agriculture.

Leclercq, Vincent. 1988. *Conditions et limites de l'insertion du Brésil dans les échanges mondiaux du soja.* Montpellier, France: INRA.

Lee, John E., and Gary C. Taylor. 1986. Agricultural research: Who pays and who benefits? In *Research for Tomorrow, 1986 yearbook of agriculture.* Washington, DC: United States Department of Agriculture.

Lee, Richard B. 1968. What hunters do for a living, or how to make out on scarce resources. In *Man the Hunter*, ed. R. B. Lee and Irven DeVore. Chicago: Aldine.

Lele, Uma J. N.d. Overall flows of official development assistance to the MADIA countries. In *Aid to African agriculture: Lessons from two decades of donor experience*, ed. Uma Lele. World Bank Discussion Paper.

———, and Arthur Goldsmith. 1989. The development of national agricultural research capacity: India's experience with the Rockefeller Foundation and its significance for Africa. *Economic Development and Cultural Change* 37:305–343.

———, Bill H. Kinsey, and Antonia O. Obeya. 1989. Building agricultural research capacity in Africa: Policy lessons from the Madia countries. Unpublished working paper presented for the Joint TAC/CGIAR Center Directors Meeting, Rome.

Lewis, W. Arthur. 1954. Economic development with unlimited supplies of labor. *The Manchester School of Economic and Social Studies* (May):139–191.

Lipton, Michael. 1977. *Why poor people stay poor: Urban bias in world development.* Cambridge, MA: Harvard University Press.

———, with Richard Longhurst. 1990. *New seeds and poor people.* Baltimore, MD: Johns Hopkins University Press.

Lorenz, Max C. 1905. Methods of measuring the concentration of wealth. *Publications of the American Statistical Association* 9:209–219.

Mabbs-Zeno, C. C. 1987. *Where, if anywhere, is famine becoming more likely*. College Park, MD: World Academy of Development and Cooperation (21 ISSN 0882–3235) (also available as an unpublished manuscript from ERS, USDA, Washington, DC, 20005).

Malthus, T. R. 1890. *An essay on the principle of population or a view of its past and present effects on human happiness with an inquiry into our prospects respecting the future removal or mitigation of the evils which it occasions*. London: Ward.

Mamarbachi, D. et al. 1980. Observations on nutritional marasmus in a newly rich nation. *Ecology of Food and Nutrition* 9:43–54.

Martorell, Reynaldo. 1980. The impact of ordinary illnesses on the dietary intakes of malnourished children. *American Journal of Clinical Nutrition* 33:345–350.

———. 1989. Body size, adaptation and function. *Human Organization* 48:15–20.

Masoro, E. J., B. P. Yu, and H. A. Bertrand. 1982. "Action of food restriction in delaying the aging process." *Proceedings, National Academy of Science* 7:4239–4241.

Maxwell, Simon J. 1978a. *Food aid, food for work and public works*. Institute of Development Studies Discussion Paper no. 127. Brighton, Eng.: University of Sussex.

———. 1978b. Food aid for supplementary feeding programmes: An analysis. *Food Policy* 3:289–298.

———, and H. W. Singer. 1979. Food aid to developing countries: A survey. *World Development* 7:225–247.

Mayer, Jean. 1976. The dimensions of human hunger. In *Food and agriculture*. San Francisco: Freeman.

Mazumdar, D. 1965. Size of farm and productivity: A problem of Indian peasant agriculture. *Economica* 32 (May):161–173.

———. 1975. The theory of sharecropping with labor market dualism. *Economica* 42 (August):261–271.

McFarland, William E., et al. 1974. *Demos, demographic-economic models of society—A computerized learning system*. Santa Barbara, CA: General Electric Tempo.

McGuire, Judy S. 1988. *Malnutrition—Opportunities and challenges for A.I.D.* Washington, DC: Resources for the Future.

McKigney, John, and Hamish Munro, ed. 1976. *Nutrient requirements in adolescence*. Cambridge, MA: MIT Press.

McLaughlin, M. 1984. Interfaith action for economic justice.

Meier, G. 1979. Family planning in the banjars of Bali. *International Family Planning Perspectives* 5:63–66.

Mellor, John W. 1984. Food price policy and income distribution in low-income countries. In *Agricultural development in the third world*, ed. Carl K. Eicher and John M. Staatz. Baltimore, MD: Johns Hopkins University Press.

———. 1985a. *Agricultural change and rural poverty*. Food Policy Statement no. 3. Washington, DC: International Food Policy Research Institute.

———. 1985b. *The role of government and new agricultural technologies*. Food Policy Statement no. 4. Washington, DC: International Food Policy Research Institute.

———. 1986a. *The new global context for agricultural research: Implications for policy*. Food Policy Statement no. 6. Washington, DC: International Food Policy Research Institute.

———. 1986b. Dealing with the uncertainty of growing food imbalances: International structures and national policies. In *Proceedings nineteenth international conference of agricultural economists*, 191–198. Brookfield, VT: Grower.

———. 1988. Global food balances and food security. *World Development* 16: 997–1011.

———, and Bruce F. Johnston. 1984. The world food equation: Interrelations among development, employment, and food consumption. *Journal of Economic Literature* 22:531–574.

Merrick, Thomas W., et al. 1986. World population in transition. *Population Bulletin* 41.

Miller, Gay Y., Joseph Rosenblatt, and Leroy Hushak. 1988. The effects of supply shifts on producer's surplus. *American Journal of Agricultural Economics* 70:886–891.

Mincer, Jacob. 1976. Unemployment effects of minimum wages. *Journal of Political Economy* 84, no. 4, pt. 2 (August):87–104.

Mintz, Sidney W. 1989. Food and culture: An anthropological view: In *Completing the food chain: Strategies for Combating Hunger and Malnutrition*, ed. Paula M. Hirschoff and Neil G. Kolter. Washington, DC: Smithsonian Institution.

Monto, A. S., and J. W. Koopman. 1980. The Tecumseh study XI, occurrence of acute enteric illness in the community. *American Journal of Epidemiology* 112:323–333.

Myers, Robert G. 1988. *Programming for early child development and growth*. Paris: UNESCO–UNICEF Cooperative Program.

———. Forthcoming. *The twelve who survive: Strengthening programmes of early childhood development in the third world*. London: Routledge.

Naiken, L. 1988. Comparison of the FAO and World Bank methodology for estimating the incidence of undernutrition. *FAO Quarterly Bulletin of Statistics* 1, no. 3:iii–v.

Nakajima, Hiroshi. 1989. World health statistics annual. Geneva: WHO.

Notestein, Frank W. 1945. Population—The long view. In *Food for the World*, ed. Theodore W. Schultz. Chicago: University of Chicago Press.

Oxford Economic Atlas. 1959. *The shorter Oxford economic atlas of the world*. 2d ed. Oxford: Clarendon Press of Oxford University Press.

Paglin, M. 1974. The measurement and trend of inequality: A basic revision. *American Economic Review* 65:598–609.

Parizokova, Jana. 1977. *Body fat and physical fitness*. The Hague: Martinus Nijhoff Medical Division.

Park, Robert Ezra. 1934. Forward. In Charles Spurgen, *Shadow of the plantation*. Chicago: University of Chicago Press.

Payne, Philip R. 1985. The nature of malnutrition. In *Nutrition and Development*, ed. Margaret Biswas and P. Pinstrup-Andersen. Oxford: Oxford University Press.

Pellett, Peter L. 1977. Marasmus in a newly rich urbanized society. *Ecology of Food and Nutrition* 6:53–56.

———. 1987. Problems and pitfalls in the assessment of nutritional status. In *Food and evolution: Toward a theory of food habits*, ed. Marvin Harris and Erick B. Ross. Philadelphia, PA: Temple University Press.

Pelto, Gretl H. 1987. *Cognitive performance and intake in preschoolers*. Chapter 30 in *Cognitive performance and intake in preschoolers*, ed. Lindsay H. Allen, Adolfo Chávez, and Gretl H. Pelto. Final report, CRSR, on food intake and human factors, Mexico Project. Mexico City: University of Connecticut and Instituto Nacional de la Nutrición.

Perisse, J., F. Sizaret, and P. Françoise. 1969. The effect of income on the structure of the diet. *FAO Nutrition Newsletter* 7 (July–September):2.

Peterson, Willis L. 1979. International farm prices and the social cost of cheap food policies. *American Journal of Agricultural Economics* 61 (February):12–21.

Pfeifer, Karen. 1985. *Agrarian reform under state capitalism in Algeria*. Boulder, CO: Westview Press.

Philippines. Ministry of Agriculture. 1981a. Food consumption and nutrition. Memo to Agricultural Minister Tanco, September 8. Manila: National Agricultural Policy Staff.

———. 1981b. National agricultural policy staff memo, September 8. Manila: National Agricultural Policy Staff.

———. 1981. *Seasonal price indices of selected agricultural commodities*. National Policy Staff Paper no. 2, Manila: Ministry of Agriculture.

———. 1983. *National consumption patterns for major foods, 1977–1982*. Manila: Special Studies Division, Economic Research and Statistics Directorate, National Food Authority.

Philippines. National Economic Development Authority. 1983. 1987–88 integrated survey of households (ISH). In *1983 Economic and Social Indicators*. Manila: National Economic Development Authority.

Philippines. National Science and Technology Authority. 1983. FNRI Publication no. 82-ET-10. Manila.

———. 1984. *Second nationwide nutrition survey: Philippines, 1982*. Manila: Food and Nutrition Research Institute.

Phillips, Marshall, and Albert Baetz, eds. 1980. *Diet and resistance to disease*. New York: Plenum Press.

Phipps, Tim T. 1984. Land prices and farm-based returns. *American Journal of Agricultural Economics* 66 (November):422–429.

Pike, Ruth L., and Myrtle Brown. 1984. *Nutrition: An integrated approach*. New York: John Wiley.

Pinstrup-Andersen, Per, and Elizabeth Caicedo. 1978. The potential impact of changes in income distribution on food demand and human nutrition. *American Journal of Agricultural Economics* 60 (August):402–415.

Pinstrup-Andersen, Per, and Peter Hazell. 1985. The impact of the green revolution and prospects for the future. *Food Reviews International* 1, no. 1:11 (also available from IFPRI as a reprint).

Pinstrup-Andersen, Per, et al. 1976. The impact of increasing food supply on human nutrition: Implications for commodity priorities in agricultural research and policy. *American Journal of Agricultural Economics* 58:137–138.

Population Information Program. 1985. Fertility and family planning surveys. *Population Reports*, Series M, no. 8 (September–October). Baltimore, MD: Johns Hopkins University Press.

Population Reference Bureau. 1970. *1965 World population data sheet*. Washington DC: Population Reference Bureau.

———. 1987. *1987 World population data sheet*. Washington DC: Population Reference Bureau.

Pullum, Thomas W. 1983. Correlates of family-size desires. In *Determinants of Fertility in Developing Countries. Vol. 1: Supply and Demand for Children*, ed. Rudolfo A. Bulatao et al. New York: Academic Press.

Quandt, Sara A. 1987. Methods for determining dietary intake. In *Nutritional Anthropology*, ed. Francis E. Johnson. New York: Alan R. Liss.

Ranade, C. G., and R. W. Herdt. 1978. Shares of farm earnings from rice production. In *Economic consequences of the new rice technology*, ed. R. Barker and Y. Hayami. Los Baños, Philippines: International Rice Research Institute.

Rangarajan, C. 1982. *Agricultural growth and industrial performance in India*. IFPRI Research Report no. 33. Washington, DC: International Food Policy Research Institute.

Rask, Norman. 1986. Economic development and the dynamics of food needs. Paper delivered at : University of Maryland Global Development Conference, College Park, September.

Ray, Anandarup. 1986. Trade and pricing policies in world agriculture. *Finance and Development* 23 (September):2–5.

Repetto, Robert. 1985. *Paying the price: Pesticide subsidies in developing countries*. Research Report no. 2. Washington, DC: World Resources Institute.

Reutlinger, Schlomo. 1983. Policy implications of research on energy intake and activity levels with reference to the debate on the energy adequacy of existing diets in developing countries. Agriculture and Rural Development Department Research Unit Discussion Paper no. 7. Washington, DC: World Bank.

———. 1985. Food security and poverty in LDCs. *Finance and Development* 22 (December):7–11.

———, and Marcelo Selowsky. 1976. *Malnutrition and poverty: Magnitude and policy options.* Staff Occasional Paper no. 23. Washington DC: World Bank.

——, et al. 1986. *Poverty and hunger—Issues and options for food security in developing countries.* Washington DC: World Bank.

Rivera, Juan, and Reynaldo Martorell. 1988. Nutrition, infection, and growth. Part I: Effects of infection on growth. Part II: Effects of malnutrition on infection and general conclusions. *Clinical Nutrition* 7:156–167.

Roberts, D. F. 1953. Body weight, race and climate. *American Journal of Physical Anthropology.* 11:533–558.

Rogers, Beatrice Lorge. 1988a. Design and implementation considerations for consumer-oriented food subsidies. In *Food subsidies in developing countries,* ed. Per Pinstrup-Andersen. Baltimore, MD: Johns Hopkins University Press.

——. 1988b. Economic perspectives on combating hunger. Paper delivered to the Second Annual World Food Prize Celebration, Smithsonian Institution, Washington, DC, September 30. (An edited version is available in *Completing the food chain: Strategies for Combating Hunger and Malnutrition,* ed. Paula M. Hirschoff and Neil G. Kolter. Washington, DC: Smithsonian Institution, 1989.)

——. 1988c. Pakistan's ration system: Distribution of costs and benefits. In *Food subsidies in developing countries,* ed. Per Pinstrup-Andersen. Baltimore, MD: Johns Hopkins University Press.

Rose, Stephen, and David Fasentast. 1988. *Family incomes in the 1980's.* Working Paper no. 103. Washington, DC: Economic Policy Institute.

Rosegrant, Mark W. 1986. Irrigation with equity in Southeast Asia. *IFPRI Report* 8 (January):1, 4.

Rountree, John. 1985. Computations done at the University of Maryland from data provided by the Egyptian Ministry of Agriculture, the Central Agency for Public Mobilization and Statistics, and the Ministry of Supply. Unpublished ms.

Rustein, Shea O. 1984. Infant and child mortality: Levels, trends and demographic differentials. In *World Fertility Survey Comparative Studies No. 45,* rev. ed. Voorburg, Netherlands: International Statistical Institute.

Ryan, James G. 1977. *Human nutritional needs and crop breeding objectives in the Indian semi-arid tropics.* Hyderabad, India: International Crops Research Institute for the Semi-Arid Tropics (ICRISAT).

Sahlins, Marshall. 1968. Notes on the original affluent society. In *Man the hunter,* ed. R. B. Lee and I. DeVore. Chicago: Aldine.

Sahn, David E., ed. 1989. *Seasonal variability in third world agriculture—The consequences for food security.* Baltimore, MD: Johns Hopkins University Press.

——, and Neville Edirisinghe. Politics of food policy in Sri Lanka: From basic human needs to an increased market orientation. In *The Political Economy of Food and Nutrition Policy,* ed. Per Pinstrup-Andersen. Forthcoming.

Salaff, Janet W., and Arline Wong. 1983. *Incentives and disincentives in population policies.* Report no. 12. Washington, DC: Draper World Population Fund.

Santos-Villanueva, P. 1966. The value of rural roads. In *Selected readings to accompany getting agriculture moving,* ed. Raymond E. Borton. New York: Agricultural Development Council.

Scandizzo, Pasquale L., and Colin Bruce. 1980. *Methodologies for measuring agricultural price intervention effects.* Staff Working Paper 394. Washington, DC: World Bank.

Scandizzo, Pasquale L., and I. Tsakok. 1985. Food price policies and nutrition in developing countries. In *Nutrition and development,* ed. Margaret Biswas and Per Pinstrup-Andersen. Oxford: Oxford University Press.

Schuh, G. Edward. 1988. Some issues associated with exchange rate realignments in developing countries. In *Macroeconomics, agriculture, and exchange rates,* ed. Philip L. Paarlberg and Robert G. Chambers. Boulder, CO: Westview Press.

Schultz, Theodore W. 1979. *The economics of research and agricultural productivity.* Arlington, VA: International Agricultural Development Services Occasional Paper. Quoted in *Agricultural development in the third world,* ed. Carl K. Eicher and John M. Staatz. Baltimore, MD: Johns Hopkins University Press, 1984.

Scobie, Grant M. 1983. *Food subsidies in Egypt: Their impact on foreign exchange and trade.* IFPRI Research Report no. 40. Washington DC: International Food Policy Research Institute.

———, and Rafael Posada T. 1984. The impact of technical change on income distribution: The case of rice in Colombia. In *Agricultural development in the third world,* ed. Carl K. Eicher and John M. Staatz. Baltimore, MD: Johns Hopkins University Press.

Scrimshaw, Nevin S. 1988. Completing the food chain: From production to consumption. Paper presented at the Second Annual World Food Price Celebration. Smithsonian Institution, Washington, DC, September 30. (An edited version of this paper is available in *Completing the food chain: Strategies for Combating Hunger and Malnutrition,* ed. Paula M. Hirschoff and Neil G. Kolter. Washington, DC: Smithsonian Institution, 1989.)

———, Carl Taylor, and John Gordon. 1968. *Interactions of nutrition and infection.* Geneva: WHO.

———, and Vernon R. Young. 1976. The requirements of human nutrition. In *Food and agriculture.* San Francisco: Freeman.

Scrimshaw, Susan. 1978. Infant mortality and behavior in the regulation of family size. *Population and Development Review* 4:383–403.

———. 1984. Infanticide in human populations: Societal and individual concerns. In *Infanticide: Comparative and evolutionary perspectives,* ed. Glen Hausfater and Sarah B. Hrdy. New York: Aldine.

Seckler, David. 1982. "Small but healthy": A basic hypothesis in the theory, measurement and policy of malnutrition. In *Newer concepts in nutrition and their implications for policy,* ed. P. V. Kukhtame. Pune, India: Maharastra Association for the Cultivation of Science Research Institute.

Sen, Amartya K. 1964. Size of holdings and productivity. *Economic and Political Weekly.* (February).

———. 1966. Peasants and dualism with or without surplus labor. *Journal of Political Economy* 74:425–450.

———. 1973. *On economic inequality.* London: Oxford University Press.

———. 1981. *Poverty and famines: An essay on entitlement and deprivation.* Oxford: Clarendon Press.

Senauer, Benjamin, et al. 1988. Determinants of the intrahousehold allocation of food in the rural Philippines. *American Journal of Agricultural Economics* 70:170–180.

Shakir, A. 1975. The surveillance of protein-calorie malnutrition by simple and economic means (a report to UNICEF). *Journal of Tropical Pediatrics and Environmental Child Health* 21:69–85.

Sherman, Adria R. 1986. Alterations in immunity related to nutritional status. *Nutrition Today* (July–August):7–13.

Sicat, Gerardo P. 1983. Toward a flexible interest rate policy, or losing interest in the usury law. In *Rural financial markets in developing countries, their use and abuse,* ed. J. D. Von Pische, et al. Baltimore, MD: Johns Hopkins University Press.

Simmons, George B., and Robert J. Lapham. 1987. The determinants of family planning program effectiveness. In *Organizing for effective family planning programs,* ed. R. J. Lapham and G. B. Simmons. Washington, DC: National Academy Press.

Simon, Julian L. 1986. *Theory of population and economic growth.* New York: Blackwell.

Sinaga, R. S., and B. M. Sinaga. 1978. Comments on shares of farm earnings from rice production. In *Economic consequences of the new rice technology,* ed. R. Barker and Y. Hayami. Los Baños, Philippines: International Rice Research Institute.

Snyder, J. D., and M. H. Merson. 1982. The magnitude of the global problem of acute diarrhoeal disease: A review of active surveillance data. *Bulletin of the World Health Organization* 60:605–613.

Sommer, Alfred, et al. 1986. Impact of vitamin A supplementation on childhood mortality—A randomized controlled community trial. *Lancet* (May 24):1169–1173.

Stackman, E. C., Richard Bradfield, and Paul C. Mangelsdorf. 1967. *Campaigns against hunger*. Boston: Belknap Press of Harvard University Press.

Steindl, Josef. 1987. Pareto distribution. In *The new Palgrave, a dictionary of economics*, vol 3., ed. John Eatwell et al. New York: Stockton Press.

Stephenson, Lani S., M. C. Latham, and A. Jansen. 1983. *A comparison of growth standards: Similarities between NCHS, Harvard, Denver and privileged African children and differences with Kenyan rural children*. Ithaca, NY: Cornell International Nutrition Program.

Stevens, Robert D., and Cathy L. Jabara. 1988. *Agricultural development principles: Economic theory and empirical evidence*. Baltimore, MD: Johns Hopkins University Press.

Stiglitz, Joseph E. 1986. *Economics of the public sector*. New York: Norton.

Stone, Bruce. 1985. *Fertilizer pricing policy and foodgrain production strategy. IFPRI Report* 7 (May):1, 4.

Streeten, Paul. 1987. *What price food? Agricultural price policies in developing countries*. London: Macmillan.

Stuart, H., and S. Stevenson. 1950. Physical growth and development. In *Textbook of pediatrics*, ed. W. Nelson, 5th ed. Philadelphia, PA: Saunders.

Tanner, J. M. 1977. Human growth and constitution. *In Human biology—An introduction to human evolution, variation, growth and ecology*, by G. A. Harrison et al. Oxford: Oxford University Press.

———, R. Whitehouse, and M. Takaishi. 1966. Standards from birth to maturity for height, height velocity and weight velocity: British children I. *Archives of Disease in Childhood* 41:454+.

Timmer, C. Peter. 1984. Choice of technique in rice milling on Java. In *Agricultural development in the third world*, ed. Carl K. Eicher and John M. Staatz. Baltimore, MD: Johns Hopkins University Press.

———, Walter P. Falcon, and Scott R. Pearson. 1983. *Food policy analysis*. Baltimore, MD: Johns Hopkins University Press.

Todaro, Michael P. 1980. Internal migration in developing countries: A survey. In *Population and economic change in developing countries*, ed. Richard A. Easterlin. Chicago: University of Chicago Press.

Traub, James. 1988. Into the mouths of babes. *New York Times Magazine* (July 24):18.

Tupasi, T. E. 1985. Nutritional and acute respiratory infection. In *Acute respiratory infections in childhood: Proceedings of an international workshop*, ed. R. Douglas and E. Kerby-Eaton. Adelaide, Australia: University of Adelaide.

UNICEF (United Nations International Children's Fund). 1982. *News* 113:9.

———. 1987. ORT and much more—Developing whole CDD programmes. CF/PD/PRO-1987-001. Memo to all field offices, January 15.

———. 1988. *State of the world's children, 1988*. New York: Oxford University Press.

United Nations. 1991. *World Population Prospects 1990*. Population Study no. 120. Department of International Economic and Social Affairs. New York: United Nations.

United States. Bureau of Census. 1961. *Historical statistics of the U.S. from Colonial Times to 1956*. Washington, DC: Bureau of Census.

———. 1987. *Statistical abstract of the United States: 1988*. Washington, DC: Bureau of Census.

United States. Congress. 1974. *National nutrition policy study—1974: Hearings before the Select Committee on Nutrition and Human Needs.* Part 3: *Nutrition and Special Groups.* 93d Cong. Washington, DC: Government Printing Office.

————, Office of Technology Assessment. 1986. *Technology, public policy, and the changing structure of American agriculture.* OTA-F-285. Washington, DC: Government Printing Office.

United States. Department of Agriculture. 1917. *Geography of the world's agriculture.* by V. C. Finch and O. E. Baker, Office of Farm Management. Washington DC.

————. 1963. *Composition of foods, raw, processed, prepared.* Agricultural Handbook no. 8. Washington DC.

————. 1970. *Feed situation report* (November).

————. 1984. *The impact of wheat price policy change on nutritional status in Egypt,* by Ibrahim Soliman and Shahla Shapouri. Washington, DC: United States Department of Agriculture, ERS, International Economics Division.

————. 1985. *U.S. demand for food: A complete system of price and income effects,* by Kuw W. Huang. Technical Bulletin no. 1714. Washington, DC: USDA.

————. 1988. *World food needs and availabilities, 1988/89: Summer.* Washington, DC: USDA, ERS.

————. 1989a. Environmental degradation and agriculture, by John Sutton. USDA/ERS *World Agriculture Situation and Outlook Report,* WAS-55 (June):35–41.

————. 1989b. *World agriculture,* by Francis Urban and Arthur J. Dommen. Washington, DC: USDA.

————. 1990. U.S. government concessional exports, commodity by country and fiscal year. Unpublished data base. Washington, DC.

United States. Department of Health and Human Resources. 1981. *Height and weight of adults ages 18–74 years by socioeconomic and geographic variables, United States.* data from the National Health Survey, Series 11, no. 224. DHHS Publication no. (PHS) 81–1674. Hyattsville, MD: National Center for Health Statistics.

United States. Department of Health and Human Services. 1987. *Anthropometric reference data and prevalence of overweight, United States, 1976–80.* DHHS Publication no. (PHS) 87–1688. Hyattsville, MD: National Center for Health Statistics.

————. 1988. *The surgeon general's report on nutrition and health, 1988.* Public Health Service Publication no. 88–50210. Washington, DC: Dept. of Health and Human Services.

United States. Department of Health, Education and Welfare. 1976. NCHS Growth Charts. *Monthly Vital Statistics Report* 25, no. 3, Supp. (HRA) 76–1120. Rockville, MD: National Center for Health Statistics, Resources Administration.

————. 1979. *Weight by height and age for adults 18–74 years: United States, 1971–74.* Data from the National Health Survey, Series 11, no. 208. Hyattsville, MD: Public Health Service, Office of Health Research, Statistics and Technology, National Center for Health Statistics (NCHS), Vital and Health Statistics.

United States. Department of State. 1976. *Clinical and subclinical malnutrition and their influence on the capacity to do work,* by G. B. Spurr, M. Barac-Nieto, and M. G. Maksud. Project AID/CSD 2943, Final Report. Washington, DC: State Department.

————. 1978. *Agricultural policies and rural malnutrition,* by Phillips Foster. USAID Economics and Sector Planning Division, Office of Agriculture, Technical Assistance Bureau, Occasional Paper no. 8. Washington, DC: State Department.

————. 1986a. *Development and spread of high yielding rice varieties in developing countries,* by Dana G. Dalrymple. Washington, DC: Agency for International Development.

————. 1986b. *Development and spread of high yielding wheat varieties in developing countries,* by Dana G. Dalrymple. Washington, DC: Agency for International Development.

United States. Federal Reserve System, Board of Governors. 1989. *Balance sheets for the U.S. economy, 1949–88*. Washington, DC: Federal Reserve System.

United States. National Academy of Sciences. 1974. *Recommended dietary allowances*. Washington, DC: National Academy of Sciences.

United States. White House. Council of Economic Advisers. 1989. *Economic indicators*. Washington, DC: The White House.

———. White House. President's Science Advisory Committee. 1967. *The world food problem*. Vols 2 and 3: *Report of the panel on the world food supply*. Washington, DC: The White House.

University of California Food Task Force. 1974. *A hungry world: The challenge to agriculture, summary report*. Berkeley: University of California Division of Agricultural Sciences.

Vergara, Benito S. 1979. *A farmer's primer on growing rice*. Los Baños, Philippines: International Rice Research Institute.

Von Braun, Joachim, and Eileen Kennedy. 1986. *Commercialization of subsistence agriculture: Income and nutritional effects in developing countries*. Working Paper on Commercialization of Agriculture and Nutrition no. 1. Washington, DC: International Food Policy Research Institute.

Von Braun, Joachim, et al. 1989. *Nontraditional export crops in Guatemala: Effects on production, income, and nutrition*. IFPRI Research Report no. 73. Washington, DC: International Food Policy Research Institute.

Walinsky, Louis. 1962. *Economic development in Burma, 1951–1960*. New York: Twentieth Century Fund.

Walker, Alexander, and Harry Stein. 1985. Growth of third world children. In *Dietry fibre, fibre-depleted foods and disease*, ed. H. Trowell et al. London: Academic Press.

Waterlow, J., R. Buzina, W. Keller, J. Lane, M. Nichaman, and J. Tanner. 1977. The presentation and use of height and weight data for comparing the nutritional status of groups of children under the age of ten years. *Bulletin of WHO* 55:489–498.

Weiner, J. S. 1977. Nutritional ecology. In *Human biology—An introduction to human evolution, variation, growth and ecology*, by A. G. Harrison et al. Oxford: Oxford University Press.

Whitney, Eleanor N., and Eva Hamilton. 1977. *Understanding nutrition*. St. Paul, MN: West.

WHO (World Health Organization) 1985a. *Energy and protein requirements: Report of a joint FAO/WHO/UNU expert consultation*. Technical Report Series no. 724. Geneva: WHO.

———. 1985b. *Fourth programme report for control of diarrheal diseases 1983–1984*. Geneva: WHO Program for Control of Diarrheal Diseases.

———. 1985c. *The management of diarrhoea and use of oral rehydration therapy*. Geneva: WHO/UNICEF.

———. 1989. Report on world health. Press release, September 25. Washington DC: WHO Regional Office for the Americas.

Winick, M., K. Meyer, and R. Harris. 1973. Malnutrition and environmental enrichment by early adoption. *Science* 190 (December):1173–1175.

Winter, Roger P. 1988. In Sudan, both sides use food as a weapon. *Washington Post*, November 19:A25.

World Bank. 1975. *Land reform sector policy paper* (May).

———. 1982, 1984, 1986, 1988, 1989, 1990. *World development report*. Six separate volumes. New York: Oxford University Press.

World Food Council. 1988. *The global state of hunger and malnutrition, 1988 report*. Nicosia, Cyprus: Secretariat, World Food Council.

World Food Program. 1989. *Food aid works*. Rome: FAO, World Food Program.

Index

About the Book and the Author

Millions of people in the less developed countries are hungry, even though there is more than enough food in the world to feed them. This book tackles the question of why—and what can be done about it.

The book begins with an emphasis on definitions and facts—for example, How is malnutrition defined and measured? What are its effects? Who is undernourished? Where?—then turns to the economic, demographic, and health-related causes of undernutrition. In looking at potential solutions, Foster not only examines short-term possibilities, such as food-linked income-transfer programs, but also analyzes policies aimed at alleviating the fundamental causes of hunger—policies that would increase employment and income among the poor and lower the price of the food they eat, reduce disparities in income and wealth distribution, control human fertility, and promote better health.

Integrating knowledge from a number of disciplines (among them nutrition, economics, demography, health science, geography, agronomy, anthropology, and public policy analysis), this highly readable and comprehensive text provides a combination of data and explanation designed specifically to be used in the undergraduate classroom.

Phillips Foster is professor of agricultural and resource economics at the University of Maryland.